The Marshall Plan From Those Who Made It Succeed

Edited by
Dr. Constantine C. Menges

Foreword by
President Stephen Joel Trachtenberg
The George Washington University

D1452841

The Program on Transitions to Democracy
and
University Press of America, Inc.
Lanham • New York • Oxford

Copyright 1999 by
University Press of America,® Inc.
4720 Boston Way
Lanham, Maryland 20706

12 Hid's Copse Rd.
Cumnor Hill, Oxford OX2 9JJ

Library of Congress Cataloging-in-Publication Data

ISBN 0-7618-1658-5 (pbk: alk. ppr.)

Dedication

This book is dedicated to:

Everett H. Bellows

Paul R. Porter

and all the individuals who worked with such idealism, dedication and skill to bring about the success of the Marshall Plan.

Contents

III. Country Missions

IV. The Marshall Plan and the People

V. The Legacy of the Marshall Plan

VI. Illustrative Lives of Public Service

Conference: The Marshall Plan, Perspectives of the Participants Fifty Years Later, June 2, 1997—
Excerpts from the proceedings

The Marshall Plan: Design, Accomplishments, and Relevance to the Present

Appendix

Foreword

Fifty years after President Harry S. Truman decided to launch the Marshall Plan, a comprehensive effort by the United States to help Europe recover from the devastation of World War II, a historic commemoration conference convened at The George Washington University. This commemoration conference was unique among others held at the time because it was initiated by the very individuals who had designed and implemented the Marshall Plan. We were pleased that virtually all the living architects of the Marshall Plan participated in and attended the conference, which led to the publication of the book.

Our involvement in the public commemoration of the Marshall Plan began in January, 1996 when President Clinton personally invited more than 500 civilian and military leaders from the 16 NATO and 27 Partnership for Peace countries to convene at a symposium jointly sponsored by the White House, the Department of Defense, and The George Washington University.

We were pleased that the men and women who were the architects and implementers of the Marshall Plan subsequently asked The George Washington University to serve as their partner and host for their own major conference and commemoration.

At this gathering, and in this book, the creative and dedicated individuals who have served the United States with distinction have provided new and important insights into the genesis, accomplishments, and history of the Marshall Plan—one of the most successful and important U.S. foreign policy initiatives of this century. In addition, the personal retrospectives written by the Marshall Plan participants provide a treasury of new information and delightful stories about this splendid endeavor.

It is thanks to the democratic reconstruction of Western Europe and Japan after World War II, in combination with the existence of credible defensive military alliances, that the democracies have avoided another world war for more than fifty years.

This book provides an opportunity to obtain new insights about our history from the Marshall Plan participants and also to express appreciation to them for all that they did in the cause of freedom and peace.

Stephen Joel Trachtenberg
President, The George Washington University

1999

Preface

In June 1947, then U.S. Secretary of State George C. Marshall proposed a cooperative program of U.S. assistance in the rebuilding of a Europe devastated by World War II. This endeavor became known as the Marshall Plan. A half century later, it is abundantly clear that the Marshall Plan launched by the Truman administration with bipartisan support from Congress, and the diligent efforts of European partners, made a major contribution to the transformation of Western Europe into a community of democratic, peaceful and prosperous nations.

There is a broad public interest in the United States and in all the Western European countries in the origin, the history, and the contemporary meaning of the Marshall Plan. This book offers a unique opportunity to learn from the Marshall Plan participants themselves. The Americans who participated directly in designing and implementing the Marshall Plan decided to hold a commemorative conference in June 1997, the fiftieth anniversary of the Plan's public announcement. At the suggestion of Mr. Paul R. Porter, these individuals established an executive committee to organize the event. Mr. Melbourne Spector represented the Executive Committee cordially and effectively. As expressed by Mr. Paul Porter, the fundamental purposes of the conference and the book were: "to enlighten the general public and to inform historians and other writers of events and insights that are generally not known."

This book accomplishes those purposes because the personal memoirs and essays gathered together in this volume are vivid, enlightening and reveal new information. We learn about work of immense significance done with great dedication and goodwill that remains an inspiration for all who seek a better future.

At the time the Marshall Plan was proposed, there was relatively little public support in the United States, or interest in its objectives. It required both political courage and political vision for President Truman to move

xiii

forward with this idea. The actual planning, implementation, adaptation, and consistency of U.S. effort, in turn, required the dedicated, creative and competent work of many men and women whose work was difficult, challenging, and, only in retrospect, destined to be successful.

At the suggestion of Mr. Everett H. Bellows, an architect of the Marshall Plan and former chairman of the Board of Trusties of The George Washington University, the Executive Committee of the Marshall Plan participants requested that the university be the partner and site for their commemoration conference. Several had participated in our symposium of 43 Euro-Atlantic nations on security and democratic civil-military relations in the context of the European post-communist transitions. That January 1996 event had been co-sponsored by the White House, the Department of Defense, and the Program on Transitions to Democracy of The George Washington University and began the public commemoration of the Marshall Plan's fiftieth anniversary.[1]

The President of The George Washington University, Stephen Joel Trachtenberg, agreed that the university would serve as the host and coordinator of this conference on a pro bono basis. President Trachtenberg in turn requested that I provide the substantive support for the university and that Ms. Lu A. Kleppinger, director of the Office of Conferences and Institutes, manage all logistical and implementation aspects. The Executive Committee of the Marshall Plan participants requested that I serve as chairman of the conference and edit the subsequent publication.

We are very appreciative for the participation in the commemorative conference of distinguished invited guests: Rep. Benjamin Gilman, Hon. Jack Kemp, Co-Director, Empower America, Hon. Peter McPherson, president of Michigan State University, Secretary of the Treasury Rubin and a large number of ambassadors from nations which were assisted by the Marshall Plan.

The following page acknowledges by name the many individuals who made the conference and this publication possible. It was an enormous pleasure to work with members of the Executive Committee in defining and carrying out the commemorative conference. The financial contri-

---

1. The proceedings of that conference have been published as: C Menges, ed. *Partnerships for Peace, Prosperity and Democracy*, New York, Oxford, Lanham, MD: University Press of America, 1997.

butions of many Marshall Plan participants, a substantial donation by Mr. and Mrs. Minos Zombanakis in honor of the late Frank Mahon, and a very generous donation by President Trachtenberg for The George Washington University ultimately made it possible to move forward with the publication of this book.

As on other occasions, it was very rewarding to work with Ms. Lu A. Kleppinger and her able staff as they assured a well functioning conference. I am also indebted to the many individuals at the Program on Transitions to Democracy who worked on this project with me. Among these dedicated individuals, the person who has worked longest and with great skill and thoughtfulness to help bring this volume to its final form has been Ms. Jill Schwartz, Executive Assistant with the Program for the last sixteen months. Her effective work has contributed to making this publication a reality.

I am also personally and profoundly grateful to all of the Marshall Plan participants, their departed colleagues, and the leadership of the United States for the wise decisions and dedicated efforts that we know as the Truman Doctrine and the Marshall Plan. Those initiatives provided the foundation for the freedom, well-being, and peace enjoyed by the democracies during the last half-century.

It has been a privilege and an immensely rewarding experience to work with the Marshall Plan participants on this commemoration.

> Constantine C. Menges, Ph.D.
> Director, Program on Transitions to Democracy
> Professor in the Practice of International Relations
> The George Washington University, 1999

Acknowledgments

The editor wishes to acknowledge the following individuals who helped to make the conference and this publication possible.

Executive Committee of the Marshall Plan Conference

Robert E. Asher
Everett H. Bellows
James R. Brooks
Manilo F. DeAngelis
George M. Elsey

Theodore Geiger
Lincoln Gordon
Philip M. Kaiser
Fordyce W. Luikart
Edwin M. Martin

Paul R. Porter
Melbourne L. Spector
Elmer Staats
Morris Weisz

Financial Contributors

Robert Asher
Everett H. Bellows
Adolph J. Bennett
Kathleen S. Bitterman
Frederick J. O. Blachy
Robert. B. Black
Blum-Kovlar Foundation
Ethel W. Brandwein
James R. Brooks
Vincent W. Brown
Weir M. Brown
Vincent Checchi
Manilo DeAngelis
Daimler-Chrysler
Peter K. Daniells
Marie-Bon de V.C. Roberts
Mary W. Donner
John A. Edelman

George Design Studio
E. Ernest Goldstein
John W. Gunter
John Grady
Arthur A. Hartman
Robert L. Hubbell
Sperry Lea
Alice E. May
John W. McDonald
Charles L. Merwin
Cornelius F. Miller
Waldemar A. Nielson
Paul H. Nitze
Janet Wilson Owens
Anita P. Paige
W. Todd Parsons
Paul R. Porter
Theodore Tannenwald Jr.

Thomas Schelling
Harold Seidman
Abraham M. Sirkin
Aristotelis D. Sismanidis
Ruth L. Sivard
Robert Solomon
Melbourne L. Spector
Julian S. Stein
David J. Steinberg
Stephen J. Trachtenberg/
  The Geo. Washington
  University
Ralph L. Trisko
Alfred D. White
Warren W. Wiggins
H. Lawrence Wilsey
Minos A. and Pia
  Zombanakis

The George Washington University

President Stephen Joel Trachtenberg

(continued)

Acknowledgments

The George Washington University

Office of Conferences
and Institutes

The Program On Transitions
to Democracy

Ms. Lu A. Kleppinger, Director
Ms. Elizabeth Castronovo
Ms. Elizabeth Arritt
Ms. Nancy Kim
Ms. Tracy Silk-Punke

Dr. Constantine C. Menges, Director
Mr. A. Vance Renfroe, Senior Associate
Mr. Michael Auten, Executive Assistant,
    1996-1997
Mr. Michael Ard
Mr. Chad Corson
Ms. Catherine Kuchta-Helbling
Mr. Bryan Kurrey
Ms. Sarah Leonard
Mr. Richard Marquez,
    Executive Assistant, 1997-1998
Ms. Jill Schwartz,
    Executive Assistant, 1998-1999

Introduction

Paul R. Porter
  The Triumph of the Democracies
The Executive Committee of the Marshall Plan Conference
  The Marshall Plan and its Consequences
Hon. Benjamin Gilman, Chairman, International
Relations Committee, U.S. House of Representatives
  Fifty Years After the Marshall Plan
Hon. Robert E. Rubin, Secretary of the Treasury
  One of America's Finest Moments

The Triumph
of the Democracies

Paul R. Porter

The Marshall Plan is perhaps best appraised in the answers to four questions: What did it accomplish? What was our purpose in undertaking it? What made it a success? What is its effect on our lives a half century later?

A simple answer to "What did the plan accomplish?" is that it was the pivotal event, the turning point, in a turbulent epoch that began with the First World War and continued until the collapse of the Soviet Union brought an end to the Cold War.

Every generation must contend with evil and folly. Our generation encountered them on a grand scale. The man-made disasters they caused in this century did far more harm to people and property than was done in the same time by all natural disasters such as hurricanes, earthquakes, and epidemics of disease. Consider the years between 1914 and 1947.

The first disaster began in Sarajevo, the Balkan city that has been much in the news during the conflict in what is now called Bosnia. It was there on June 30, 1914 that a fanatical Serbian nationalist assassinated the Archduke Francis Ferdinand, heir to the throne of the Austro-Hungarian Empire. Austria-Hungary declared war on Serbia. Then like tenpins tumbling, Germany declared war on France and Russia, Great Britain declared war on Germany, and Russia declared war on Turkey. After the United States entered the war in 1917 on the side of Great Britain and France, an Allied offensive in the following year forced Germany and Austria to accept an armistice. In the meantime, a revolution in Russia replaced the arbitrary rule of a Czar with the arbitrary rule of a tightly disciplined communist party.

Then came what Churchill aptly called "the follies of the victors." An enduring peace could have been obtained by what he called "reasonable common sense and prudence." Instead, Great Britain and France, driven by a desire for vengeance, demanded reparations from the losers on a scale so large that their payment was impossible. The United States, which might have exercised a stabilizing influence, turned to a policy of isolationism. The war damaged the economy of all nations that participated in it. Their governments tried to repair the damage at the expense of others. The result was a numbing worldwide economic crisis known as the Great Depression.

In Germany, runaway inflation, resentment against unrealistic reparations, and widespread unemployment combined to bring to power one of the most evil men of all times, Adolph Hitler. It was a distinction he shared with Josef Stalin. Though enemies later, they were partners in the aggression aimed at dividing Poland between their countries which began the Second World War.

That war resulted in the loss of 50 million lives, including some six million killed in the Holocaust. The two years that followed Germany's unconditional surrender were a time of a sharpening conflict between the Soviet Union and the other victors.

That was the setting for the Marshall Plan that launched Western Europe on the road to a phenomenal economic recovery and the restoration of a confidence in the future that had been lost a third of a century earlier. In 1947, the Soviet Union rejected an opportunity to participate and prevented the nations of Eastern Europe from participating. For the next 44 years there followed a tense standoff known to history as the Cold War.

How future historians may describe the epoch between the start of the First World War and the end of the Cold War, we cannot say. I would call it *The Time of the Trials and the Triumph of the Democracies*. That does not mean that democracy prevails everywhere. It of course does not—not in China, not in the Middle East other than Israel, nor in most of Africa. But there is no longer a serious external threat to the very existence of the democracies.

Why did we undertake the Marshall Plan? Our motivation was succinctly stated by General Marshall in a commencement address at Harvard. "The truth of the matter," he said, "is that Europe's requirements for the next three or four years of foreign food and other essential products—principally from America—are so much greater than her ability to pay that she must have substantial help. . . . Any assistance that this Govern-ment may render in the future should provide a cure rather than a mere palliative."

His proposal resonated with the deepest feelings of the American people. All Americans but the very young had vivid memories of the war just past. Many also remembered clearly the First World War. They were determined to avoid a third. That meant rejecting vengeance which had destroyed the peace after the First World War. Specifically, it meant co-opting Germany and Italy, our defeated enemies, as partners in the creation of prosperity and peace. We are now so accustomed to our former enemies as partners that we fail to marvel at the magnitude of the American achievement.

What made the Marshall Plan a success? It was an undertaking for which there was little precedent. The Congress created an independent agency, the Economic Cooperation Administration, to administer our aid. Besides its headquarters office in Washington, it established a mission in each of the participating countries and a coordinating operation in Paris directed by an officer known as the United States Special Representative in Europe. For the first two years that office was filled by Averill Harriman. In my opinion, it was he, among the many able participants, who made the largest single contribution to the success of the Marshall Plan. As Secretary of Commerce, he directed the studies that established the anticipated volume of aid and played a major role in obtaining the support of Congressional leaders. As the plan's coordinator in Paris, he demonstrated high skills as a diplomat in inspiring cooperation among European leaders. The Europeans jointly created the Organization for European Economic Cooperation, or OEEC. In it they scrutinized each other's recovery plans.

At different times, I had three roles in the administration of the plan. I think I can best give a glimpse of how it worked by recounting a few experiences. My first was chief of the mission to Greece. That country was the "basket case" among the countries aided by the Marshall Plan. It was poor to begin with, was not well governed, and had suffered badly from a communist-inspired civil war. For a long time, the British had subsidized the Greek government as a part of their policy of maintaining friendly nations in the vicinity of the Suez Canal, but now could no longer afford it. A year before the Marshall Plan began, the American government began aid to Greece to prevent a communist victory.

We helped the Greeks to modernize industries, improve their agriculture, build power plants and roads, and in general do things that would enable them to become self-supporting. As mission chief, I was often obliged to say no to the requests of the Greek government. It wanted a steel mill for instance and we refused because Greece lacked the resources for an efficient operation.

I hated to leave Greece. My wife and I liked the Greek people, and on my way to work it was an inspiration to raise my eyes to the top of the Acropolis and see the marble Parthenon gleaming in the rays of the morning sun. However, after I had been there 15 months, William C. Foster, who had succeeded Paul Hoffman as administrator of the Economic Cooperation Administration, asked me to become the assistant administrator of the program in Washington.

The assistant administrator was responsible for preparing an annual program for submission to Congress. I once calculated that one quarter of the time of the Washington staff was devoted to preparing the annual program and other information for members of Congress. Sometimes it was to explain why we could not approve the use of aid funds to benefit some of their constituents.

The first week in my new job I was visited by five United States senators from tobacco-raising states. They asked me to revoke an agreement I had reached while in Greece with our military authorities in Germany who were then in charge of our aid program there. Before the war, Germany had imported most of its tobacco from Greece. Our military authorities, however, had authorized imports from the United States. That meant a double burden for the American taxpayer—once to pay for Germany's imports and then more aid to Greece than would be necessary if it could sell its tobacco to Germany. The Senators wanted American exports of tobacco to Germany to continue. I told them that we would not pay for any tobacco exports unless directed to do so by legislation. That was one of the ways in which we were able to hold the cost of the Marshall Plan to $13.3 billion—23% less than had originally been expected.

My final job was that of Acting United Special Representative in Europe at the regional office in Paris. Fear among the nations of Western Europe that the Soviet Union might cross the Iron Curtain led them and the United States in 1949 to create the North Atlantic Treaty Organization which promised mutual support in the event that any one of them might be attacked. However, it lacked an effective organization to provide the defense the treaty promised. After North Korea invaded South Korea in 1950, President Truman recalled General Eisenhower to active duty and told him to plan the level of forces that would be needed to protect Western Europe in the event of a Soviet attack.

Soon after arriving in Paris, I called on Eisenhower at his headquarters near Paris. He received me cordially, but I was troubled to learn that his staff estimated that the NATO forces would cost about twice what our Marshall Plan staff thought the member countries could afford.

When the Marshal Plan ended on December 31, 1951, I became deputy chief (for economic affairs) of the American team that conducted the negotiations to organize and finance NATO. The cost that was eventually agreed upon was close to what our Marshall Plan staff had thought would be feasible. As President, Eisenhower seemed comfortable with that amount.

A half century has now gone by since the start of the Marshall Plan. How are we affected by what it accomplished? Besides our freedom which is no longer under assault, we enjoy a standard of living that would not have been possible without the success of the plan. Our economy is strongly affected by the success of our trading partners. When they, too, enjoy a high standard of living, they support the creation of American jobs and a rising income.

As a measure of the economic success that began with the Marshall Plan, I quote from figures assembled by the World Bank. They are given as a percentage of the purchasing power per person in the United States. In 1995, the average purchasing power per person for all countries aided by the Marshall Plan was 64% of the per capita purchasing power in the United States. It was 74% for France, Germany and Italy, but Portugal, Greece and Turkey brought down the average. The average for the countries of Eastern Europe which were held captive in the Soviet Bloc was 21% or one third of that of the Marshall Plan countries as a whole. The average in the former Soviet Union was 13%. The figures speak eloquently of what the Marshall Plan accomplished and of the great harm that the Soviet Union did to the standard of living of its own people and those of Eastern Europe.

NATO stopped any further Soviet expansion in Europe. It was the Marshall Plan that created the pattern of cooperation that made NATO possible and that created a democratic prosperity that the Soviet Union could never match. In these essential respects the Marshall Plan was the keystone in the triumph of the democracies.

The Marshall Plan
and its Consequences

MARSHALL PLAN CONFERENCE PARTICIPANTS, JUNE 1997

"The most unselfish and unsordid financial act of any country in all history," said Churchill. He referred to the Lend Lease Act and the occasion was a speech to the House of Commons after Roosevelt's death. His words apply with equal, if not greater, aptness to the Marshall Plan that was launched and successfully completed in the Truman Administration.

The external food, industrial raw materials and critical machinery that enabled Western Europe to recover from grave economic wounds of war came inevitably from the United States, but the genius of the Marshall Plan was that it was constructed so that each recipient, in obtaining what it needed, was also required to contribute according to its ability.

General George C. Marshall, then U.S. Secretary of State, set the pattern in a commencement address at Harvard University on June 5, 1947, inviting European nations to take the initiative in determining their needs. The American role would consist of "friendly aid in the drafting of a European program and later support of such a program so far as it may be practical for us to do so. The program should be a joint one, agreed to by a number, if not all, European nations." The 16 nations that accepted the invitation initially calculated their combined needs to cost $29 billion in prices prevailing then. An American committee pared the estimate to $17 billion. As conducted, the Marshall Plan beneficiaries generated during the next four years a performance that held the actual cost at $13 billion.

A century after the start of the Marshall Plan, its consequences endure. Most notably:

1. The economic recovery of Western Europe was spectacularly successful with large mutual benefits to its people and the people of the United States.
2. Peace now prevails among major powers that had repeatedly made Europe a battleground. Old rivalries have been subordinated in a now substantial European Union. In the perspective of a half century, the achievement has been large.
3. Democratic government in the participating nations has been made secure. Threats from communist and fascist parties, once a source of major turmoil, have receded into history.
4. The NATO alliance, which was probably not possible without the example of the Marshall Plan, stopped further Soviet aggression and in time expedited the collapse of an Iron Curtain that separated East from West.

We had the good fortune to participate in the planning, implementation or reporting of the Marshall Plan. Two generations later, problems of a different character confront our nation. But the need remains to encourage transitions to democracy in formerly unfriendly nations, provide humanitarian assistance, strengthen our ties with like-minded nations, assure our security and promote trade.

Fifty Years after the Marshall Plan

Hon. Benjamin A. Gilman*

It is a great honor for me to join in this commemoration of the fiftieth anniversary of the Marshall Plan.

While the Marshall Plan bears the name of our distinguished former Secretary of State, General George C. Marshall, we recognize that he did not conceive nor implement the Marshall Plan all by himself. He had a great deal of help along the way, and we are privileged to have with us today many of those who contributed to the success of the Marshall Plan. To them I want to express a special word of thanks on behalf of the Congress and the American people.

Your extensive work and your vision set us on what was unquestionably the right course for our nation after World War II. By pursuing that direction, America not only preserved the freedom of Western Europe, but also—after decades of struggle—successfully brought about the demise of communism and the triumph throughout most of the world of America's vision of democracy, political pluralism, and free market economies. In no small measure, today's world was shaped by your earlier efforts. We are deeply indebted to you for it.

As a Republican member of Congress, I have always had a special admiration for Senator Arthur Vandenberg, who made his reputation

---

* Representative Benjamin Gilman is Chairman of the House of Representatives, International Relations Committee, and delivered this speech to the conference of Marshall Plan participants at The George Washington University on June 2, 1997.

working with Secretary Marshall and President Truman to forge our nation's post-War foreign policy. Senator Vandenberg's name, of course, has become almost synonymous with bipartisanship in foreign policy. And for good reason.

Let us not forget that the Marshall Plan was proposed by a Democratic Administration and approved by a Republican Congress. It was, in short, a bipartisan policy, and certainly the bipartisan support it enjoyed was essential to its sustainability and ultimate success.

Senator Vandenberg did not rest once the Marshall Plan was approved. In June of 1948 one year after Secretary Marshall's speech at Harvard University proposing the Marshall Plan—he offered the so-called Vandenberg Resolution, endorsing the formation of a military alliance between the United States and the free countries of Western Europe. Senator

Vandenberg's resolution passed overwhelmingly—64 in favor to just 4 against—and this show of political support contributed to the momentum that culminated, less than ten months later, in the signing of the North Atlantic Treaty and the founding of NATO.

On the occasion of the Marshall Plan's fiftieth anniversary, President Clinton and others have pointed out that the strategic challenges facing our nation in the post-Cold War era are similar to those we faced in the last post-war era fifty years ago. But there are also important differences. An op-ed in yesterday's Boston Globe by David Warsh put it well:

Instead of a world hobbled by war, the United States looks outward to a world pretty much at peace with itself. Instead of relatively easily repaired physical damage, the harm done to many of the world's great nations—Russia, China. India—has been self-inflicted. It is institutional regeneration that is needed, not spare parts and heating oil.

Just as we needed to create NATO after World War II in order to consolidate the fragile democracies in Western Europe, we need to expand NATO today in order to consolidate the fragile democracies that have recently emerged in the former captive nations of Central and Eastern Europe.

Most commentators have overlooked another parallel between 1947 and 1997—the fact that, once again, control of our government is divided between a Democratic President and a Republican Congress. One might think that this could spell trouble for NATO enlargement. I believe, however, that just as divided government provided fertile soil for the Marshall Plan and the creation of NATO fifty years ago, it will provide fertile soil for NATO enlargement today.

The fact is we in the Congress have already passed today's equivalent of the Vandenberg Resolution. And we've done it more than once.

Three years ago we passed the NATO Participation Act, creating a military assistance program to facilitate the admission of new members to the Alliance. Two years ago in the House of Representatives we passed the Contract With America, which called for NATO enlargement. And last year, Senator Dole introduced in the Senate, and I introduced in the House, the NATO Enlargement Facilitation Act, which set aside special assistance for Poland, Hungary, the Czech Republic, and Slovenia to join NATO. Our bill passed the House by a vote of 353 in favor to 65 against, it passed the Senate by 81 in favor to 16 against, and President Clinton signed it into law last fall.

In the House we're getting ready—perhaps as early as this week—to take up another measure I have offered, the European Security Act, which will do for Romania and the Baltic States what our bill last year did for Poland and the other front runners for admission to NATO.

The fact is, we in the Congress believe that it was initially our idea to enlarge NATO, and the Clinton Administration came late to it. But we're glad they've joined us, and we look forward to working with the Administration in the spirit of Senator Vandenberg to make certain that our nation rises to the challenges of the post-Cold War era.

One of America's Finest Moments

HON. ROBERT E. RUBIN*

I am pleased to have been invited to speak to you today on the occasion of the 50th anniversary of the Marshall Plan, and I am honored to be with those of you here who worked on the Marshall Plan.

Let me start by looking back for a moment, and then I would like to discuss the carrying forward of the spirit and vision of 1947 to the world of today and tomorrow.

Fifty years ago, George Marshall spoke at Harvard and proposed the outlines of the relief plan for Europe that would bear his name. At a time when we were exhausted from war, a time when the temptation to withdraw from international engagement was strong, we reached out with a dramatic infusion of aid for a Europe in crisis. The costs of the Marshall Plan were immense—$13 billion over three years, nearly 10% of the federal budget at the time. But the return on our investment was equally immense. The Marshall Plan was crucial to the rebuilding of Europe and the strength and prosperity of the Western economies. That Plan, its spirit and vision, marked one of America's finest moments.

There is no doubt that, in moral terms, the Marshall Plan was the right thing to do. But the Marshall Plan was also vitally in our economic and national security interest. America needed then, and needs today, a prosperous and thriving world to remain prosperous and thriving herself.

---

* Secretary of the Treasury Robert E. Rubin delivered this speech to the conference of Marshall Plan participants at The George Washington University on June 2, 1997.

Visionaries such as George Marshall understood that. Though Marshall was a military man, he knew that victory does not come when the guns are laid down and the flag is raised, but rather when the conditions for long term peace and prosperity are established. He knew that stability today could quench conflict tomorrow, that the most effective diplomacy is preventive diplomacy.

Today the legacy of the Marshall Plan is clear. It helped build a European continent both prosperous and free, one moving ever closer to integration. It firmly set the Uruted States on the course of leadership and engagement in international affairs. And it showed that we had learned the lesson from our decision after World War I to withdraw from global affairs.

The imperative for U.S. leadership and engagement in the global economy has not changed since the Marshall Plan, though the circumstances obviously have. In fact, in some respects that imperative has increased, just as the centrality of economics to foreign policy, which was great then, has also in some respects increased. In 1947, 12% of our economy relied on trade. Today, that figure has more than doubled. In 1947, the vast preponderance of leading U.S. corporations viewed themselves as American companies with offices abroad. Today, they see themselves as global corporations based in United States. In 1947, capital markets were national, with very little flow across country borders. Today, there is an enormous integrated global capital market, with vast cross-border investment and financing flows every day. Technology, political change, and market openings have sped our economies toward integration and created new opportunities for growth, and also new risks. It is no exaggeration when we say that our economic well-being is enormously and irreversibly linked to the rest of the world. I saw a column the other day in which the author was decrying the globalization of economic life. I think he might as well have been decrying the rise and fall of the tides. The reality in my view is not at issue. The only question at issue is whether we turn this to our advantage—with the great benefits that can flow therefrom—or we turn our back on reality, with the results that usually flow from that. There is no question where George Marshall would have come out on that issue.

Fostering a healthy global economy is enormously in our interest in 1997, as it was in 1947. At that time, to confront the economic challenge of post-war Europe, Marshall laid out a three-part strategy: providing much needed capital to reconstruct devastated nations; conditioning that assistance on key economic policy reforms; and integrating Europe in the international community. That conditionality and that vision of integrated economies are now sometimes forgotten, but they were an integral part of the Marshall Plan.

The strategy for promoting growth and economic well-being in both the developed and the developing countries of today's economy is very similar: supporting sound economic policies in conjunction with providing assistance, now largely through the international financial institutions and their policies of conditionality; breaking down barriers to economic integration, including through the trade liberalizing efforts of NAFTA, GATT/WTO, APEC and the "Free Trade Area of the Americas;" and providing capital, though today this is increasingly through promoting conditions that attract flows of private capital.

That highlights a central difference between the challenge of rebuilding Europe in 1947 and the challenge of spurring development and growth around the world today. In the 1940s, there were no global capital markets. The Marshall Plan's $13 billion in direct government-to-government lending was critical to the reconstruction of Europe. Now, the key to development and growth is less official aid, whether bi-lateral or through the international financial institutions, than creating the environment that will attract private investment.

Key to creating that environment is another product of this remarkable period of international vision and leadership in the late 1940s, the Bretton Woods Agreement institutions, the International Monetary Fund and the World Bank, and their more recent companion institutions, the regional development banks and the GATT/WTO.

Take the case of the developing countries around the globe which have undergone a remarkable transition over the last twenty-five years. In Asia, Latin America, central Europe, in country after country, there is an emerging, almost universal, consensus that free-market economics is the key to prosperity. Many countries in each of these regions have achieved great improvements in economic conditions in recent years or, in some cases, particularly in Asia, in recent decades. The international financial institutions have been central to this by investing in education, health care, and other underlying requisites for a successful market based economy, and encouraging sound financial and other policies by conditioning their assistance, just as the Marshall Plan did fifty years ago. This in turn is critical to our country, to prosperity in developing countries and in the countries transitioning from communism, and to further political stability and democracy, all of which contribute to economic activity in our county and enhances our national security.

However, despite all of the progress with respect to the developing and transitioning countries, the challenge of bringing the whole of the world's population into the economic mainstream and our future, our economic well-being, our national security, our environment, and our public health, depend upon meeting the challenge. The World Bank estimates that 1.3 billion people live on less than one dollar per day, and even in many of the countries where significant progress has been made, those gains are not irreversible

Many parts of Asia have achieved economic conditions unimaginable 30 years ago, but a vast number of Asians still live in poverty. And in Africa, a whole continent has remained mired in poverty, though some countries have started to adopt reformist regimes and have begun to experience real economic improvements. Applying the spirit and vision of the Marshall Plan to Afica, I do not think that there is any question that an economically successful Africa is not only in the interest of Africans, but is important to our interests as well.

Towards these ends, the Administration is working with a bi-partisan group in Congress on developing a vigorous Africa strategy and with the international financial institutions to greatly increase their focus on Africa. An Africa that succeeds in a commitment to democracy, economic reform, and sustainable development will provide higher standards of living for its people and be more stable politically and socially. That in turn, will benefit American businesses and workers, and it will strengthen our national security by lessening the need to respond to crises in Africa.

However, every component of forward-looking international economic policy immediately encounters the debate about our country's role in the global economy, and more generally in the world, just as the Marshall Plan triggered an enormous debate in its day. That debate can be seen on a number of fronts. One is the area of resources.

We are the world's largest and richest economy by far, and yet we are the largest debtor to the United Nations, and we account for the lion's share of the arrearages to the World Bank and its sister multi-lateral development banks. We were instrumental in creating those institutions, and now we threaten their health.

Similarly, on trade liberalization, as nations around the world join together in all sorts of ways, with the European Union, MERCOSUR in Latin America, and AREA in Asia, the United States seems increasingly resistant to trade liberalization. This movanent towards integration will continue, with us or without us; the only question is whether we will be inside, and receive the benefits, or on the outside, much to our detriment.

To secure the political support to maintain our leadership abroad requires building public support for these forward looking policies. This, too, George Marshall understood very well. When he spoke at Harvard in 1947 about his proposal to help Europe, he recognized the political challenge ahead when he said: "An essential part of any successful action on the part of the United States is understanding on the part of the people of America of the character of the problem and the remedies to be applied. Political passion and prejudice should have no part." After he made the proposal, President Truman, Republican Senator Arthur Vandenberg and members of both parties launched a campaign to educate the public about the Plan and build support for it. The Marshall Plan, which was initially met with skepticism and opposition, eventually passed overwhelmingly in both houses of Congress.

Today, we face that same challenge of building in Marshall's words, an understanding on the part of the people of America of the character of the problem and the remedies to be applied. Those in government who are committed to meeting that challenge cannot do so alone. All who understand how vitally our well being is linked to the well being of the rest of the world need to join together in building a shared understanding among all Americans of that vital linkage.

After World War II, much of the support for the Marshall Plan came as a result of the urgencies of the Cold War. Today, there are also great urgencies for American leadership in the world, but they are less obvious and more difficult to understand, making the challenge of building public support all the greater. I would like to conclude by urging that you leave today's program at George Washington University not only with a deepened understanding of the Marshall Plan and General George Marshall, but with a commitment to honoring his spirit and vision in facing the challenges of today, including helping to build a shared understanding among all of our citizens of our common interest with the rest of the world. I have focused primarily on economic interdependence this afternoon, but today national security, public health, environmental protection, crime and terrorism have all become issues that no nation, even the richest and most powerful, can face alone. Surely one of the great lessons of the 20th century, a lesson George Marshall clearly understood, is that withdrawal from international affairs cannot work. When we withdraw, we suffer; when we engage, we prosper.

Personal Retrospectives

I. Background: Launching the Plan

Everett H. Bellows
Bringing New Productivity Ideas to Europe
Theodore Geiger
The Path to the Marshall Plan and Beyond
Arthur Goldschmidt
*The Marshall Plan—Answering Liberal and
Conservative Objections*
Robert L. Hubbell
*Participating in the Prologue and Epilogue
of the Marshall Plan*
Ben T. Moore
A New Trade Policy for Europe
Paul R. Porter
From the Morgenthau Plan to the Marshall Plan and NATO
Harold Seidman
The Management Structure for the Marshall Plan
Melburne L. Spector
A Transcendent Experience

Bringing New Productivity Ideas to Europe

Everett H. Bellows

From April 1948 until January 1954, I worked in the Marshall Plan on three very different assignments. Initially, I was asked by the Director General of the Foreign Service, Chris Ravendahl, to take a temporary assignment on the newly created Economic Cooperation Administration to help set up its personnel system. The "powers that be" had decided that the administration of the Marshall Plan would be outside of the State Department, but the Foreign Service structure would serve as our model. An established bureaucracy would have to have rules and precedents to be followed, but we didn't have the time to instill such a culture. I asked only that I would be permitted to take along one other person from State. Receiving permission to do so, I chose Melbourne Spector—one of the best decisions I ever made.

Paul Hoffman in Washington and Averell Harriman in Paris were given Cabinet rank. This fact greatly facilitated the actions Mel and I took. For instance, when Mel and I sat down with "Ma" Shipley to negotiate the status of American staff serving abroad we would have to haggle over each and every assignment. We asked that all appointees in the Foreign Service Reserve Class III and above be given diplomatic passports—all other staff would be issued special FS passports. Additionally, those assigned to the Office of the Special Representative (OSR) would be validated for travel throughout Western Europe. "Ma" balked. I responded, "OK. Let's go up and see Assistant Secretary Peurifoy." She thereupon withdrew her objections but afterwards always referred to the Paris staff as "international gypsies!"

Hoffman, Harriman, and William C. Foster, Harriman's deputy in Paris, picked the country chiefs of missions—David Bruce in France, Tom Finletter in the UK, David Zellerbach in Italy, Harvey Collisson for Germany, etc. In turn, they empowered the country chiefs to pick their own staffs. It was Mel's job and mine to expedite the processing of these people and get them on their way, which often meant families as well. By September, the crunch was over and I joined Leland Barrows, Executive Assistant to Harriman, as his deputy in OSR.

One of the inspired actions of the Marshall Plan was the creation of counterpart funds matching the dollar amount of aid to each participating government. Five percent of these counterpart funds were made available to provide for administrative costs. Although they were not appropriated money, Leland and I decided that we would treat them as such and promptly set about establishing budgets and financial controls. We didn't want people behaving as if these monies were wooden nickels.

Towards the end of the second year, our administrative routines were well established and I thought it was time to move on. Charley Marshall offered me the post of Deputy Chief of Mission in Denmark—a very tempting offer indeed. Meanwhile, Leland had written to Bill Foster, who by then had replaced Paul Hoffman as administrator of the Economic Cooperation Administration (ECA), indicating that I was available. Foster offered me the opportunity to be his Executive Assistant in Washington—who could resist that offer? I thanked Charley Marshall, but I accepted Mr. Foster's exciting offer. Of the many interesting incidents in that post, I particularly recall the afternoon that Congresswoman Rogers called Mr. Foster and I had to tell her that Mr. Foster was not taking calls because he was in conference with the Austrian Foreign Minister. Mrs. Rogers told me to tell the Administrator that if he did not return her call in 15 minutes, she would go down to the well of the House and make her remarks there. Disobeying the Boss, I got on the intercom to Mr. Foster and told him what had transpired. Mr. Foster instructed me, "Everett, you call the Congresswoman back and tell her to go ahead—that's why she was elected." I did and she didn't.

Meanwhile the matter of European productivity had become a salient issue. I'm not sure of the whole history of that issue, but I do know that shortly after the OECD had issued a report entitled "Eight Principles of European Recovery," a group of second echelon people in OSR had gathered in the Talleyrand snackbar and over coffee and croissants formulated a proposition they called "Productivity, the Ninth Principle."

I estimated they were thinking in terms of what today would be called micro-economics. The idea was scorned by some of the macro-economists who presided at OECD and OSR. Nevertheless, the idea caught on.

Without telling me what was about to happen, Bill Foster asked me to take over what had now become the Productivity and Technical Assistance Division within ECA. To my surprise two weeks later, Foster became Deputy Secretary of Defense under Bob Lovett.

The Washington office was well staffed, but the OSR office was leaderless and drifting. My presence was requested in Paris and I returned. It is doubtlessly very difficult to quantify the full impact of our efforts to promote industrial and commercial productivity. That we had a real impact from time to time is clear. Many local entities, such as the Jeunes Patrons in France, took on the task of educating their members and anyone else who would listen. You may or may not consider it a blessing, but we were responsible for the first self-service grocery stores in Denmark.

We promoted advances in the foundry work in the Netherlands and Italy, just as the newly created NATO was searching for so-called "off-shore" procurement sources. We encouraged the introduction of business administration courses into European university curricula. We encouraged trade unions to think in economic rather than political terms. This list is endless. These examples are illustrative.

Along the way, we Americans learned some amusing lessons ourselves. I recall one of our textile manufacturing experts coming into my office, completely bewildered. "What's the problem?" I asked. He told me that he had recently spoken to a manufacturer in Lyons. He had asked the French patron, "Wouldn't you like to make more money?" and the answer came back, "No. Not particularly." "So what do I do now?" was this expert's question. In another incident, a British executive was asked, "Wouldn't you like to see more competition in England?" His answer was, "On the whole, no."

In any case, however we were judged in the 1950s, it is fundamental today to talk productivity both here in the U.S. and in Europe.

The Path to the Marshall Plan and Beyond

THEODORE GEIGER

M y connection with the Marshall Plan began in September 1945 when I was discharged from the Army at the request of the State Department and sent to London to join the staff of the U.S. Mission for Economic Affairs (MEA). MEA was headed by Thomas Blaisdell, for whom I had worked in the War Production Board before entering the Army in 1943. He had recommended my appointment to the Mission.

Stationed for administrative purposes at the U.S. Embassy in London, MEA represented the United States on three intergovernmental organizations established in the wake of the Allied victory to help the liberated European nations rebuild their economies. These were the so-called "E" organizations: the European Coal Organization (ECO), which allocated scarce supplies of coal among the participants; the European Central Inland Transport Organization (ECITO), which tried to ensure the efficient use of the available stock of locomotives and freight cars within the region; and the Emergency Economic Committee for Europe (EECE), which provided a forum for discussion of common recovery problems and attempted to bring about an equitable distribution of supplies of other scarce commodities among the members. Served by a small number of national civil servants seconded by the participating governments, these bodies had no staffs and budgets of their own and did not dispense aid in money or goods. Given its predominant military, economic and political position in Western Europe, the United States played the role of problem-solver and arbitrator in these organizations.

My work was exclusively with the EECE, which was headquartered in London, but various sub-committees usually met on the Continent at the invitation of member governments. Although I served on several of these sub-committees, my main responsibility was the EECE's timber sub-committee, which was concerned with lumber for rebuilding or repairing war-damaged housing, factories, railroads, mines, and other essential facilities.

A week after I arrived in London, I was preparing to attend the sub-committee's first meeting when Tom Blaisdell informed me that I would be chairing it. This proved to be a challenging assignment. I was the youngest member of the sub-committee; most of the others were twice my age and some had held cabinet posts in their prewar governments. Yet, being a representative of the U.S. Government conferred enormous prestige and influence in Europe during the early postwar years, and the deference accorded to me by the other members was owed in no small measure to my official position. Fortunately, however, I knew enough about the lumber industry from my experience in the War Production Board to be able to act as an arbitrator and expediter in carrying out the sub-committee's responsibilities.

Our work with the "E" organizations required the staff of the MEA to travel frequently on the Continent and we became reasonably well acquainted with the economic difficulties of the West European nations and the Allied-occupied zones of Germany. We reported regularly to the State Department on these developments and briefed every official who passed through London on them. Thus, we helped make Washington aware of the developing European economic crisis.

Until the fall of 1946, economic recovery was fairly rapid. Most countries gave top priority to using their available resources for rebuilding basic industries and transportation facilities and providing emergency shelter and food for the millions of people left homeless by the war. By the end of the year, however, the imports required for this effort had drained their already war-depleted reserves of gold, dollars and other convertible currencies, and they lacked the means for producing exportable goods that could earn them dollars in the United States, Canada and Latin America.

This dollar shortage became increasingly severe during the early months of 1947, as an unusually cold winter gripped Western Europe. The winter wheat crop failed, food rations were cut below already austere levels, fuel was so scarce that homes and offices could be heated for only a few hours a day, and icy conditions disrupted transportation systems. As the weak, centrist, coalition governments seemed powerless to cope with the deepening crisis, a general mood of hopelessness settled over the region, and popular support for the communist parties grew rapidly, especially in France, Italy and Allied-occupied Germany.

The dollar shortage not only cut off imports from outside Europe but also drastically curtailed trade among the European nations. Since the 1930s, most West European currencies had been inconvertible; after the war, governments permitted exports to one another only if they were paid for in U.S. dollars or balanced by imports of equivalent value under bilateral barter deals. One consequence was that there were often significant quantities of scarce commodities available for export within the region that could not be sold to importers because they were unable to pay in dollars or to offer desired goods in barter.

As a first step toward restoring a multilateral market system of trade and payments in Europe, I suggested to the State Department in September 1946 that the United States should consider the establishment of a European Clearing Union, which would balance off all bilateral surpluses and deficits in intra-European trade on a quarterly basis. This would eliminate bilateral barter and preferential trade arrangements. It could also increase the volume of intra-European trade to the extent that external sources of long-term funding, such as the United States or the World Bank, could be found to balance the Clearing Union's books at levels higher than the totals of the credits the surplus members were willing to provide, and the dollars the deficit members were able to pay, toward settling their accounts with the Union. I was politely thanked by the Department for my memorandum, but no action was taken on it.

By the spring of 1947, the severity of the economic crisis in Western Europe and the potentially disastrous political consequences were fully recognized in Washington. Having persuaded the Republican-dominated Congress to support the Greek/Turkish Aid Program, the Truman Administration and the State Department turned their attention to the needs of Western Europe. The result was the proposal for a European Recovery Program (ERP) in Secretary Marshall's speech at Harvard on June 5, 1947.

In July 1947, I returned to Washington both for personal reasons and because all important decisions affecting Europe's future would be made there. The Administration was organizing itself to cope with the formidable task of convincing the American people and the Congress that the proposed

ERP should be authorized and funded. In turn, the Republican Congress was determined to equip itself with the ability to make an independent evaluation of European needs and U.S. capabilities for meeting them. As part of this effort, the House of Representatives appointed a Select Committee on Foreign Aid chaired by a highly respected Republican Congressman from Massachusetts, Christian A. Herter, after whom the committee soon came to be called. He chose as staff director a Harvard professor, William Y. Elliott. He had learned of my European experience and asked me to become a full-time consultant to the committee. I accepted, eager to have the opportunity to work for Congressional approval of the Marshall Plan.

The members of the Herter Committee decided to see conditions in Western Europe for themselves. Divided into groups of three, they visited all of the countries during the early fall of 1947. I remained in Washington, charged with the task of drafting a general introduction to the country and the commodity sections of the projected final report which other staff consultants accompanying the Congressmen would prepare on their return. The introduction would explain the reasons for the European crisis and what needed to be done for European recovery.

After nearly two years in Europe, I had concluded—as had other young analysts in the U.S. and European governments—that the difficulties of the region and its uncertain future prospects could not be decisively improved simply by an emergency relief program. Undoubtedly, the current dollar shortage could be alleviated by grants and loans from the United States to finance needed imports of food, fuel and scarce materials. However, such aid would only be a palliative and would not be likely to prevent the recurrence of similar crises. In addition to emergency aid, structural changes in West European economies and in the relations among them were required. Only structural changes would enable these countries to achieve and sustain a rate of productivity growth that would make their exports large enough and sufficiently competitive in price and quality to restore their prewar capacity to support themselves at politically acceptable levels of living.

Productivity growth depended on more than adequate capital investment, labor skills and technological innovation. Equally critical were the elimination of the big budgetary deficits that were pushing up inflation and the abolition of the myriad of prohibitions and regulations, inherited from the Great Depression and the War, that were restraining investment, innovation and internal and external trade. By drastically lowering—and eventually removing—tariffs and quantitative restrictions on intra-European trade and restoring currency convertibility, the progressive integration of the European economies would create a freely trading regional market large and competitive enough to develop the capabilities required for competing successfully in world markets with the United States. Thus, European recovery depended essentially on what Western Europe could do for itself.

The draft of the introduction elaborated on this thesis and supported it with facts and figures. It explained:

- the basic imbalance between population and indigenous raw materials;
- how Europe had been self-supporting before the War;
- the effects of the Great Depression and the War on agricultural and industrial production and foreign trade;
- the crucial roles played in the regional economy by the United Kingdom and Germany and the necessity of reviving their capacity to do so again;
- the need to coordinate national recovery programs;
- the importance of currency stabilization and convertibility;
- the desirability and feasibility of European clearing and customs unions, and;
- the dangers of a complacent expectation that the European nations could be restored to economic self support and political stability by emergency relief alone.

Chris Herter and Bill Elliott liked the draft and made some changes and additions in it. The Herter Committee authorized its publication first as a separate twenty-page preliminary document under the title "What Western Europe Can Do For Itself," and then as an introduction to the final detailed report, which was issued early in 1948.

The Herter Committee terminated at the end of 1947 and I returned to the State Department to help with what was called "ERP preplanning" pending the passage of the authorizing and appropriations legislation. This process was completed by the end of March 1948 with the creation of a new, independent agency to administer the European Recovery Program (ERP). The new agency, the Economic Cooperation Administration (ECA), was activated early in April by the appointment of Paul Hoffman as Administrator, reporting directly to the President.

Hoffman immediately hired Richard M. Bissell, an MIT economist, as Assistant Administrator for Program and delegated to him the responsibility of directing the substantive economic work of the ECA.

The State Department had expected to transfer to the ECA the staff already working on ERP preplanning. However, given congressional insistence on ECA independence, Hoffman cautioned Bissell not to accept a wholesale transfer of personnel from the Department but only selected individuals. Bissell had served in Washington during the fall of 1947 as staff director of the group of eminent private citizens appointed by the President and which, under the chairmanship of Averell Harriman, had issued an influential report recommending the adoption of the Marshall Plan. During that time, Bissell had read the preliminary report I had written for the Herter Committee and had asked me to lunch to discuss it. Seeing my name on the list of people working in the Department on ERP preplanning, he called and asked if I would like to become one of his three special assistants. "Would I!" was all I could reply. The next day, I moved over to the Miatico Building where the new agency—then less than a week old—was located.

So began the most exciting and stimulating period of my years in public service. Working for Dick Bissell was the greatest intellectual challenge of my life. The depth and keenness of his analytical capabilities were awesome. Pragmatic by nature, he was oriented toward solutions to real-life problems rather than to theoretical insights. The rigor of his logic, the pertinence of his information, and the clarity of his spoken and written expression set a high standard for the performance he expected from those who reported directly to him. Yet, Bissell wasn't arrogant or condescending, and he treated everyone with courtesy, even those of whose intentions or abilities he had a low opinion. However, he didn't suffer fools or time-wasters gladly, and dealing with them was soon delegated to his special assistants. I have never known another person who could have discharged as brilliantly as he did the responsibilities he bore. The broad authority delegated to him by Hoffman gave Bissell the final word on how much aid both in dollars and in counterpart funds (the local currency accruing to participating governments from the domestic sales of ECA-financed imports) each of the 16 countries would receive and for what purposes. Controlling the purse strings, Bissell also set the general policies governing the operations of the substantive divisions of ECA headquarters in Washington and of the Office of the Special Representative (OSR) in Paris and the ECA missions in the participating nations.

Averell Harriman had expected that he, as the Special Representative to the Organization for European Economic Cooperation (OEEC), would have final authority over the division of aid and the country missions, and there was some tension between him and Bissell at the beginning. But Hoffman was firm and the deference with which Bissell treated Harriman soon reconciled him to the situation. Moreover, Harriman felt it was beneath his dignity to deal with anyone in the participating governments and the OEEC below the rank of cabinet minister or ambassador. This effectively excluded him from direct contact with the very able Robert Marjolin, the Secretary-General of the OEEC, who ran the organization on a day-to-day basis. Harriman delegated this responsibility to the person he had initially appointed to head the OSR's Program Division, an obscure economics professor from Iowa. With little experience in international economics and policy making—and a poor manager as well—this man quickly lost the respect not only of his own staff, but also of Marjolin and the heads of the resident European delegations to the OEEC, who began to look directly to Bissell whenever serious issues had to be discussed. It was not until June 1949 that the appointment to the OSR of Milton Katz (as Deputy Special Representative) and Lincoln Gordon (as Program Director) provided it with leadership of the requisite intellectual and managerial capacity.

As Bissell's special assistant, I had two major responsibilities. The first was to handle relations with the OEEC. All cables and memoranda from the OSR regarding the operations of the OEEC were addressed to Bissell. Those on regional problems or with regional implications were my concern. I drafted replies to them—often after conferring with people in the operating divisions—and submitted them to Bissell, who usually wanted some changes and additions made. Conversely, we in Washington frequently initiated queries and suggestions regarding the work of the OEEC, most of which I drafted for Bissell's signature.

At the request of the heads of the resident national delegations to the OEEC, Bissell attended their monthly meetings, and I always accompanied him to Paris. We met, of course, with Harriman and his staff to go over the agenda. But, the most productive part of our visit was invariably the small dinner, arranged by Marjolin in a private room at a three-star restaurant, and attended only by the heads of the British, French, Italian, Dutch, and Belgian delegations. The discussions over the good food and wine were in confidence and ranged from frank evaluations of program successes and failures to sharp critiques of possible new policy initiatives contemplated by the Europeans or the Americans. Knowing the nature of my work for Bissell, Marjolin always invited me, but until Lincoln Gordon came to the OSR, no one on Harriman's staff was ever asked to attend the dinners—or was even aware they took place.

My second area of responsibility, related to the first, was to stimulate the development within ECA headquarters of new ideas for and approaches to the structural reforms at the regional level that would help the West European nations achieve and maintain self-support at politically acceptable levels of living. At an early stage, I established an ECA Policy Series, for which anyone in the agency could submit a paper for possible inclusion. Many of the most insightful, forward-looking or provocative ideas produced by individuals or teams within the agency were published in the Series. My workload on idea generation and OEEC relations, as well as on other assignments from Bissell eventually grew so heavy that he permitted me to hire John C.L. Hulley, a very bright young Harvard graduate student in economics, as an assistant.

Of my own contributions to the ideas on regional restructuring, only the two most significant may be briefly noted here, both done in collaboration with others. I had already urged in the Herter Committee report the importance of a customs union for the future prosperity of the West European countries. Singly and together, Harold Van Buren Cleveland (a friend from the State Department who was head of the France/Italy section in ECA headquarters) and I wrote several papers in the Series explaining the problems confronting Western Europe in the years ahead—including how to reintegrate Germany into the regional economy—that could be substantially mitigated by a customs union and beyond that by a European political and economic union. As a first step in that direction, we recommended that Paul Hoffman propose to the OEEC's ministerial-level governing Council the immediate abolition of quantitative restrictions on imports and exports within the region and the progressive reduction of tariffs and other trade barriers to create an integrated European market.

Bissell liked the proposal and discussed it with Hoffman, who approved. Van Cleveland and I drafted the relevant paragraphs of the forceful "single market" speech, which Hoffman delivered at the Council's meeting on October 31, 1949. The OEEC initiated a program along these lines some months after.

The second collaboration was on the necessary monetary complement to the trade-liberalization program. Updating and substantially elaborating my clearing-union proposal of three years before, Van Cleveland, John Hulley and I (with help from Albert Hirschman of the Federal Reserve Board) drafted a detailed plan for an Intra-European Clearing Union. Bissell's critique of the draft significantly improved its substance and persuasiveness, and his name rather than ours had to appear on the proposal if it was to be taken seriously by the OEEC. Known therefore as the Bissell Plan, he presented it at the monthly meeting of the OEEC heads of delegations on December 10, 1949. After prolonged negotiations in the OEEC, in which the OSR participated, a revised version of the plan was implemented in July 1950 as the European Payments Union (EPU).

I do not wish to imply that ideas about trade liberalization and payments arrangements were generated exclusively by Americans. Quite the contrary. Both subjects had been discussed during the summer of 1947 at the Paris Conference on European Economic Cooperation, which prepared the European response to Secretary Marshall's speech. That dialogue was continued in its successor organization, the OEEC. But, as late as the spring of 1949, these desultory deliberations were leading nowhere, stymied by the Europeans' unwillingness to make the concessions to one another needed for a common approach to regional trade liberalization and new payments facilities. It was then that Bissell concluded that the ECA had to take the initiative if anything was to be done. Paul Hoffman's single-market speech in October was a wake-up call to the Europeans, emphatically placing the influence and prestige of the United States behind the goal of European economic integration and promising U.S. support for a plan of action capable of accomplishing it. This was followed two months after by the presentation of the Bissell Plan, a detailed blueprint on which the Europeans could focus their efforts. Their response to both U.S. initiatives was energetic and productive.

To my mind, this experience exemplifies the second of the two necessary contributions of the United States to the success of the Marshall Plan. The first contribution was, of course, the billions of dollars that financed the importation into Western Europe of goods and services that were required by the immediate emergency and that guaranteed an adequate, if still austere, level of lying to its people until self-support could be achieved. Equally important, these imports included new machinery and equipment that added an important increment to the Europeans' own much larger capital investment in restoring and continuing to raise the productivity of their factories and fields.

Many Americans and Europeans persist in equating the Marshall Plan with this physical contribution, which was certainly more photogenic and easier to grasp than the second contribution. But, the second had much deeper and longer-term consequences for the future of Western Europe. The formal commitment of the United States to supporting the economic integration of the region was a necessary—though not in itself a sufficient-condition for the eventual success of the movement toward European union then being organized by Jean Monnet, Altiero Spinelli and others on the Continent. While drafting Hoffman's single-market speech, Van Cleveland and I urged that it include an explicit endorsement of the movement toward European union as the long-term goal of economic integration. Bissell was skeptical of such an outcome, and the State Department wouldn't even allow us to use the term unification, let alone refer to a European union. However, in his posthumous memoirs (*Reflections of a Cold Warrior*, Yale University Press, 1996), Bissell wrote, "I have to admit, that I did not have as strong a sense of the tide of history as these two men did."

In the 1950 renewal of the authorizing legislation, the Congress did add to the purposes of the ERP the encouragement of European unification. And, when the Eisenhower Administration took office in 1953, Secretary of State John Foster Dulles, long an advocate of European union, made support for it an official policy of the United States.

The Marshall Plan— Answering Liberal and Conservative Objections

Arthur Goldschmidt

Introduction

I remember the two elder American statesmen, each a leading figure in his respective party, who questioned the feasibility of the Marshall Plan upon its unveiling in June 1947. This was a jolt to President Truman who needed to get the plan through a newly elected Congress with a Republican majority—the first in almost two decades. He called for prompt answers to the doubts they raised.

Former President Herbert Hoover, the Republican predecessor to Franklin Roosevelt, simply objected to its drain on the treasury. This knee-jerk reaction had been expected. Responsibility for answering his arguments was turned over to the staff of the new Council of Economic Advisors, who eventually rebutted it with a fiscal study.

However, Bernard Baruch, prominent wealthy Democrat and adviser to several presidents, had raised a more complex question of whether the demands of such massive aid would outstrip American capacities, especially when considering dwindling non-renewable resources and eroding topsoils. To answer Baruch, President Truman appointed a Cabinet Committee to mobilize the entire Executive Branch, including independent agencies such as the TVA and the Federal Reserve, into interlocking task forces that would determine the effect of the proposed foreign aid on the domestic economy. It would be chaired by the Secretary of the Interior,

Julius A. "Cap" Krug, a "Baruch man." Krug, an engineer who had risen to top management in the War agencies, had just recently been appointed Secretary of the Interior, replacing my old boss, the feisty Harold L. Ickes.

Cap called me into his inner office and related the objections delivered by Baruch and the interdepartmental structure being corralled to answer them. The huge organization chart he sketched seemed awkwardly balanced on a small box labeled "Economic Editorial Group." He wanted me in that box.

As the director of the Power Division in the Office of the Secretary, I asked, "Why me? I'm not an economist any more."

"Maybe not, Tex," he answered candidly, "but you're the nearest thing we've got!"

Our small drafting bloc dwindled in that sweltering summer to Chandler Morse of the Federal Reserve, Mary Keyserling of Commerce, and me. Despite our size, we made enormous progress and celebrated the fact that our report—a hundred-page folio-sized volume with lots of tables and charts, reviewing the status of all raw materials and industries of the country—was the first to be completed and published. It led the parade of reports that would include those of a joint Congressional committee and its expert staff, headed by the brilliant Richard Basal, which became the epicenter of the Marshall Plan drive.

Later, as Secretary Krug presented me with the department's highest honor, the Distinguished Service Award (usually reserved for dead heroes of rescues in the field services), he included the fact that I had "served as chairman of a committee to analyze information gathered by approximately twenty committees, and supplied to them by as many government agencies, for a study of the relationship between the foreign assistance program and our domestic economy, which the President had requested me to conduct. His committee, within a short time, had to review and assimilate voluminous data for presentation in accurate, concise and lucid form. The resulting report, National Resources and Foreign Aid, published in October, 1947, received international circulation and gratifying acceptance."

1948-1950

An immediate result of the Krug report was the involvement of the Department of the Interior in the network of committees of the Department of State, including the Executive Committee for Economic Foreign Policy

headed by Assistant Secretary Willard Thorp. I served on these committees, reporting to the Secretary of the Interior and keeping its bureaus
informed. The debates in Congress and the executive branch conference
rooms during the winter of 1947-48 continued in our living rooms and at
our dinner tables. Could we or couldn't we? Will we or won't we? The
topic monopolized the media at home and abroad.

Similarly, confrontations erupted in the parliaments abroad. In
February 1948, I heard the French National Assembly debate the question
of joining the plan—opposition voices were met with chanting of "The
Volga Boat Song" and pro-Marshall Plan speakers were shouted down
with cries of "Coca Cola, Coca Cola!" Such was often the level of the
discourse.

The ghost of John Maynard Keynes haunted our own consideration
of the Marshall Plan. It was however, the earlier Keynes rather than the
author of the *General Theory*. Indeed, many of us veterans of the New
Deal who had struggled with unemployment during the Great Depression
felt he had merely put a scientific label after the fact, on what should
have been done with common sense. The CWA and WPA really deserve
more plaudits from Keynes. Unaware of his advice to the British
government in the 1920s, we saw his visit to Washington in the mid-
1930s as a case of teaching grandma to suck eggs in the good old British
tradition. Whatever our petulance in the 1930s, all was mercifully forgotten
by Bretton Woods as the war waned in the 1940s. It was thus the sharp
reasoning of the young Keynes in his 1919 book and the mess at Versailles
that remained in everybody's mind in the Marshall Plan discussions.

Most of us had been brought up on "The Economic Consequences of
the Peace." Would we become entangled with European reconstruction
debts? Would the new Republican Congress take us back to the days of
Calvin Coolidge and quotesmanship such as, "They hired the money,
didn't they?" Before it was clear that Vandenberg would become a
statesman, we all played games thinking up ways of getting cash into
European hands without collecting a lot of IOUs. I had a couple of schemes
such as sending our armed forces on leave, especially shore leave for the
navy, with bonus payments for past deeds and advances on future ones.
This would give a jump start to the European economy without straining
their capital account; as a popular tune of the time put it, "You won't
miss what's gone!" But, as estimates of requirements ran from 12 to 20
billion dollars, meeting bottom lines of such magnitudes could potentially
exhaust our armed forces if not the treasury to the point of endangering
our defenses.

My less labor-intensive scheme simply entailed the United States buying outright certain fixed assets that Americans generally would easily agree were worth owning, such as Mont-Saint-Michel, Chartres, West-minister Abbey, Stonehenge, some bridges in Venice and Florence, and similar real estate and infrastructure in participating countries, on which we could fly the Stars and Stripes. We might give their present owners the right to redeem them at some later time. In view of the advances in our technology for moving things and past history of rich Americans carrying off whole castles, some Europeans might have questioned the validity of our promises to keep these treasures where they were, ultimately frightened by the prospect of the glories of Europe disappearing across the broad Atlantic highway.

My Junket Plan grew out of these crude attempts to avoid a debt problem. It was the only one of my inventions that was given any attention in the press; it was featured as the major part of the column, "Under the Sun," in *Holiday* magazine for April 1948. Roger Angell, then still in his only farm league assignment before hitting the majors, was the columnist who had dinner with us in Georgetown and wrote up the scheme under the title: "Solution:"

American tourists can save the world. That's the opinion of a man we know in Washington, DC who—like everyone else these days—has been worrying about the future of Europe and the Marshall Plan. Quite without intention, this man has come up with a plan of his own . . . it is called the Junket Plan. The big sticker in the current European Recovery Plan, explains our friend (whose name is not Mr. Junket), is the little matter of how the 16 European nations are to repay the money we vote them without going broke all over again. He estimates that Europe needs roughly $14,000,000,000 to get on its feet. Under the Junket Plan, money will be sent to the participating nations, but not as an outright gift. The minute each country gets its bundle of cash it will issue bonds or certificates in the same amount. These will be worth $100 each and preferably should be handsomely printed jobs . . . like small travel posters. Illustrated with tourist attractions, like the Tower of London, Chartres . . . and the Doges palace. They will be sent to this country, and every man, woman and child will receive one $100 nest egg that will take five years to hatch—before that time they can not be cashed or sold. Sometime in 1953 they will mature, whereupon they can be dusted off and spent, but only in Europe.

That's where the junket comes in—a junket to Europe by thousands and thousands of Americans, all shareholders in the future of the 16 participating nations . . . [which] actually are paying back in the commodity which they can best afford: services like hotel rooms, railroad tickets."

Angell's column goes on celebrating the benefits to all concerned, including fighting U.S. inflation, educating Americans and insuring that "many thousands of Americans and many thousands of Europeans will get to know each other better, with peace, prosperity and good will as the result."

As we know, the Junket Plan was never adopted as such. But, like the case of the Asian Co-Prosperity Sphere of the Japanese, its aims came quietly into being, if not quite as democratically spread as I had proposed.

When the Marshall Plan was finally adopted, the expertise of the Bureau of Mines, Geological Survey, Reclamation and other bureaus of the Interior Department were made available to the Marshall Plan. We thus became part of the latest fad that had started in Washington with the closing of the war—flaunting the foreign or international aspects of the activities of domestic agencies. Some Departments created posts of Assistant Secretary for Foreign Affairs and everybody engaged in encouraging their relevant Specialized Agencies in the new United Nations system. They wanted to catch up with the Labor Department that inherited that relic of the old League of Nations the International Labor Office (ILO). So, in time, the ILO was joined by Food and Agriculture Organization (FAO), World Health Organization (WHO), UNESCO, the Bretton Woods twins and the other satellites of the UN system.

The Department of the Interior never was quite so fashionable. To be sure, we were suspect because of our promotion of the United Nations Scientific Conference on the Conservation and Utilization of Resources, which Truman had suggested to the United Nations in 1946. In heading the U.S. effort on the preparatory committees of this first big UN conference, I made use of the network of scientific bureaus of the government and their counterparts in universities and the private sector that had been set up for the Krug Report. We achieved a high level of American participation in papers for the Conference. But, there was always a State Department officer at my side to ensure that the meeting would not give birth to a Planetary Organization of Home Offices, Interiors, and other "Ministries of the Miscellaneous."

In the course of 1948, I became convinced that the parameters of the Marshall Plan idea should be widened to include help to the poorer countries of the world and that such development was essential to curb their rampant population growth. I presented my views in an address to the American Academy of Arts and Sciences in Boston that was widely circulated by the interior press office and placed into the Congressional Record by Congresswoman Helen Gahagan Douglas. By happy coincidence, my speech on January 12 was followed by President Truman's repetition of the same points in his triumphant inaugural address eight days later. An Advisory Committee on Technical Assistance was thus added to the State Department network to develop the Truman proposal for submission to the Congress and to the United Nations. I represented the Interior Department on ACTA, too.

In August, the United Nations Scientific Conference on the Conservation and Utilization of Resources began at Lake Success and was front page news around the world for three weeks. It spurred interest in international economic cooperation for development and the creation by the United Nations of the Expanded Programme of Technical Assistance (ACTA). I joined in the administration of that program in the fall of 1950.

L'Envoi—1968

In the Spring of 1968, Paul Hoffman and I, as the Administrator of the United Nations Development Programme and the American member of its Governing Council respectively, met privately over dinner on a Friday evening in Geneva to talk about the session to begin the following Monday. Hoffman seemed uncharacteristically tired. Deeply concerned for my friend—one of the really great men I have known—I was glad to hear that his wife was flying in that evening. Anna Rosenberg was an important public official long before their unlikely autumnal marriage. (Incidentally, she had been considered a "Baruch man" in her heyday). Paul spoke warmly of missing her, but that was not the cause of his condition.

Paul was simply exhausted from being feted for the past couple of weeks at national celebrations of the twentieth anniversary of the Marshall Plan in the various capitals of Europe. As we dropped any pretense of working on the following week's agenda I realized once again that he always kept his eye on the ball. If his close personal friendships made it impossible for him to turn down any of these invitations he would use them to further the work he was now doing for the United Nations. He had taken these occasions to drive home the lesson of the value of international economic cooperation, especially his current concern for increasing the voluntary contributions of governments to the UNDP. What a man!

Participating in the Prologue and Epilogue of the Marshall Plan

ROBERT L. HUBBELL

My experiences with the Marshall Plan were of three quite different types. In 1947, I was a member of a team of Harvard graduate students who prepared recommendations on how to administer the Plan, some of which were adopted. My next two experiences were in Europe with successor organizations from the Marshall Plan.

Marshall Plan Organization

In the fall of 1947, the Bureau of the Budget, the State Department and Congressional committees were busy preparing plans and legislation to authorize the structure and financing for the European Recovery Program proposed by Secretary of State Marshall in his Harvard Commencement speech the previous June. At the Graduate School of Public Administration in Harvard (then known by the name of its building as the Littauer School and presently as the Kennedy School), Professor Merle Fainsod presented his seminar in public administration with a list of problems for which solutions should be proposed. Five of us took on the topic of organizing the administration of the Marshall Plan. Two of the five, Bartlett Harvey and Harry Kahn, went to work for the Economic Cooperation Administration (ECA) immediately after leaving Harvard. I went first to the Bureau of the Budget and then to the Foreign Operations Administration.

Fainsod thought our paper had useful ideas and passed it on to two colleagues who were providing consulting services in Washington about the Marshall Plan. Professor Lincoln Gordon of the Business School was working with the State Department and Professor W.Y. Elliott of the School of Arts and Sciences was working with the House of Representatives Foreign Affairs Committee headed by Christian Herter. Both professors reported that ideas in the paper found their way into authorizing legislation or executive orders. I no longer have a copy or the paper, but even if one could find parallels between it and the authorizing legislation, one could not be sure that the ideas had not also come from other sources.

A key proposal was that the existing structure for financing and arranging exports should be used for commodities financed by the Marshall Plan. That is, the Economic Cooperation Administration should not purchase, ship and deliver commodities. The scheme was that banks from which a European importer would normally purchase foreign exchange would now issue a letter of credit chargeable against the nation's Marshall Plan allotment to buy supplies or equipment on the approved list for that country. In this manner, the European importer would make arrangements with an American exporter just as if the foreign exchange had come from regular sources.

Our paper also dealt with the other side of that transaction, namely the counterpart funds. The local currency which an importer would use to buy foreign exchange went into a special account. These funds were then used to finance local development activities, with the joint approval of the U.S. economic cooperation mission in that country and the economic coordination ministry of the country. Another feature of our paper was that the U.S. should have a mission outside the embassy in each country which would operate with a minimum of control from Washington headquarters. This pattern worked, partly because strong people were recruited to head the country missions.

Labor Division in SRE

Paul Porter's paper, "From the Morgenthau Plan to the Marshall Plan and NATO," says the Marshall Plan ended December 31, 1951. That would mark the end of its 4-year authorization. However, the structure of U.S. Missions in European countries and a Special Representative in Europe (SRE) headquartered in Paris persisted for a while after that. I believe some countries still received assistance which had been previously obligated. I know there were still technical advisors in several countries and also counterpart funds to use. The Office for European Economic Cooperation (OEEC) continued to operate to promote cooperation between nations. At some point, the U.S. organization became part of the Foreign Operations Administration which embraced the Technical Cooperation Administration (Point four) as well as the ECA. Even today the OEEC endures as the Office of Economic Cooperation and Development, a coordinating body for donor nations.

In the summer of 1952, David Christian, the Manpower Advisor in the Labor Division of SRE, recruited me to be his assistant. The Labor Division basically consisted of people who worked with European trade unions to help them resist Communist infiltration and to be positive forces for democracy and development. The Division had a kind of functional supervision of labor officers in several U.S. Missions around Europe. The Division was a bureaucratic home for the manpower function. Dave Christian was U.S. representative on the OEEC Manpower Committee and operated with little supervision. The Manpower Committee exchanged information on operations of vocational training and employment services. It endeavored to negotiate on movement of workers across borders and to promote some parallelism of national social insurance systems. The U.S. interest was to encourage cooperation both to help development and to build toward European union. It seems likely that some of the tentative steps taken under the OEEC Manpower Committee helped the groundwork for the later closer manpower cooperation of the European Union.

Dave Christian and I also represented the U.S. on the NATO Manpower Committee and attended meetings of the International Committee of European Migration in Geneva, which dealt with refugees.

When Harold Stassen took over the Foreign Operations Administration, he set out to reduce staff. All positions in the Labor Division were eliminated except for the labor economist Morris Weisz and myself. In the summer of 1954, I declined to return to the Budget Bureau and Morris Weisz became responsible for manpower duties.

The Economic Cooperation Administration, like other special wartime agencies, had special recruiting power. Federal civil servants who transferred from old-line agencies to the ECA had reemployment rights. I had left the Labor-Welfare Division but reentered the Budget Bureau in the International Division.

Operations-Aid Mission in Greece

In 1959, I transferred from the Budget Bureau back to the FOA. At first I was in Washington in charge of the Greece-Turkey-Iran Office. In the summer of 1960 I went to Athens as Deputy Director of the U.S. Operations Mission there.

Greece had received aid before the Marshall Plan under the Truman Doctrine to defend Greece and Turkey. It continued to receive assistance after the Marshall Plan. We observed the 15th anniversary of the Truman Doctrine in March of 1962 and closed out the Mission at the end of the fiscal year, June 30, 1962.

Although it had been part of the Marshall Plan, Greece was publicized as the first less developed nation to be "graduated" from the program of the United States Agency for International Development (the new name under President Kennedy). The judgment was that the Greek economy could be self-sustaining and competitive. Later, other "graduates" included Iran, Korea, Taiwan, and, I believe, Argentina, Brazil and Mexico.

During the last two years, Greece still received about $20 million a year in financing for imports. It was difficult to distinguish whether this was justified by a foreign exchange gap or as support for a defense effort. During the processing years, our assistance, both financial and technical had done much to help increase agricultural, electrical, and industrial production. We had also helped with a network of roads.

We had a few technical advisors during those last two years. The ministries receiving the advisers seemed pleased to have them but the Coordination Ministry and Foreign Ministry seemed insulted that Greece was still getting "advice."

One of the advisors, George Summers, was helping with agricultural marketing. Greece, despite its climatic advantage, was having trouble exporting tomatoes and fruit to Europe because it lacked inspection, grading and quality control. Summers persuaded seven different agencies with overlapping responsibilities such as agriculture, commerce, transport, and customs to cooperate with a Cretan farm association to start grading tomatoes. The graded tomatoes brought premium prices in the Athens market, demonstrating that the effort was worthwhile. When I left, the Greek officials were talking about grading for other commodities for the European market.

Another technical assistance project was a contract with Harvard University and its Professor Edward Mason for a team to help with economic policy and planning. Mason recruited as team chief a holder of a Harvard Ph.D. who was chair of the Economics Department at Berkeley, Andreas Papandreou. A Greek native, he was an American citizen with an American wife. His father headed the opposition party in Greece. Unfortunately, Andreas used the return to Greece as an opportunity to get into politics and eventually succeed his father, renouncing his U.S. citizenship. He was an opportunist who espoused a policy of semi-socialism and anti-Americanism. His years as Prime Minister undid some of the good from the Marshall Plan and may well have delayed Greece's full membership in the European Union. If the United States had not financed Papandreou's return, he probably would have found another way to get there, but, it is ironic that the contract to bring him was one of the last USAID projects.

A New Trade
Policy For Europe

BEN T. MOORE

The plans for the post-war economy did not include anything like the Marshall Plan. Instead they called for three institutions: the International Monetary Fund (IMF), the

International Bank for Reconstruction and Development (IBRD), also called the World Bank, and an International Trade Organization (ITO). All three were to be "specialized agencies" under the United Nations, global in scope and open to all members of the UN. The Bank and the Fund were agreed upon at the Bretton Woods Monetary and Financial Conference in July 1944, although they were not ratified until the end of 1945. A UN Committee was created to prepare for the International Trade Organization at the beginning of 1946, but it made slow progress, especially after the Republican party took control of the American Congress in the election of November 1946.

I was assigned to the Division of Commercial Policy (CP) in the Department of State. CP was responsible for drafting a Charter for the ITO and the planning of multilateral reductions in tariffs and other impediments to trade. My section in CP covered trade policy for Europe. I worked closely with an officer who was responsible for financial policy toward Europe, Harold Van Buren Cleveland (d. 1993).

European production and exports were hit hard by the Great Blizzard of January 1947 and the European balance of payments deteriorated. The British decided that they could no longer subsidize Greece and Turkey to prevent chaos and communists from overwhelming them. President Harry

Truman was thus forced to proclaim the Truman Doctrine: the United States would come to the aid of countries whose independence was threatened by subversion from outside. The Congressional reaction to Truman's request for emerging aid to these two countries made it clear that a new approach which would treat Europe as a whole and provide a solution to its economic problems was required.

Van Cleveland and I had already begun a paper based on such a comprehensive approach. After Charles P. Kindleberger, an expert on the economy of defeated Germany, returned from the Moscow foreign ministers meeting (March and April 1947) which had failed to persuade the Russians to treat Germany as a unit and merge their zone with the British, American, and French zones, Van Cleveland and I asked him to add a section on Germany to our paper. The paper was not widely circulated until after Marshall's Harvard speech. However, it led to an eloquent speech by Under-Secretary of State Dean Acheson on May 8, 1947 to the Delta Council at the Cleveland Teacher's College in the heart of Mississippi cotton country. This speech was intended to alert the country to the need for the Marshall Plan. Dean Acheson resigned as Under-Secretary of State on June 1, 1947, but he continued to support the Marshall Plan by speaking around the country as a private citizen.

Meanwhile William L. Clayton, the Under-Secretary of State for Economic Affairs, had been in Geneva conducting the negotiations on the International Trade Organization and tariff reduction with Clair Wilcox, the Director of the Office of International Trade Policy in the Department of State, as his deputy. Clayton moved about in Europe and was frightened by what he saw as a breakdown of the exchange of goods between farmers and city dwellers caused by the decay in value of key currencies. He wrote a memorandum on the appalling state of the European economy which he gave to George Kennan, Director of the State Department Planning Staff. Kennan sent this memo and his memo on the political situation in Europe to Secretary of State George C. Marshall. Charles E. Bohlen, a career foreign service officer who had been President Franklin Roosevelt's interpreter at the Yalta Conference in 1945, incorporated much of Clayton's memo word for word and provided Marshall with the text of the June 5, 1947 speech at Harvard.

The speech was intentionally vague but it was clear on one essential point. The Europeans had to take the initiative and determine what they required from the United States for a recovery program. Both Earnest Bevin, Foreign Minister of Great Britain and Georges Bidault, Foreign

Minister of France, understood this. Bevin flew to Paris on June 17 to discuss the next steps and agreed to plan a conference to be held in Paris. In return Bidault agreed that Britain should have the chairmanship of the conference. They also agreed to invite the Soviets to participate in the planning. Bidault felt it was essential to invite them to placate the French left, and Bevin went along with this. They both hoped the Soviets would back out, fearing American domination. France would then agree to proceed with a conference without them.

Vyacheslov Molotov, the Soviet Foreign Minister, arrived in Paris on June 27, 1947 with a delegation of around 100 officials. Stalin had instructed him to insist on finding out from Bevin and Bidault their stance on three points: (1) ascertain the type and amount of aid, (2) insist that it be offered on a country-by-country basis, avoiding a Europe-wide cooperative program, and (3) permit the participation of the Germans only if Soviet demands, particularly for reparations, would be met. When it became clear that the Plan still had no firm guidelines and that the Western powers would *not* agree to Soviet demands (2) and (3), Molotov terminated the discussions. On July 4 Bidault and Bevin issued invitations to all European countries except Spain, still considered fascist. Sixteen countries convened in Paris on July 12, 1947. The Eastern European Soviet satellites had been forced by Moscow to decline after an acute display of bitterness, particularly by the Czechs.

On July 22, 1947 Britain made the pound convertible for current transactions, as was required by the agreements signed at the end of 1945. These put into effect the Bretton Woods agreements (IMF and World Bank) and provided Britain with a large loan in dollars from the United States. Other countries, particularly Belgium and Argentina, which were holding sterling balances as a result of exporting more to Britain than they imported, converted these balances into dollars causing a substantial drop in Britain's gold and dollar reserves. On August 20, 1947 the British stopped what amounted to a run on the pound and made sterling inconvertible again. The British economy obviously had not recovered enough to restore confidence in its currency and this strengthened Bevin's determination to press ahead with the Marshall Plan.

The Committee on European Economic Cooperation (CEEC) began its effort to respond to Secretary Marshall's request that Europe, now limited to Western Europe, draw up a plan, a request for American aid issued on July 12, 1947. On April 3, 1948, eight months later, President

Harry Truman signed the Economic Cooperation Act making the Marshall Plan a reality. In this period the following actions were taken.

1. The CEEC under the chairmanship of Oliver Franks, an Oxford Don transformed into a brilliant civil servant by Britain's problems in the war and the post-war period, drew up a program of cooperation and a request for aid, which was clearly too large. The State Department sent a delegation to Paris in September 1947, of which I was a member. In the course of providing the friendly aid that Secretary Marshall had offered in his Harvard speech, this group managed to reduce the amount of aid requested in the CEEC report by several billion dollars.

2. The CEEC report was further received by the State Department's working Committee on the Marshall Plan, of which Charles P. Kindleberger was Executive Secretary. The committee used a commodity approach, listing twenty-six commodities and commodity groups which were exchanged among participating countries and provided by the United States. The residual amounts to be provided by the United States were supposed to meet the dollar deficits of the participating countries but they fell short, thus reducing the amount of U.S. aid further.

Commodity and country committees were formed and they included not only the State Department experts on each country and commodity, but also experts from other departments. In addition there were massive reports by special committees like the committee under Secretary of Commerce Averill Harriman which agreed to the political necessity of the European Recovery Program (ERP). Senator Arthur Vandenberg, converted from being an isolationist by the Japanese attack on Pearl Harbor and since the Republican victory in the 1946 election Chairman of the Senate Foreign Relations Committee, commented that, "The preparations the State Department has made for this next showdown are amazing. Indeed they overwhelmed us with documentation. It is a magnificent piece of work. But it is three inches thick."

3. The hostility of the Soviet Union helped to get the program passed by the United States Congress. In addition to their walkout in Paris and forcing their satellites not to participate, they encouraged the communist parties, particularly in France and Italy, to mount strikes and demonstrations against the United States and the Marshall Plan. Both Georges Bidault and Alcide de Gasperi, the Prime Ministers of France and Italy, were having difficulty forming governments leaving out their numerous communist deputies. De Gasperi did not succeed until the Christian Democrats won the Italian election shortly after the Marshall

Plan legislation was passed by the American Congress. De Gasperi was undoubtedly helped by the threat that the United States might eliminate Italy from the program if the communists came to power. The Pope, the Italian priests and the recently formed American Central Intelligence Agency also contributed to the Christian Democrats. Also the Czechoslovak coup in early 1947 which brought the communists to power and ended democracy in Czechoslovakia boasted support for the Western democracies participating in the Marshall Plan.

4. Congress also insisted that the State Department not administer the European Recovery Program. The legislation provided for an independent agency, the Economic Cooperation Administration (ECA), headed by and staffed primarily by businessmen. The ECA also decided to establish its own missions in all sixteen of the participating countries. Each mission was required to assemble detailed monthly reports on their country.

Then there was the problem of counterpart funds. These funds were created by the sale of U.S. goods for local currency. Countries like Britain, which claimed to manage their economies properly, did not admit that the U.S. had any say over the disposition of the local currency. The U.S. insisted that the use of these funds required the agreement of the ECA country mission. For Britain this procedure was simply an automatic formality, but for a country like France, withholding of counterpart francs could be used as pressure to curb deficits and hold down inflation. A further problem was the insistence by Congress that five percent of the counterpart funds belonged to the U.S. and should be used at its own discretion. Some of this local currency was used to build new embassies, but more went to pay for trips to Europe by Congressman and their hotels and entertainment while abroad.

5. When I joined the staff of the State Department's working committee on the Marshall Plan shortly after the Harvard speech in June 1947, I was the only officer transferred from the Division of Commercial Policy. As I have pointed out, CP's task was to create the third institution for postwar economic policy, the International Trade Organization (ITO). The negotiations on the ITO were going slowly. As a way to give impetus to trade policy, we conceived the idea of going ahead with multilateral negotiations on tariff reductions before the charter of the ITO was completed rather than wait for the ITO to be established and ratified. Therefore, long before Marshall's speech, almost the entire staff of CP went off to Geneva to engage in multilateral tariff negotiations with many

UN members, including European countries involved in the Marshall Plan without the Soviet bloc. These negotiations were conducted on the basis of non-discrimination. If a tariff was reduced by one country in return for a reduction by another country, these reductions would be extended to all countries participating in the negotiations, the principle of most-favored-nation trading status (MFN). These reductions also were bound against subsequent increases. The General Argument on Tariffs and Trade (GATT) came into force on January 1, 1948, before the Marshall Plan began fully functioning. The Charter for the ITO was drafted later in the year, but when it became clear that the necessary ratifications, including that of the U.S., would not be forthcoming, the plan for the ITO was dropped. GATT became a multilateral treaty and its members were called "the contracting parties." Its headquarters were in Geneva, and although it never became a full-fledged specialized agency, it went on to negotiate "rounds" of tariff reductions which drastically lowered these obstacles to trade over the years.

Working with Clair Wilcox, I made an effort to make a connection between the Marshall Plan and GATT. However, the first was based on a regional approach, while the other was from the beginning global. There was also another problem. Tariff reductions could not really take effect until currencies were stabilized and convertible. The Marshall Plan required that the two other UN specialized agencies, which were already ratified, the IMF and World Bank, be put on hold. They were, like the stillborn ITO, open to all UN members and were supposed to be global rather than regional in scope. Before the Marshall Plan came into effect, the World Bank made only one loan to a European country, the Netherlands, to get started on the rehabilitation of the Port of Rotterdam. Before the war, Rotterdam had been the principal gateway from the Atlantic Ocean into Europe, and had been completely devastated by the Germans.

On December 19, 1947, the State Department submitted a document of 131 pages of small print entitled "Outline of European Recovery Program—Draft Legislation and Background Information." It required the establishment of an Economic Cooperation Administration independent of the State Department, and it spelled out in detail how this new agency should be constituted and operate. It included a request for four billion dollars for the first year of a program estimated to last four years and amount to a range of between $15.1 and 17.8 billion.

The State Department's draft of the Economic Cooperation Bill had to go through the complex process of review by the Congress, which Under-Secretary of State Will Clayton had explained to the Europeans immediately after the Secretary of State's Harvard speech: hearings by the Senate Foreign Relations Committee and the House of Representatives Foreign Affairs Committee and the Appropriations Committees of both Houses, followed by debate in the Congress. There was opposition from the isolationists led by Senator Robert Taft of Ohio, but both the Economic Cooperation Bill and the necessary appropriation of funds were approved by wide margins.

In the course of the hearings and debate, important supporters of the bill became convinced that if the European participants would effectively integrate their economies this would speed their recovery and reduce the need for U.S. aid. In the preamble to the Economic Recovery Act, the Congress inserted its most positive contribution to the legislation, a passage urging the participating countries to join in a United States of Europe.

The State Department would not endorse such a highly political step, but it had been urging the Marshall Plan participants to turn the OEEC into a permanent organization to promote economic integration. The convention creating the Organization for European Economic Cooperation (OEEC) was signed by seventeen countries, including West Germany (represented by the occupying authorities), on April 16, 1948, thirteen days after President Harry Truman signed the Marshall Plan legislation. The OEEC convention did not commit the "contracting parties," as the members were called, to go very far toward integrating their economies. They refused to promise a customs union, agreeing only to "study" such a step.

The ECA shared the enthusiasm of the Congress for the aim of going beyond simply adding up the "shopping lists" of the individual participating states. Paul Hoffman, the Administrator of ECA, became increasingly inpatient and frustrated with the OEEC's lack of progress, and when the participating countries were unable to agree on the allocation of U.S. aid among themselves, he took on this task himself. In September 1950, the third year of the aid program, he earmarked $600 million of the year's aid program to force the participants to create a European Payments Union (EPU). This institution provided an incentive to move trade away from the straightjacket of bilateral balances to the more efficient multilateral pattern that had prevailed before the war. The Payments

Union continued for eight years after Marshall aid had ceased, and contributed to the establishment of full currency convertibility on a multilateral basis. This certainly was one of the important legacies of the Marshall Plan.

From the Morgenthau Plan to the Marshall Plan and NATO

Paul R. Porter

I joined the Economic Cooperation Administration (ECA) in September, 1949, as chief of its mission to Greece. In November, 1950, I became assistant administrator of the agency, and in August, 1951, I became acting U.S. Special Representative in Europe (SRE), coordinating the work of all country missions.

I believe that my most decisive input was in the summer of 1951 when as assistant administrator I supervised the assembly of estimates from our country missions concerning the support their respective host countries could give to an expanded defense effort planned by the fledgling NATO without crippling the recovery that had already taken place. In response to growing alarm about Soviet intentions, a NATO committee proposed a force that would have been three times the strength of the Western allies at the peak of World War II. Eisenhower was recalled to active service from the presidency of Columbia University and made Supreme Allied Commander for Europe. He and his staff began a major paring of the proposed force levels.

When I was appointed Acting SRE, I conferred with him and found that the revised cost estimates were still about twice what our agency believed to be feasible. In January 1952, I was appointed deputy chief (for economic affairs) of the American team that negotiated new force levels and supporting infrastructure for NATO. Eventually, the lower cost estimates prevailed. As President, Eisenhower seemed comfortable with it.

The input I found to be the most interesting was a conversation with Ernest Bevin, British foreign minister, and Hector McNeil, his deputy, two days after Marshall's speech at Harvard, but I cannot say that anything I contributed was decisive since the result might have occurred anyway. At the time I was chief of the U.S. Mission for Economic Affairs attached to the American Embassy. The day after Marshall's speech, I was jubilantly reading to my wife the cabled text when McNeil phoned to ask me to lunch with him the next day at the House of Commons. Bevin joined us and after coffee, the day being sunny, we walked back and forth on the terrace beside the River Thames while they plied me with questions. McNeil's memorandum of our conversation, included in Foreign Office archives since made public, said that he had asked who we expected to take the initiative and I had said the British. I had no instructions of any kind, but I was confident that my answer was a safe one.

As I remember the conversation, they were visibly relieved that I had not said that we looked to the UN Economic Commission for Europe (ECE) to take the initiative. A fortnight earlier, McNeil and I had represented our respective governments at the founding session of the ECE. It had begun with high hopes, but the obstructionism of the Soviet delegate made it evident to our government that it could not be an instrument for recovery.

Bevin asked me what the United States expected of governments that might participate in a recovery program. I said that I thought the European Coal Organization (ECO) was a good model. The organization allocated scarce supplies of coal, including large temporary imports from the United States. Each participating nation was required to justify its needs to the other nations, and all decisions had to be unanimous. That pattern was adopted by the Organization for European Economic Cooperation which the participants in the recovery program created to help implement the Marshall Plan.

**The following is a memoir written for the
President Harry S. Truman Library in 1984:**

I

An improbable chain of chance events carried me to roles in the creation and administration of the Marshall Plan and the organization of NATO. The chain began in the late 1930s, when I concluded that if

Hitler's behavior resulted in war, as seemed likely, the United States would be drawn into it and that after contributing to Germany's defeat, the American objective should be the creation of a United States of Europe capable of avoiding a third world war. Then came a wartime job in Washington and carpool conversations with the author of the Morgenthau Plan which caused me to seek and obtain a position in our military government with a resolve to seek the rejection of that plan. A third chance event was a brief survey I made of the labor situation in the Ruhr region at the end of the war that brought me an undeserved reputation as a coal expert. My previous experience with coal had consisted of shoveling it into a home furnace.

I cannot remember when the idea of a United States of Europe entered my consciousness. It must have come from some magazine article and lodged in my mind without stimulating any further thought at the time. In later years I read that Churchill had proposed the idea in 1931, but he was not the first. The chance circumstance that made me an advocate of this idea was a policy dispute within the Socialist Party concerning the approaching war. Most members of the party ardently supported the isolationist view of its esteemed leader, Norman Thomas, who became a principal spokesman for the broadly based "Keep America Out of War" movement. Within the party's national executive committee and in *The Kenosha Labor,* a small weekly newspaper I edited, I argued that our national interest required that Nazi Germany should not dominate Europe. Defending that position, I felt obliged to hold forth a vision of a stable and democratic political order in Europe when the war was over. By the time the war had begun, a yellowed clipping from *The Milwaukee Journal* reminds me, I was calling the envisioned new order a United States of Europe. *The New York Times* also briefly took note of this advocacy when it reported the resignation of myself, Arthur McDowell and Leonard Woodcock (who later became president of the United Automobile Workers and the first United States ambassador to the People's Republic of China) from the party and its National Executive Committee in March, 1941. In retrospect, I recognize that my advocacy, whose only effect was to fix an idea in my mind that would influence me later, was another, if less pure, version of isolationism. In the simplistic view I had at the time, at war's end the victors and the vanquished, influenced by ourselves as a model, would create a United States of Europe that would thereafter preserve the peace on that long troubled continent, freeing us from any need for further intervention. What actually happened was beyond my wildest imagination.

In the summer of 1941 I accepted a job offer in the agency that became the War Production Board. My wartime work—chairman of an interagency committee (War Production Board, Navy, Army, and Maritime Commission) that also included members from management and labor—is irrelevant to this memoir except as it opened my eyes to the resourcefulness and huge productive capacity of the American economy. It was a revelation that I carried into my views of the potential of the Marshal Plan and NATO when they were conceived.

Wartime gasoline rationing forced urban automobile riders into carpools. A carpool organized among neighbors in Bethesda, Md. included myself and Harry Dexter White, Special Assistant to the Secretary of the Treasury, and Henry Morgenthau. White was a hard-driving and imaginative civil servant. He and John Maynard Keynes for the British were the principal creators of the International Monetary Fund and the International Bank for Reconstruction and Development, more commonly known as the World Bank. White was also the architect of a breath-taking plan for the future of Germany which the Secretary embraced and championed. The Morgenthau Plan, as it was soon known, proposed that "all industrial plants and equipment not destroyed by military action shall either be completely dismantled and removed from the area or completely destroyed, and all equipment shall be removed from the mines and the mines shall be thoroughly wrecked." Morgenthau and White accompanied Roosevelt to a meeting with Churchill at the Second Quebec Conference and offered a memorandum that declared an intent of "converting Germany into a country primarily agricultural and pastoral in its character." Churchill at first opposed it, remarking that "Europe would be chained to a dead body," but yielded to his adviser, Lord Cherwell, after White presumed to suggest to Cherwell that support for the plan would make it easier for Britain to obtain economic aid when the war was over. He and Roosevelt initialed the memorandum on Sept. 15, 1944. Later, both had second thoughts in response to other advisers. The President told Henry L. Stimson, Secretary of War, that he did not know why he had accepted the "particular language" and that it must have been "without much thought." The draconian plan was pared in the directive (JCS 1067) that the Joint Chiefs of Staff gave to the American military government, but a policy of reducing the capacity of German industry prevailed even into the third year of the Marshall Plan. I learned the story of the meeting in later years, but I learned the contents of the Morgenthau Plan in carpool conversations and was appalled at the idea of destroying resources needed for reconstruction.

Since Pearl Harbor, I had given no thought to what would come after victory, but the harshness of White's purpose impelled me to begin thinking about a post-war policy more immediate than a potential United States of Europe. The obvious central fact was that for some time the United States, the United Kingdom and the Soviet Union would occupy a conquered and devastated Germany. (The decision giving France an occupation role lay in the future). I asked myself: What effect would their joint occupation have on restoring democratic rule in Germany? If it was not restored, what would be the effect on the future of Europe and indirectly our own? In the 1930s, I had acquired a profound distrust of the Soviet Union because of its Marxist-Leninist doctrines, its seizure of the Baltic states, and its initial participation in the war as Hitler's ally. It did not seem plausible to me that the Soviet rulers would agree to grant conquered Germans democratic freedoms that they denied their own people. The more probable course, I thought, would be to exploit post-war disorganization and misery in an attempt to bring all of Europe under their own rule. If this analysis was correct, then anything that caused more misery in countries that Germany had occupied and plundered would make it easier for the Soviet Union to dominate Europe through communist-controlled governments. But even if the somber estimate was wrong and the most optimistic reading of Soviet intentions could be accepted, German factories and steel mills should not be dismantled for reparations or vengeance, but should be used to help supply the urgent needs of a devastated Europe, including, necessarily, German needs.

An early revival of democratic institutions that the Nazis had crushed and banned would be essential to a re-establishment of German democracy. German trade unions had been staunchly anti-Nazi before Hitler had destroyed them. I reasoned that if allowed to reorganize at an early date, they would be a buffer to a potential Nazi revival. Guided by these views of what I thought our policy toward Germany should be, I obtained appointment as a labor adviser to the army's military government organization then being formed.

The policy at that time was still fluid. The basic directive was in dispute among senior advisers to the Secretaries of the War, State and Treasury Departments, despite Morgenthau's temporary victory at Quebec. White told me that Treasury favored a policy of"no responsibility" after Germany had been reduced to an agricultural society. The other departments favored "extensive controls." It was the latter policy that was adopted, but with controls setting low "industry levels" that preserved much of the Morgenthau Plan without its name.

II

In March, 1945, I reported to headquarters of the Manpower Division, U. S. Group, Allied Control Council, at Bushey Park, near London. Although not required, I also called at the American Embassy where I met Thomas C. Blaisdell, Jr., Chief of the Mission for Economic Affairs; Samuel D. Berger, the Embassy's Labor Officer; and, John W. Tuthill, Assistant to Robert Murphy, Political Adviser to Eisenhower. Berger arranged an appointment with Ernest Bevin, the Minister of Labor. I told him that I hoped both we and the British would allow an early revival of German trade unions in our zones of occupation. I received an impression that if the idea was being considered at all, his ministry was not involved. But as he escorted me to the elevator, he spoke feelings that foreshadowed British policy when he became Foreign Minister. "I hate the Germans for what they have done to us," he said. "But I know we have to learn to love the bloody bastards. It may take us a year or two longer than you to do it."

I was impatient to get into Germany and after a few weeks at Bushey Park, I obtained a temporary transfer to the 12th Army Group headquarters at Verdun. A week before the end of the war in Europe, I moved with it to Wiesbaden in a two-mile-long convoy of command cars open to the chill wind. East of Verdun we saw army tanks lost in the blitzkrieg five years earlier rusted among memorials to soldiers who died on the same fields in the wars of 1870 and 1914-1918. The abandoned tanks were only a prelude to the war damage seen in Metz, but even what I saw there was small compared to the ruins of little Saarlautern. In the days ahead I saw the same sort of jagged walls protruding from great heaps of rubble in Frankfurt, Berlin and a dozen other cities. But that of course was before the Marshall Plan.

Soon after arriving in Wiesbaden I obtained authorization to survey the labor situation in the Ruhr. In the chaos of the early days of the occupation, travel from one area to another required the permission of area commanders, not unlike that which princes required in medieval times. En route by jeep I had to make a roundabout swing through Fulda, Kassel, Braunschweig, Hannover, and Bielefeld, stopping in each long enough to have my travel papers validated for passage to the next command post. These approvals added three days to the journey, but also as in the middle ages, hospitality in the form of a billet of admission to the army mess was freely given at any post and the time on the road produced unforgettable pictures of the ending of the war. Westward from Hannover on every mile of the road was a stream of Belgians, Dutchmen and Frenchmen who had been drafted into compulsory labor in German factories and were now walking home with small bundles of personal possessions slung over their backs or occasionally loaded into a liberated cart. No doubt they celebrated when reunited with their families, but on the road they seemed dispirited and apprehensive of what they would find. I also noted how thin they were.

The occupation zones agreed to by the wartime Allies corresponded to the expected disposition of national troops at the end: Russians in the East, Americans in the South, and British in the North. Recognizing a need to maintain coal production, the British had organized a Rhine Coal Control and manned it with mining engineers. The Battle of the Bulge, however, had drawn American forces into the Ruhr and they were responsible for security at the time of my visit, a circumstance that led to a dispute with the British in charge of the mines. An American colonel had established a curfew that began before the end of the work day in the mines and when German miners came out of the pits, military police arrested them and held them in a stockade. After mediation the miners were exempted from the curfew long enough to get to their homes, but that was not the only obstacle to production that could be readily overcome. The shortage of miners was acute. Young miners had been conscripted into the army and their places were filled with slave laborers from occupied countries. The latter had quit as soon as the German troops retreated. The British supervisors told me that much of the mining machinery was worn out and no new machinery was available. Stocks of timbers to support mine roofs were nearly exhausted and foreign exchange was no longer available to import them from Sweden. Many miners' houses had been destroyed. Already there were food shortages. The British supervisors thought they would be lucky to increase production in the coming year equal to one fifth of the pre-war level.

III

Back in Wiesbaden, I wrote my report, not suspecting that it would determine my career for the next eight years. The report quickly attracted attention at high levels. A Piper Cub was sent to fly me to Supreme Headquarters where I briefed American and British officers. There, I met Maj. Gen. William H. Draper, Jr., in civilian life an investment banker soon to become head of the economics division of military government. Six and a half years later when he became chief of the American team to negotiate the organization of NATO, I became his deputy for economic affairs. But at the time, the consequential event for me was an invitation by Blaisdell to join the Mission for Economic Affairs as the U. S. representative to the European Coal Organization. While in London to discuss his offer and before returning to Germany to obtain release from military government, I described the alarming situation in Germany to Bevin and George Isaacs, president of the Trades Union Congress. We had dinner the evening before ballots were counted in the recent national election. (The tally had been delayed to await the votes of overseas soldiers). Isaacs was confident of his re-election to Parliament and expected the Labor Party to gain, but not enough to form a government. Bevin was non-committal, but within 48 hours Bevin was the new Foreign Minister and Isaacs had been named to Bevin's former office.

The European Coal Organization was the most effective of three emergency organizations that the Americans and British had initiated a few months before the end of the war to allocate scarce commodities equitably and to relieve the scarcity to the largest extent possible. The other two were the European Central Inland Transport Organization, which began a return of railway cars to the country of ownership, and the Emergency Economic Committee for Europe, which tried to restore intra-European trade in food, fertilizers, timber and a few other commodities. All European nations, except Spain, had been invited to participate. Poland and Czechoslovakia took part, but the Soviet Union did not and it excluded its occupation zone in Germany. In the beginning, while the American and British governments actively sought a unified administration of all of Germany through the Allied Control Council, their occupation zones made no contribution to the work of the three "E organizations," but when the hope for unity receded, the American and British military governments jointly decided how much of West Germany's coal would be retained for its industries and homes and how much would be put into the pool for others.

The United States was a member of each of the organizations because of its role as a supplier of scarce commodities which before the Marshall Plan were financed by loans. Before long we were shipping two million tons of coal a month to Europe. But it was not enough and because oil was then little used as a fuel in Europe, the allocations that my European colleagues and I made once a month when we met in a sometimes unheated office at the British Ministry of Fuel and Power were in effect those of jobs and a minimum of household comfort. The Mission for Economic Affairs represented the United States in the three organizations. It was attached to the Embassy for administrative purposes, but otherwise reported directly to the State Department. During the war, the mission had been responsible for coordinating non-military supplies to Britain, but when Blaisdell became its chief in early 1945, he foresaw a balkanized Europe emerging from the ruins of war unless aggressively countered by positive measures to restore intra-European trade. He moved quickly to establish the mission as an American instrument of reconstruction. Historians, so far as I am aware, have overlooked the work of the "E organizations." An inquiry would disclose practices that became the foundation of the Marshall Plan. Blaisdell, who at the age of 90 is still teaching at the University of California at Berkeley, was its earliest prophet.

My experience in helping to allocate scarce supplies reinforced my determination to overturn the American policy of imposing a ceiling on German industrial capacity. In one of the six papers I sent to the State Department beginning in early 1946, I noted that the plans for dismantling much of German industry then being considered in the Allied Control Council "take no account of the impact . . . on the economy of other countries" and I challenged the propriety of the occupying powers reducing the capacity of German industry without the consent of other nations dependent upon it. I argued that if the price of reaching an agreement with the Soviet Union on the future of Germany was the impoverishment of the rest of Europe, then the United States should pursue an independent course. Concerning the Russians, I wrote:

> There are many indications that in addition to their known interest in obtaining maximum reparations in the form of capital goods the, desire the weakening of the whole of Western Europe. Major emphasis is given by the U.S. control authorities to getting along with the Russians. But it often appears that they conceive of getting along with the Russians as a program in itself rather than as a means to an end. . . .

> The best offset to Russian domination of Europe will be an economically unified Europe, whose resources will be adequately used to provide steady and full employment and a rising standard of living. The aim should be an economic federation within which goods would move

through a minimum of barriers; with, if not a common currency, at least currencies which are freely convertible; with coordinated investments directed toward giving all members equal access to sufficient coal, electric power, basic industrial and agricultural products and transport routes; and with maximum mobility of labor. . . . Russian expansionism now lends it a special urgency. . . .

The basis of economic union should be the federal principle: begin with as many states as may be prepared to accept the basic propositions and keep the door open for prodigals. Participation initially by the countries which are now Soviet satellites is improbable. But their early entry is neither essential to its success, nor need their absorption into the Soviet system be conceded."

I wrote the above paper, titled *The German Problem in the Light of Soviet Policy,* in the summer of 1946, and having succeeded Blaisdell as chief of the mission, I took it to Washington for discussion. The State Department backstops for the mission, Wayne Jackson, Miriam Camp, and Doris Whitnack, were not unsympathetic, but the paper raised political issues outside their responsibility. I did not then meet others whose thinking was parallel to mine, although there was a growing number.

IV

I found encouragement, however, in another quarter. Soon after my return to London, Robert Murphy, by then Political Adviser to General Lucius Clay, American Commander in Germany, asked me to prepare a paper for the American delegation to a forthcoming meeting of the foreign ministers of the four occupying powers. I complied on Jan. 14, 1947 with *European Dependence on the German Economy* (this and other papers noted in this memoir are deposited at the Truman Library). I cited requests that Germany's neighbors were making in the "E organizations" for German exports of "nitrate fertilizers, basic chemicals, replacement parts, building materials, transport equipment and electric power." I noted that the trade with Germany which they sought would not be possible under the "level-of-industry plan" then supported by the American occupation authorities. I commented that:

This plan, if accepted as a permanent pattern, will impoverish the whole of Europe for many years to come . . . and it may give to the Soviets the domination of Europe which the Nazis sought and lost.

I noted that the restrictions on Germany's industrial production were not only preventing European recovery, but were resulting in actions by its former trading partners that would lock them into a lasting autarchy. During the 1950s,Jean Monnet justly won renown for his leadership in helping to create the European Economic Community, but an earlier and less known Monnet Plan was pointed in the opposite direction. It proposed a major development of French coal mines (with American loans) that would depend upon high-cost coal seams. I argued that the required capital should be put into lower-cost Ruhr mines since

> Both French and German interests would be better served if maximum use were first made of the Ruhr reserves. Given reasonable security as to supplies from the Ruhr, the French could, and probably would, modify the Monnet Plan away from an uneconomic self-sufficienyv and toward a more integrated *European* economy.

I proposed a special authority to ensure Germany's neighbors permanent access to its output of coal and steel and a clearinghouse for payments. New capital was needed in nearly all European countries. So I proposed also the preparation of an "investment plan, possibly for submission to the World Bank, for the most economical allocation of capital in light of European requirements." I suggested that the proposed new United Nations Economic Commission for Europe might be an "appropriate forum" for determining needs for imports and investment. The proposals, Murphy wrote to me, were "useful and provocative."

The Economic Commission for Europe (ECE) had a large potential. Vaclav Kostelecky, a Czech national who was a member of the ECE staff for many years, had nearly completed a history of the early ECE which he sent to me for comment shortly before his death in 1982. His study benefits from access to British official documents and interviews with some East Europeans who helped overcome initial opposition by the Russians. It throws new light, I believe, on the Russian rejection of an opportunity to participate in the Marshall Plan. Walt W. Rostow initiated this idea in a State Department memorandum in March, 1946. He proposed a UN regional agency to promote an "all-inclusive European . . . collaboration in the fields of trade, finance and economic development." When the proposal was introduced in the UN Economic and Social Council, Hector McNeil, Minister of State in the British Foreign Office, at first was doubtful, but agreed to support it in "a hope that the U.S.S.R. would cooperate with real good will." The Russians offered numerous objections. Joseph Winiewicz of Poland confided to McNeil that Vlacheslav Molotov, the Russian Foreign Minister, feared that "the Soviets would be forced to provide economic statistical information" and the sending of "observers inside the Soviet Union on economic subjects." After "three extended meetings with Molotov and Vyshinksi," Winiewicz won their consent that the Soviet Union "should be neutral and that Poland and Czechoslovakia should be permitted to support it."

The ECE held its first session May 2-12, 1947 in Geneva with 18 countries represented. Heads of delegations included McNeil, Andre Philip, a recent Minister of Finance for France; Jan Masaryk, Foreign Minister of Czechoslovakia; Valerian Zorin, Ambassador to Czechoslovakia and soon-to-be Vice Foreign Minister for the Soviet Union; and Will L. Clayton, Undersecretary of State for Economic Affairs for the United States. I was his deputy and alternate. Since Clayton was also attending the conference that created the General Conference on Tariffs and Trade (GATT), I attended the ECE meeting in his stead after the first day. Our objective was that ECE should become an all-European economic recovery organization. McNeil and Philip spoke in favor of this objective. Privately, Masaryk and Tadeuz Lychowski, the chief Polish delegate, favored it. In a conversation with Leo Mates of Yugoslavia, I could have discerned then, had I been sharper, early signs of the later break with the Russians. The Russian objective seemed to be to ensure that the ECE would be ineffectual. Besides denouncing the United States, the United Kingdom and France, Zorin engaged in long procedural wrangles. The main result of the meeting was an agreement to meet again July 6-16. At the start of the session, I had invited Zorin to lunch, but he delayed acceptance until the day after adjournment. When my colleague Robert Asher and I did have an opportunity to talk to him, we found him to be unresponsive.

My most vivid memory of the first meeting in Geneva is a dinner that McNeil hosted for Masaryk, Philip and myself. Masaryk told us of the "intense pressure" he was under from the Russians. Then looking down and pointing to his crotch, he remarked in poignant anguish, "I wonder if I am still a man." Remembering his despondency when he was found dead the following February, having jumped or been thrown from a window in his Foreign Office apartment, I could not dismiss the possibility of suicide, as claimed by his communist opponents. Many years later I read Robert Mayne's *Post-War*. I think he has made a convincing case that Masaryk was murdered.

While I was in Geneva I met at 7:30 each morning with Clayton to inform him of what had happened at the ECE meetings the previous day. We talked about Europe's worsening condition. He was sympathetic to proposals I had made in my papers and was particularly attracted to the idea of an economic federation. He emphasized it in a memorandum that he gave to General Marshall on his return to Washington.

V

General Marshall's brief commencement address at Harvard on June 5, 1947 changed the future of Europe. Its most important words were these:

> It is already- evident that before the United States Government can proceed much further in its efforts to alleviate the situation and help start the European world on its way to recovery, there must be some agreement among the countries of Europe as to the requirements of the situation and the part those countries themselves will take in order to give proper effect to whatever action might be undertaken by this Government. . . . The initiative, I think must come from Europe. The role of this country should consist of friendly aid in the drafting of a European program and of later support of such a program so far as it may be practical for us to do so. The program should be a joint one, agreed to by a number, if not all, European nations.

I was jubilantly reading to my wife the cabled text when McNeil phoned me at home to ask me to lunch with him the following day at the House of Commons. His memorandum of our meeting, in Foreign Office archives and since made public, reported that he had asked me whom we had expected to take the initiative and I had said the British. Actually, I had no information beyond what was in the text, but I felt my answer was on safe ground. We were both skeptical that the floundering ECE could be an effective instrument for the European response. Bevin joined us for coffee. His excitement was evident and as the three of us paced back and forth on the terrace besides the Thames, relishing the June sunshine, I felt that he had already decided to seize the initiative. I said that I thought the practice of the European Coal Organization of requiring all claimants to justify their needs to other claimants was a sound precedent for preparing a joint recovery program.

On June 17 Bevin went to Paris to consult his French counterpart, George Bidault, and the two invited Molotov to a further meeting.

Molotov, accompanied by a large delegation, joined them on June 27, but he was prickly from the outset. Germany should be denied aid until the occupying parties had agreed on reparations. Italy should also be excluded. He proposed that other countries separately declare their needs and that the United States then be notified of the total dollar costs. He was adamant against a common European plan which Bevin and Bidault felt to be necessary. After four days of deadlock, Molotov walked out. Bevin was convinced that he had come to the conference to sabotage it. He and Bidault then invited all other European countries, except Spain, to a conference on July 12 to prepare a response to the Marshall offer. Czechoslovakia accepted, whereupon Stalin summoned Masaryk and Klement Gottwald, the Communist premier, to Moscow and ordered the Czechs to withdraw. They did. Even after that, the Poles intended to participate. In Geneva for a renewed meeting of the ECE, Lychowski told me on the afternoon of July 11 that he had a reservation on the night train to Paris. When I saw him the next morning, he lamely said that he had received new instructions.

In later years, a school of historians has blamed the Marshall Plan for the division of Europe. Some have argued that Bevin and Bidault, in response to American direction, manipulated events to exclude the Russians from the Marshall Plan. Even if they had sought to do so, Molotov could have outfoxed them by proposing that responsibility for a European response be entrusted to the ECE. It was Bidault, however, who in his opening statement to the conference proposed using the ECE and Molotov rebuffed him. Despite the fumbling first meeting of the ECE, the United Nations had a standing in public opinion at that time that would have made it impossible for the British and French governments to have spurned use of the agency if it had appeared to be a means of obtaining Soviet cooperation. I think the same could be said of American public opinion then. George F. Kennan wrote in his *Memoirs* that "our hopes for the possible use of ECE as a center for European recovery received a severe setback from the account Will Clayton gave us, on his return from Europe, of the behavior of the Soviet delegation at the first meeting of that body." Still, Marshall's speech which he helped to prepare *after* that meeting said unequivocally, "it would be neither fitting nor efficacious for this Government to undertake to draw up a program designed to place Europe on its feet economically. This is the business of the Europeans." The ECE option, if Molotov had chosen to use it, had the United States, the United Kingdom and France over a barrel.

It can be argued that the Russians made a tactical blunder. I think a less patronizing interpretation of their behavior is that they understood clearly what they were doing. The recovery of Europe would foil their hopes of extending communist rule west of the line reached by their troops. Politically, the tide was already running against them in the West. France, Italy, and Belgium had ousted communist ministers from their governments. In the ECE, the Soviet Union had six votes and two of these were the dummy votes of the fictitiously sovereign Ukraine and Belarus. Poland, Czechoslovakia, and Yugoslavia were eager for economic aid and were not yet fully disciplined. The West had 12 votes. The Soviet Union could not dominate the ECE and did not wish to cooperate in it or any other organization for European recovery. Given the Russians' long-term purposes and these circumstances, their strategy was to consolidate Soviet control behind the Iron Curtain, promote political opposition in the West, increase military threats such as the blockade of Berlin, and shrilly blame the United States for the division of Europe (which neither Caesar nor Napoleon could unite).

The nations that met in Paris on July 12 appointed an Executive Committee and various technical committees to compile their combined needs for food, fuel, machinery and other essentials, but only with great difficulty were they able to set aside suspicions and rivalries to project a $29 billion four-year program. Kennan reported from Paris that most of the governments were "afflicted at just this time with abnormal weaknesses, fears and prejudices. . . . The work of the Conference cannot logically be stronger than the political and psychological fabric of the war-torn, fear-wracked, confused and maladjusted area which is the object of its labors."

Even so, the idea of a joint program was radically new. An American committee headed by Averell Harriman pared the projected cost to $17 billion. This was the figure presented to the Congress which created the Economic Cooperation Administration to administer American aid. It held the American costs of a robust European recovery to $13 billion, a satisfying underrun of 23%.

I watched the recovery from such vantage points in the Economic Cooperation Administration as chief of the Marshall Plan mission to Greece, Assistant Administrator for Program, and the Paris-based coordinator of 17 country missions. Soon, on any day 150 ships were crossing the Atlantic or unloading at port with goods purchased with Marshall Plan funds. In my 15 months in Greece, American economic and military aid was nearly a quarter of the Greek national product. By 1950, the value of production in the Marshall Plan countries was a quarter greater than in the year before the war. In the Organization for European Economic Cooperation and its committees, representatives of the participating governments presented their claims for aid to the scrutiny of their peers and from the scrutiny came discoveries that many things being imported from the United States could be obtained in trade from each other's expanding production. The European Payments Union was created as a clearinghouse as a result. At a meeting of mission chiefs in the spring of 1950, I proposed that we invite the participating governments to explore the possibility of a common currency. Harriman, who was then coordinator of the country missions, was sympathetic to the idea, but it was laid aside as premature.

VI

The North Atlantic Treaty Organization, otherwise known as NATO, began as a British idea. Bevin proposed it to Marshall on Dec. 16, 1947, at a dinner in Bevin's Foreign Office flat. The sixth meeting of the Council of Foreign Ministers had ended that day and Molotov had been more truculent and abusive than ever. Marshall was sympathetic, but could not promise American support at that time. He reminded Bevin that the Congress had not yet approved the recovery program. Also 1948 was an election year. He suggested that Bevin begin with a European nucleus, which he did. The fear that the Russians might send their troops across the Iron Curtain was strong enough that France and the Benelux nations quickly joined the British in the new Western European Union. It was not until April 4, 1949 that the United States was ready to sign the North Atlantic Treaty which superseded it. Canada, Norway, Denmark, Iceland, and Portugal also signed. Greece and Turkey adhered to it two years later. The treaty declared that:

> . . . an armed attack against one or more of them . . . shall be considered
> an attack against them all, and consequently they agree that . . . each
> of them . . . will assist the Party or Parties so attacked by taking
> forthwith . . . such action as it deems necessary, including the use of
> armed force, to restore and maintain the security of the North Atlantic
> area.

Committees were named to assess the defense needs of the defined sectors, and they floundered badly. They proposed a total of 307 divisions which was three times the Allied strength at the peak of World War II. Eisenhower was recalled to service from the presidency of Columbia University and was made Supreme Allied Commander for Europe. He and his staff begin deflating the estimates to a more practical level. At this time, I was Assistant Administrator of the Marshall Plan agency and responsible for approving aid to each participating country. Reports to Washington from our country missions shared the alarm of finance ministers that the projected buildup would reverse the recovery that had been achieved and could cause a reduction in living standards. When I went to Paris in August, 1951, as coordinator of the country missions I called on Eisenhower at his headquarters at St. Cloud. His staff-prepared estimate of the buildup cost was roughly double the amount our Marshall Plan staff thought would be feasible. Eventually, the approximate lower estimate prevailed and as President, Eisenhower seemed to be comfortable with it.

The Marshall Plan ended Dec. 31, 1951. I remained in Europe for another 14 months as a member of the American NATO negotiating team with the long-handled title of Deputy United States Representative in Europe for Economic Affairs. Differences within and between governments concerning the required level of forces and supporting infrastructure were resolved only after protracted negotiations. Every major decision touched sensitive political issues, but none was more sensitive than rearming Germans. By now the Soviet Union had remade East Germany in its own image and in the Western occupation zones a democratic government had taken form under the tutelage of the United States, the United Kingdom and France. Although the French were deeply divided, the lessons of recovery and the needs of mutual security persuaded them that the Federal Republic of Germany should be accepted as a partner in all respects. The construction of air force bases in Spain was another sensitive issue. The State Department was opposed, fearing that it would be construed as an endorsement of the Franco regime. Knowing that the French Socialists maintained a relationship with the underground Spanish Socialists, I asked Andre Philip if he could learn what the latter thought of the proposed bases. A few weeks later he asked me to lunch at a home where I met two Spanish Socialists, who at considerable risk had illegally crossed the border to meet me. I expected them to chide me, but they said that they would welcome the bases because they would help to "open up" their closed society.

I asked the visitors how soon they thought democracy might be restored in Spain. They said five years. It took a quarter of a century. When it is said that communism in Eastern Europe and the Soviet Union will endure permanently, I am reminded of that time gap between hope and actuality. Though time lags beyond what we wish, hope should not be surrendered.

VII

Early in 1953 as I made ready to return to America and private life, I reflected upon eight intense, crowded years, seven of them lived in Europe. Now that NATO had been fashioned into a credible instrument of mutual security, while recovery, instead of being retarded, had grown apace, it seemed to me that a new risk might be a budding complacency. I looked for historical precedents and remembered a league of Greek city-states organized in the Fourth Century B. C. to resist Persia. I stated my concern in a talk to the Anglo-American Press Association in Paris. Theodore White, who was present, reported my remarks in *Fire in the Ashes: Europe in Mid-century.*:

> The politics that wrecked the Confederacy of Delos are as vivid today as when the archons of the city-states wrestled and debated them as live issues. For it immediately became apparent that there was a fundamental imbalance in the Confederacy. Its mainspring and leader was the great democracy of Athens; its lesser members vrere the Greek city-states of Ionia, no less proud, but infinitely weaker and living cheek-by-jowl with the enemy on the frontier of Persian power. . . .
> The lesser states argued that the success of the Confederacy lessened the peril and thus its burdens might be reduced. Athens argued that only constant exertion and effort kept the Persian peril contained.

In less than a generation the Confederacy fell apart and was replaced by the Athenian Empire.

Anniversaries are anchors for reflections and resolves. From whatever ugly event one chooses as a beginning- Munich, the Hitler-Stalin pact, or Pearl Harbor- it will soon be a half century since the fates of America and Western Europe were joined on the battlefield as ally or enemy, in recovery and in mutual security. Since NATO began, a third of a century has passed. Former enemies have long since been reconciled. Entrepreneurial economies have produced beyond what optimists expected. Democratic societies have advanced to larger freedoms and an armed alliance has preserved peace in Western Europe. Joint decisions reached with utmost difficulty in the early aftermath of a terrible war have held up well and enriched the lives of millions.

For a few years in the mid-1950s it appeared that a United States of Europe might be emerging. Men of vision and stature strove to create institutions that would be its foundation: Jean Monnet, Robert Schuman, Andre Philip and Rene Pleven in France; Paul-Henri Spaak in Belgium; Konrad Adenauer and Walter Hallstein in Germany; Churchill occasionally; and many others. France, the Benelux counties and Germany created the European Coal and Steel Community. These five plus Italy created what became the European Union, later joined by the United Kingdom, Ireland, Denmark and Greece. These countries send popularly elected delegates to the European Parliament, a parliamentary body without power. The institutions fall far short of a federal union, however, and the momentum has slowed. Unfortunately, most of the creators were elderly men. Monnet, the most resourceful, was past 80 during the critical years and men of lesser vision succeeded them.

We should not deprecate what they achieved, but the reality that confronts the United States is that for some years to come the imbalance of power between it and its European allies will persist. Such unity as democratic Europe has achieved derives mainly from a resigned acceptance of what is seen to be the least unsatisfactory choice and very little from a spirit of innovation. Two devastating wars, the loss of empires, and the proximity of the Soviet Union have induced a caution that reinforces Europe's dependency and leaves to the United States a larger leadership responsibility than is in the best long-term interest of either it or the allies. Under these circumstances, cooperation is bound to be more difficult in practice than it is presumed to be in principle. Not only are the allies often divided among themselves, but in the latter half of the twentieth century at least, they are more disposed than we toward settling for things as they are. Some resentment arises on one side from disparity of power and on the other for disparity in burdens.

The fact that NATO has survived well for a third of a century does not ensure its vitality in the future. As presently constituted, it exemplifies the strength and weakness of the welfare state. It has provided security against a formidable risk, but it reflects, and perhaps fosters, a self-perpetuating dependency. Time is also bringing new uncertainties. Both the United States and its allies are changing. As our population becomes more Latin American and Asian, new Americans will not have the ethnic and cultural affinities that have helped to sustain the Alliance. The emergence of a world economy that began with the creation of GATT in Geneva in 1947 has produced severe economic faultlines in America and Europe which exacerbate trade rivalries. Shared sympathies are no longer as strong as they were at the time of the events I have related.

I still believe that a democratic United States of Europe would be in the best interests of ourselves and its members. Together, the nations of Western Europe have a population that is comparable with that of the Soviet Union and an industrial and inventive strength that is significantly greater. It is their lack of unity that makes their political strength so inferior. We and a united democratic Europe would have political differences, but a partnership would be a compelling need for both. In the absence of a United States of Europe, NATO is the next best alternative for mutual security, but an imbalance of power and burdens like that which destroyed the Confederacy of Delos will continue to haunt it.

The Management Structure for the Marshall Plan

HAROLD SEIDMAN

O rganization, structure and location were major controversial issues that divided supporters of the Marshall Plan. Republicans, led by Christian Herter, wanted the Plan administered by a business-like government corporation independent of the State Department. Traditionalists within the Bureau of the Budget argued that any agency concerned with foreign affairs should be in the State Department to assure that the United States spoke with one voice abroad.

As the Bureau of the Budget's government corporation specialist, I was assigned to the White House working group drafting legislation. I prepared an analysis of the proposal, published by the House Committee on Foreign Aid, which examined various organizational options. The Marshall Plan did not meet the accepted criteria for a government corporation in that it was not designed to be revenue-producing and potentially self-sustaining. I proposed a compromise authorizing the Administrator of an independent Economic Cooperation Administration (ECA) to create a corporation if and when he found such action desirable. The compromise was accepted. President Truman also assured bipartisan support by advising the members of Congress that Paul Hoffman, a leading business executive, would be the ECA administrator.

Later, as Chief of the Bureau of the Budget's International Organization Branch, I was concerned with implementation of the Marshall Plan, particularly the role of the Ambassador and the working of the country teams. Problems were caused by the Ambassador's delegating to the Deputy Chief of Mission (DCM) chairmanship of the country team.

It became clear that establishment of the ECA as an independent agency was the right decision. The foreign service officers believed that all relationships with a foreign government should be through the foreign ministry. They were appalled at the Marshall Plan's "interference in domestic affairs" and the by-passing of the foreign ministry to deal directly with the Treasury, Commerce, and Trade ministries. The most effective staff of the ECA were those recruited from the outside and the Treasury and Agriculture attaches.

A Transcendent Experience

MELBOURNE L. SPECTOR

E verett Bellows was responsible for my participation in the Marshall Plan, and I can never thank him enough.

It was early March of 1948 when Everett with his usual jauntiness and buoyancy walked into my office at the State Department where we both worked in the Office of the Director General of the Foreign Service. Everett worked directly for the Director General, and I was a position classification analyst in the office's personnel division. Everett explained that a new organization was being created to administer a vast foreign assistance program, mainly for Europe. The organization was titled the Economic Cooperation Administration (ECA), and the program to be administered in Europe was the European Recovery Program, popularly called the Marshall Plan. To carry out the plan the administrator had been given the option of setting up his own administrative machinery overseas, including a personnel system, or using that of the Department of State. The administrator, Paul Hoffman, had opted to use the system of the Department. Hence, the Department was lending a team of experts to set up the administrative system—finance, communications, administrative services, personnel and so on. Everett was picked to set up the overseas personnel system. Everett felt he needed someone to do position classification and compensation, for which he felt he did not have enough experience. Luckily for me he chose me. We had known each other from previous assignments in the war support agencies during 1941 and 1942.

That day we moved in to the Maiatico Building at the corner of Connecticut Avenue and H Street, the Northwest caddy corner from the White House across Lafayette Park. The building was just being completed. It had floors and elevators and nothing else. Thanks to Don Stone, the acting Assistant Administrator for Administration, and his staff, hundreds of desks and chairs were moved in and telephone lines were strung along the ceilings and dropped to the desks. Meanwhile workers were putting up partitions to make offices using rivet guns with live ammunition to drive in the rivets. One would be on the phone when a gunshot would go off and raise the person a foot off his or her seat!

Everett's and my assignment was to devise a version of the Department of State's foreign service for use by a new, emergency-driven organization. The actual organization patterns of the regional office in Paris and of the missions to the individual countries were being outlined by another team. It was my job to spell out the duties and responsibilities of every individual position, give it a title, and assign to it a grade level. We used Foreign Service Reserve and Foreign Service Staff authorities for the positions. Due to an agreement between the ECA administrator and the Assistant Secretary of State for Administration, Jack Puerifoy, all persons at FSR-3 and above automatically got diplomatic passports and those below got official passports. This agreement gave Mrs. Shipley, the legendary head of the passport division, a great deal of heartburn. A situation I will go into later.

In addition to our jobs of devising the system, Everett and I had to legally sign off on all appointments since we were State Department officers. This was strictly pro forma as long as all legal requirements were met as to citizenship, security and medical clearance, and so on. However, being physically housed in the ECA Personnel Office meant that applicants came to Everett and me looking for jobs, so we assisted in the actual recruitment of staff from time to time. Everett was soon recruited to go to Paris as Leland Barrow's deputy in the management part of the Special Representative's office. Soon after Barrows' arrival, he asked that personnel authority be delegated to the Regional Office so that actions could be taken there as well as in Washington. This meant a big upheaval in the State Department since this had never been done before. I had the help of two wonderful individuals to prepare a personnel manual so that the necessary actions could be performed in Paris. They turned out a complete manual in sixty days. It was an amazing piece of professional work. Their names were Jane Ganeshan and Elizabeth Biggus. Of course, this had to be approved by the State Department, which was done in very short order, another indication of the priority the program was given in the highest quarters of the government.

A word should be written here about the effect of the Marshall Plan on the Foreign Service. The service had been developed and shaped from the earliest days of the republic, even before we had a constitution, so it wasn't designed for an emergency driven, hard-hitting organization. This meant that Everett and I and our State Department successors assigned to ECA had to urge the Department to reinterpret the Basic Legislation to make it more useful to our type of an emergency, short-lived program. One example was the regulation on home leave: every U.S. citizen foreign service employee was entitled to be returned to the U.S.for home leave after two years of uninterrupted service overseas. The Department took uninterrupted to mean quite literally that if an officer returned to the States for emergency leave, to be with a dying parent for example, the two-year waiting period began again with the officer's return to duty. We argued that this was patently ridiculous and got them to change the rules. Much of State's thinking stemmed from its chronic limited budget, whereas lack of funds was not an ECA problem. For many years Foreign Assistance Legislation has been used to modify State Department Basic Legislation.

An indication of Secretary Marshall's wise decision to separate ECA from the State Department was when the Director General of the Foreign Service called me into his office one day and told me to keep my eye open for positions that could be occupied by regular State Department foreign service officers for whom the Department could not find jobs. Actually, some officers were used, but they were very well qualified for whatever positions they occupied. In fact, a word should be said about the complete lack of political or other outside influence in the hiring of staff. There was none.

Back to Mrs. Shipley for a moment. The personnel office of ECA under Virgil Couch's leadership was trying to set up a streamlined, one-stop hiring process. The aim was to interview, grant medical and security check, and hire a candidate in one day. For those going overseas, this also meant the issuance of a passport and the obtaining of travel and transportation documents—all on the same day! We had obtained the services of the U.S. Public Health Service to give physical examinations at the Maiaitico building and we had decided to give tentative security clearances based on the security people's perusal of the Attorney General's and House Committee on Un-American Activities list. People were thus hired with a tentative security clearance pending the full FBI clearance, which took a minimum of ninety or more days. Obviously we could not tolerate such delays.

The policy worked very well, and only a very small fraction of employees had to be terminated based on the full-field investigation. This policy was retained by the subsequent foreign aid agencies and was only halted in 1964. The only hold-up to setting up a one-stop service was Mrs. Shipley, who insisted that passport applicants personally apply for them at her office in the Winder building on Seventeenth Street. (Mrs. Shipley was very proud of her offices in this building, the very same building President Lincoln often visited during the Civil War to read the latest telegraphic dispatches on the progress of the war.)

Everett and I went to call on the great lady, who let us know where we stood by keeping us waiting for forty-five minutes before seeing us and then greeting us with: "You are about as welcome as the flu!" She was furious with Puerifoy for giving blanket, automatic approval for the issuance of official and diplomatic passports, telling us that she even maintained two passports for every official of the Department stationed in Washington, up to and including the Secretary, and worked only on a case-by-case basis. She personally determined which type of passport the official would be allowed to use based on the type of trip the official was taking. She made clear to us that she had made the U.S. passport a very important, almost sacred, document. For example, during the time she had been in charge of passport issuance, she had succeeded in making the U.S. passport legally acceptable as proof of U.S. citizenship. At this point I told her how much I agreed with her reverence for a passport, and said that I had just read Rebecca West's book called *The Meaning of Treason,* in which she described how Lord Haw-Haw had been executed in Britain as a traitor because he had broadcast from Germany during the war holding a British passport. He was thus held to be a British citizen and could be tried as a traitor. This seemed to carry the day with Mrs. Shipley and she granted us the authority to issue passports at the ECA headquarters.

I was recalled to duty in the State Department later that fall, assigned to be the Executive Secretary to the Foreign Service Selection Boards. I married my long-time girl friend Louise Vincent in November of 1948, and thought I was settling into the usual career of a State Department personnel function. But in early March of 1949 I was recruited by Edward McMenamin, Director of Personnel in the Office of the Special Representative in Paris, to be his deputy. Ed was an old and dear friend whom I respected as much as liked. It was a wonderful experience. After a very satisfying year as Ed's deputy I was transferred to be the chief of the Organization and Management division, replacing Jack Kubisch, who had left to return to private business in the United States.

While in the Organization and Management job, I hired a psychiatrist, Dr. Mottram Torre, to work with my staff and myself in a type of sensitivity training setting. This was an attempt at building better team spirit and better sensitizing us to our clients' needs. Jonathan Yardley recently wrote that the Peace Corps was the first Executive Branch agency to use psychiatrists. I beat them by several years, and I am sure the Defense Department and CIA did as well. I used psychiatrists as consultants again when I returned to Washington as the Deputy Director of Personnel of the Foreign Assistance Agency.

While in the management job, I took on the leadership of a task force suggested by Lincoln Gordon. Lincoln, who was the Special Representative's Chief of Program, had made a tour of all of the missions as preparation for his return to Washington, where he was to serve as Averell Harriman's Chief Program Advisor. Harriman was then the president's Special Assistant for Foreign Affairs. Lincoln felt that the organization chart for our missions was too uniform. We had the same organization for each mission, whether it was Ireland, France, or Belgium. I remember him stating that it was like saying every man could be fitted with a size 38 coat. With this in mind Harry Fite, the new Administration chief who had replaced Barrows, brought over Hirst Sutton from the U.S. Bureau of the Budget and John P. Robinson from the ECA headquarters staff. To this group, we were lucky to add the services of Hellene Granby who had served the Greek mission so well. We were going to try to devise an organization and budgeting system that was tailored to the program rather than financial allocations or some rigid, standard idea of how a mission should be organized. This was one of the first attempts to achieve what would come to be called "program budgeting."

Another Marshall Plan innovation was to set up a unified Information and Cultural Organization in each diplomatic mission. This was the brainchild of Waldemar Nielson, who asked me to set one up in Turkey. Prior to that time, each embassy had a cultural section while the Marshall Plan mission had a large Information Program. The then U.S. Ambassador was a first-rate, experienced foreign service officer who readily agreed, and thus a test precursor to USIA was created.

I don't recall too much more from this experience than to recall that my staff and I fought and won battles to retain tourism and small business as legitimate concerns for the Program. After two wonderful years in Paris, I was reassigned to the headquarters of ECA. My assignment to Washington as the Deputy Director of Personnel was a mostly happy one for me. My chief was Robert Rupard, a professional and experienced public administrator. Bob was eager to try new approaches, which suited me to a tee. The Assistant Administrator for Administration was still Don Stone, another experienced administrator who too wanted to try new things and especially to utilize what we could from the field of social sciences.

A central concern of all organizations with overseas operations is the performance of its employees in an alien environment. A person's previous record of working within the continental United States usually is no indication of how that person will perform abroad or how his family will fare. We attempted to approach the problem from two perspectives, that of recruitment and that of training. When recruiting, how could one foretell how the employee would fare abroad? Of course, one could be fairly certain concerning the candidates's professional or technical competence, but one could not predict how that person would perform abroad, how the employee would be able to relate to his or her host country, a co-worker or a host country organization. How would he or she—or their family—would adjust to the customs? There were no easy tests or exams that could be given. It was rumored that during the war OSS had tested people by putting them through simulated living and working conditions. This method, for us, was too expensive and time-consuming. One thing we found we could do was to very accurately and painstakingly spell out the job requirements and desirable qualifications, not only the detailed duties and responsibilities, but the types of persons and organizations the employee would be required to work with and in what kind of environment. We also attempted to get better State Department Post Reports on the customs and mores of the countries where our people would be assigned. Up to that time we were recruiting from something not much more than a one phrase or one sentence job title. Ernest Barbour of our staff designed a more detailed and comprehensive position description and qualifications requirements document, dubbed an AIRPAR, which vastly improved the basis not only for recruitment but also for subsequent training.

On the training issue, Washington was lucky at that time to have cultural anthropologists on the staff of the Foreign Service Institute of the State Department. One was Edward T. Hall who worked closely with us to better prepare our people for overseas service. At Don Stone's suggestion we also used M. L. Wilson of the Farm Security Administration and others from the Agriculture Department's Extension Service. At this point, more and more of our personnel were engaged in technical assistance. In addition to Europe, ECA had programs in Indo-China, Formosa, India, and the Philippines. In these early days, along with the newly created Technical Cooperation Administration (Point IV), we were grappling with how to provide technical assistance effectively.

A small digression here. Sometime in 1951 or 1952, at the request of the director of the United Pueblos Indian Service Agency in Albuquerque, New Mexico, I was detailed by Harriman to make a study of how the institutions of higher learning in New Mexico could be used for training ECA and TCA personnel before going overseas. Dr. Sophie Aberle, the Indian Service director, herself a physician with a doctorate in cultural anthropology, understood that New Mexico with its three cultures—Native American, Hispanic, and Anglo-Saxon—was an ideal training ground for people going abroad to provide technical assistance. With the leadership of Dr. Aberle and the excellent cooperation of all of New Mexico's institutions of higher learning, we were able to set up a consortium of the institutions ready to give language, cultural awareness, and other types of training. Unhappily, neither ECA/MSA nor TCA (the big potential user) availed themselves of the opportunity. Much later the Peace Corps did essentially the same thing.

As a result of the election of 1952 the Eisenhower Administration came in to being and Harold Stassen was appointed to the position of Special Assistant to the President for Mutual Security and administrator of the Mutual Security Agency, the successor to ECA. I was acting Director of Personnel during this period and assisted Governor Stassen in setting up the Foreign Operations Administration, which took over all of the functions previously performed by ECA and TCA, including the Institute of Inter-American Affairs.

Special Note: Some Administrative Innovations of the Marshall Plan Agency

I am taking advantage of this opportunity to note briefly some of the administrative innovations, which were introduced by the Economic Cooperation Administration.

Comptroller

This function, usually dubbed the audit function, was traditionally a part of the administrative function in an agency or department: for example, a part of the duties of the Assistant Secretary for Administration. Setting up a separate, enhanced over-all audit function stemmed from the U.S. government's experience with the United Nations Relief and Rehabilitation Administration (UNRRA) during and after World War II. The U.S. Congress had been highly critical of UNRRA's operations in 1944 and early 1945 and there was a chance of greatly reduced financial support for the agency. Will Clayton, the U.S. Assistant Secretary of State for Economic Affairs, moved to calm Congressional fears by telling them that he would see to it that UNRRA elevated the audit function to the highest level, setting up an independent comptroller who would report directly to the head of UNRRA. He even provided the actual person to fill the job, Harry Howell, whom Clayton had known in his own firm of Clayton Anderson in Texas. Howell did very well in the job and calmed congressional fears. To reassure Congress that this new, richly funded agency would be run properly, the independent comptroller was copied for ECA. The title was later changed to "controller."

Executive Recruiter

One of the first actions by the new administrator, Paul Hoffman, was to bring in his brother-in-law, Tex Moore, to help him recruit the best talent he could find to run the new agency and its programs. The position was institutionalized as an adjunct to the Office of the Administrator and has remained such ever since. In most other government agencies this function has been and remains a part of the duties of the Director of Personnel or Assistant Secretary for Administration. I do not believe that any other agency or department handled its recruitment of top managers in the same way at the time.

Executive Secretary

This function originated with the military. It was utilized during World War II by the Chief of Staff of the Army. When James Byrne became Secretary of State, he asked the military to help him in his new duties. The position of Executive Secretary was created in the State Department and filled by Carl Humelsine, who had held the same position in the Office of the Chief of Staff of the Army. The position was adopted for ECA, the first civilian agency to use it besides the State Department.

Regional Office for Foreign Affairs

A regional office was established in Paris to oversee and coordinate the activities of the 15 missions and to relate to the OEEC. During the war, Nelson Rockefeller had a small staff which was called a Regional Staff in various countries but no full-scale non-military organization had been attempted before. Incidentally, during the Kennedy Administration some thought was given to setting up a regional office for the Alliance for Progress somewhere in Latin America.

My experience in the Marshall Plan was one of the most, if not the most, satisfying experiences of my life. It was rare for a government employee to work in an agency that had not only complete and unswerving support from the White House, but from the Congress and the public. As Charles L. Mee, Jr. wrote of Marshall Plan service in Europe: "To be young, to be American, were wonderful things in the late forties; to be one of Averell Harriman's sides—or an aide to one of his aides—was transcendental."

And so it was transcendental!

Personal Retrospectives

II. The View From Washington and Paris

Ringside at the Marshall Plan

ROBERT E. ASHER

My role in the Marshall Plan may have been tangential and inconsequential but, for me, it was instructive and enjoyable. From 1946 through 1950, I was based in London and Geneva in the Foreign Service Reserve of the State Department. Thanks largely to Averell Harriman, however, I was also able to observe at first hand and, on occasion, participate in, Marshall Plan activities. During World War II, I had worked in Washington for the War Production Board, in North Africa for the Lend-Lease Administration, and in Europe for the United Nations Relief and Rehabilitation Administration (UNRRA). In my UNRRA capacity, I was attached, or as the British say, "seconded," to Supreme Headquarters Allied Expeditionary Forces (SHAEF) in Versailles and then Frankfurt.

In 1946, I became a State Department employee, assigned to the Mission for Economic Affairs in the U.S. Embassy in London. One of my duties there was to represent the United States in the Emergency Economic Committee for Europe (the EECE), a rather informal temporary agency in which most of the countries of Western Europe, other than Germany and Italy, were represented. The accomplishments of the EECE were modest, but the exchanges of economic information were frank, friendships and trust were established, and the way was to some extent paved for the more formal and intensive cooperation of the Marshall Plan period.

In 1946, while I was in London, a Temporary Subcommission on the Reconstruction of Devastated Areas was established under the Economic and Employment Commission of the United Nations Economic and Social Council. The "devastators," as the subcommission members soon became known, subdivided into two working groups: one for Europe and Africa, and one for Asia and the Far East. When the Europe/Africa group came to London, the U.S. member, Isador Lubin, enlisted the help of our Mission for Economic Affairs and, as a member of that mission, I had the opportunity to work briefly with him. The report of the "devastators" led to the creation in 1947 of the UN Economic Commission for Europe (ECE). The distinguished Swedish economist, Gunnar Myrdal (later a winner of the Nobel Prize in economics), was appointed Executive Secretary of the ECE. He quickly assembled an excellent international staff.

The first session of the ECE was held in May 1947. Paul R. Porter, then Chief of the Mission for Economic Affairs, and I were members of the U.S. delegation, which was headed by Under Secretary of State Will Clayton. Until that session got under way, there was hope in its secretariat and among some of the delegations that the ECE would play a major role in coordinating European recovery. The tasks of the EECE and two other "E" organizations, the European Coal Organization and the European Central Inland Transport Organization, were assigned to the Economic Commission for Europe. Unfortunately, the behavior of the Soviet Union at that first ECE session ended our high hopes for the ECE.

Shortly before the second session of the ECE, Secretary of State George Marshall made his electrifying speech at Harvard University. Czechoslovakia and Poland, among others, were desperately eager to respond affirmatively to the Secretary's invitation (via Bevin and Bidault) to join in devising a joint recovery program for Europe. Unfortunately, the USSR was extending its reach and tightening its noose around them. One of my most vivid and poignant memories is of Jan Masaryk, then the Czechoslovakian Foreign Minister and ECE representative, pleading with the U.S. delegation for time and assistance in holding the door open for Czech participation. During his pleas, his face grew tense and his tone almost hysterical. He was obviously in despair. Seven months later, he was dead. Whether he committed suicide or was the victim of a political murder remains unknown.

The head of the Polish Delegation, Tadeusz Lychowski, was an old school diplomat; he replied to Russian speeches in Russian, French in French, and English in English. Although he was more restrained than Masaryk, he was equally eager to have his nation become part of the Marshall Plan.

By the end of the second session, it had been agreed that the United States would station a resident delegation to the ECE. Paul Porter and I were transferred to Geneva, Switzerland; Paul was designated Chief of the U.S. Resident Delegation to the ECE. We did our best to relay the Polish and Czech desires to Washington, London and Paris, but the Soviet Union not only rejected the opportunity to participate as the Soviet Union, it also made participation by its western neighbors, including Poland and Czechoslovakia, impossible.[1] In spite of Soviet hostility toward the Marshall Plan, a back door relationship of Poland to the Plan with respect to coal production and export, and of Czechoslovakia with respect to steel production, subsequently came into being via the ECE Coal and the ECE Steel Committees.

The Marshall Plan got under way in 1948 and Ambassador W. Averell Harriman was named head of the Office of the Special Representative (OSR) in Paris. By that time the staff of the U.S. Resident Delegation to the ECE had acquired considerable familiarity with the problems and prospects of the European economy. Paul Porter, Chief of the U.S. Resident Delegation, therefore went to Paris to meet Ambassador Harriman, inform him of our activities, and offer the delegation's help until Harriman's own staff could be assembled. The ambassador took advantage of the offer; Mr. Porter, several of his colleagues and I went to Paris to review and facilitate the drafting by the Europeans of the initial European Recovery Plan. After several busy days in Paris, I returned to Geneva and the rest of our team followed soon thereafter.

Paul Porter kept in close touch with Averell Harriman and members of the U.S. delegation to the ECE, most notably our coal and transport specialists, became frequent commuters to Paris. Mr. Porter and I attended meetings of the Marshall Plan's country mission chiefs. Our role was to brief Ambassador Harriman and his country mission chiefs on what was going on in Geneva (the European Headquarters of the United Nations), listen to the reports made by the mission chiefs, participate in the discussions and, insofar as possible, ensure that the work undertaken in Geneva complemented the work carried out under Marshall Plan auspices.

Compared to his phenomenally articulate deputy, Milton Katz, or to the ebullient Paul Hoffman, Averell Harriman appeared inarticulate. He was a poor but earnest speaker, disinclined to go out on a limb or express himself carelessly in public appearances. However, he was receptive to bold ideas and more than willing to back vigorously those he believed to be good. He had no capacity for small talk and, if he had a sense of humor, he kept it hermetically sealed during the three years in which I knew him best.

In 1949, while continuing to serve as head of OSR in Paris, Harriman was appointed U.S. Representative to the ECE. I once telephoned him from Switzerland to remind him that, upon arrival in Geneva for an ECE session that he had agreed to attend, he might have to say a few words to the press. I knew at least that the *New York Times* correspondent would be on hand. "Looking forward to a productive meeting and some useful discussions with fellow-delegates" was the type of "extemporaneous" statement I suggested. "Fine," he said, "I'll put my secretary on and you can dictate it to her." I said I would call her back in an hour, which I did.

The next morning at 6:30 a.m. at my home in Geneva, the phone rang and it was Averell. He suggested a few completely inconsequential modifications in my draft, such as changing "but" to "however." When I readily agreed, he said, "Don't agree with me just because it's 6:30 in the morning, I want your considered opinion." When I later mentioned his meticulousness to his Information Director, Alfred Friendly, he said, "Don't forget, you're dealing with Honest Ave, the hair-splitter." By way of postscript, I should add that in his long career of service to his country, Averell Harriman made almost none of the verbal gaffes produced by virtually every other person in public life.

The Marshall Plan operated in Southeast Asia as well as in Europe, but its heart and soul were in Europe. The rehabilitation of the European economy was its raison d'être, an objective that was understandable, measurable, and ardently desired by virtually all of the non-communist world. World War II, still fresh in the memory of all Marshall Plan participants, had also had a clear and understandable focus—the defeat of fascism—that brought forth prolonged and heroic inter-allied collaboration.

There were differences of opinion about how to carry out the Marshall Plan, particularly about the priority of global versus regional machinery and institutions, of alternative approaches to the convertibility of European currencies, of agriculture versus industry, and of dependence on international trade versus greater national self-sufficiency. In addition, there were personal incompatibilities. But the differences tended to be honest ones, overcome without the wild charges, rancor and pettiness that characterize so much of public debate today.

By all but the far left and the far right, the sizable American presence in Europe was accepted and appreciated, not only as an inescapable concomitant of vitally needed imports, but also because the American invaders brought to a weary continent energy, imagination, a can-do spirit, and a credible version of a better world. They espoused and believed in free markets and the free-enterprise system. But, they also recognized that it was not unfettered free enterprise that had extricated their nation from the depths of the Great Depression and carried it to victory in World War II—government, business, labor and academia had worked in concert. (Senator Joseph McCarthy, through his Committee on Un-American Activities had begun but not yet succeeded in undermining public confidence in the federal government.)

Our Conference Statement, "The Marshall Plan and Its Consequences" rightly highlights four enduring consequences of the period. How sad that the extraordinary collaboration of business, labor, government and academia that prevailed from early World War II through the Marshall Plan period cannot also be included as an enduring legacy. The captains of industry and finance who held high posts in the Marshall Plan worked hand-in-glove with the academics and civil servants assigned to serve them. Organized labor supported the Marshall Plan and provided some of the most capable personnel involved in its execution. Many of the "bureaucrats" and academics had entered government service during the exciting days of the New Deal and World War II. Like their colleagues, they were willing to work imaginatively for long hours without overtime pay.

I have probably said enough by now to demonstrate that, as stated in my opening sentence, my role in planning and implementing the Marshall Plan was tangential and inconsequential. I had worked for the U.S. Government at home and abroad since 1934. By 1947, I could claim at least a superficial knowledge of the potential of the U.S. economy and the problems of the European economy. That knowledge was enormously enhanced by my ringside seat at the meetings of the Marshall Plan's country mission chiefs while I had a full-time job in Geneva, first as Deputy Chief and then as Chief of the U.S. Resident Delegation to the ECE, after Paul Porter vacated the top post to become Director of the Marshall Plan Mission to Greece.

I enjoyed immensely all of my government jobs and take great satisfaction in having been in public service during some of this nation's finest hours. It saddens me to think that it took a catastrophic depression and a devastating world war to evoke this sense of mission, civility, and collaboration so characteristic of those bygone years. How, I ask, can those attitudes be restored and preserved in a vigorous functioning democracy in "normal" times?

Note

1. Now that the secret Soviet archives are being declassified, it would be interesting to learn more about the thinking in the Kremlin with respect to Secretary Marshall's speech and its aftermath. Was Soviet hostility due to the expectation that, in the absence of early economic recovery, the opportunities for local communist parties in Western Europe would be greatly enhanced? Was it the USSR's usual refusal, made clear to me in my Lend-Lease and UNRRA days, to provide essential information on the state of the Soviet economy and to allow nationals of other countries to review or verify the data being provided? Or was it a desire to conceal from outsiders the extent of its military readiness?

From Traveling Student to Marshall Plan Participant

VINCENT W. BROWN

Touring Europe as a Student in 1949

My friend, Bob Arnold, and I left Los Angeles for Washington DC by Greyhound bus in mid August. (The third member of our group, Bob Berdahl, had already left for England.) After checking out Washington DC, we headed for Montreal, Canada, where we picked up a British austerity vessel headed for Birmingham, England. Accommodations and food were spartan, but we didn't mind. When we arrived in England, we bought bicycles and toured around Wales, Stratford-on-Avon, London, etc. for a month. The U.K. was still under rationing, and we were issued ration cards. Most of the damage from the German bombing raids had been cleaned up, but the vacant lots in downtown areas still showed. Reconstruction was just beginning.

We then took a small ship across the channel to Denmark, and bicycled across it. We stored the bicycles in Copenhagen and proceeded to hitchhike and train through Sweden, Norway and back. We stayed mostly in youth hostels, and sometimes overnight in jails at no cost. Everyone was very accommodating and many shared their meager rations with us.

We then left for Germany and cycled down the Rhine valley via Bremen. It was devastated. In Coblenz not a building was standing, and we slept in the basement of what had once been a fifteen-story hotel. Everyone was very nice to us, especially since we were on bicycles, as was the population. We did not find any German citizens who felt personally responsible for the war or the Holocaust. In fact, many thought that the problem was not due to Hitler himself, but rather to the bad influence of his advisors. By this time it was early November, and we had frost on our eyelids as we cycled down the Rhine. We were anxious to see Paris, so we put ourselves (3rd class) and our bikes (baggage car) on the train in Coblenz and went to Paris.

We really enjoyed Paris, and stayed in a little hotel called "Mon Reve" (My Dream). There was no heat in Paris during the winter of 1949, and we almost froze to death. I remember sitting up in bed trying to keep warm, typing letters home wearing gloves and my old navy fur jacket. But we loved it, and decided to see Paris in the spring.

I signed up at the Alliance Française to learn French under the GI Bill and we all applied for work at the main offices of the Marshall Plan, which were on the Place de la Concorde in the Hotel Talleyrand. It took considerable persistence to get hired and to obtain our security clearance. In the interim, we had time to visit the Louvre, go to the theater, concerts and opera, and see most of Paris's fabulous museums which were just beginning to be refurbished after the six years of neglect during World War II. It was cold work since none of the museums were heated. It was easy to get around since the subway and buses were fully operational, although many Parisians still used their bicycles to get around. Hot water was in short supply, and our hotel rooms had no showers and the toilet was down the hall. So we went to the public bath twice a week to bathe. We usually had to wait in line, and took books to read as we waited our turn. All in all, we had a fabulous time.

My first job for the U.S. government in Paris was as a security guard protecting NATO secrets. As a World War II veteran, I was supposedly qualified. I was very uneasy loading my "38" revolver, and unsure what I would have done if I had encountered an intruder. After a few weeks one of our guards shot himself, and they decided to replace the civilian guards with U. S. Marines—a wise decision, in my view. Almost immediately after the Marines arrived in the spring of 1950, I was hired by the Economic Cooperation Administration's regional office based in Paris.

The Marshall Plan Years (1950-1957)

I spent a total of seven short years at the Marshall Plan's overseas headquarters of the Economic Cooperation Administration (ECA), the Office of the Special Representative (OSR), in Place de la Concorde,

Paris. I was hired as a Technical Assistance Specialist working for the Marshall Plan on technical assistance and productivity activities. The name of the agency changed over the years beginning with the Economic Cooperation Administration and its successor agencies, the International Cooperation Administration and the Foreign Operations Administration (1950-1957).

Technical Assistance and International Cooperation in Europe

Little did I know when I joined the ECA in June 1950 that this was the beginning of a career that was to span more than a quarter of a century. My first job was Technical Assistance Specialist in the Technical Assistance section of the Industry Division, OSR, Paris. I was recruited by Scott L. Behoteguy, deputy head of the TA section, who went on to become an Office Director in Washington, D.C. and a USAID Director. Our offices were in the Hôtel Talleyrand at the corner of the Rue de Rivoli and the Place de la Concorde. The U.S. Embassy was on the opposite corner of the Place. Our office was a large room filled with desks, chairs, and telephones which were constantly ringing with calls from all over Europe. My job was to process applications for technical assistance from southern Europe, and my co-worker, Norman Schoonover, processed applications for northern Europe. He also went on to become a USAID Director. Norm and I were to see that the applications met the criteria for technical assistance. The head of the Technical Assistance section was John T. Quinn (retired from ITT), and the Division head, Mr. Gihlcrest, had been head of a chemical processing plant. Many of the professional staff were from the private sector or on loan from other government agencies.

In September, I was reassigned and became the Technical Assistance Specialist for Organization for European Economic Cooperation (OEEC) operations and was assigned the responsibility for the development and implementation of an effective OEEC Technical Assistance program. The OEEC was the international organization set up by the nations receiving Marshall Plan aid to divide it up, assign priorities among countries, complete economic analysis, etc. Its headquarters was at the Chateau de la Muette near the Bois de Bologne in Paris. Its successor agency exists today as the Organization for Economic Cooperation and Development (OECD).

As part of this exercise, the governing council of the OEEC had set up a Technical Assistance Group (TAG) to coordinate and organize this multi-country activity. My job was to work with them in developing an annual TA program and budget and to secure approval from OSR. I was also the focal point in OSR and the principal coordinator for all OEEC Technical Assistance projects. This activity was so new, that based on operating experience, I was to suggest standard operating policies and procedures. The TAG consisted of representatives from the OEEC countries, and the meetings were translated into French and English. I spoke for the U.S. for most meetings with my bosses coming for the policy/budget approval sessions.

It was felt that in the ten years since World War II began in 1939, most countries had fallen behind the U.S. in critical technical, social and applied research fields. Both the national and multi-national TA programs at that time were designed to help the European countries close this gap. International conferences and seminars in selected fields were held in Europe and the U.S., as well as consultant teams provided from the United States. Some of the fields we worked in were: metallurgy, chemistry, banking, marketing, labor/management, productivity and applied research. However, the applied research was carried under the aegis of a separate sub-committee that I also monitored. I arranged for representatives from the National Academy of Sciences (NAS), the National Science Council (NSC), and the Department of Commerce's Office of Technical Services (OTS) to attend the research committee sub-committee meetings.

While the major theme was to develop ways of coordinating information and to avoid duplication of government financed applied research, I believe our unique U.S. contribution to Europe was the introduction of the concept of non-profit applied research organizations which were jointly financed by universities and major private sector companies such as Stanford Research, Southwest and Batelle. These organizations were supported in good part by contracts from U.S. government departments and agencies. We fielded technical assistance teams manned by the directors of these institutes, who went around the major European countries showing governments, universities and industry how to set them up. As a result organizations were set up in Germany, France and the UK.

I'd like to insert a parenthesis here. In 1954, a big event occurred in my life. I decided to marry a Parisian girl, Françoise Durand. It was necessary to get permission from both the Paris and Washington offices. Françoise received a thorough review by our Embassy security services, as did the French of me in retaliation, but we both passed with flying colors. We had a few anxious moments waiting for Washington's approval, which finally came in a telegram signed by Harold Stassen (then Administrator of the Mutual Security Agency), which read "Permission granted for Vincent Brown to marry." We were married in a civil ceremony by a communist mayor in a suburb of Paris [Issy les Moulineaux] on April 12, 1954. I'm pleased to report that we are still married today.

While most of the Marshall Plan activities were beginning to wind down by 1954, that year the technical assistance "transfer of know-how" section got a new lease on life. Congress passed an amendment to the Foreign Assistance Act called the Benton/Moody Amendment which called for a specific program to assist the European countries and the OEEC in improving its labor/ management relations and subsequently improve its productivity. The legislation also provided the grant funds to go with it. Improved labor/management relations in Europe was the objective, and the sharing of the experience in the U.S. was designed to facilitate this transformation.

One of the big activities designed to implement the Benton/Moody Act (1954/55) was the establishment of a European Productivity Agency under the OEEC. By this time our little Technical Assistance section in the Industry division of the OSR had grown to a full division—The Productivity and Technical Assistance Division (PTAD), headed by Everett Bellows and Don MacPhail. A lawyer heading up the OEEC section, Hugh Smith from Oregon, was tapped to develop the charter for the European Productivity Agency (EPA). A young officer on the PTAD staff, Eugene Abrams (who stayed on with ECA and its successor agencies and eventually became a USAID Director), was selected to write the first draft of the charter, and worked with the Europeans in bringing it to fruition. At the national level, many of the bilateral programs benefited from this legislation and created National Productivity Centers in their respective capitals. My OEEC technical assistance activities were integrated into the European Productivity Agency, and the Technical Assistance group was replaced by the OEEC Productivity and Technical Assistance Committee.

The European Productivity Agency

The U.S. initiated EPA was one more tool in the attempt to convince European businesses to adopt modern labor/management techniques, management strategies and marketing techniques. As mentioned above, this work had been started bilaterally, and most European countries, including Iceland, had already set up National Productivity Centers. The EPA provided a forum for the Center Directors to meet, exchange information, organize inter-European teams and so forth.

European management in the early 1950s looked very much as it had in the Depression years of the 30s. While the U.S. had made great strides in labor management relations and in the whole area of marketing and advertising, little had changed in Europe. There was great skepticism on the part of European management, particularly the French patronat. However, once they got into it, they perceived the benefits and were eager to know more. Lasting relationships were established with private U.S. management groups and labor unions. Under the EPA numerous conferences, teams to the U.S., consultant teams, documentation, and other services were organized.

In a broader perspective, European economists, political scientists and intellectuals in general were beginning to think about a European common market, a "United States of Europe." The multi-nation European Coal and Steel Community had already been initiated. The OEEC's European Productivity Organization (EPA) was very much part of this thrust.

Throughout the 1950s, the names of our aid agency changed a number of times. The ECA had become the Mutual Security Agency (MSA), which was transformed into the Foreign Operations Administration (FOA). By 1956, it was called the International Cooperation Administration (ICA) and it didn't become the Agency for International Development until after President Kennedy's inauguration. I believe Congress had hoped that the assistance effort would disappear except for the Latin America-style "Point IV" programs once the main objectives of the Marshall Plan were achieved in the mid-fifties. However, by 1957, it was becoming clear that foreign assistance was not going to disappear, but would have its focus on assisting developing countries. As a result, a more permanent and rational system of assigning personnel was instituted.

A personal anecdote comes to mind. Bill Kontos, later USAID Director and an ambassador who was with ICA Personnel in those days, came out in early 1957 and informed me that I had been working in Paris for seven years—far too long! I replied that I had no objections to moving, but had just not been able to bring myself to apply for a transfer. In light of my Paris office's recommendation that I be sent to a francophone country to take advantage of my fluent French, the Washington bureaucracy, with its usual insight, proposed that I be sent to Liberia, an English speaking country. Fortunately, I was rescued by Don MacPhail, the past head of the Productivity and Technical Assistance Division in Paris, who by this time had been named Deputy Mission Director in Tunisia (a francophone country). I was transferred to Tunis in September 1957 as an Assistant Program Officer.

Establishing Technical Assistance In Europe

WILLIAM COLEMAN

I applied in the Organization and Management (O&M) Division because I had gotten into organization matters in Greece, and I wanted to broaden my public administration experience. The person who interviewed me was Robert Rupard. He thought that the fact that I had organizational experience in Greece and had been in the various executive positions in personnel management in the United States might qualify me in O&M. The head of the O&M Division, Harry Fite, who had joined the organization from the Budget Bureau, interviewed me and appointed me as both an analyst and an assistant to him in running the division.

The division was one of four reporting to the Director of Administration, Donald Stone. The other divisions making up the whole administrative area were Personnel, Budget, and Administrative Services. The Personnel Division was headed by Virgil Couch, we had adjoining offices with the Budget Division. The Administrative Services head was Orbun Powell.

The O&M Division tackled various management problems that would arise in divisions throughout the agency. We would go in, look at them and make some recommendations. For example, because the Budget Bureau was imposing agency personnel ceilings throughout the government at that time, we had a system of personnel ceilings for the various organizational units of the ECA. Don Stone would have periodic meetings with the division heads under him about how to handle the personnel caps. At O&M we, along with Budget, looked at various divisions and departments, giving them suggestions as to how they could meet the personnel caps and still be effective.

For example, we devised and helped establish a small unit in the agency called the Program Methods Control Staff (PMCS). They developed new forms and various program processes for different departments, but were not part of the Department of Administration. They were under Tyler Wood, the Assistant Administrator for Operations. Dick Bissell was Assistant Administrator for Programs.

Don Stone also asked me to give some study to the provision of the Economic Cooperation Act that dealt with technical assistance. As far as Western Europe was concerned, we would give assistance wherever we could in the reconstruction and rehabilitation problems that those countries were facing.

At the outset it was separate. The British and the U.S. had agreed to form an Anglo-American Productivity Council and my recollection is that it was pushed by Philip Reed, President of General Electric, who had been in negotiations with British industrialists. They thought it would be a good idea, and I took it up with Hoffman, thinking that it would be a good idea. It was formed with a small council made up of U.S. and British officials, comprising not just public sector but some private sector representatives as well. It was a discrete part of the Economic Cooperation Administration (ECA) Technical Assistance Division.

I thought that the technical assistance provision had great importance, and I sent Stone some memoranda on it. I don't know what the elements of the internal debate were, but Hoffman decided that there ought to be a division of technical assistance (TA) and that was assigned to the jurisdiction of Ty Wood, who was Assistant Administrator of Operations. Technical assistance involves bringing people to this country and taking them around to see our processes, along with sending our experts to other countries. A very able person out of the General Counsel's Office, William (B.Y.) Hoff, was named head of that division and he recruited an assistant working in Don Stone's office, Jack Fobes.

Hoffman set about organizing the TA division and, because of the memoranda that I had written for Stone, he asked me to take over the operations side of the division while Jack Fobes would take over the program side. That may seem overlapping, but it was divided in such a way that if a decision was made on the Program side that, for example, we ought to let half a dozen teams from half a dozen countries come over here and look at such and such a subject, the offer would be made known through our missions abroad. The handling of these people and the working up of their itineraries and so on would be taken care of by my team in Operations.

I had a staff of about thirty program managers in four sections. For the handling of every delegation that came over, a project manager would be in charge. Sometimes they would handle more than one delegation at a time, because if it were a fairly simple itinerary, after making advance arrangements, they would let one of the people in the delegation look after the rest. Sometimes, not very often but sometimes, a Project Manager would be handling two or even three different projects at the same time. In terms of personnel, that was the largest of the sections. I had a recruitment section of two or three professionals to work with the Personnel Division in getting the right kind of American experts that the overseas country had asked for.

A third section had to do with the logistics and other supporting services, such as what visiting delegations would need in such-and-such a field. What kind of books ought to be provided, and what kind of other services were needed. That section was tied in with the Budget Bureau Division, headed by Bernie Rosen, whose job it was to be a reservoir of knowledge about how the U.S. Government worked. Finally, we had the equivalent of a fourth section, the Anglo-American Productivity Council, located in New York City. I visited there an average of every ten days or so.

Two Marshall Plan Techniques

JOHN E. FORBES

S ubsequent to my four years experience with the Economic Cooperation Administration and the Mutual Security Agency, April 1948 to December 1951, I enjoyed assignments in Europe involving multilateral cooperation over a total of 17 years. Friends in that region have reminded me over the years of the spur to practical cooperation in Europe which came from the basic motivation and the spirit embodied in administration of the Marshall Plan.

Seminars

They emphasized, for example, the dialogues/multilogues in 1947-50 when countries presented and defended specific aspects of their development policies and plans before panels of the then OEEC. Those mutual criticism and appreciation sessions constituted valuable learning opportunities for the participants, for their governments, and for leaders in their civil societies. All national partners shared in the responsibilities and benefits from discussions which touched upon a wide range of social and economic questions and promoted mutual understanding and respect. Such techniques could well be applied more generally today in multilateral cooperation.

Technical Cooperation

Only a few days before Paul Hoffman, ECA Administrator, was scheduled for testimony before committees of Congress in the spring of 1948, Donald Stone came back from a directors' staff meeting. The need, he explained, was for a briefing for Mr. Hoffman on a paragraph in the Marshall Plan legislation which authorized a small amount of funding for technical assistance. What was this intended to cover? What did he expect to do under this authorization?

Stone directed a consultant, with my assistance, to prepare (under a four-day deadline, as I recall) a statement of purpose, policy and strategy, together with the elements of a work plan on the subject of technical assistance. The consultant and I worked in his hotel room in Washington. We produced an annotated list of eight or nine types of such assistance and a statement for the record, and designed graphics for a presentation.

The proposed appropriation was approved. I believe that the Marshall Plan materials contributed to Executive Branch discussions both before and after President Truman's "Point Four" statement in his Inaugural Address of January 1949, which stressed the importance of technical assistance for economic and social development.

From Cameraman in the War to Radio Producer in the Marshall Plan

ROBERT HOPKINS

As a U.S. Army combat cameraman in World War II, I witnessed and filmed for the official record, the war in Western Europe. In the process, I recorded the devastation of cities, the demolition of factories, the eradication of railway marshaling yards, rolling stock and locomotives, ports, ships, highways, bridges and tunnels. I saw rich farmlands sown with mines. I observed the despair etched on the faces of refugees uprooted from their land and homes in Italy, France, Belgium, Holland, Luxembourg and Germany, as Allied forces brought the Nazi regime to its knees. These scenes and images are still burned into my memory. When the war ended, I returned to America and went to work as a production assistant and screenwriter at a major film studio in Hollywood.

In 1949, I had the good fortune to land a job with the Economic Cooperation Administration (ECA) in Paris. Here was an opportunity to participate in rebuilding the economy of Europe from the ruins of war via the inspired European Recovery Program, popularly remembered as the Marshall Plan.

The Marshall Plan offered economic cooperation to all European countries affected by World War II. War-torn nations with no hard currency were permitted by the ECA to buy urgently needed American machines and technology with their own national currencies. Reduced to simple terms, this meant that a French farmer could buy an American tractor to cultivate his land, by paying the French franc equivalent of the dollar cost. This gave the farmer a true sense of participation in the recovery effort, crucial to bolstering his self-respect.

These local currencies, called "counterpart funds" were pooled and used in-country to pay for labor and raw materials to rebuild housing, schools, municipal buildings, factories, and the country's infrastructure. Fifteen percent of counterpart funds were set aside to pay for the administration of the Marshall Plan.

Sixteen countries, ranging from Norway to Greece, welcomed the Plan. Czechoslovakia also expressed a desire to join, but the Soviet Union, which controlled that country, viewed the Marshall Plan as a means of weakening its influence there, and forced it to rescind its acceptance.

The Marshall Plan championed ideas virtually unknown in Europe at that time. It proposed and actively promoted the Common Market and the Council of Europe. With the Point Four program, it encouraged new productivity techniques. It fostered the desirability of a common currency in Europe to promote trade. It urged the creation of free trade unions and successfully helped organize them in order to counter nascent Soviet influence in Western Europe. As the Soviet Union tried to thwart the Marshall Plan projects, the contours of the Cold War began to emerge.

I was assigned to the Information Division in the Office of the Special Representative where, among other tasks, I collaborated with Roscoe Drummond in writing speeches for Ambassador W. Averell Harriman, the ECA Special Representative.

Then, because I had produced a documentary radio series in America, I was placed in the Radio Section. Here, I produced a number of weekly radio programs, which were broadcast in the vernacular by local radio stations throughout the sixteen countries participating in the Marshall Plan. They were designed to inform Europeans of their own progress in rebuilding their economies.

I also produced periodic programs in English for audiences in the United States. These took the form of roundtable broadcasts, chaired by Ambassador Harriman in which he, seated in our studio in Paris, received a report from each ECA Country Mission Chief. One by one, they reported to him by radio their progress in fulfilling the mission assigned to them. He commented on their reports and gave them guidance. These broadcasts were transmitted to NBC or CBS in the United States to inform Americans of progress being made in Europe with the cooperation of the United States through the mechanism of the Marshall Plan.

Those days were exciting for me—for all of us—because we could see that it was working. Although it was years after the Marshall Plan ended before the Common Market and the Council of Europe became a reality, these entities are firmly established and taken for granted. Europe is united, prosperous and economically sound because of the Marshall Plan.

I believe there is a place for the Marshall Plan today. It should be reconstituted and applied to resolve the economic crises in Russia, Bosnia, Albania and other trouble spots in the world. Foster a healthy economy and strife becomes obsolete.

Three Simple Lessons

ALFRED REIFMAN

I joined the State Department after my service in the Army in 1946 and worked on the economic issues of Western Europe—notably the Monnet Plan and the Blum-Byrnes loan to France. Then George Marshall made his commencement address at Harvard, beginning a long period of intensive work—seven days a week, more than eight hours a day—preparing the estimates and analysis for the French role in the Marshall Plan.

I wrote the economic part of the Bluebook on France's role in the European Recovery Program; Val Lorwin did the political analysis. We argued that France and Italy might voluntarily opt for communism unless living conditions improved and there was hope for the future, as the French and Italian communist parties represented the largest organized political forces in their respective countries. This was the standard line. Equally important to me were two other factors. One was a feeling of guilt, since America had been spared the devastation of war and occupation. The other was the fear that unless another way could be found to help Europe, the lending that we were doing would come back to haunt us when payment came due, much as was the case with the inability of Germany to pay reparations after World War I that did so much to bring on Hitler. Cumulatively, these reasons were sufficient for me to wholeheartedly support Marshall's proposal.

Several anecdotes from the planning period, 1947-48, may be interesting.

First is the "Kindleberger surplus," named after Charles Kindleberger, the chief economist working on the Plan in the State Department, later a professor at MIT. In estimating trade flows, analysts, working independently, had projected more exports from European countries to each other than imports from each other, which was a physical impossibility. To resolve the problem, Charlie called a meeting of all the country analysts. Each offered exports of a commodity for others to take. Speaking for France, I was very liberal; I took almost all offers. Thus, we balanced the intra-European trade accounts.

The aid figures were supposed to be based on estimates of a country's "needs" for the import of particular commodities, after taking into account their exports of the same commodities. At the request of a Pennsylvania congressman, we even had to estimate the demand for carbon black, a commodity I couldn't find in the trade statistics, but we came up with a number for it anyway. Yet, the specific commodities we were required to project such as coal, wheat and oil covered only some 25% of a country's imports. Clearly, to me, aid should depend on how much we wanted a country to receive. I chose to keep France's balance-of-payments deficit at the level funded. When questioned whether I had correctly estimated France's aid requirements and balance-of-payments deficit for 1948, I asserted confidently that at the end of the year, France's deficit would equal the amount of aid I had projected. I had taken Economics 101, but my questioner, a Senior State officer, had not. The deficit had to equal the amount of aid France was about to receive. That's all the dough they had to spend over their earnings.

At the meeting of the country analysts, I was criticized for calculating that France ought to get more aid than any other country. In response, I submitted a paper showing the aid estimates on a per capita basis. France was in the middle and Iceland led the list by far.

After finishing our work, we were told at State that we would have to do it all over again under the auspices of the National Advisory Committee on Monetary Affairs (NAC), a committee chaired by Treasury. We were to do this on Sunday—another Sunday!—at Treasury. The results were unchanged, but it was an interagency product and George Willis of Treasury led the way.

Congress felt that it could not evaluate the estimates, so it asked for the professional qualifications of each of the analysts and our names and bios were published in the Congressional Record. That was our brief moment in the sun.

A good deal of credit for the Plan should go to three individuals: Charles Kindleberger, James "Scotty" Reston, and Leonard Miall. They rode to work together in a car pool as gasoline was rationed to save rubber. On the drive down, Charlie kept insisting that Marshall's speech was significant and not just another commencement address. Reston kept writing about it in the *New York Times*, building support in Congress and the public. Leonard Miall broadcast news and analysis over the BBC. Bevin, the British Foreign Minister, heard his broadcasts, asked for a copy of the speech and was told that it was only a commencement address and was coming by sea mail in seven to ten days. Shocked, he asked for and received a wireless copy, called Schumann, the French Foreign Minister; and suggested a meeting in Paris to discuss Europe's reply. The Plan was on its way.

After the Plan became operative, in August 1948, I went to Paris to serve as Deputy Chief of the Program Review Division of the Economic Cooperation Administration (ECA) Mission to France. David Bruce was the Mission Chief. I stayed until 1950. There I was involved in the evaluation of French economic policies. I can't say that I had any impact on them. If anyone had an effect, it was the Treasury team headed by Tomlinson.

Impact

Despite the impressive economic achievements of the French in 1948-1950, we thought they were lagging. We worried why France was not recovering as fast as we had hoped. We looked for reasons, such as low investment or the persistence of the family firms undercutting the spirit of entrepreneurship. The reason we could find no factor explaining French economic sluggishness, was that there was none. France was doing well.

The major accomplishment of the Marshall Plan was political. Western Europe united. Successively there was intra-European trade liberalization, a payments union, the Common Market, the Community and now the European Union. Germany was reintegrated into Europe. Antagonism among the European powers was replaced by cooperation. The major exception was the refusal of the U.K. to join the Common Market, the European Economic Community, when it was first formed.

The impetus for European cooperation and integration came from many sources, American and European. The U.S. Congress included in the original legislation a clause reminding the Europeans of the success that the forty-eight American states had with their economic union, a suggestion I thought at the time, was presumptuous. Marshall Plan workers did influence the policies of the European governments. Jean Monnet played a crucial role in advancing the dream of a united Europe.

How significant were the funds we supplied to Europe? Some were important. For example, H. Van Cleveland, a former State Department official who played a key role in the events leading up to Marshall's speech, argued that aid was unnecessary, that an exchange-rate change by Europe would have done the trick. Clearly, Europe would have recovered anyway. Moreover, U.S. aid was some 3% of European GNP over the period 1948-51, and it supported consumption as well as investment. Thus, the impact on investment and, consequently, long-term growth, was quite limited. But our financing did speed the process of economic recovery and growth. The aid helped Europe over a period when it would have had great difficulty maintaining its imports. Economically, Europe might have lost one year's growth without aid. But even such a small decline in, or failure to increase, living standards might have had serious political repercussions. Aid did give the Europeans hope that they were not alone and that America would help.

I draw a number of simple lessons from the Marshall Plan:

1. The change in policies was the essential factor in the long-term economic and political recovery of Europe. Marshall Plan people and European leaders played a key role in this endeavor.
2. Financial assistance was necessary to get the attention of the governments to make these changes. But it was not sufficient. Governments do not change long-established policies and practices easily. To affect change there had to be sympathetic ears in the government. In such cases, and only in such cases, U.S. support for their views could be decisive.
3. The existence of an infrastructure of laws and practices conducive to a market economy as well as a trained labor force and industrial capacity made it possible for the Plan to achieve its economic goals in four years.

Men and Women of Good Will

HILDEQARD BLANKEN SHISHKIN

My experience in the Marshall Plan began in the spring of 1948 when I was a clerk newly assigned to our Embassy in Paris. Happily for me, Averell Harriman arrived shortly thereafter to set up the Office of the U.S. Special Representative in Europe, the Economic Cooperation Administration (ECA)'s European headquarters. He invited me to join his staff as his secretary. Thus began a fascinating experience, a working relationship, and a friendship which lasted almost a lifetime.

Of course, my job was not that of a policy-maker or implementer. I stayed close to our headquarters office in the Hotel Talleyrand, the elegant 18th century building off the Place de la Concorde. Over time, its occupants included the Comte de St. Florentin, Talleyrand, the Rothchild family, in World War II the German Admiralty, and at war's end the French government, including Maurice Thorez.

From my perch, I had a unique opportunity to observe those involved—the great, the near-great, the professionals, and the clerks— all joined in this extraordinary undertaking, the Marshall Plan. I had spent the previous year on Foreign Service assignment in Reykjavik as well as Switzerland, relatively calm waters. But here, I was face to face with extraordinarily impatient people. Everyone in and out of government was eager to participate in this joint U.S./European recovery effort.

What I saw in terms of the success of the Marshall Plan in the two years I worked there was the joyous replacement of dry, weevil-infested brown bread by the white French baguette and the sight of shabby doors being painted in fresh colors, brass being polished, shops brightened and food stalls filling with goods.

On October 25, 1948, the Paris edition of the *New York Herald Tribune* published the results of a survey it had undertaken, and declared the Marshall Plan a success:

". . . success as an historic effort toward economic recovery,"
". . . success as a newly learned habit of practical international cooperation,"
". . . successful as an American investment,"
". . . success as American foreign policy."

Twenty-five years later, in a discussion of the factors contributing to its success, Jean Monnet declared that the accomplishment would not have been possible "without a continuing day-to-day collaboration by men of good will who knew what they wanted and how to achieve it."

Foremost among these were Paul Hoffman, operating out of Washington, and Averell Harriman, working in Paris. Their exceptional talents and mutually supportive working relationship established the non-partisan tone which so greatly benefited their efforts. It was said of Hoffman that none got so much money out of Congress when there was not one single voter in support of the program. In a tribute to Hoffman, Harriman declared that few men in history had done so much for so many, in such a brief span of years.

Harriman contributed his exceptional negotiating skills, human understanding and extensive foreign experience, including pre- and post-World War I and during World War II in Moscow and London. The writer E. J. Kahn, Jr., said of Harriman, that he was one of the few world statesmen who think not in terms of masses, but of individuals: "You can sense from what he says that he perceives human beings behind problems."

The Marshall Plan was a program focused on the people. It provided for the active participation of labor. Of course, I am sorry that there were so few professional women. I do remember with admiration Evelyn Scheyer, who worked so skillfully on refugee and displaced persons matters. I also recall a Women's Advisory Committee on Information in Washington. I wish I knew more about women's participation in and support for the Marshall Plan.

I believe future policy makers will draw strength and guidance from the experience and achievement of the concept of the Marshall Plan. In its attack on hunger, want, and chaos, it is an example of power used to its best ends.

The European Payments Union

ROBERT SOLOMAN

A s a young economist fresh out of graduate school, I joined the staff of the Federal Reserve Board in December 1947. I worked on France and the Benelux countries and attended Congressional hearings on the proposed European Recovery Program at which Dean Acheson, among others, testified. My work included following and writing papers on economic and financial developments in the European countries as well as attended inter-agency meetings on the various problems that arose.

In the autumn of 1952 I was loaned to the Office of the Special Representative (OSR) in Paris for three months. The part of OSR to which I was attached was concerned with the European Payments Union (EPU) and with the eventual convertibility of the currencies of the Marshall Plan recipients. In particular, we studied the exchange rates of the European countries and considered whether adjustment of those rates was a necessary pre-condition for convertibility.

The Marshall Plan was a major historic event. How Europe would have fared without it is virtually impossible to imagine. The benefits were many. In addition to the most obvious one, the provision by the United States of financial aid which in turn made it possible for Europe to import and reconstruct, the arrangements regarding counterpart funds had a positive effect on the macroeconomic policies of the recipient countries.

Another major benefit was the encouragement of free trade and payment among the European countries which, immediately after the war, were using quantitative import restrictions and bilateral payment arrangements to protect their slim foreign exchange reserves. The Intra-European Payments Agreement and then the EPU accomplished the aim of freeing trade and payments and introducing greater competition into European economies. I was able to observe the positive effects on the French economy of the competition from imports from other European countries.

A Trap that Led to a Window of Opportunity

Thomas W. Wilson, Jr.

It was an afternoon in early March of 1948, as I recall it, when I received a telephone call in New York from Alfred Friendly in Washington. I had known him in my newspaper days and had been glad to learn recently that Averell Harriman had chosen him to head Public Information Services for the American headquarters of the Marshall Plan that Harriman was preparing to establish in Paris. As it turned out, however, Friendly was calling with the ridiculous notion that I should do the same thing for the Marshall Plan mission in London.

I explained at once why this was just impossible. The Second World War had kept me separated from wife and children for more than two years and we were just reunited when I was packed off to Moscow to work with the Allied Commission on Reparations. Following that I spent a year in Egypt, and now at last I was settled, with a great house on Long Island Sound and a wonderful job, with a chance to make some real money. The last thing in the world I wanted was to leave the country again. Besides, I understood that the Marshall Plan was to be run mainly by businessmen, who were not likely to look for help from New Deal fans like me.

Friendly put up a vigorous argument. We had won the war, he said, but the way things were looking in Europe we might very well lose the peace. The outcome would depend upon the success or failure of the Marshall Plan. And Congressional support could depend upon whether American generosity is known and appreciated in Europe. Friendly also stressed that the head of the U.S. Mission to the United Kingdom was not a provincial businessman but Thomas K. Finletter, a prominent New York lawyer, a Democrat, and a good internationalist.

There was much more discussion, but I held my ground. Finally, Friendly told me that Finletter was, at that moment, en route between Washington and New York with the understanding that I would meet him in his office at ten o'clock the next morning. So, Friendly said, do me the favor of explaining in your own words why you cannot join him in London. I could see no harm in that and agreed to do so.

The next morning I met Tom Finletter for the first time and immediately felt that I had known him for years. I tried to report briefly on my discussion with Al Friendly, apologized for meeting with him under false expectations, and offered to help in finding a more available candidate for his staff. Finletter said that it was easy to understand my problem. Indeed, he had at first declined his own appointment for strong personal reasons. But he went on to explain how he concluded, upon careful thought, that he really did not have a right to turn away from a chance to help undo the wreckage left by Hitler. He talked at length about the Marshall Plan as a test of U.S. leadership in world affairs, about the special role of Britain in post-war recovery, and about Republican opposition to the Marshall Plan in Congress. And then he set a trap: Congress had authorized the Marshall Plan for four years but would appropriate funds only one year at a time. This put a special emphasis upon public understanding in the very first year of the program. "How would you approach this problem," he asked me, "if you were in my shoes?"

I walked straight into the trap and began an impromptu monologue on what I thought were the answers. When I ran out of steam, Finletter said something like, "I am glad to have your judgment because you see it exactly the way I do. Now, I am leaving on the Queen Mary tomorrow, but if you decide to join us you could come by air and we could start this job off together." My firm position dissolved on the floor of his office. That very day I arranged a one-year leave of absence from my company and began the process of selling the car, getting rid of the house, taking the kids out of school and packing up for a trip that got the family to London about the time Finletter arrived.

London was the worse for wear. The bomb damage seemed everywhere. Buildings were in bad need of paint; windows were still taped against marauding V-1s and V-2s—food, gasoline, tobacco and alcohol were still tightly rationed, and newspapers were full of warnings about the tough times still ahead.

I soon discovered there would be no problem in informing the public about the Marshall Plan. The British Treasury already had begun a multimedia campaign of economic education about the problems of post-war adjustment. The Marshall Plan, of course, was a key source of hope for the future, and so our story became a regular chapter in the Treasury's public education program. This worked so well that when visiting Congressmen wanted to know whether the British public was aware of our help, I could hand them an editorial complaining bitterly about the torrents of praise in newspapers, magazines, radio, newsreels and official speeches about the Marshall Plan. The editorial ended with a sour prediction that the Marshall Plan message would soon be converted into a Sunday sermon from every pulpit in the United Kingdom. The clipping came from *The Daily Worker*, the official newspaper of the communist party, and most visitors asked for a copy to take home with them.

Our small staff in London was a pick-up team, a mixture of businessmen, bureaucrats, labor unionists, academics and others with nothing in common except a taste for public service and a talent for working in harness for something they believed to be worthwhile. By the time my year was up and I was scheduled to go home, Averell Harriman asked me to shift to the headquarters staff in Paris. This time there was no agony of choice. I resigned from my job in New York and prepared to move the family once again.

One of the first things to strike me in Paris was the effect of geographic location on political outlook. In London it was easy to understand British reluctance to be drawn into joint operations with countries across the Channel. From Paris, this seemed to be a threat to the whole enterprise. Time and again, I was to find that a one-hour plane trip could shift the whole argument about European integration.

Yet it was from the headquarters in Paris that I began to sense the political implications and the sheer boldness of the Marshall Plan. That the technically advanced nations of Western Europe might repair the damage of war within a few years was not such a wild idea. After all, the Industrial Revolution was born there, and they could rebuild damaged plants and railroads provided, of course, that they could obtain the needed imports of food, machinery and materials which could only come from America. But the U.S. offer to contribute that critical margin was contingent: the Europeans would first have to get together, combine their separate needs, and collaborate on the design of a single, multi-national European recovery program. And this would have to happen among culturally diverse societies; nations at different stages of economic development, with various levels of national resources and governments of contrasting competence; and, nations, worst of all, that for centuries had fought each other on grounds of nationalism, religious dogma and realpolitik.

Today, there is no serious doubt that this precondition of the Marshall Plan eventually led, painfully but directly, to the European Coal and Steel Community; a payments union; the Common Market; and, the European Parliament, the Court of Justice and the other institutions of the European Union. More than that, traditional enemies are convinced of their interdependence and no longer depend upon the conventional wisdom of power politics to serve their national interests in the contemporary world. None of this, of course, was visible or predictable in the early days of the Marshall Plan.

Indeed, for the first few years, France was the strategic center of a knockdown, drag-out propaganda battle between the friends and foes of the Marshall Plan. The attack was led by the communist parties of Western Europe, which still held some public respect for their war-time struggle against occupying Nazi forces. But after the Soviet Union refused to participate in the Marshall Plan, they did their best to sabotage the recovery program, acting mainly through the trade unions they controlled. The dock workers refused to unload the first ships to arrive in France with Marshall Plan cargo; the coal miners struck to undercut industrial productions; the walls of cities were plastered with propaganda posters; rocks were thrown through screens at movie theaters showing progress in recovery; and, of course, the central villain was the American conspiracy to colonize Europe through the Marshall Plan. Against all this, the Marshall Plan information office in Paris responded with an unprecedented output of documentary films, elaborate systems of traveling exhibits, radio programs, posters and publications for schools, trade unions and other groups as well as the general public. It was a strenuous contest but one that was never in doubt. Not many Europeans wanted to oppose the European Recovery Program—or even the foreigners supporting it.

After two years at the Paris headquarters and another year with the mission to France, I finally headed for home, feeling that we had done a good job—good for the Europeans, good for us, and good for the world-at-large. The sheer joy of working at an international enterprise with enthusiastic people committed to a common goal was to linger on. And I remained grateful for that to Al Friendly and Tom Finletter and others too many to name for an exciting and rewarding four years.

Since then I have sometimes wondered whether later generations ever will have opportunities comparable to service with the Marshall Plan. But with fifty years of perspective, my opinion is that what the Marshall Plan proves, above all else, is the need for more political ingenuity in a world with problems that make the European Recovery Program look like small potatoes.

Personal Retrospectives

III. Country Missions

From Denmark to Pakistan

JOHN O. BELL

As a relatively senior civil servant in the Department of State, I was fortunate enough to attend the second year of the National War college in 1947-8. When I returned to duty in the Department I found I was to assist Ambassador Achilles, who was engaged in the negotiation of what became the North Atlantic treaty, NATO, and from which emerged the Military Assistance Program to meet the need for developing a new international military power.

This was cause for concern because of the effect the military buildup had on the struggle to foster and promote economic recovery. It was obvious that economic recovery and the defense build up of the allied nations required balancing these needs in such a way as to promote both and threaten neither. The pursuit of these goals required and obtained the full cooperation and the best talents of the Departments of State and Defense and the Marshall Plan administration. I was involved in these matters, which gave me daily contact with officials of the three agencies as issues arose. My belief is that each had a respect for the needs and views of the others and that we felt ourselves partners in a great venture.

At this stage, I decided that I wished to pursue a career in the Foreign Service rather than continue as a civil service member of the State Department. I was fortunate enough to be admitted and was then sent to Denmark as an economic officer. I protested that I had but one three hour course in economics and was told that I was expert enough on the Marshall Plan and that the agency had agreed that I should serve not only as the Embassy Economic Officer but also as Deputy Chief of the Marshall Plan mission. This was exciting, off I went to Copenhagen on New Years Day 1960!

It was also a new sort of assignment as the Ambassador told me that she had heard nothing from the Marshall plan chief there (Charles Marshall—a splendid man). I said that I had been assured of my duties in Washington and that we just needed to be patient. Not long thereafter Mr. Marshall invited me to join him in Paris at a meeting of mission chiefs and told me that he really did not need a deputy for operations but welcomed the chance to discuss policy and exchange views which was most kind of him. We became fast friends and I got a good education in the process. When Mr. Marshall retired, I became the director and remained until the Danes said, "Thanks, we do not need any more help."

I was then advised that I would be sent to Pakistan to serve in our Embassy there, but to my surprise, my duty was to be director of the aid mission at the request of USAID, now involved in many non-European areas. I spent two years in Karachi and then returned to Washington where State advised me that I would serve in the economic agency as the deputy administrator for the Near East and South Asia, which I did for a year or so. I was then drafted by Under Secretary Douglas Dillon to head his staff as a delegate of the Presidential commission for the various aid programs. In this way, I served him and also his successor, George Ball when Kennedy took over from Ike. I later served as Ambassador to Guatemala and as Political Adviser, concerned with some 64 countries, to the General commanding Strike Command.

A long and wonderful experience is how I view my government service. I was lucky to have had a small role. General Marshall and many other great men have my deep gratitude for what they did. Those years featured the vigorous pursuit of policies and activities which sought to advance and balance the political, economic and military interests of our nation and to play a constructive role in the world. Wise leadership promoted vigorous debate and produced mutual respect and intelligent results—a model for emulation.

Not to be overlooked, in my opinion, is the contribution made by the many persons outside the government establishment who gave generously of their time and abilities to assure the success of an enterprise which coordinated not only the branches of government but cooperation with our nation's academic and business organizations.

The Marshall Plan in the United Kingdom

THOMAS T. CROWLEY

P rior to my commenting on the U.S. Mission to the United Kingdom, a brief summary of our backgrounds seems appropriate. I grew up in southern New England, attended MIT for four years and graduated in April 1942 with a BS Degree in Mechanical Engineering and Business Administration. Then I and several other ROTC classmates were activated as second lieutenants and assigned to the 1st Engineer Battalion, a unit of the First Infantry Division.

The Division sailed for England in August 1942 and for the next three plus years I was actively engaged with the 1st Engineers in the campaigns of that Division in the European Theater: the North Africa landing, Tunisia, Sicily, and returning to England to prepare for and undertake the assault landing at Omaha Beach. I survived that day and went on with the Division, fighting in battles in Normandy, northern France, Belgium, Aachen, the Bulge, the drive across Germany to the Elbe River and the Hartz Mountains, ultimately ending the war in western Czechoslovakia. At the very least, my experience familiarized me with Western Europe and provided first-hand exposure to the chaotic conditions raging in many of the European countries in the immediate post-war period.

After several months of occupation duties, I returned intact to the United States mainland in September 1945. Although I had achieved the rank of Lieutenant Colonel, I opted not to remain in the military and became an assistant to Professor Erwin Schell, head of the MIT Department of Business Administration. In this capacity I was also able to earn an MS in Business Management and re-acquaint myself with the functions and vocabulary of the industrial world.

In the early fall of 1946, I was employed by U.S. Steel in Pittsburgh with a staff group responsible for the analysis of products, markets, facilities, and recommendations for future action by the corporation. Over the following two years, this work provided me with a broad background covering U.S. Steel and the steel industry in general.

Meanwhile, after over a year's courtship, Julia (Jay) C. Deane and I were married in February 1948. Jay was a Boston girl, a graduate of Radcliffe College, who had spent the war years working in the United States Office of War Information, including a tour of duty in South Africa. She had been fortunate enough to attend the Harvard Graduation in June 1947 and heard General Marshall's famous speech which led to the formation of the Marshall Aid Program. We settled in a Pittsburgh suburb and have been happily married ever since.

That summer in late August 1948, we were on vacation in Marion, CT with nothing but sailing in mind. The phone rang and it was an official from the Marshall Plan Aid Mission in London who asked me to meet him in New York to discuss going to London to join their staff as their steel specialist. I met the official in New York who outlined the Mission's need for someone to evaluate British requests for steel and steel processing equipment coming from the United States. Britain had plenty of bricks and mortar but was desperately short of dollars to buy U.S. products and equipment to rebuild and modernize their industries. The Mission Chief was Tom Finletter, a prominent New York lawyer. The offices were in the London Embassy, and I would have full diplomatic status as a Foreign Service Reserve Officer, Class 3. It was easy to say yes.

A few days later, Jay and I, on our way back to Pittsburgh, stopped in Washington DC where I received further orientation on the Economic Cooperation Administration (ECA), which was the U.S. agency set up to handle the Marshall Aid program. While there, I met Clarence Randall, head of Inland Steel who had just made a major survey of the European steel industry for Paul Hoffman and Averell Harriman. He liked my background, briefed me on the status of the steel industry abroad and asked U.S. Steel to put me on a leave of absence; he thought that would enhance my role in dealing with the British steel industry. It did.

Given my wartime experience in Western Europe, Jay and I were excited by the objective of helping the European countries work together to rebuild their economies with U.S. assistance. This approach seemed to offer a far more attractive future than the relationship that had ensued for three successive generations, which had led to the Franco-German wars of 1871, 1914-18 and 1939-45.

In September I flew to Paris to meet appropriate officials at Averell Harriman's ECA headquarters and then went on to London. Jay followed a few weeks later. Life in London was not simple, as the British were still under wartime rationing. Jay joined a group of wives organized by Mrs. Douglas, the American ambassador's wife, to give talks when asked at Women's Institutes all over the country. In this pre-TV era the British were curious about what life was like in the United States. Mrs. Douglas' program filled a definite need and was very beneficial to our relationship with the British people. It should be realized that Britain had a tightly controlled economy since the beginning of the war. The country had a highly trained civil service. Moreover, the infrastructure was in place to direct recovery resources to the economic sectors, which were given priority. Thus, administering the aid program did not experience some of the difficulties encountered in other countries.

Meanwhile, at the Mission, my job was to get acquainted with those officials at the Ministry of Supply who dealt with the steel industry and with members of the industry itself through the British Iron and Steel Federation. The Labor Party was in power at the time and one of its tenets was to nationalize the steel industry, as well as coal and several other industrial sectors. Relations between steel and other business leaders and the Ministry were delicate to say the least.

One unique activity which sped up Britain's recovery was Paul Hoffman's early decision with British leaders to establish the Anglo-American Council on Productivity. It's objective was to send British teams from specific industries to visit U.S. factories to see how they were equipped and how they functioned to produce in their specific fields. While this Council was technically outside direct ECA control, our group in the Mission was involved in coordinating team plans. Each team had an equal number of management and union representatives who would go to the United States and visit factories in their field. As I recall, upwards of forty such teams participated and the reports published on their return to the United Kingdom provided a major stimulus to the modernization of British industry.

Over the next year or so I visited about every major steel plant in the United Kingdom and a number of smaller ones, too. I became familiar with their modernization plans, especially those likely to involve the use of dollars for United States equipment. A procedure was evolved along the lines of a capital budget routine in United States industry. Projects would be brought to the Mission's attention after first processing through the appropriate screening controls used by the Ministry of Supply. We would then analyze the project, consult with the industry, and satisfy ourselves that it was sound in a business sense and that dollar resources were essential. We sent our recommendations on to the Paris European Headquarters and then on to Washington. Trips back and forth to ECA Paris were frequent. Tom Finletter and successive Mission chiefs, John Kenny and Bill Batt, were all of the view that Marshall Plan dollars should go into modernizing facilities rather than to buying such products as tobacco. For example, ECA funds were allocated for U.S. made equipment that went into the new steel plant built in South Wales to provide the country with its first modern continuous strip mill.

When Jay and I went to London, we expected to stay no more than two years. It proved to be three, for in the spring of 1950, I was promoted to head the Mission's Industry Division with responsibilities over such diverse fields as petroleum, machine tools, textiles, coal, et cetera, as well as steel. I had a small staff of specialists with appropriate industry backgrounds and consultants on call. Then, when the Korean War broke out, the Cold War intensified and NATO came along, we found ourselves spending more and more time on defense-related matters.

It was interesting work and, by virtue of our industrial backgrounds, we were of considerable help to our embassy colleagues. However, by the end of the summer of 1951, it seemed to me we had accomplished what ECA set out to do—help Britain get back on its feet. I resigned with everyone understanding my desire to return to private business at home.

Jay and I thoroughly enjoyed our three years in London. Our oldest son, John Gifford, was born there in February of 1950. We traveled all over the country and made many friends and acquaintances. We even did some sailing (our sport), joining the Royal Lymington Yacht Club and becoming members of their dinghy sailing team for two summers.

With our diplomatic status we enjoyed typical embassy functions. Yes, we were presented at Court and attended several Buckingham Palace garden parties. All in all, it was quite an experience for a growing young family.

From our perspective, the Marshall Plan was an outstanding success. It speeded the recovery of Britain and other European countries. It provided a solid foundation for the region to deal with the pressures of the Cold War and facilitated joint efforts by the nations to live together, peacefully, for more than a half-century.

Greece and the New International Situation

MANILO F. DE ANGELIS

I had ten years of personnel and general management experience when, completely unexpectedly, I was asked to be one of four personnel experts to go to Tokyo over the winter of 1946-47. We were to consult with a special group of thirty key Japanese Government officials on possible and desirable reforms in their personnel system. General MacArthur's staff had recommended that the Japanese personnel system would need to be substantively converted to a more democratic model to insure the post-occupation continuity of the new policies sponsored by the Supreme Allied Command.

This assignment gave me a vision of the real challenge facing the U.S. in organizing for the new world-wide international situation that had to be met. My desire to be part of that effort in whatever capacity I might be effective was also aroused. I was completely surprised, however, when on return to the United States in the Spring of 1947, the State Department offered me a program planning assignment in the Office of the Chief of the new American Mission for Aid to Greece (AMAG) under the Truman Doctrine, which would start in the summer. It was to be a limited one-year diplomatic job and I could be accompanied by my family. We debated about taking our two children, 3½ and 1½, to a civil war-torn Greece, but eventually agreed to go.

In September, 1947, I flew into Athens, Greece to begin my assignment as a member of AMAG. The objective was to help the Greek military end the threat of the communist-supported invasion and civil war and to restore the prostrate economy of the country after it had endured practically ten years of foreign occupation. The $400 million program was divided, with $300 million going to Greece and $100 million for a mission to Turkey. The Truman Program was intended to help Greece and Turkey limit the expansion of Soviet power into the Mediterranean Sea area.

AMAG was a combined military and civilian mission. I arrived without a specific assignment because only one week before my scheduled departure I was called to the Office of the Assistant Secretary for Near Eastern Affairs, George McGhee, and told that a cable had arrived from AMAG saying that the position I was slated to occupy had been eliminated through a reorganization. My choice was to proceed to Greece without a specific assignment (since the State Department had already made all the travel arrangements for me and my family), or simply forgo participating in AMAG and remain in my position in the U.S. Civil Service Commission as Chief of the Program Planning Staff. My wife, Priscilla, and I decided we would go to Greece. I would fly out from New York on the night of September 14. My family would follow in two weeks, departing New York for a twenty-one day trip by ship. On the ship were twenty other wives and families of AMAG members who were also coming to join husbands who had flown in during July and August.

The Mission Chief assigned me to the Finance Division with unspecified duties. I was to do whatever was needed as problems arose— and they did quickly. For example, the Athens Power Co. was unable to provide enough power to industries because a $250,000 generator it had ordered was being held in customs, and could not be released for lack of dollar exchange to pay for it. In two days, I learned how to open a letter of credit against the AMAG dollar fund in the Bank of New York and the generator was released to the power company and put to work immediately, vastly aiding the local industry.

Another time, our Agriculture Advisor found a severe shortage of seed grain needed for planting in the fall, if Greece were have a harvest in the spring. We therefore arranged financing for a cargo plane to fly in enough seeds for the fall planting. Since the local yield of winter grain produced a significant crop, this saved a great amount of grain that would have needed to be directly imported that spring.

In another instance, the U.S. Army Corps of Engineers had sent a team to work under Mission Financing to restore ports, airports, roads, railroads, and reopen the Corinth Canal, which the Germans had blocked for more than seven years by blowing up the railroad bridge crossing it. They had U.S. dollar funds for the imported equipment, but had no way to pay in local drachmas for rental of a building, local help, local allowances, and so forth. The Engineers Administrative Officer came to me with this problem. In very little time, I had our Mission Chief ask the Greek Minister of Finance to lend the Engineers 15 million drachmas as an advance against the drachma counterpart funds that were to be generated equivalent to the grant assistance furnished Greece by the United States. This purely paper transaction created non-existent funds with which the engineers were able to get to work.

The Marshall Plan provided U.S. dollar financing for manufactured goods and commodities that were not available in Europe because of the destruction caused by the war. A portion of the financing was on a loan basis to be repaid in the long term, but for poorer countries, like Greece, the major share of aid was on a grant basis. For each dollar equivalent of grant aid delivered, the country was required to deposit local currency into a counterpart fund of which 95% was to be used by the country to finance activities approved by it and AMAG. The other 5% was to be deposited in a Mission account for U.S. use in meeting local costs, rather than having to purchase drachmas with U.S. dollars.

This creation of counterpart funds policy was applied to the grant aid under AMAG before the Marshall Plan also adopted it. In 1947, as a post-UNRRA Aid program, the U.S. provided food grain grants of $50 million each to three countries with serious shortages: Greece, Italy and Yugoslavia. The first shipload of such grain arrived in Piraeus shortly after I did. Thus, I got the job of drafting the "Drachma Agreement" between Greece and AMAG spelling out the counterpart details involved. Upon the Agreement's approval, a few days, it's implementation fell to me. I had to obtain the delivery ship's bill-of-lading and ascertain the value of the grain (CIF Piraeus—cost, insurance, and freight). Then I drafted a letter from the AMAG Chief to Finance Minister Chelmis citing the dollar value multiplied by the 5,000 drachma/dollar official exchange rate and requesting deposits of 95% and 5% in the respective accounts.

I thus became the keeper of the counterpart accounts generation records and also the budget officer for their disbursement as AMAG had a tax advisory team helping them to reconstruct an effective tax system. Meanwhile, the 95% counterpart was the only source of local cost financing for the reconstruction projects that employed more than 12,000 workers on the roads and other infrastructure projects. Local currency was also needed for agriculture, housing, relief, and other joint projects designed by the Ministry of Reconstruction and AMAG. As Special Assistant to the Assistant Mission Chief, I served as liaison with the Ministry.

When the pace of Greek/AMAG projects accelerated, so did inflation with the drachma/dollar exchange rate, in three years rising from 5,000 to 30,000 to the U.S. dollar. To restrain inflation we were required to "freeze" or hold back a portion of the 95% counterpart and could not distribute all of it for projects.

Secretary Marshall made his speech at Harvard on June 5, 1947. By that fall, Greece was one of 16 European countries which had responded, eager to participate. AMAG then made plans for the integration of our AMAG Program with the Marshall Plan when it would be in operation. Congress and President Truman swiftly completed the legislation and the Marshall Plan began on April 1, 1948. AMAG was divided into its economic and technical assistance side which was transferred to the European Recovery Program, the Marshall Plan's official name. The military side was continued as a separate program. To support both sides, a Joint Administrative Group (JAG) operated by the State Department was created. As Special Assistant to the Mission Chief, I became the administrative liaison with JAG. Our original State Department appointments were converted to ERP appointments and we were treated as foreign service officers with regard to home leave, etc. My family was granted home leave since we had agreed to return to the USAID Mission for another tour.

In one year, AMAG military had re-equipped the Greek military, and with 13,000 kilometers of rebuilt roads reaching to all areas, the communist threat had largely subsided, especially since Yugoslavia stopped giving refuge and aid to the rebels. The airports were working, the Corinth Canal had been reopened, the main railroad line was functioning again, and the Truman Dock had been constructed in the port of Pireus so ocean liners could once again dock normally. The Marshall Plan greatly increased intra-European trade because the Regional Office in Paris screened all requests for items. If such items were available in another member country, that source was used rather than U.S. aid. Thus, German coal was exchanged for Greek tobacco at no dollar cost to the United States.

The U.S. aid program in Greece clearly demonstrated the essential requirement of military security to insure opportunity for economic growth and recovery. At one point, the rebels had driven nearly 800,000 refugees out of their mountain villages and home, creating a huge relief burden on the economy. Monthly sustenance rations were sent to each refugee center to feed the approximately 10% of the Greek population which they represented. The climate for close cooperation between the U.S. and Europe stimulated a great expansion of trade each way and the understanding that mutual security was best for the entire Atlantic community.

After my home leave we returned for a second tour, which was cut short by the outbreak of the Korean War. I was transferred back to the Mutual Security Agency headquarters in Washington, DC and appointed Deputy Budget Director. One of my first duties was to establish an overall budget system for estimating the generation of counterpart local currencies in each of the participating countries and also for controlling the use of the 5% portion accruing to the United States. Because these funds were not appropriated and considered "free," there were many claimants for them. The U.S. Information Agency wanted the counterpart to fund projects abroad requiring local funds. In this way, the U.S. Strategic Stockpile program requested, and I released, more than $100 million of the 5% counterpart available from the aid given the European countries. Thus the Stockpile acquired chrome, manganese, titanium, and other such materials from the European countries' former colonies at no U.S. dollar cost. Other claimants for this counterpart were the many Congressional delegations which discovered that they could use these funds to cover their travel and living expenses while abroad.

My service as Deputy Budget Director lasted four years, during which time the European Recovery Program changed to the Mutual Security Agency and then in 1953, with the addition of the Technical Assistance Agency and the Development Loan Fund, to the Foreign Operations Agency. We had to prepare annual budget presentations for seven different Congressional authorizing and appropriating committees. During these years, United Sates Agency for International Development (USAID) programs were added for Korea, Taiwan, Iran, and India, and technical assistance teams were sent to many Latin American countries. The Food for Peace and the War on Hunger programs also became U.S. offerings. All of these required coordination both in Washington and in the countries being aided.

In 1962, with the creation of USAID, I was asked to become Deputy Assistant Administrator of the Africa Bureau. The newly independent

African countries all wanted USAID missions and programs. We could not effectively use full missions in all the countries, therefore I was authorized to establish and head a regional USAID mission in Washington to operate the programs and projects jointly agreed upon by each of the thirteen former French colonies and the Bureau. In response to our Ambassadors' and the specific country's request that we undertake a specific project, we would send out a technical specialist and a program officer team to develop with the local officials a work plan that we might approve and finance. In the first year of operation, the regional USAID reduced administrative expenses and doubled the number of operating programs. My assignment required considerable travel; on one trip I visited seventeen countries over a twenty-two day period.

In 1965, I was sent to our largest Mission in Latin America, Brazil, to be Assistant Director for Management. A major task I faced was merging seven separate locations of USAID staff into a new thirty-two story high building in which we had rented the top sixteen floors for five years. The programs in Brazil included the large agricultural, health, and education regular programs and many specialized technical ones. By 1967, I had consolidated the staff and was ready to return home.

In the Washington headquarters, my job was to head the Management Planning Division. We were constantly monitoring the manpower needs of the several USAID overseas missions and the Washington office. USAID was annually given reduced personnel ceilings and Management Planning was charged with recommending appropriate ceiling allocations to the various organizations. We also were constantly considering suggested overall reorganizations of the entire Agency received from Congressional Committees. In 1971, after 32½ years of federal government service, I took early retirement and for twenty years was a self-employed management consultant.

As I review the Marshall Plan's impact and implications for the future, I believe that very real economic recovery occurred in the member countries, although progress was uneven. There was a major expansion of intra-European trade which has continued over the years. Many other links between the OECD countries were also forged including the European Payments Union and the European Coal and Steel community. Additionally, the increased flow of exports from the U.S. to Europe created many new jobs in the United States. Technical exchanges of personnel have developed mutual understanding and tourism has expanded steadily over the years as a result. The recovery of Europe and of Japan enabled them to also become donor countries to the lesser developed world to the extent that now the U.S. is no longer the major or largest donor nation.

Colonial rule in Africa by Germany, France, Belgium, Portugal and the UK gave way to independence movements and self-government. The effects were felt also in Southeast Asia as Indonesia became independent from the Netherlands and the UK withdrew from India. The U.S. similarly pulled out of the Philippines. The Organization for Economic Cooperation and Development (OECD) became a continuing body in Paris, stimulating bilateral aid from the former colonial powers to the new countries and others. The World Bank and the International Monetary Fund largely succeeded in stabilizing foreign exchange and the currency markets while providing long-term loans for development. The United Nations and its specialized agencies added their shoulder to the wheel by helping to maintain peace while promoting economic growth and political stability.

As the USSR challenged the West during the post-war period with the "Iron Curtain," the Berlin Blockade, nuclear power, and "Sputnik," the U.S. and Europe created the North Atlantic Treaty Organization. NATO has rightly been credited with maintaining fifty years of peace in a Europe that had drawn the U.S. into two world wars in the 20th century. American participation and leadership has been and is critical to the success of NATO. I strongly believe that the concepts of mutual assistance, cooperation and security stimulated and demonstrated by the Marshall Plan's success are generally and widely held.

The U.S. is now the only superpower in the world and must continue its leadership in multilateral bodies and through bilateral relations to build a climate of trust, peace, and improved living standards. Support of new bodies such as the World Trade Organization (WTO) and the International Court of Justice as well as of existing United Nations and other multilateral heirs of the Marshall Plan is required of all nations. Peacekeeping by members of the UN Security Council is needed to keep small local conflicts from becoming major problems. We must stimulate the growth of the less developed world and help reduce the great inequalities in Gross Domestic Product and per capita income that exist.

The globalization of multinational corporations and the vast expansion of rapid communications and air transportation are providing more ties among the world's people. With greater contacts and understanding of each other, we are creating opportunities for advanced research and education for many who previously were unable to develop their capacities fully. Continued people-to-people exchanges and exchanges promoted by the Fulbright Program, the German Marshall Foundation and international student exchanges have grown in scope and have shown positive results. Non-governmental organizations such as the Red Cross, CARE, and many church supported humanitarian programs will continue to supplement the work of the International Refugee Organization (IRO) and governments. The World Health Organization has virtually wiped out smallpox everywhere. The spirit of the Marshall Plan lives on in the current generation motivated by its basic concepts of mutuality, cooperation, and peace to create a better world.

Life in Greece During the Marshall Plan

PRISCILLA GRINDLE DE ANGELIS

Introduction

On September 27, 1947 the Nea Hellas, a converted troop ship, sailed from Hoboken, New Jersey for Piraeus, Greece. On board, in addition to the European crew and passengers, was a small group of American women and children. We were bound for Greece to join our husbands who only a few weeks earlier had flown to Athens to form the American Mission for Aid to Greece. Most of us had never left the United States before and few had any notion of the demands of overseas and diplomatic life. The eighteen-day trip was the first step in our pioneering adventure in American foreign policy.

During the three years that followed, I wrote weekly letters to my family in New England. I have used these letters to jog my memory about some of the high spots in our three-year assignment. I hope to point out some of the problems women faced in coping with overseas life after World War II. The Greek Mission was a model for the United States aid mission that followed. Our group had unique experiences in the pleasures and headaches of living in a strange culture.

Our decision to go to Greece was not taken lightly. It began one June night in 1947 when my husband, Manilo, and I were lingering over coffee after dinner in our Virginia apartment. The children were asleep and we were comparing notes on the day's events. "How would you like to go to Greece for a year?" Manny ventured. "I have been asked to be part of a new mission to give economic assistance to help the country recover from the war."

Manny had returned three months earlier from a government assignment in occupied Japan. I had spent six months with my family in Massachusetts. Rick, who was then four years old, was recovering from polio and Nancy had just turned two. I was worried about the health of the children in a country where famine and civil violence were rampant. I was also anxious about the changes that living abroad would make in our style of living.

However, I had always wanted to travel and had studied both Italian and Ancient Greek in college. Manny, a first generation Italian-American, also saw this as an opportunity to visit Italy, as well as an opportunity to travel while we were both young enough to enjoy it. Our doctor advised us to keep our family together and reminded us that children in Europe had somehow been surviving for generations. We decided to take the plunge.

Why We Went

Greece was close to collapse after World War II. Civil war had broken out between pro and anti communist Greeks and the Soviet Union was exploiting the division in the country through its Yugoslav allies. The Communist core of the Greek Resistance Movement, EAN/Elas, was openly subsidized by the Tito government. One of the few forces for stability was the British Army, which had given aid to the Greek Armed Forces throughout the war. However, Great Britain itself was weakened by the war and in 1947 notified the United States that it must withdraw assistance to Greece as of March 31, 1947. The United States had provided welfare through UNRRA but more than sustenance help was needed. The Greek government appealed to the United States to help in bringing stability to the country.

On March 12, 1947 President Truman appeared before the Congress of the United States to ask for a commitment to assist the Greek nation in recovering economically. After two months of intense and controversial debate, a bill was finally approved and on May 22, 1947 Public Law 75 was signed by President Harry Truman. The government provided for the establishment of an American Mission For Aid to Greece. This group of American advisors from many professions was assigned the task of assisting the Greek nation in its economic and military recovery.

It was a historic decision for the United States. We had turned our back on a policy of isolationism and embarked on a program of assisting other countries with their internal problems. This policy would later be extended to undeveloped countries all over the world. The historian William Hardy McNeil has written the following summary of the situation in Greece in 1946 and 1947: "The nature of Greek society and the shortcomings of the Greek government, together with the constellation of internal relations in 1946 and 1947, made a communist revolution possible, indeed probable. But the injection of a massive new force, United States aid, changed the events and prevented the consummation."

In this account I can neither assess the merits of the original program nor the achievements of the Mission to Greece. I have neither the qualifications nor the will to do so. Instead I hope to tell something about our life as dependents of mission personnel (most of the members were men) and to describe the pleasures and problems we met. Out of this will, I hope, emerge a picture of what this experience meant to me and the other women in the American Mission For Aid to Greece.

Getting Ready to Go

Once we decided to take the plunge and go overseas for at least a year, we discovered that we needed several months to prepare ourselves. Our destination was Greece—a country ravaged by war. There was a critical shortage of food, fuel and medicine and no luxury items available except on a flourishing black market. Most of us agreed to go only if we could provide our children with adequate care and ourselves with some of the elements of comfortable living. In short, we wanted new adventure, but not wartime deprivation.

One of our first steps was to get typhus and typhoid shots as well as new vaccinations for ourselves and the children. This took the better part of the first two months and the Navy did this for us. Then we had to arrange to rent our apartment and to store most of our furnishings. We were allowed to ship 2,000 pounds of household goods and 700 pounds of air freight and other baggage. Our household goods included such items as linens, dishes, books, lamps, medicines, toilet paper and so forth. We also took a refrigerator and an electric heater, which was to come in very handy in the chilly winter ahead.

I shopped for a year's supply of clothes for ourselves and the children. This took ingenuity because the children were two and four years old and growing very fast. Shoes were especially a challenge. Rick was still recovering from polio and at this point wore two sizes of shoes. I solved this problem by making arrangements with Michelson's Shoe Store in Lexington, MA to keep a record of our sizes and current purchases so that he could order them shipped APO when we needed them.

Our lives were governed by long lists: items to go airfreight, goods to be stored in Washington, luggage to go by boat freight, addresses to be changed and financial matters to arrange. The U.S. government assured us the use of the Army PX and the Navy Medical Service. We were going to be able to buy some basic canned and dried foods at the PX but for the rest of our food supply we would have to rely on the Greek economy.

During our packing days I sometimes hired a baby sitter for Ricky and Nancy. I had to take a bus to Washington to shop for clothes and household materials and the children were no help when it came to organizing trunks and shopping.

In the midst of our preparation, Manny was called home by the serious illness of his father who had suffered from heart trouble for many years. He recuperated briefly, but died in September on the same day that Manny flew to Greece. He went three weeks ahead of us because his services were desperately needed. I spent the month visiting my mother and dad in Lexington.

One other aspect of our preparation that we had not anticipated was money. A large outlay was involved in buying household goods and clothing supplies in addition to trunks and other luggage. We borrowed on our insurance to meet these bills and paid ourselves back over the next year from the extra money we made from overseas service.

Aboard the Nea Hellas

The children and I took the overnight Pullman sleeper from Boston to New York so we could board the Nea Hellas in time for a noon sailing from Hoboken, NJ on September 27, 1947. Fortunately, my mother came with us and was a wonderful help in coping with Ricky and Nancy amid the hubbub of the baggage handlers and people crowding on the pier. Somehow we managed to get settled in our outside cabin with bunkbeds in time for farewells. I was very excited and also very apprehensive. What were we getting into? Fortunately, there was too much going on around to dwell very long on the future.

I was deluged by a continuous stream of new experiences and acquaintances—the unfamiliar sounds of Greek, Italian, French and other languages challenged my mind and exhausted my nerves. I realized very soon that I was the only American aboard alone with small children. Elizabeth Howard had four children with her, but her sister was a companion to help her on the trip.

The Nea Hellas (New Hellas) was constructed by the Fairfield Co. of Glasgow in 1922. Until 1939 she had been called the Tuscania but at that time she was converted to a troop carrier and was used in that capacity for the duration of the war. From 1946 to 1947, the English Ministry of Transport ran the ship through the Anchor Line Ltd. Transport. The ship was a twin screw with three decks, radar and periscope and its gross tonnage was 16,991 tons. This was a relatively small ship, compared with the tonnage of the Queen Mary (81,235 tons) and the Queen Elizabeth (85,000 tons). I was dismayed when I saw the size of the Nea Hellas at the time of boarding. Could we trust her to get us across the Atlantic?

The Nea Hellas was managed along lines of the old grand tours. Dinner was served formally and in several courses at eight o'clock p.m. Tea was offered on the decks at four in the afternoon. There were no children's facilities at all so we lived in our cabin and on the decks in good weather. Food was a problem for Nancy—we had been assured that there would be a complete line of baby foods on board. However, there were only pureed carrots so she lived very well on carrots and mashed bananas for the duration. Nicos, our waiter in the dining room, loved the kids and was very helpful—especially in giving me a chance to practice my elementary Greek. Gastronomically, it was no treat for me, however, because I was preoccupied with seeing that the children got enough to eat and remain on some sort of a schedule.

Rick, who had rapidly recovered his mobility after his polio attack of the previous year, loved to roam and explore all the decks. This was a worry to me for there were several places on the decks where he could have easily slipped below to the waves. Dot Sponsler and her teenage children, Snooky and Bing, were wonderful friends. They put up with the children's antics at the formal dinners and often played with Rick and Nancy when we were out on the decks. After several tries at dinner with Rick, I decided to feed both children in the stateroom. My rest and relaxation came at night after they were asleep.

It was great to wake up at night to the motion of the ship and to stare out at the endless waves through the porthole by my pillow. I looked forward to meeting Manny at the end of the trip. I was also mad at him for having gone first and leaving me to cope with two small children aboard ship.

On several days the going was very rough—at the stern you could see the bow dipping and cresting the angry swells of the Atlantic. Almost all the passengers were sick. There were several moments when I felt queasy, but I couldn't afford to get sick because of the children and thankfully I didn't.

Several times during the voyage a gong in the night called us to fire drill. We rushed down to the lounge with our sleepy kids, hair curlers, nightgowns and orange life preservers. One thing is certain—we became well acquainted with our shipmates and by the time we docked in Piraeus we had made several life long friends. Over thirty years later, we still call it the "Greek Group." This fact made going by ship more attractive than flying.

The other women with me on the Nea Hellas were from all over the country. Most of us were dependents of Mission personnel but there were several like the White sisters who were going to work for the Mission as medical advisors.

Lois Hermansen was a young bride from Pennsylvania going to join her husband, John, who was to work in the Public Administration Division. Dorothy Sponsler and her two teenage children, Bing and Snooky lived in Harrisburg, PA where her husband, Bill was the Director of the Budget for the State. Nancy Booth was with her two young people, both in their teens. Her husband, Loomis, was a specialist in water management. From the Society of Public Administration in Chicago came Charles Conlon—his wife, Dorothy, was on board with us. Kay Iverson and her two daughters were from Salt Lake City, Utah and her husband Kenneth was a close associate of Manny's. Irene Jay and her husband, Ed, had been overseas in Japan with the Army and seemed more sophisticated about the way things were done overseas. She had the first big cocktail party when we arrived and always knew where to shop for the best bargains. They had no children.

Dorothy Howard had four children with her and her sister, Louise, traveled with her to help, for she had one small baby still in a carriage. Evelyn Strachan and one daughter were also with us. They were from Detroit, where her husband, Alan, had been an executive in the United Auto Worker's Union. He was to be in charge of labor relations for the Mission and was a native of England. There was also an Army wife, Dot Tuttle, hale and hearty who introduced us to "spinactopatopas" and "tyropatas" at one of the first parties. Also with us were Nancy Jones and her two children.

Of course, there were others who joined the American women's group from time to time. Several dependents had come on an earlier voyage of the Nea Hellas and others came later by airplane and other ships. In general, most of the women were very well educated and committed to helping Greece recover. However, most of us had not traveled outside the United States before and were relatively naive.

Arrival in Lisbon was a landmark; the monotony of the voyage gave way to the excitement of seeing Europe and going ashore. I arranged for the stewardess to baby-sit Nancy and Rick and I joined the tour of Lisbon, Estoril and the mountain castle of the Kings of Portugal at Sintra.

We rode like royalty in black American sedans, parting the crowds of fisherman, bicyclists, and donkeys as we sped along. I couldn't believe that I was in this ancient land of pastel tiled bungalows, olive trees and medieval castles. The first impressions of a new culture are the most vivid and my feeling of good fortune to be in Portugal was immense. The tour was a success aside from my temporary panic at losing Rick in the labyrinths of Sintra. However, he soon appeared on the shoulders of one of the guides and we were off in the limousines down the steep slopes, past the lavish beach resort of Estoril to our ship at the docks.

Our mood changed drastically when we arrived at Genoa and Naples three days later. This was our first exposure to the devastation of the war. Also, we were tired of being cooped up on shipboard and the novelty of sailing had worn off. The sight of entire blocks of Genoa gutted by bombing was shocking. Poor and ragged Italians swarmed the ships docks carrying on a brisk trade in cigarettes and begging for alms from travelers bold enough to venture ashore. Boats of hungry scavengers circled our ship, fishing out the refuse from the Nea Hellas. I decided that going ashore was more of a trip than I could face. I decided to spend the two days in port keeping the children happy on board. There would be better times to see Italy, I hoped.

Four days later we rounded the Cape of Sunion and sailed into Piraeus, each of us tense with the excitement of meeting our husbands. This one experience of traveling alone with small children has made me very sensitive to the plight of refugee mothers and children.

The kids and I grabbed Manny as soon as he poked his head in the door of the cabin lounge. Greek officials were busy checking our passports and medical certificates in preparation for landing. After eighteen days on board in close confinement, we eyed the spouses with curiosity. "You mean that's her husband?" "How did she ever land that gorgeous man?"

Not all of this marital puzzle-solving was instant. Several enterprising husbands had rented a speedboat and were cruising around the Nea Hellas yelling "yaaso" and otherwise showing off their new Greek.

The descent from ship to shore was another shock. The harbor of Piraeus had been gutted by bombs and even at this date all loading was done by small craft. The sailors helped us jump from the lowest rung of the ships ladder to the small boat below. Nancy and Rick were gently tossed to the waiting hands of Greek crewmen.

What We Found in Greece

We drove in an army car from Piraeus directly to our new home in Kifissia, a summer resort nestled at the base of Mt. Pentelikon. On the way we gaped at the gray, drab buildings pockmarked with bullet holes from the recent civil war. I was thrilled to see the Acropolis high over the whole city, still dominating Athens as it had for centuries. Here was the city I had studied and read about since I was small.

Manny had not been idle in preparation of our arrival. He had found us a desirable house to rent and was trying to find out if our household goods were on the Nea Hellas. He had sent me several frantic telegrams aboard ship inquiring as to their location. I was never able to get any information from the purser except that he thought our goods were at the bottom of the hold. Manny decided to gamble that they were indeed on board and rented us a house from Vasilaous, a real estate man and small business operator. How fortunate we were! The weather was very cool that fall and coal was in short supply. Our small house had a wood burning stove on the ground floor so we were able to keep warm. The other Americans who were housed in hotels had no heat though October and were very chilly.

The house had two floors, was made of brick and stucco and was ringed by a balcony with boxes of geraniums, which bloomed most of the fall. It faced the marble quarries of Mt. Pentelikon. In the early morning and late afternoon shepherds prodded their flocks of sheep up and down the dirt roads to the mountain pastures. The hooves of the sheep sounded like rain in the cool air. Kifissia means "wind" in Greek and on the hillside we often felt the torrents as they rushed down the mountain.

The two stories of the house at 31 Levidou Street were arranged without regard for convenience. The main floor had a living room and a salon which combined, a bath, a pantry and two bedrooms. There were no closets but armoires were provided in each room—a standard European practice. Downstairs was a kitchen with an iron stove, a small dining room and a maid's room and bath. The house was designed for "live-in" help, which everyone who could afford a house even of this modest size expected to have. After Manny had rented the house, he learned from the landlords that a Greek couple was using the garage and had been told they could stay on because they had nowhere else to go. Panyotis, an unemployed dentist, and Irene were very good to the children, but we soon learned that they were extreme leftists. He was seized by the police at Christmas time in a round-up of suspected communist sympathizers.

The hall on the ground floor led outside to a portico, which ran around the back of the house. This was very convenient for the children who stored their bicycles there and played under the balcony in safety in all kinds of weather. Here in Kifissia they couldn't play outside unsupervised, as they had in our apartment complex in Alexandria, VA.

For the first week we ate dinner every night at the army mess at the Palace Hotel. Other members of the Mission lived here until they found houses. After supper, we drove home with the children in a horse and buggy that waited for us in the village square.

Our maid, Sophia Avros, had not yet arrived from the islands where she had survived the hardships of the long war in Greece. Also our household goods had not yet been delivered from the hold of the Nea Hellas. We camped out at 31 Levidou Street.

We cooked breakfast and lunch over a sterno set positioned on the iron stove in the kitchen. Since tap water was not yet safe from pollution, we learned to boil our water for drinking or to purify it by dissolving Halazone tablets. We also treated all the fresh fruits and vegetables that were to be eaten raw with the same Halazone mixture to avoid pollution from fresh produce.

Soon we explored the local markets where we were shocked to see bloody carcasses of animals hung on hooks in the meat stores. Greek cuts of meat were unlike any we had known in the United States so purchasing any meat was an adventure in eating, sometimes with weird results.

We were also delighted with the garden fresh broccoli and cauliflower and by the ever-present yogurt store, which turned out this Greek staple. Our greatest pleasure, however, was visiting the bread ovens where we bought long, hot fresh loaves of bread. The children loved to tear off the hot bread as a treat on the way home. The local baker insisted in wrapping our loaves in newspaper since he knew that bread was packaged in the United States.

For the first time in my life, I learned the value of clean, pure water and the luxury of a steady supply for cooking, drinking and bathing. When we first arrived, the water supply was rationed and we learned to pump water to our outside storage tank on the roof. This tank provided an extra supply when the town pipes were shut off.

Most of the people in Kifissia looked relatively healthy, but we knew that this was rare in the countryside. Deprivation of every sort was the general lot in most villages. It was cold when we walked to town to shop and I felt sorry for the children in their bare, red, chaffed legs. Everyone looked with interest and envy on the long overalls that Rick and Nancy wore to keep warm.

We were able to purchase most of our staples in the Army PX in Athens and this trip took up one day of my week. In the States, we had been promised all sorts of goodies in the PX and some of them were there. However, it was far from a shopper's paradise. The eggs were frozen and peculiar tasting so we bought local eggs. Ice cream mix came in gallon tins, which were difficult to adapt to family use. There were also Army issue gallon cans of spinach, which no one in our family liked despite all the ads from Popeye.

In our second year in Greece, frozen milk was brought in from Germany. Until that time, however, we used canned or powdered milk because the Navy doctors felt the local milk was too unreliable for children and that, if it had been pasteurized, it had been leached of many nutrients. I got acquainted with a product called Avoset, a bottled cream which would whip if given a lot of encouragement. I also discovered that my kitchen stove cooked only on high heat so that I could regulate it only by putting successive pans of hot water on the bottom shelf. I'm amazed that anything came out at all. Of course, ovens were a luxury in Greek houses. Most people used communal ovens for baking meats, vegetables and pastries.

In the fall of 1947, the local transportation had not yet been repaired from the ravage of war. Buses, when they ran, were in rickety condition and badly overcrowded. As a result, our Mission set up a motor pool to supply transportation to personnel for work, school and recreation. We called the motor pool whenever we needed transportation and we were usually able to get some kind of a vehicle to carry us to the doctor, school, or shopping. Top Mission personnel had cars and personal drivers. We were encouraged to double up for these expeditions, which was more fun and helped us to get acquainted with other wives and members of the Mission. We also learned Greek faster as we practiced with the drivers.

One of our first trips to Athens was to the Navy Doctor who was charged with the care of American families. Doctor Niforopoulus was a Greek-American, undoubtedly one of the reasons he had been assigned to Greece. Americans of foreign extraction were often not assigned to countries where they spoke the language because in some cases it was felt that they would have divided loyalties in some matters, making their nationality a drawback. However, in the case of medicine, Greek was necessary. Fortunately, we kept very healthy our first year and it was not until I became pregnant that we had any need for local doctors. Emergency cases were flown to the Army hospital in Frankfurt, Germany.

At first, most of the Greek friends we made we met in connection with the work of the Mission. An exception to this was our neighbors, the Barthis, who called on us the first few days and were helpful in many ways. They explained local customs to us and invited us to their home for religious feasts such as the Easter midnight feast. Vasilaous, our real estate man, invited us to a party of young people where they did round dances, drank oozo and retsina, and served kataif and baklava, those delicious Greek pastries.

I hired an Army widow, Madame Zachou, to teach me Greek since there were no formal lessons as part of the Embassy program—they were too busy getting on with the business of aid. Necessity made me a rapid learner because Sophia knew no English and I had to communicate with her about the house and the children and also shop in the local market. At the end of the six months I was quite fluent, although it was "demotiki" or "kitchen Greek," not "katherevesa," the language of the print and to some extent that of the upper classes. Some of our most frustrating experiences and the most amusing had to do with language.

We Organize to Meet Our Needs

Wherever Americans are living together, they organize themselves in groups for various purposes. We American wives were no exception. Those of us with small children wanted to provide them with playmates. Also, we needed to get a chance to get together to share our good and bad experiences and to learn from each other. At first, we met informally in each other's homes so that the children could play together and we could visit with each other in between spats. Of course, most of us had household help for the first time in our lives and we had more free time from domestic chores. Eventually, we decided to send a group of the children to Athens to a well-recommended Greek kindergarten. This experiment was not successful with Ricky. He rebelled at the regimentation and strange language and religious rites. One day, he refused to go and I decided that we had to make other plans.

Through the Greek YWCA we formed a cooperative kindergarten with both American and Greek children. Transportation was provided by the mission carpool. Nancy and Ricky both went to this school and they loved carpooling with other children. They also practiced their Greek with the drivers who were tolerant of the children, and also with the teacher who was Greek, but knew enough English to make the children comfortable.

I remember the difficulty we had trying to get equipment for the playschool—especially a sandbox. At one meeting someone suggested that our husbands would build one on a free Saturday. This was a customary division of labor in our families. The Greek women were horrified at the suggestion. They explained that Greek professional men not only knew nothing about carpentry but they considered it improper for them to do any such work. This was one of our first brushes with cultural differences.

In September 1948, I helped to organize a women's guild at the Protestant Union Church in Athens. In a letter to my parents I wrote, "This week we had the first meeting of the new woman's guild at the Protestant church in Athens. Five of us had started it and were pleased to have a turnout of forty-five. We plan one lecture meeting per month and one service meeting sewing for hospitals, distributing clothes, etc. This is really the first organized group of American women to do a job besides playing bridge and attending cocktail parties."

And two months later one Friday afternoon, our church guild met at our house to sew toys for the children's hospital for Christmas and nightgowns for the maternity wards. It was quite a job to collect enough chairs and sewing machines for forty people. One of the women from the hotel helped me with the baking for the tea we served as people worked.

One of our projects was with the YWCA and its secretary, Clara Wheeler. We arranged through her to send clothes and supplies to a girl's boarding school in Athens. This school housed needy girls in very primitive conditions, for many of them were destitute because of the war and subsequent guerrilla fighting. In later years, many such relief works were coordinated with or superseded by the Welfare Department of the American Women's Organization of Greece.

In July 1951 Evon N. Clark wrote the following in the *Washington Post* about the organization of AWOG, as it was soon called. "AWOG was founded during the guerrilla war in 1948 at the suggestion of General George Marshall, the Secretary of State. General Marshall, visiting with Mrs. Henry Grady, wife of the then Ambassador to Greece, remarked, 'There are enough American women here to make or mar any program. Are they organized?' Mrs. Grady who had already formed the nucleus of a club immediately called all the American women to the embassy residence and AWOG was formally organized. In 1949, it became affiliated with the General Federation of Women's Clubs, and in 1950, a member of the Federation of American Women's Clubs Overseas." The primary purpose was "to gather together for enlightenment and study in the international field and to support the existing nonpolitical, nonprofit institutions working for the benefit and welfare of Greece."

In addition to the educational and charitable projects, various activities provided a support group for the women in a strange country. American women were away from home and family and in many cases were tied down by the care of small children. AWOG provided the opportunity to meet other adults—both men and women—and the chance to participate as full partners with their husbands in the total program of the Mission.

Collecting and distributing clothes for Greek refugees was one of AWOG's main projects. We all wrote to various church and social groups in the United States asking for good used clothes. Thousands of tons of goods arrived through the APO in the next years. American women gathered to sort and clean the clothes and then took turns helping to deliver them to villages and refugee camps.

The following is from a letter written home in June, 1949.

A group of us visited the local refugee camps in Lamia with our Economic Cooperation Administration (ECA) field representative John Hare. The impressions we gained from this visit I thought would interest all of you, particularly those who have sent boxes of clothing and food. The need is very impressive and really has to be seen to be appreciated—even here in Athens we feel very far away from the front.

The city of Lamia has a normal population of 20,000 people, but with the onset of guerrilla warfare people from the villages have crowded into the town until now there are 32,000 refugees straining the facilities of the town. That there have not been serious outbreaks of disease and starvation among these people is indeed a tribute to the various aid programs, which have cared for them since they came penniless with few worldly goods. At that, however, their situation is grim to say the least. The first refugees and those with some money or goods were able to make small straw huts scattered in every available spot of land in the town.

We visited one of these villages and went into several huts. One of the smallest of these housed a family of four children and several adults and their few possessions—no furniture, of course. Their clothes were in all states of repair and included anything that would cover the body—in fact most of the younger children and babies wore no underclothing. In spite of all this, however, the people with whom we talked seemed fairly resigned and cheerful. This country is used to calamities and the poor people expect and receive very little in the way of comforts.

The refugees in these straw huts were comparatively well off as compared to another group we visited. These late-comers had been housed in large buildings that looked like Quonset huts. There were thirty-five families in one of these buildings and absolutely no partitions to separate them and give even a semblance of privacy. Rolled blankets marked off the spots of each family and in spite of the number of people and lack of facilities, the place was quite neat. We were struck by the lack of young men and were told that all, who were not away with the Army, went out each day to find firewood to bake the bread. This took longer and longer each day as the woods became stripped. Five open fireplaces outside are the only means of cooking the little oil and vegetables they can buy with their meager allowances. Fortunately, American funds are supplying the children with canned milk daily.

All of us who visited the camps came away with the feeling of wishing there was something we could do as individuals to alleviate the suffering of these people. So I am writing to tell you about these refugees and hoping that some of you can find old clothes that you can send to us APO or that you can get various groups to which you belong to make up packages. Many of the villages that have been recently liberated from the guerrillas are much worse off than those we visited in Lamia.

An important part of the A.W.O.G. program was organizing educational projects such as lectures held in the Acropolis or at other accessible sites such as Elusis, Corinth, or Mycenae. We heard the greatest scholars of the American School of Classical Studies lecture at historic places. One morning I was present when the tomb of a small child from the 9th Century BC was opened. The smallest rocks and cups of dirt were saved to aid in dating the tomb. Generally, however, I was limited in the number of lectures I could attend because of the children. Paul's birth in February 1949 limited my participation even more. However, we were lucky to have household help so that we could go out more freely than was possible in the United States. Such help came with headaches—more of that later.

In retrospect, it seems to me that our various groups were important to the smooth functioning of the American Mission. They provided the necessary support for the American women and their families although at the time we didn't define it that way. The social life that came from these groups was necessary for women who were often abroad for the first time and living in isolated locations in the Athens area. Husbands were often gone all day and sometimes kept very late hours. (There were very few women working professionally then—in or out of the government.) Our welfare and educational work was coordinated with the programs of the American Mission for Aid to Greece. It provided another way for Americans and Greeks to work together and thus understand each other better.

Coping With Life Overseas

For most of us the Greek Mission was our first experience living in another culture. We knew intellectually that the Greeks had an old and established culture. By and large, however, we were the products of a self-satisfied American culture and felt that we were on a kind of missionary venture to bring the best of American know-how to the country. I don't think that this unconscious attitude of ours was always appreciated by the Greeks.

We were well educated—many of us had been to college, but had given up any thought of using our education in an active way and were devoting ourselves to our husbands' work and our families. The women's movement had not yet impinged on our awareness.

We were, in many ways, the first line of American contact with the average Greek citizen—the farmer, maid, electrician and peddler. We learned enough Greek to supervise our maids and to see that our children were safeguarded when they were left at home. We needed the language to help us buy food and to bargain with the plumber and dressmaker. We provided the backup service to our men so there would be food when they returned from work, so that their children would be well cared for, and that there were social events for the Mission and their Greek counterparts.

Our spare energies were used in welfare kinds of projects. In the process we came in close contact with Greek people and had the immense satisfaction of learning well another language and culture. And it often wasn't easy.

Sometimes the end results were comic, but other times they were more serious. My friend, Sally Rock, and I had learned a little Greek. One day I called her number and inquired in my best Greek "Einay kyrea mesa? (Is the lady of the house in?") Sally answered and, hearing Greek spoken, called her maid to take the call. "Embros" boomed her maid. I thought I had the wrong number and called my maid, Sophia, to help me. Of course, if we had both spoken English there would have been less confusion, but we loved to practice our newly learned language. And this is why, of course, they had professional interpreters doing Embassy and Mission business because many mistakes could be and were made.

After eight months in Greece, I discovered to my surprise that I was pregnant. Actually, I was very pleased and had a very easy and happy pregnancy. However, after the baby was born I experienced postpartum depression that ultimately required that I go through psychoanalysis. I will never know if this illness was caused by the tensions of living overseas away from familiar surroundings or whether it might have happened anyway back in the States. I managed to survive by the love and care of my husband and friends—especially Sally Rock who was a trained psychiatric social worker. I was delivered by Dr. Panyotu, a Greek obstetrician well trained in England. He practiced the natural childbirth method, which was fine with me, because I always had easy labors.

My problems began in the nursing home where I was delivered—the Atheniki Kliniki. I had a problem communicating with the nurses about the bottles for milk. I had never nursed a baby and the Greek nurse couldn't believe that I had no milk. They decided to sterilize the bottles by pouring plain hot water into them and then filling them with evaporated milk. I solved this problam by sending the bottles to Marcia Leet who had a small baby at home and knew the process for sterilizing bottles. I was happy to get home to my own kitchen and, by that time, to two maids—Sophia and Despina.

Much of our conversation and many of the traumas of overseas living centered around the "maid problem." This is not a situation that lends itself to much sympathy from housewives back in the United States, who picture life with servants as idyllic. In reality, there were good and bad features to it. It was necessary to have help if one did not wish to get bogged down in the drudgery of housekeeping. Shopping was inconvenient and foods unfamiliar. Water had often to be boiled or treated and fresh fruits and vegetables soaked. Also it was pleasant to have help in the house for entertaining and also for babysitting.

The drawbacks were several. Greek girls, raised in the primitive life of the Greek village, especially during the war, had sketchy ideas of sanitation and no idea about how to use our washing machines and other labor saving devices. They also were not used to our food. I must also say here that many of us grew to love Greek cooking, especially the "dolmathes," stuffed cabbage and grape leaves stuffed, and the "avgolemone," soup made with eggs and lemon.

Sometimes dangerous situations came up which involved the use of our appliances. Manny and I took a trip to Turkey and an American couple agreed to come and live in the house while we were gone. We had a pressure cooker which I had warned Sophia not to use because she didn't really understand the principles of using it. I was horrified, therefore, to arrive home to find Sophia at the door with an ugly burn mark on her face. She had forced open the cooker before the pressure had been reduced. Fortunately the burn mark was not permanent and neither she nor the children were hurt.

Our first Thanksgiving we planned to have guests and the commissary had provided American-style turkeys. I asked Sophia if she knew how to stuff a turkey and she said "malesta" (but of course). Sometime later I came into the kitchen to check her progress and discovered that she had sliced the bird from stem to stern and I had to sew it up again before proceeding to the stuffing. Perhaps it was my Greek, which caused the confusion, but to this day I can't imagine how she planned to cook the turkey that way.

Many Americans choose to have only one maid because of the "infighting" that inevitably came with several in the house. Even if it wasn't fighting, a lot of loud yelling in a strange language sounded like arguments and was disruptive in any household.

We soon became used to the many inconveniences of life in post-war Greece. Electricity often failed—usually at the most inconvenient times. I remember vividly one party that was being given by Ken and Kay Iverson. They had invited many high ranking dignitaries and had just started with drinks when their whole electrical system blew out. They called us to see if their maids could bring all their food down to our house to be cooked and heated in our stove. While we were doing this, they served a lot of extra drinks and many of the guests didn't know that there had been a delay.

Cooking itself often called for ingenuity. The vegetables and fruits were delicious and very fresh. However, you could get only what was in season so that there was no lettuce all summer and an oversupply of cauliflower and cabbage in the fall. Ice cream was non-existent except if you made it at home. I treasured the few mixes that appeared in the Commissary and developed a caramel pudding that could be cooked by boiling condensed milk for three hours.

We certainly never lacked for adequate food and, in fact, the diet must have been similar to what our parents had eaten a generation before us. One made what one needed from one's own garden and kitchen and often had additional help in the kitchen. Some Americans did have cooks. We did for a very short while, but we found our lifestyles just didn't mesh, especially when the cook put a heavy dose of liqueur in Paul's birthday cake.

Greece was my first experience as a diplomatic wife—luncheons, cocktail parties, and teas—a constant social swirl and a heady experience. I'm glad that I had the experience. For us, it continued over a period of twenty years when we returned to the United States and then again in Brazil. However, I learned early that there are hazards to that life. One of the biggest is to the figure. In Greece my weight rose to 180 pounds with the steady intake of sweets and alcohol. I also found that cocktail party talk is boring and superficial and that jockeying for position is endemic to the institution. Cocktail parties may serve a useful purpose, but I far prefer a small dinner party where decent conversation can take place. Diplomatic professionals find it too easy to get involved in the alcohol regime and often stick to short stays and carrot stick refreshments.

We met many educated and wealthy Greek people, although at the time we were there, several families were living in straightened circumstances. For the first time I had become aware of the dangers of being used. Americans had largesse to be given—PX goods, licensed imports and so forth and many scandals arose at different times from this donor-recipient relationship. The temptations for abuse were great and one became wary of one's relationship with Greek businessmen and others who stood to benefit from a close relationship.

In many ways, our deepest relationships were with maids and others who gave us service. We were living very closely and there was little room for deception. I remember how touched I was when I discovered that Sophia had saved all of her month's salary to buy a violin to send to her brother on Mykonos Island. She and her family had barely survived the famine of the German occupation.

We actually felt very little danger when we were in Greece. Now as I reread the story of the Greek Mission, I realize that it was a very tenuous situation. I think that the only time I felt afraid was on Christmas Eve, 1947. We had just returned from a party at John and Lois Hermanses's. It was one o'clock and we had just dropped off to sleep. Suddenly, there was a scuffle in the courtyard and we rushed to open our window to face the loaded rifles of the local Police Militia. "Don't shoot," I yelled. "We're Americans."

"We know that" they replied. "We want Panyiotu down here." With that they dragged off Panyiotu from his garage home with his wife, Irene, weeping and pleading with them to spare him from prison. The local police were taking communist sympathizers into preventive detention because of rumors of a coup. In all the time that we were in Greece, Panyiotu never returned from the island where he was sent for re-education. I have often wondered what happened to him for I felt quite sympathetic toward him and his concerns for Greece. He was warm with the children and his criticism of Greek society valid and honest.

Summing Up

We stayed three years in Greece and in that time had many extraordinary opportunities for travel and sightseeing. In June 1949 we were guests of the state-controlled SEK railway on its first run from Gravia to Lamia. This was the first trip taken since 1944, when the Germans retreating from Greece had blown up and destroyed its main road and railroads. For those of us who had been in Greece since the start of the reconstruction period, it was a particularly satisfying experience.

I quote from a letter home:

The trip took us through some spectacularly beautiful country with rugged mountain peaks still covered with snow, deep gorges, and rich valleys dotted with olive trees and ripe wheat fields. Traveling through the ancient towns of Thebes and Levadia we were in stations with crowds of people out to see the momentous occasion. The train engineer kept up a steady hoot of the whistle throughout the trip, calling the peasants from their work in the fields. Arriving in Gravia, we picked up a convoy of soldiers to escort us the rest of the way, for although the area was relatively secure, one of the most notorious of the bandit leaders had his headquarters in the neighboring hills.

At the new Brallo and Gorgepotomas bridges, there were contingents of soldiers standing at attention for review and workmen everywhere were waving their approval of the occasion. The trip included passing through some thirty tunnels, and we found this a distinctly unromantic experience because of the fine film of coal dust that was sprinkled on our faces, clothes and seats. I found that I was very popular because I had brought along a jar of cleansing cream and some kleenex, which helped to keep the blackness under control. Upon arrival of the train in Lamia, we found the whole town out for the occasion. The modest station was decorated with oleander branches and the local mayor and committee made speeches for the occasion.

One July we were on the boat trip that stopped to visit the shrine on the island of Tinos where the sick from all over the country came for a cure at the sacred church. When we were back on board ship and watching the crowd on shore, someone called attention to something on shore. Everyone rushed to the starboard side and created such a list in the boat that the captain appealed on the loudspeaker for some people to rush to the port side to prevent the ship from tipping over. The same ship had taken us to the island of Rhodes where we wandered through the beautiful resort that Mussolini had made his own. The hotel of the Roses was not fully restored to its pre-war glory but was certainly elegant enough to please us. We also visited the Spa of Kalithea, which was famous for the cures of its laxative waters. In fact, the cures were so speedy that over fifty toilets of both eastern and western varieties were provided adjacent to the dance floor and bar. One of the greatest joys of early post-war travel was the lack of crowds and the lack of pollution all along the

Mediterranean. The amenities were limited but the sheer beauty of scenery was everywhere.

In April of 1948, our turn came up for a free ride to Italy on the Army plane. This was only my second plane ride and I was so nervous that I couldn't sleep the night before. The small plane took only two hours to Italy, but the cabin was unpressurized and swooping down over Mt. Vesuvius and the Po Valley was a real thrill to me. In Rome, we stayed at the Hotel Nationale and after eight months in Greece, I felt that I was back at the pinnacle of European civilization. The hotel was elegant with good service and comfortable rooms. It was still early after the war and Americans were still novelties.

We spent many hours with Manny's family in Rome and his uncle, the priest, literally ran us through the Vatican Museums and arranged a private audience for us with the Pope. Private meant that the Pontiff stopped and greeted each of us personally—slipping naturally from English to German to Italian. We also took a train to Norcia in Umbria, which was still suffering from the war. My one vivid memory is the numbing cold. (On one of these trips Manny's relatives put a "priest in bed" to keep us warm. This was a wooden frame that would prop up the covers so that hot coals could be put in the bed to warm it up.) Aunt Nazarena lived in Rome but she had spent many years in America and visiting her was a warm family reunion indeed.

Later that year we were also able to visit Paris and on our return trip to Europe, after home leave in the fall of 1949, we arranged a stop of a few days in London. All of this travel was possible because we had reliable help in Greece where we felt the children were safe in the care of Sophia and Tassia. They were both very good help and I regret that we have lost touch with both of them.

Momentous Decisions

GLORIA GARDNER

In July 1950, as a civilian employee with the U.S. Air Force Intelligence Headquarters in occupied Germany, I received a surprise call from the Office of the Special Representative in Paris. She regretted that there was not likely to be an opening in the U.S. Operations Mission in Paris for some time, as I had hoped when applying. There was, however, an opening in the U.S. Operations Mission to Greece. In the hope that at some later date I might be able to transfer to the Paris Mission, I accepted. Never in my wildest dreams would I have realized what a momentous decision was made in that five minute phone call. It certainly changed the course of my young life for at least the next twenty years. I was about to become a part of history, albeit a small part.

Arriving in Athens on a warm night in August 1950, I was first assigned as secretary to the Deputy Director of the Industry and Transportation (IT) Division, Harper M. Sowles. In 1951, I was reassigned to the Chief of the Ports and Shipping Branch, Bill Wild. During the final months of my tour, I served as secretary to the Director of IT, Cecil Calvert. So I was to spend my entire first tour in this fascinating division, constantly learning about the industrial and transportation program for what was then the Kingdom of Greece.

I believe our mission was one of the largest in the Marshall Plan. It was certainly a busy one. Mr. Paul Porter was our Mission Director at the time. After three devastating wars from 1939 to 1947, the Greek economy was in shambles. As representatives of the American taxpayer, we were there to lend a helping hand to its brave people struggling to survive. Working in IT, reading the files, it was perhaps easy to recognize the result of our efforts in the gradual restoration of the transportation system. The port of Piraeus was once again bustling with ships and boats of all sizes. Greek longshoremen were now busy unloading incoming cargoes and loading such traditional commodities as Greek olive oil, fish, hides, wines, sponges, and later bauxite, cement, etc.

The CAA had a group of technicians in place to advise Greek aviation and the airport at Hellenikon was operating a busy flight schedule bringing the first tourists and businessman to the country. Railroads, which had been demolished, were somewhat slower to go into full operation, but trains were running to many towns in the outlying areas. Local buses and street cars were certainly operating in Athens so that the Athenians could now depend on local transport to get to their offices, shops and markets. Some long distance buses were operating in the more politically stable areas so that it was now possible to visit some of those famous classic sites such as Corinth, Mycenae, and Delphi. Vehicles were in less than top condition, but they were running under supervision of the IT technicians—sometimes even on schedule! The Mining Branch, with its two advisors, was involved in several projects—such as the restoration of the bauxite mines in the area.

So far, the tourism industry was represented by a single advisor with a single Greek secretary in a small office. Business was slow until the transportation systems began to function. The existing Greek hotels and travel agencies started to gain momentum, laying the foundation for a highly successful tourism program throughout the country.

The crafts advisor, the only woman on the staff, was responsible, at least in part, for the reappearance of the beautiful Ceramikos and Laurium potteries in the gift shops along with items such as colorful textiles from Mykonos. Small businesses were encouraged to return to production. I remember a tour to one of the local factories before the war; the Dardoufas Brothers had created beautiful women's gloves in the French style and were now manufacturing their first products for export. The tailors and shoemakers were busy again, supplying the needs of the Greeks and foreigners. I've always wondered if they were ever able to eliminate the squeak from their shoes. Perhaps the Greeks preferred their shoes with this unique feature!

While the communists were still able to raid the villages in the north, kidnapping the children for indoctrination behind the Iron Curtain, most of the country was finally able to find food and shelter, return to work, send their children to school, and celebrate their religious and national holidays in safety. After a decade of constant hardships and suffering, the people were at last free to live as Greeks—to congregate once more in their sidewalk cafes and taverns, to argue politics or to sing and dance to their mandolins and bouzoukis, enjoying their ouzo and regional flavorful cuisine. After fifty years of relative peace and serenity in Western Europe, I still believe that this was one of the great legacies of the Marshall Plan in Greece and a measure of its overall success. For those of us participating in this economic transformation, it was a remarkable experience. Now more than ever, I marvel at the farsightedness of those who conceived and planned the bureaucratic structure of the Mission to implement the program. In a sense, we were all like missionaries or explorers or both, setting out to traverse terra incognito.

Fortunately, our Mission was blessed with an outstanding group of civil servants and technicians to accomplish this. The range of their professional backgrounds and experience remains impressive. In our division, economists, lawyers, automotive specialists, and railroad men rubbed elbows with journalists, bankers, geologists, an Army general and a commercial artist. This was true of the Greek staff assigned to IT as well. In the process, I know we all benefited from this diversity of talent and culture dedicated to the recovery of the economy. As for the clerical staff, IT was again blessed with an outstanding group of young American women, eager for an opportunity to work and travel. This was the case throughout the Mission and the friendships we formed endure to this day.

At that time, it's doubtful that any of us realized our historical role as the first American women to serve the U.S. government as civilians in such an undertaking overseas. Most of us so enjoyed our first tour that we continued to serve with ECA's successor agencies, and some would devote their entire career to this supposedly "temporary" worldwide organization.

Certainly our relationship with the Greek clerical staff, male and female, was also groundbreaking. In a sense, we served as role models for many of the first Greek females ever allowed to work in an office situation involving foreigners. We introduced them to U.S. office procedures and taught them English in our spare time. In turn, they invited us to their homes, took us shopping and traveling, and acted as our interpreters. In general, we became part of each other's lives as they often confided their concerns both at work and at home. It is only as I write this that I realize what an enriching experience it was for all concerned.

Implications For The Future

My hope is that there is some concerted effort to bring the Marshall Plan and its achievements to the attention of our contemporaries as well as posterity. Since the 1970s, I've been asking young people in the U.S. and abroad what, or if, they have heard about the Marshall Plan. I don't recall anyone who was aware of its existence. What about a television or video documentary dealing with this subject in a way that will fascinate as well as educate these young people? Perhaps on the order of the excellent PBS series on World War II—on a smaller scale? History brought to life. . . . Certainly with the recent worldwide information explosion, all sorts of media approaches could be possible for the classroom and/or home.

Thank you for the opportunity to express some very precious memories concerning the Marshall Plan and my own experience. As one of its participants, I remain grateful and proud to have witnessed its overwhelming success even today. May its legacy continue to endure. As the Greeks might say, "Zito the Marshall Plan!"

From London to Athens

John W. Gunter

I believe that I can reasonably claim to have been a Marshall Plan participant, although I was never employed by the Economic Cooperation Administration. At the time of Secretary Marshall's speech in June 1947, I was the U.S. Treasury Representative at the Embassy in London. As I recall, the British were the first Europeans to react to the Secretary's invitation and immediately sought guidance on how to proceed most effectively. The Undersecretary of State for Economic Affairs Will Clayton was sent to London to discuss the matter with the U.K. Government.

Secretary Clayton was invited to meet with the British Cabinet at 10 Downing Street on the evening of his arrival. Harry Hawkins, the Minister of Economic Affairs in the Embassy, and I were designated to accompany the Secretary. While the meeting was chaired by Mr. Attlee, the principal British spokesman was Ernest Bevin, the Foreign Secretary. In fact, the meeting turned into a brilliant dialogue between Bevin and Clayton, who obviously liked each other. The importance of these two men in getting the Marshall Plan off to a good start should be remembered by all of us.

Several months later I was recalled by the Treasury to become Deputy Director of the Office of International Finance. Frank Southard was the Director. I found the Treasury greatly concerned with providing effective backing for the Marshall Plan. With this objective in mind, the Treasury was strengthening its overseas representation, particularly in Europe.

In 1949 I became involved in the operations of the Economic Cooperation Administration (ECA) mission in Athens, which was headed by Paul Porter. I was nominated by the Treasury to be the U.S. member of the Greek Currency Committee. This Committee, which consisted of three Greek Ministers, the Governor of the Bank of Greece, and two foreign "experts", one British and one American, controlled Greek monetary policy. I was on the payroll of the Bank of Greece, but was expected to be in contact with the American Mission on an informal basis. Paul Porter and I had, I think, a very effective relationship from the viewpoints of both the Mission and the Greek Government.

Rescuing Austria

Lloyd Jones

Introduction

Although I joined the staff of the ECA in July, 1949, my experience with the Marshall Plan was quite limited in one sense: that my service was in the ECA Section of the then American Legation in Bern. Switzerland, of course, did not receive any financial assistance from the United States under the Marshall Plan. The Economic Cooperation Administration (ECA) section consisted of two officers (after 1951, one) and two secretaries. The purposes of our reporting and liaison presence in Bern were largely to:

1. Provide regular reports on Swiss economic relations with the other European nations to ECA headquarters in Paris and Washington.
2. Keep Swiss officials and the public informed of all aspects of the development of the Marshall Plan.
3. Encourage the Swiss to provide a maximum of credits as their share in the recovery program of their European trading partners.

The last of these was within the context of the European financial clearing systems initially and, from 1950, of the European Payments Union. We also conducted a small technical assistance program for Switzerland which the Swiss funded and through which they were able to send managers, technicians, and others to the United States for study tours and plant visits.

Effects of the Marshall Plan

My principal impression of the Marshall Plan to this day is of its enormous psychological impact and the degree to which it provided economic and political hope to a Europe that had largely despaired of the future. As a very young combat infantryman, I had fought across France, Luxembourg, Germany and Austria in 1944-45, in the course of which I saw the enormous physical destruction of war. Returning in the fall and winter of 1948 as a student at the University of Zurich, I travelled occasionally through the same countries. The mood I found was of deep discouragement, in many instances the obvious consequence of the physical effects of war.

Moreover, the war had come on the heels of ten years of economic depression and political turmoil through much of the continent, and hopes for the future had waned. But with the Marshall Plan, people were beginning to realize that they could perhaps deal with their problems and were entertaining the possibility of hope. This undoubtedly was the initial impact of our assistance, a tremendous psychological and political stimulus. Ultimately, however, the promise alone would not be enough. The program had achieved that which it set out to do: to assist Europe to reach economic stability and viability. By 1952, with that success the nations of Western Europe were reinvigorated. Their development, supported in part by the assistance of the United States, had reached the point at which they could begin the process of charting the profound political and economic changes that since that time have produced today's Europe.

Austria's Success Story

After almost four years of duty in Switzerland, I was reassigned to Vienna in 1953. While the Marshall Plan technically ended in mid-1952, the aid program to Austria remained in place and the country was still occupied and divided by the Allied powers. One of my first tasks as an economic analyst was to prepare a balance-of-payments forecast for Austria for fiscal year 1953. My analysis provided the extraordinary forecast that the country was indeed achieving economic independence in the sense that its external accounts were in surplus and foreign exchange reserves were rising rapidly, meaning that Austria soon would have no further need for assistance.

Through 1953, Austria received just over a billion dollars in immediate post-war and Marshall Plan aid from the United States, almost all of which took the form of grants. In return, it provided a model case for the utility of external financial assistance. Following the war, the expectation was that Austria would be on the international dole for the indefinite future. The country had been riven by civil war in the 1930s and then annexed by Germany. Prior to that, the economy had never recovered from the shock of World War I and its aftermath, the collapse of the Habsburg Empire.

Three factors explain much of the achievement of Austria's economic take-off in this period. First, there was the domestic political stability. For a variety of reasons, the nation's political parties were able for the first time to reach a consensus on a democratic political system. Second, the German takeover of the country in 1938 had led to substantial new investments (primarily for Germany's war economy) in iron and steel making, non-ferrous metal production, and in a wide range of machinery output. Third, our assistance made it possible for Austria to refurbish much of that investment and provide needed foreign exchange for new investment. An additional final factor was the economic recovery of Europe itself. As a consequence, Austria's exports began to increase and tourism particularly became a major factor in the economy.

By the time of the State Treaty in May 1955 (under the agreement, the occupying Allied powers agreed to unify the country and respect its neutrality), the nation's economy was in excellent condition. Today, although Austria has problems similar to those of other European nations, the country is an extraordinarily pleasant contrast in political and economic terms to the Austria from 1918 to 1945 which is a benefit to Europe, the United States, and itself.

Our Accomplishments In Greece

C. WILLIAM KONTOS, AMBASSADOR (RET.)

I was recruited for the Marshall Plan Mission to Greece while working on a Ph.D. at the London School of Economics. My wife and I arrived in Athens in October 1949 and we left in September 1953.

Initially, I was assigned to the Civil Government Division with the task of helping the Greek government reorganize its administration. The staff consisted of six professionals, including myself, who were busily engaged in assisting the reform and streamlining of the new, post-war Greek government. The civil war had just ended with, the communists in northern Greece being defeated by the Greek army with considerable U.S. military advice and materiel.

The role of the Civil Government Division in reshaping a country's public administration was a novel task for Americans. We concentrated on organizing a civil service code and commission, strongly advocating decentralization to local governments by strengthening the role of their "monarchs" and prefects. We helped determine the number and functions of ministries. My job was to support the senior officers of the division, all experts in public administration. Among my other assignments, I was given the task of reorganizing the Greek postal system and introducing new methods to their patent office. Our endeavors were only modestly successful because, despite the extraordinary influence the mission wielded in a country completely dependent on the U.S. financially, the old Greek ways of discharging the business of government were firmly entrenched and highly resistant to change.

The primary task of the U.S. economic mission was to deal with the chaotic situation left in the war's wake. The country's infrastructure was in a shambles: there were few good roads, a mediocre communications system, erratic power supply, and many villages had been destroyed, leaving a sizable number of people lacking adequate shelter and food. Essentially, our job was one of reconstruction. Roads and bridges were built, power stations erected, agriculture revived, and village housing programs launched.

Beyond the successful reconstruction of public works, our scope was both ambitious and comprehensive. The mission's engagement moved from reorganizing ports and railways to civil aviation, the establishment of democratic trade unions, the recasting of the tax collection policy, and control of the level and types of goods imported into the country with U.S. funds. The total approach was much too bold. While there were some successes, the inability to achieve reform in these areas was considerable. Nevertheless, over the four years I spent in Greece, I saw the emergence of palpable material progress and a consequent rise in the living standard of its people.

Since much of the work of reconstruction was done outside of Athens, the collaboration of local authorities was crucial, and lent impetus to our goal of government decentralization. I personally took charge of a program of voluntary self-help whereby villages were given materials such as roofing, bags of cement, pipes, tiles, and reinforced steel rods. The inhabitants undertook supplying the labor needed to build small public works. In close cooperation with the Ministry of the Interior, we set priorities among villages and disbursed local currency funds for the purchase of materials.

The local currency was drawn from "counterpart funds." The fund held drachmas deposited to a U.S. account by the Greek government from its sale of commodities that were imported with U.S. dollars. This technique of generating local currency through the sale of U.S. goods was one of the most creative and useful devices initiated by the Marshall Plan staff. We were able to allocate millions of drachmae from counterpart funds for work done voluntarily by villagers at a fraction of the cost of a project built in the normal way by a contractor. When engineering skills or other technical assistance was required, we were able to have them supplied through the monarch's office.

For a sum equivalent to two million dollars, we funded schools, bridges, culverts, roads, watermains, clinics, slaughter houses, and other small infrastructure projects throughout the villages of Greece. I traveled extensively all over the country observing the work in progress for myself. It was gratifying to see first hand the creation of these small works by the people who would benefit from them and who came forward in great numbers. It is important to note that the villagers themselves determined the choice of projects. We followed their desires as to whether a road or a school was of the first importance.

The director of the Mission when I arrived was John Nuveen, a Chicago financier. He was succeeded by Paul Porter who had been the U.S. Representative on the Economic Commission for Europe. He, in turn, was succeeded by Roger Lapham, former mayor of San Francisco. Leland Barrows, who took over from Lapham, asked me to become his Special Assistant. This position, to which I devoted my last two years in Athens, entailed a variety of tasks and a whole range of relationships linking the Director with his staff. I sat in on all of his staff meetings and frequently accompanied him on his calls on Greek government ministries.

The central concern of these two years was to bring about the stabilization of the very volatile Greek economy. The Mission proposed a major currency reform along the lines of the U.S.-backed economic policy that was the centerpiece of the "German miracle." The Embassy backed a much less radical approach, namely, a straight devaluation of the drachma. The debate within the U.S. government in Athens and Washington, as well as with the Greek government, went on for months. It was a fascinating time to observe a policy evolving in which the livelihood and wellbeing of an entire population depended on a successful outcome.

In the end, the Greek government opted for a straight devaluation, although there were advocates for currency reform. The decision was made and announced without a word leaking beforehand. The drachma dropped from 30,000 to a dollar to 3 to 1, and in time, became a relatively hard currency. Production was enhanced and inflation, in due course, sank sharply. Along with curbing inflation and other measures, Greece's financial house was put in good order. This was a major accomplishment of the Marshall Plan.

The mission also pioneered certain internal administrative innovations, such as setting up a Joint Administrative Service that gave support— vehicles, maintenance, personnel and other services—to all U.S. government entities (embassy, Marshall Plan Mission, military, and other smaller agencies of a very large U.S. presence in Greece). The Embassy's

Economic Counselor wore a second hat as economic advisor to the director of the Marshall Plan Mission. The concept of an Ambassador's "country team" had its beginnings in Greece. Its members were the heads of the principal agencies and met regularly to coordinate all U.S. programs.

The mission had good relationships with the regional office in Paris and headquarters in Washington. The Paris regional office was quite helpful on the whole, sending us short-term advisors such as productivity or industrial experts and economists who reviewed various sector programs, e.g. power and agriculture. There were also useful inter-mission exchanges, notably with Turkey and Italy. Washington's Greek desk was a powerful and persuasive advocate for mission policies, which they supported and had, in part, engendered.

Much of the way the U.S. conducted its economic aid programs through the Marshall Plan exercised a profound influence on the methods used by successor agencies, such as Point 4, the Mutual Security Agency, the Foreign Operations Administration, and the Agency for International Development. These independent agencies, whose heads reported to the President, enjoyed extraordinary freedom of action. As time passed, however, this was moderated by greater policy control from the Department of State and a more dominant role by ambassadors over USAID field missions.

This was a heady experience for a young man and, though I went on to a varied and fulfilling career in USAID and the State Department, the fascination and great challenge of those years in Greece remain the most memorable of my career.

Managing Occupied Germany— All From One Desk

AMBASSADOR JOHN W. MCDONALD (RET.)

Introduction

P ost-World War II Europe was a remarkable turning point in history and I wanted to be a part of it. My goal, since high school, was to become a U.S. diplomat, but I had been frustrated because the foreign service examination process had been shut down during the war years. In the spring of 1946, my last semester in law school, I read a newspaper article which talked about Washington's plan to create a new, career Military Government service for Occupied Germany. The article encouraged recent college graduates to apply and become the nucleus of a service which would, over the next twenty-five years, insure that Germany would never become a threat to peace again because its industry would be dismantled and it would become an agricultural nation. I wrote and applied for a job.

In November 1946, I was notified that I had been selected as the fifteenth person in a new, one hundred person program, that had just been established by the War Department. By implication, at least, they had dropped the agricultural nation idea. I would be a Military Government Intern (trainee) at the P-1, Junior Professional Assistant, entry level and would report to Berlin as soon as possible. I was sworn in on December 27, 1946 and arrived in Berlin on January 15, 1947.

Berlin

My first memory of OMGUS (Office of Military Government-United States) was rather dramatic. There were twenty of us in the first "class" of interns. We were marched into the office of the Chief of Personnel the next day and lined up in front of the Colonel. His first words were "Who in the Hell are you and what are you doing in Berlin!" The War Department had forgotten to tell Berlin about their new innovative program, which would have us spend our first year in training, moving every few months from office to office in Berlin, the U.S. Sector of Berlin, and then the U.S. Zone, from Headquarters to the State and County levels, to learn how to manage occupied Germany.

Obviously nothing had been organized, but I was lucky. As the only lawyer in the group, I was assigned to the Legal Division and became Deputy Secretary of the U.S. Delegation to the Law Committee of the Allied Control Council (ACC). I became immediately involved in multi-lateral diplomacy, working regularly with the Soviets, French, and British on new laws and other legal issues before the Committee.

By May 1947, Personnel had organized an excellent program and I rotated through the various offices in Berlin, Wiesbaden and then spent two months as Deputy Kreis Residence Officer in Hamburg. I was then sent off for a month for training at the European Command Intelligence School at Oberammergau. In November I was appointed, at the age of 25, to be the Chief Prosecutor for Frankfurt, Germany!

Frankfurt

OMGUS quite wisely decided to establish a Military Government Court System at the end of 1947, which was designed to bring some legal order out of the chaos of post-war occupied Germany. The courts had jurisdiction over all Allied civilians, all displaced persons, and all German nationals who violated Military Government Law. All the available experienced lawyers wanted to become judges, because of the higher pay and prestige. When Personnel began to look around for potential District Attorneys, they found the likes of me, and I was delighted. In court every day for almost two and a half years, I prosecuted over 500 cases personally and managed the prosecution of 4,500 more. I saw the impact of the Marshall Plan, indirectly and from a grass roots perspective, through the nature of the crimes that were committed. During 1947-48 most cases dealt with the theft of food or material goods from the occupiers, black-marketing and document falsification. People were struggling to stay alive. After the currency reform of June 1948, the break away of the Soviet Zone, and the creation of East Germany, counterfeiting of currency became a big issue. There were also fewer crimes of violence because West Germany was gradually beginning to re-build itself, with Marshall Plan assistance, and directing its energies towards that end.

In October 1949, without changing jobs, or even my desk, I was transferred to the State Department, as a temporary Foreign Service Staff Officer with HICOG (High Commission Germany).

Bonn-Petersberg

In April 1950, I became the fifteenth American in Bonn-Bad Godesberg and was assigned to work with my second international organization, the Allied High Commission, which was officially established in September 1949. It was tripartite in structure—U.S., U.K., and France—and basically ran West Germany. I worked for Joe Slater, the U.S. Executive Secretary to John J. McCloy, the first U.S. High Commissioner. As U.S. Secretary to the Law Committee I dealt daily with my British and French counterparts, helping to lead Germany back to democratic nationhood. I had my offices at The Petersberg, a beautiful former hotel on top of a hill opposite Bad Godesberg, and crossed the Rhine daily, by car ferry, to get to work.

Here too I had the opportunity to see the massive impact the Marshall Plan was having on West Germany. The barge traffic on the Rhine, outside my window, seemed to grow daily. Construction was everywhere. People were better dressed and better fed. Fear was gone. Prosperity was gradually returning. The economy was growing, and the people were becoming more interested in the politics of democracy and concerned about how to build a new nation, based on freedom and human rights.

Paris

Following the NATO Foreign Ministers' Meeting in Lisbon in February 1952, the U.S. Government decided to try an organizational experiment by creating its first regional organization in history, the Office of the United States Special Representative in Europe (SRE), to be based in Paris. SRE was designed to allow the United States Government to speak with one voice in Europe, i.e., to represent the Departments of State, Defense, Treasury, and the Mutual Security Agency, which was responsible for the Marshall Plan. The first SRE was Ambassador (formerly General) William H. Draper, who had two Senior Ambassadors on his staff. He was the U.S. Representative to NATO and to the Organization for European Economic Cooperation (OEEC) and was responsible for the allocation of all Marshall Plan assistance to Europe. This man had power.

In April, 1952 I followed Joe Slater to Paris, at his request. He had just been asked by Ambassador Draper to be his Executive Secretary, and I became Assistant Staff Secretary. We were directly involved with the issues at NATO, the OEEC, and of course with all of the problems associated with implementation of the Marshall Plan. It is difficult to imagine today that in 1952 the United States spent 3.25% of its GNP on the Marshall Plan! In 1996 we spent 0.16% of our GNP on our world-wide aid program, and many Americans complain that this is still too much.

Bureaucratically this was an interesting period in our history. On arriving in Paris I was transferred to the Mutual Security Agency, from the State Department. When Mr. Stassen came to office in Washington he changed MSA to FOA, the Foreign Operations Administration, and I was duly shifted, still doing my same job. In April 1954, having survived Stassen, I was transferred back to the State Department, never changing desks. I did enjoy working with my third and fourth international organizations, NATO and the OEEC and was committed to the SRE regional approach. I believe the office of Executive Secretary was an important unifying force in this bureaucratic structure.

Unfortunately the concept of SRE was too powerful for Washington to bear. Many of the interagency disagreements over turf and money were transferred from Washington, DC to Paris. Everyone seemed to be jealous of General Draper, who did a superb job with the power and authority he had. The office acronym was changed in June 1953, from SRE to USRO (U.S. Regional Organization), having lasted less than a year and a half. Ambassador John Hughes took over from Ambassador Draper. Ambassador Hughes was still U.S. Representative to NATO and the OEEC, but the money and power reverted to Washington and to the U.S. Economic Missions throughout Europe. SRE was a noble experiment however, that worked in spite of Washington.

Before closing I would like to honor the families, the wives, and the children, who followed in the footsteps of their spouses, during those difficult years. My wife and two children arrived in Frankfurt in October

1947. They, and their peers, had to learn how to adapt to the rubble and desolation of war torn Germany. They deserve special credit for giving up an easy life in the United States and coping with education, housing, and food problems and learning how to interact with poverty, hopelessness, barbed wire and hungry people surrounding their homes.

Postscript

In November 1954, after eight years in Europe, I was posted to Washington, DC and assigned to the Office of the Executive Secretary, during Secretary Dulles' term of office. I had subsequent assignments with ICA; in the Middle East; with the Bureau of International Organization Affairs, as Deputy Director General of the International Labor Organization in Geneva; and, with the Foreign Service Institute. I was appointed Ambassador twice by President Carter and twice by President Reagan, to lead U.S. Delegations to Global UN Conferences.

I retired in 1987, after forty years with the U.S. Government, and became a Law Professor at George Washington University Law School. I then became the first President of the Iowa Peace Institute in Grinnell, Iowa and five years ago co-founded the Institute For Multi-Track Diplomacy, here in Washington, DC. The humanitarian aspects of the Marshall Plan have had a major impact on my life to this day because our Institute takes a systems approach to peace and focuses on the non-violent resolution of international ethnic conflict.

A Perspective from Scandinavia

HERMAN L. MYERS

B y coincidence, General Marshall proposed his Plan at the Harvard Commencement ceremonies at which I received an MPA. Staying at Harvard as a Littauer Fellow for another year and returning to the Department of Agriculture for the next four years, I came late to the Marshall Plan.

From 1952-1954, I was the Scandinavian Desk Officer in Washington; the USOM (Mission) Deputy Director in Norway from 1954-1956; and the U.S. Representative to the Netherlands in The Hague in 1956. Since project benefits are readily available in official records, and the basis for the Plan in articles[1] and books, these notes are limited to random memories and observations.

As Scandinavian Desk Officer, an assistant and I were the conduits in Washington from and to Missions in Iceland, Denmark, and Norway. Iceland took up about 80 percent of our time and effort and as a distinctive straight balance of payments replacement program, highly dependent on fisheries earnings. Iceland was of strategic value to the U.S. because of its location as a military base (Keflavik Airbase), and, therefore, was less project-oriented. I do not remember the need to repair or reconstruct prior German damage. Indeed, Iceland still benefits from German engineering which supplies the island with free thermal power for heat and drying uses from the 17 mile pipeline to the volcano.

Norway, which had lost half of its shipping to torpedoes during the war, sunk the first German ship to appear in its harbor, destroyed its heavy water to prevent its use by the enemy, and was subject to occupation as the German army moved toward Russia, was a worthy ally and beneficiary. As a literate and advanced nation, Norway hardly needed to be told where and how to use its counterpart of close to $1 billion.

Our Mission by 1954 was primarily one of assisting the Norwegians to find and bring in competent technicians and material at reasonable cost. During my two year tour, I was impressed by the lack of political "pork" as the decision-making was left to Norwegian Commerce Department officials, well-trained economists. These officials opted to use the counterpart funds in addition to replacing fishing and shipping fleets to start new industries. For example, the Government underground ammunition factory was converted to producing parts for the Swedish Volvo automobile). At Kirkenes material and machinery were financed to install an open face iron ore factory and to rebuild housing and other facilities for three thousand people left homeless by the Germans and then living in caves. A new metallurgy laboratory was financed at the Technical University of Trondheim, and agriculture was modernized by new technology and machinery.

Interestingly, the officials with whom I was working on a day to day basis were also the ones who headed up the Government's interest in the Scandinavian Integration Movement.

Returning from Norway, I was asked to go to The Hague to reconstruct the record on the use of the "counterpart funds." I spent eight months on this, with the cooperation of a Netherlands Treasury economist, at the end of which it was revealed that about $20 million of long term projects remained in the pipeline. An agreement with the government shifted the long-term projects to the budget and one-year projects were assigned to counterpart financing. This effectively eliminated the need for the government to report on the use of unspent funds to the United States. The Netherlands government even printed a book showing all projects financed by U.S. counterpart funds.

With such success in the Netherlands, I attempted to apply this experience to the program in Austria, which was virtually finished. Unfortunately, the counterpart funds made up practically the entire monetary stock of the country. Since two relatively equal political parties existed at the time, turning over the counterpart funds to either one was paramount to taking sides, an unnecessary and untenable U.S. position. I suggested the formation of an independent equivalent of the Federal Reserve Bank, but it takes more than a few weeks to do this, leaving termination to others at a later date.

My experience with Marshall Plan programs, in particular technical assistance, balance of payments analyses underpinning aid, and interaction with economic agency personnel was a natural preparation for my work with the U.S. Agency for International Development (USAID).

Note

1. See Charles S. Maier, "From Plan to Practice: The Context and Consequences of the Marshall Plan," *Harvard Magazine*, May-June 1997, pp. 41-43.

Germany: Solving Problems

Jacques J. Reinstein

I was assigned to the Policy Planning Staff of the State Department under the leadership of George F. Kennan when it was first set up at the beginning of May 1947, with the initial task from Secretary Marshall of addressing the critical economic situation in Europe. We were a small group, hastily assembled. Since September 1945, I had been assigned to the U.S. delegation to the Council of Foreign Ministers, which had been set up by the Potsdam Agreement. It was located in London and designed to fashion the post-World War II peace arrangements. As the March-April 1947 Moscow meeting had led to a complete breakdown over how to deal with Germany, I returned to Washington, DC.

The economic situation in Europe had been dealt with already by a number of people of great ability, but the enormity and urgency of the task seemed to me, as almost a newcomer to the current Washington scene, to have only been fully grasped by many of the experts in April. (Representatives of the State Department were then testifying before Congress on an aid appropriation for France for several hundreds of millions of dollars and giving assurance that this would be their last request). General Marshall perhaps had a clearer overall view than many of them. The clarity of his perception of the problem perhaps made him open to bold initiatives.

The Planning Staff had barely three weeks to prepare its recommendations, work which has been well described by George Kennan in his memoirs. They were not unique in many of their essentials, but they had several merits. One was that they laid out an overall approach which required cooperation by the Europeans and avoided the need by the U.S. to balance individual country requests. Another was that they envisaged action which would fix a termination to U.S. aid. This was essential to obtaining vast new appropriations from the Congress. Although they were a collegial product, they benefited from being expressed in the words of a single drafter in the articulate prose of George Kennan.[1]

I brought to the discussions, besides my general background, the personal experience of having been in London in the early months of the year and having witnessed and experienced the breakdown of the British economy in that bitter winter. One element in the recommendations for which I pressed very hard and successfully was the need for immediate action to break major bottlenecks without awaiting a general European plan. Although I had several in mind, the only one which emerged was coal. With the help of the State Department's experts and with the benefit again of vigorous discussion in the Planning Staff, I was able to put together by June 2, "Increase of European Coal Production," which laid out comprehensive action proposals. These led to the U.S.-U.K. coal talks of August 1947 and the adoption of a major program to increase Ruhr coal production.[2]

The European reaction to the Harvard speech (Bevin's initiative, the Paris meetings, and the decision of the Western Europeans to respond without Soviet and satellite participation) confronted the United States with a need to formulate ideas of its own. Wording in the Harvard speech lifted from the Planning Staff paper stressed that any initiative should be European in origin, and that the U.S. should confine its role to giving "friendly advice" with regard to the plan. As the Europeans began developing their response, they gave notice that they would send a delegation to Washington with proposals on which to seek this "friendly advice" in the summer of 1947.

Two exercises were launched to formulate the U.S. position and I participated in both. One was in the Planning Staff, which produced its recommendations in PPS 4.[3] One of my principal contributions to this paper was to raise the issue of whether the United Kingdom should be given special treatment in whatever program emerged. In our discussions in the Staff, we felt that the situation in the U.K. was deteriorating at a very alarming rate and suggested that, unless this process could be halted soon, the U.S. might be confronted with the need to propose remedial measures of a far-reaching character in concert with Canada. Happily, this need did not arise, but the paper may be interesting for historical reasons. It was classified Top Secret and its distribution within the State Department was limited. However, it was seen by Secretary Marshall.

The other exercise to formulate positions for use in discussions with the Europeans was carried out in the economic offices of the Department under the chairmanship and guidance of the Assistant Secretary for Economic Affairs, Willard L. Thorp, to whom I was a special assistant. A small staff headed by Charles P. Kindleberger and including John DeWilde prepared papers on various policy issues which would be confronted by the U.S. in dealing with what was becoming identified as the "recovery program." These were discussed in meetings of the top officers of the economic segment of the Department which were held at night several times a week, that being the only time at which such busy people could be assembled for thoughtful discussions.[4]

While there were several officers involved in the drafting of these papers, the presentation to the "Board" was made by Kindleberger, which ensured unity in the consideration of the policy issues. These papers, revised in the light of the discussions, in due course provided guidance for the U.S. participants in their discussions with the Europeans. It is my impression that there was no major policy issue of an economic character which arose during the implementation of the European Recovery Program which was not touched on during these discussions. The foresight and depth of analysis involved in the preparation of the papers by Kindleberger and his staff is impossible to underestimate.

After the preparation of these papers, I became involved in various problems in Germany and Austria arising from the occupation, and had no further connection with the Marshall Plan until the State Department took over the occupation of Germany from the military in 1949 and I was assigned to its new German office. However, I did have the unique experience of hearing an explanation of the recovery program in an informal setting by General Marshall himself in December 1947. We were meeting again with the Soviets in the Council of Foreign Ministers in London in November and December. I learned that, despite the key role played by Ernest Bevin, the U.K. Foreign Minister, in leading the European response to the Harvard speech and the important role which he had played in the British trade union movement, there were serious reservations toward the recovery plan on the part of at least some leaders in the Trade Union Congress. Ambassador Lewis Douglas arranged a lunch with them to meet Secretary Marshall, and I was one of two Americans from the delegation accompanying the Secretary who were roped in to fill up the table. At the end of lunch, General Marshall outlined the American approach and objectives in general and simple terms in a masterful way. It must have been persuasive, because I don't believe that there was further trouble from this quarter.

My next and basically last connection with the Marshall Plan was in 1949. After the State Department took over responsibility for the occupation in Germany, I was sent to Germany by agreement between High Commissioner McCloy and Henry Byroade, Director of the Bureau of German Affairs, to begin a process of establishing effective working relations between the staff in Germany and that in Washington. Relations during the military period proved to be extremely difficult and this difficulty had extended to participation in the European Recovery Program.

The European Recovery Act required that the U.S. have a basic agreement to regulate its relations with each recipient country under the program and to ensure its acceptance of the objectives of the program. There being no German government, the United States had a bilateral agreement through the ECA with each of the military governors of the three Western zones of occupation. A complicating factor in relations with the U.S. zone was the fact that the U.S. was also providing basic relief aid as a function of military government, in theory in order to prevent disease and unrest which would threaten the occupation forces. This aid was separately appropriated to the Army by the Congress, and the military authorities were anxious to maximize German foreign exchange earnings and to minimize the need for appropriations under this heading. This led to policies on the part of the U.S. military authorities which created difficulties in the recovery plan. Indeed, it was a popular saying in Washington that the least cooperative member of the Organization for European Economic Cooperation (OEEC) was the U.S. occupation zone in Germany.

With the creation of the government of the Federal Republic in the Western zones after the elections which led to Chancellor Adenauer's accession to power, it became necessary to conclude a bilateral Economic Cooperation Administration (ECA) agreement with the new government, in the first international agreement made by that government. Although the previous agreements with other countries had been negotiated in Washington, the new agreement had to be negotiated in Germany since relations between the German government and the occupying powers were conducted exclusively through the Allied High Commissioners.

Since I happened to be in Germany when this matter came up and since I was familiar with the policy objectives set out in the ECA bilaterals, I was instructed to participate in the negotiations. They were conducted by the ECA mission chief, Norman Collison, and me. We assumed that they would present little difficulty, but received a rude shock when the German negotiators asked us to spell out in detail precisely what was involved in their taking over "the rights and obligations" of the military governors under the previous bilateral agreements, a provision which we had assumed was merely a technical one.

At that point, the skeletons came tumbling out of the closet. The military governors had had a free hand in using the proceeds of the sales of "disease and unrest" aid, known as "local counterpart funds." Under the ECA bilaterals, they were required to obtain the consent of the U.S. Government through the ECA mission to use ECA counterpart funds, as a condition for which they were required to lay out for discussion the economic programs which would be supported by the use of these funds. This was an essential element in the granting of U.S. aid to all (European Recovery Program) ERP aid recipients.

What we discovered was that the military governors had exhausted the counterpart funds which were not subject to the ECA requirement, for some good reasons and also by bad management in handling foreign trade transactions. Unwilling to deal with the ECA mission in exposing their economic policies to discussion, they had gone around the mission and violated their agreements with the U.S. Government by using the ECA counterpart funds indirectly. They did this by borrowing against them from the fledgling German central bank in which the funds were deposited and which was under Allied control, the "Bank Deutscher Laender," which in due course became the present Bundesbank. The scale of what was, in effect, deficit spending by the Military Governors was vast, and the borrowing was still continuing by Allied agencies as we were negotiating. The amount involved rose to 400 million marks.

While Collison and I put a stop to this, what had happened created a major policy issue in our negotiations with the new German Government. The American economic office of the U.S. High Commissioner, a joint ECA/State Department office, had counted on use of the large ECA counterpart balances to launch major projects to stimulate the German economy. One was a major housing program, badly needed to provide housing where industry was being rebuilt. In our negotiations with the Germans on the new bilateral agreement, we proposed to fund the deficit in the military governors' accounts, an obligation which we were asking the German government to take over, by a loan from the central bank. The Germans resisted this, because of an understandable, but basically pathological fear of inflation. The Americans ultimately prevailed. Fortunately, the German fears were unfounded.

ECA aid was used effectively in Germany, and the German economy flourished during the Recovery Program. Exports were stimulated by the undervaluation of the Deutschemark though an exchange rate was established in an agreement with the Allied authorities, who at the time still maintained control over foreign exchange matters, but without discussion in the IMF, of which the Federal Republic was not yet a member. While the German government followed a quite cautious and conservative fiscal policy, the Korean War probably had a stimulating effect on the German economy, and the "German miracle" continued.

Impact of the Marshall Plan—Conclusions

The effects of the Marshall Plan were far-reaching and laid the basis for many subsequent achievements. The immediate objective of meeting the dollar gap crisis was attained. Conditions were created which facilitated the movement of European currencies toward convertibility at a later date and European cooperation in the dismantling of trade barriers in GATT/WTO. The foundations were laid for international economic cooperation, which led to the evolution of the OEEC into the Organization for Economic Cooperation and Development (OECD). An atmosphere was created which helped the transition of French policy toward Germany which was reflected in the Schumann Plan. Perhaps even the origins of the Common Market can be dimly foreseen in the development of the new relationships which were being forged. From a political viewpoint, the Marshall Plan played a decisive role in rolling back the domestic threats of Communist political power, particularly in France and Italy.

It is fashionable from time to time to suggest a new Marshall Plan for dealing with new economic problems which require imaginative solutions. The original plan was tailored to meet the needs of a specific time and situation. Its methods are not readily adaptable to new and different problems half a century later.

What is clear is that the international problems which will confront the world in the coming century will require active and timely American participation in dealing with them, not necessarily by the contribution economic or military resources through a government which is in control of its fiscal and monetary policies. That government will need the support of an informed citizenry. Creating the domestic basis for effective foreign policies is one of the top priorities for American national security.

Notes

1. Paper PPS1.
2. See *Foreign Relations of the U.S.*, 1947, Volume III, p. 514.
3. This document has not apparently been published by the State Department. However, it is presumably included in Anna Kasten Nelson, ed.*The State Department Policy Planning Staff Papers, 1947-1949*, 3 vols., 1983.
4. This group had a formal name, which I forget. Informally, it was known as "The Board of Directors."

France: An Exhilarating Experience

JULIAN S. STEIN, JR.

I will refrain from writing profundities on the impact of the Marshall Plan, leaving such endeavors to those who will eagerly embrace them. I can only say that my good fortune at being hired as an information officer, first for OSR and then in the French Mission, was and has remained, one of the most exciting events of my life.

The sheer thrill of landing at LeHavre, checking in at the Hotel Bristol and reporting the next morning to the Talleyrand are twenty-four hours that are as vivid to me today as they were nearly fifty years ago. The unique smell of Paris—sad to say virtually non-existent today—can still be summoned up from my olfactory memory bank. Finding my place in the scheme of things, looking for a place to live with my wife and child, meeting my information colleagues, and practicing my hitherto hibernating French engaged me in a kaleidoscopic whirlwind of new sights, sounds, and experiences.

And the work itself- challenging and urgent from the start—made me feel that perhaps it was really true that one could become engaged in an endeavor of positive and lasting significance for humankind. Involvement with the French press, putting out the magazine *Rapports*, burrowing into the highways and byways of France to further the objectives of the productivity program, and the mobile exhibits were immeasurably rewarding assignments. The American press corps in Paris, the people I worked with—Tom Wilson, Harold Kaplan, Roscoe Drummond, Wally Nielsen, Ned Brandt, Sam Rosenberg, George Bernier and many others—

who are all friends as well as colleagues, contributed to a heady existence. As a part of the productivity program, I marveled to see individuals of French management and labor literally astounded to report they had seen American managers roll up their sleeves and actually join their employees on the factory floor.

I even survived what seemed at the time a free fall in a coal hoist one mile deep into the Borinage, only to be confronted there by emaciated ex-Polish prisoners of the Germans who weren't exactly sure whether the war had ended.

I, like my information colleagues, was new to government service, and I quickly and happily learned that the Marshall Plan was unlike your standard government bureaucracy. New ideas were encouraged and welcomed, red tape was virtually non-existent. Moreover, you were left alone to get the job done. Almost everyone I worked with had come from the private sector and intended to return to it in the near future.

Life in Paris was a delight. My three-year-old child learned to speak French, even though it was the Patois spoken by the concierge's children. I learned to drink wine with meals. I walked and walked all over Paris; I reveled in the difference and the sameness of each street and boulevard. I soaked up scenes, the cafes, the traffic, the Seine, the night life. The Marshall Plan created not the ugly American but the welcomed American. Finally, there was the joy of driving in the country, watching the sun shining through the poplars after a rain.

In short, my life was changed. I not only came to appreciate the Europeans and what they had endured, I also became a better and more effective American. The Marshall Plan touched and improved many lives. I am grateful that mine was one of them.

Those Who Made the
Stabilization Program a Success

JAMES C. WARREN JR.

Nineteen forty-seven and forty-eight may have been the dawn of the Marshall Plan in Western Europe—and with that the dawn of the rebirth of hope—but for Greece it was a period of unrelieved calamity. The country was literally broke. Foreign exchange earnings covered less than one-third of civilian foreign exchange needs. Meanwhile, the communist-led rebels stuck the dispirited Greek National Army with impunity while the political establishment in Athens fiddled and the merchant/industrialist elite hid their inflated profits in gold sovereigns.

Nevertheless, the situation was not only stabilized by 1949, but had turned around by 1952, and a new, secure and prosperous equilibrium was achieved by 1954. From that base, or starting point, Greece went on, essentially on its own, to rack up almost the best growth record over the next decade and a half of any country in the OECD, save Japan and Germany.

What had made the difference were the American programs which supported the Greek Armed Forces, fed, clothed, and fueled the Greek nation, supported the balance of payments, and at the same time invested in the reconstruction of the heavily damaged pre-war Greek economic sinews. Through additional Marshall Plan-financed investment, the development process was extended, raising living standards to a level 50% above prewar levels. Finally, in the last chapter of what had been a program of massive U.S. assistance, a rigorous currency stabilization effort was engineered, with currency reform and devaluation as its ultimate goal.

I believe that my several, youthful years with the Marshall Plan (I was 22 years old and just out of college when I joined the ECA Mission to Greece) have left me with a distorted view of the U.S. government and of governmental processes in general: for we had a goal; we had fire in our bellies; we worked like hell; we had tough, disciplined thinking; and we could program, strive for and see results.

If the gentle reader here detects a wistful, nostalgic, perhaps invidious note creeping into these recherches du temps perdu, I should have to confess that he is not entirely wrong. Look at the record: between the end of the Second World War and the beginning of ERP, the United States dribbled $15 billion into uncoordinated relief & rehabilitation efforts in Western Europe with nothing to show for it. The winter of 1947-48 was a crisis of frightening severity. By contrast, the concatenation of disciplined, structured programs which we call the Marshall Plan expended a slightly lesser sum, $13 billion, and got results that confounded even the optimists! The difference lay in results-oriented planning of a tough and imaginative, taut and inspired character. And there was another difference: there was a certain "moral authority."

There is occasional talk these days of "recreating a Marshall Plan" for Eastern Europe and the former Soviet Union, and perhaps there really is such a strategic need. Certainly we have been leaking monies into the old Soviet bloc countries at a very substantial rate in a fashion similar to those efforts undertaken immediately after the Second World War and before ERP. But there appears to be little analysis in this loose talk, certainly no program accounting, and it appears to be little more than attractive propaganda to shore up the flagging bureaucratic fortunes of USAID. The results, if one is to rely upon newspaper reporting, are simply awful, and USAID possesses no moral authority whatsoever. If indeed one were to be serious about a coordinated recovery and development plan for the former Soviet bloc, the first step would have to be USAID's termination, simply taken out root and branch.

"We Have Met the Enemy, and He is Us" or The Marshall Plan's Currency Stabilization Program in Greece and What it Did, Not to the Greek People But to the American Proconsuls

One of the structural problems of the American program of aid to Greece was that there was such a merry-go-round at the top: seven Mission

Chiefs in seven years and, in parallel, an almost equally rapid succession of men holding the post of Principal Economic Advisor to the Chief. This was a prescription for eventual trouble, for it sometimes meant a loss of command and direction and balance in the programming. It also placed excessive power in the hands of the necessarily more parochial money-spending division heads (agriculture, public health, industry, labor, mining, transportation, and so forth). Many of these men had been in place for a long time and could, as a consequence, talk circles around the newcomers. Each of these division heads—by and large good, creative, progressive New Dealers with a sense of a leadership and a creative role for progressive government—developed "his" program to "transform" Greece; to lift "his" constituents, "his" Greek peasants out of the dust. And, by God, he was going to drive that program forward to completion. He had been transmogrified into a proconsul/advocate/special pleader instead of cool, dispassionate, expert reviewer and advisor. It became very personal.

And so it was that when the Maiatico Building HQ imposed on the Marshall Plan for Greece a formal and tough currency stabilization program, it was the Americans, the division heads of the mission, who howled most loudly. (It was perhaps an anomaly of the Greek program that the main line of communication and authority ran, not from Paris (OSR/SRE) to Athens, but from Washington to Athens.) They simply could not accept the notion that the whole, a national currency of real worth, was to be deemed more important than the sum of the parts, sectoral investment and development programs and projects. The conflict became a near-revolt, carrying with it the then incumbent Mission Chief who at one point actually tendered his resignation. These were not just bureaucratic skirmishes. The battle emerged from heartfelt beliefs. The Mission Division Heads, the American Proconsuls of Greek Agriculture, Industry Labor and Land Reclamations, felt very strongly that what they were doing for Greece was being subverted by Washington bean-counters who knew nothing of Greece itself and Greece's real needs. And in their battle they found allies in both the Embassy and the State Department.

The Embassy did not understand the stabilization program. In a very real sense they were terrified of it, and their colleagues in State were equally uncomprehending. Together, they did everything possible to scuttle the Program. The Ambassador himself even maneuvered to have the officers on the Greek Desk in the Marshall Plan Headquarters fired!

The stabilization program, however, prevailed. And if this memoir has a purpose, it is to do honor to the three men who were really the authors of that effort and who were steadfast and effective in piloting the program through some very difficult shoals, Ed Tenenbaum, Frank Mahon and Victor Sullam. Each of the three brought special talents to the task. They were wonderful fellows, emblematic of the spirit, zest, brains, drive and disciplined inspiration, which to me was the very essence of the Marshall Plan in action.

Ed Tenenbaum was a great big bear of a fellow and, of the three men, his was the role of brilliant "technician." He had been the principal author of the German currency reform of June 1948. Despite a technical prowess of the kind that makes most people's eyes glaze over, Ed possessed an additional exceptional, extraordinary talent: he could speak and write to lay audiences like an angel. He possessed a rare ability to treat abstruse, complex economic matters in terms that were fluid, fluent, and comprehensible.

I shall call Vic Sullam here the "enforcer." He knew exactly the levers of bureaucratic power which were available to him and which would be essential in developing, and then holding, the stabilization program in the face of well-entrenched adversaries. He could be, by turns, either witty and charming, or mean as a billy-goat, and he lined up an unbreakable phalanx behind the program.

Frank Mahon's great gift was that he invented something that converted good intentions into practical results. The word "stabilization," a policy-level code word for fiscal and monetary restraint to slow down and perhaps even cure the dread disease of inflation, had appeared in literally hundreds of messages and cables flying back and forth between Athens and Washington. And this had been true in every one of the years of the American program in Greece, going all the way back to 1947. Yet in practice, the policy injunction had been violated right and left. It was not a case of outright insubordination. It is just that the word was too squishy. It left room for "judgment," for "best efforts," for "promises." And the "judgements" and the "best efforts," piled one on top of the other, meaning simply that too much money was being pumped into the Greek economy. Suppressed, potentially explosive inflation and worse was being partially concealed by the U.S.-sanctioned import and public sale in Greece of British Gold Sovereigns which came from the Fed in New York City. Even as late as January 1952, we were on the precipice of a national, total repudiation of the Greek drachma as panic drove the gold rush.

It was Frank Mahon who put spine into the word "stabilization" and thereby brought an end to the gold psychosis. He did so with an invention that was remarkably simple, both in concept and in use. It was the "Inflationary/ Deflationary Balance Sheet." It was a tool for quantitative monetary and fiscal management and left little room for "promises" or evasion. It worked brilliantly.

Frank would be with us all today were it not for the fact that he is just getting over a bout of pneumonia. Vic and Ed, I am so sorry to say, both died twenty years ago—much too young. Tonight at our reception for all the old Marshall Plan war-horses, I propose to raise a toast to Frank and to the memory of great, exciting days; great camaraderie; and, the great work accomplished by the Marshall Plan.

Personal Retrospectives

IV. The Marshall Plan and the People

Waldemar A. Nielsen
Information to Win Public Support and Sustain Morale
Albert M. Prosterman
The Caravan of Modern Merchandising and Other Inventions
Ralph L. Trisko
From Europe to Asia
John D. Walker
Encouraging Democratic labor Movements
Herbert E. Weiner
Observations on Labor and the Marshall Plan

Information to Win Public Support and Sustain Morale

WALDEMAR A. NIELSEN

My recollections of the Marshall Plan begin in the months immediately after General Marshall's speech at Harvard in June 1947 and the passage of the authorizing legislation by Congress soon thereafter.

I was a special assistant to Averell Harriman and Bill Foster at the Commerce Department at the time, and Averell undertook a very active part in the effort to persuade the American public to support the proposed program. This was a period when isolationism was a strong influence in many parts of the country, particularly the Mid-West and the Far West.

Averell, after his earlier experience as Ambassador to the Soviet Union, was a passionate supporter of the Marshall Plan proposal. Almost immediately, he took off on a relentless personal campaign of speech-making to inform the public about the urgency of the problems in Western Europe and the great need for American initiative to give some financial assistance, to rebuild morale and to encourage Western European cooperation, even integration. If such an effort were not made, he acutely feared the possibility of Soviet and communist advances in the region.

He was not the world's greatest public speaker, as those of you who knew him, or heard him, will attest. But he was deeply committed and indefatigable in his efforts of advocacy in that period when the Marshall proposal was being debated.

We traveled the country together in the old DC-3 Department of Commerce plane as he made his personal all-out effort to help win public support for it. We made at least three stops every day for several weeks, a breakfast speech, a luncheon speech, and a dinner one, in places in the Mid- and Far-West, ranging from Chicago, home of the influential isolationist *Tribune*, and Los Angeles, to stops like Fargo, North Dakota; Boise, Idaho; Walla Walla, Washington; and Ottumwa, Iowa; Denver, Colorado; Kansas City, and other places.

For every one of these stops, Averell compulsively wanted to make changes and adjustments to his basic appeal, and to back up his case with the latest data available. I vividly remember one night as we flew over the Rockies in an electrical storm, just after he had finished a speech in Utah. Averell was pressing me to add in the latest figures on the drop in Britain's gold reserves for his next speech in Iowa, while lightning flashed along the wings of the old DC 3.

We had been on the go eighteen straight hours at that point, and the plane was bouncing like a basketball. So I suggested we might put the papers aside and get some sleep, since we had a breakfast stop where he had to give another talk.

"Oh, all right," he said, "if you are a little tired." By then, I think I was already asleep.

With the benefit of his efforts and those of a good many others at the time, the legislation was passed, and a new phase of our work began.

As soon as the program was authorized, he was named to head its European aspect. He then moved quickly to assemble a staff—Bill Foster as his deputy, Milt Katz from Harvard as General Counsel, and other distinguished appointees.

It was in that context that he asked me to serve as his special assistant and as Deputy Director of the European public information program, whose first head would be Al Friendly, then managing editor of the *Washington Post*. In less than two months a Continent wide program to explain and help implement the recovery program was underway.

The mandate for the program was very broad. Our task would be to keep the American public fully informed about the progress of the European recovery in order to help sustain its political support. It was also to keep the European public informed of the progress of the recovery effort to help rebuild morale and encourage European cooperation and collaboration.

Perhaps more than any other senior figure in the program, Harriman was aware that the problems of European economic reconstruction were only in part financial and material. They were equally psychological and political. I recall the day a senior Soviet general made a speech in Poland that was in effect a Russian declaration of all-out political and propaganda war against the Marshall Plan. Harriman called me in immediately afterward and expressed his deep concern.

"If we can not restore some hope and confidence here along with some economic recovery" he said, "then Italy and France and maybe even Germany will go down the drain. And that will be a political catastrophe that could shake the world. The job of your program is to help keep that from happening."

Bill Foster put the point to me in even fewer words. "One thing I have learned already on this job," he said in one of our early conversations in Paris, "is that there is a hell of a lot more to the job of economic recovery than just economics."

I remembered those words again and again in the following weeks. There were violent communist-led demonstrations every day along the rue St. Florentin when we moved our temporary headquarters from the Embassy annex to the Talleyrand. We had to fight our way through the protesters' lines to get to our offices for a week. And for a good many days thereafter, the noise of angry crowds of demonstrators in the narrow street beside our building could be heard as we tried to work.

Shortly thereafter, a wave of Communist-led strikes in the coal fields of Northern France left the factories of the country idle and our homes and offices cold for many days, a sharp reminder of the political realities in which our efforts had to operate.

One of the effects of the outbreak of strikes on the information effort was to strengthen our "Labor Information Program" directed to the non-communist labor unions of Europe. It was headed by Harry Martin and John Hutchison, two experienced journalists who were leaders of the American journalists trade union.

Information and Labor Information officers were installed in all the major Western European countries as the program was quickly put in full operation. In every major industrial Marshall Plan country vigorous initiatives were taken, in cooperation with the Labor Division, under Boris Shishkin. Close collaboration was also developed with the European Association of Free Trade Unions and with representatives of both the AFL and the CIO from the United States. In time, the fear and panic generated by the communist labor offensive was decisively overcome. This was one of the less publicized but very effective initiatives of the Marshall Plan in Europe.

At the Information Program headquarters in Paris, a full apparatus of media services was assembled: a Press office under Sid Fine, to service the American and the European press; a documentary film unit under Lothar Wolff; a radio section under James Fleming, a photography section under Sam Rosenberg; an exhibits section under the architect and designer Peter Harnden; and an opinion research section under Ruth Sivard. All these creative individuals, after their service in the Marshall Plan, became notable figures in their fields, film, television, radio, architecture, and social research in the United States.

Among the outstanding information officers installed in the major capitals of Europe were Frank Gervasi in Italy, Walter Ridder in Germany, Tom Wilson in Paris, and Abe Sirkin in London, all journalists of outstanding reputation.

In Paris, Al Friendly served as director of the program the first year and then had to return to Washington. He was succeeded as director by Roscoe Drummond, a columnist of powerful influence from the *Christian Science Monitor*, and after his return, I headed the program for its last two years.

A few of the program's highlights and accomplishments: the press section won the highest praise from the leading journalists and broadcasters of that time, Eric Sevareid, Walter Cronkite, Edward Marrow, Charles Collingwood, and many others. Theodore H. White called it the finest press office the U.S. government ever had.

The documentary film unit under the great Lothar Wolff, who had been the chief editor of the *March of Time*, produced some 125 documentary films of the outstanding recovery projects in Europe. They were shown to millions of Europeans, won numerous prizes, and are now in the U.S. National Archives in Washington.

For radio, dozens of programs broadcast regularly throughout Europe were produced. They became extraordinarily popular, and one of them made a particular impact on farm productivity. Called "The Answer Man," it was based on an American program of the same name. It was broadcast daily in several languages. In response to questions mailed in from listeners, it provided practical information to farmers about new methods of improving their crops and productivity. It also reported on the progress of various recovery projects throughout Western Europe. Our research showed that it drew millions of regular listeners, and the volume of mail we received confirmed that impact.

A program of traveling exhibitions was also developed, some mounted on trucks, some on canal barges, that traveled through the smaller communities of the region. Conceived by architect and designer Peter Harnden, it combined the spirit of a carnival with solid information about the progress of the recovery program and about new ideas for increasing agricultural production.

To engage families in every part of the region, including the major cities, a program of Children's Art Competitions was organized. School children were invited to paint pictures of any new recovery project that was improving life in their localities. Thousands entered and modest prizes were awarded for the winners selected in each province, followed by higher country-wide awards, and finally grand prizes for the Marshall Plan area as a whole.

Selections were made by committees of art teachers. The winning pictures in all categories proved to be charming and original in ways never anticipated. In the drabness of life in the region at the time, newspapers and magazines throughout Western Europe eagerly printed them in full color so they were seen by millions of viewers. As a result, the Marshall Plan got a flood of heartwarming responses which were never anticipated.

Individual country projects also proved valuable. For example, a special Marshall Plan magazine was published in France, containing everything from advice to farmers to reports on the progress being made in economic recovery. It was so well done and was so well received that it became the most widely circulated publication in the country in those years.

At least as important as any of these media projects in terms of industrial recovery and production was the special "Labor Information Program," headquartered in Paris and operative in the major industrialized countries of Western Europe.

It was specifically a counter effort to the huge Soviet-backed drive to sabotage the recovery program by the organized agitation of the many powerful Communist-led trade unions, especially in France, Italy, and Germany.

The Labor Information Program was led by Harry Martin and John Hutchison, two leaders of the American CIO newspaper employees union. Working in close cooperation with the non-communist trade unions of Western Europe, the program made a solid contribution to European industrial peace and productivity and thereby to economic recovery.

After Al Friendly and Roscoe Drummed returned to the United States, I was given leadership of the Information Program for its last two years. At that time a new element was added, namely a drive to increase European industrial productivity by disseminating information about new American techniques of plant organization, worker motivation, and collaborative efforts on behalf of greater output.

The program, led by a Chicago industrialist, Bill Joyce, was generally applauded as a significant contributor both to labor peace and to industrial output in Western Europe in the final years of the Marshall Plan.

Speaking personally for myself and my wife, Marcia, and, I believe, for all of us who served to carry out the Marshall Plan, the whole four year effort was a glorious and deeply satisfying adventure. It was service in accomplishing an important historical objective. I think it improved not only the morale but the well-being of Europeans. And it helped consolidate the democratic character of the countries of Western Europe. It surely provided the basis for the considerable progress and social peace in Western Europe since then.

For us and all who participated in it, it was an opportunity to serve an important historical objective. It was a noble experience of working with talented and highly motivated colleagues in eighteen countries on behalf of the effort of a great civilization to recover and rebuild itself after a terrible war and to defeat an effort to destroy democracy and impose totalitarian control over that region.

I was a naval officer for four years of desperately hard and dangerous service in the Pacific in World War II. And I have had very gratifying experiences in my work in business, philanthropy and public service ever since. But nothing compares in drama, adventure, and deep satisfaction to those four wonderful years of the Marshall Plan, a truly a glorious historical moment.

The Caravan of
Modern Merchandising
and Other Inventions

ALBERT M. PROSTERMAN

I served in Paris 1952-1954 as chief of the Marketing Branch of the Productivity and Technical Assistance Division of United States Representative Office (USRO). The division was headed by Everett Bellows at first and then by Don McPhail. My connection with the Marshall Plan, however, began much earlier than 1952. In fact I was involved even before it was enacted into law.

In the autumn of 1947 I was in London attending the first post-war meeting of the International Sugar Council representing the Food and Agriculture Organization of the UN (FAO), which was then headquartered in Washington. My director was Denis A. Fitzgerald who later became, after Paul Hoffman, the head of the Marshall Plan agency. Fitzgerald asked me to stay on in London for a few weeks to brief and advise a group of U.S. congressman who were in London to evaluate the need in England and Europe for the proposed Marshall Plan. I do not believe my role was of earthshaking importance, but I must not have done any harm since the enabling legislation for the Marshall Plan was approved later.

In 1948 the FAO moved to Rome. Denis Fitzgerald was named director of the Food and Agriculture Division of the new Marshall Plan and, as mentioned, eventually became head of the agency.

I went back to the Foreign Economic Agency at the Department of Commerce, where I headed a branch which had a contract with the

Marshall Plan to develop technical assistance programs in the U.S. for Europeans studying American methods of marketing and distribution.

Late in 1951, Ev Bellows recruited me to come to Paris and head up a branch in his division. We would essentially do the mirror image of my work in the States, that is, conduct a program in the field of marketing and distributing technical assistance, bringing American specialists in to participate with their business counterparts in the Marshall Plan countries. Also, we set up demonstration projects showing how new methods worked and how they could help in the war devastated countries.

One of the most innovative of the projects which I supervised had its genesis before I came to Europe. This was called the Caravan of Modern Merchandising. It was an actual small traveling super market stocked with the merchandise of the country it was in. The exhibit would be set up in a city in Europe for several days and made open to the public and trades people, then dismantled and set up elsewhere.

Along with the exhibit went five U.S. specialists in various food and grocery fields who spoke to trades people and demonstrated the advantages and economies in modern packaging and self-service. This exhibit eventually visited over 200 European cities.

It is hard now to realize that at that time self service marketing was virtually non-existent in Europe and the costs of distribution were excessively high. I believe that this project was conceived by George Lindahl, who preceded me in this work. In any case, it was a major success, and the precursor to the remarkable development of low cost distribution in all of the Western European countries.

Looking back, it was relatively easy to engage and work with the Europeans. They were eager to learn, and as we all know, they soon equaled and even surpassed the U.S. in many areas. Yet I believe, and there is a case that can be made, that without the timely stimulus and helping hand in all fields, Western Europe might never have recovered in the direction and to the extent that it has.

Essential to this whole process was the really brilliant concept of counterpart funds, making funds available for trade balance needs, yet making certain that everything that the people and governments needed had to be paid for in local currencies. This avoided the deadening aspects of outright giving. Dozens of times I was told by Europeans that the Marshall Plan wasn't giving anything because everything had to be paid for. It was difficult to explain that they were in fact getting something.

The Marshall Plan was a noble enterprise and I am proud to have been a part of it. However, along with all this nobility most of us managed to have fun and generally we ate well, even outside of France.

Years after I returned to the U.S., I met one of the younger men who had worked in my branch. After the usual reminiscences, he said to me "Before I left France you gave me some of the most valuable advice I got while abroad." My chest swelled and I preened myself, thinking that finally my wisdom had been recognized. I said "Well, John, what was it that I told you?" He said, "You told me that the best place to find good veal in the U.S. was in a Kosher butcher shop."

From Europe to Asia

RALPH L. TRISKO

M y direct experience with the Marshall Plan in Europe and in
Washington commenced in February 1948 when I was assigned
by the State Department to Geneva as Coal Advisor to the U.S. Delegation
to the Economic Commission for Europe (ECE), a regional body of the
United Nations. In that assignment I served as a representative of the
United States to the Coal Committee of the ECE and its subcommittees.
Simultaneously, I had similar functions in the Coal Committee of the
Organization for European Economic Cooperation in Paris, and as a
member of the Coal Branch of the Marshall Plan headquarters in Europe,
the Office of the Special U.S. Representative (OSR).

Coal supplies were critically short in Europe after the war, due to
the destruction of production and transport facilities, as well as normal
distribution facilities. The restoration of coal supplies was essential to
the economic recovery of Europe. The U.S. had a leading role to play in
alleviating the crisis as a major coal producer and exporter; as a member
of the Tri-Partite Coal Control Group with France and Britain—which
controlled the distribution of Ruhr coal production in occupied West
Germany—as a major source of technical and supply aid to European
coal producers; and, as the marginal source of financial aid under the
Marshall Plan.

The Coal Committee of the ECE and the OEEC were key organizations in the distribution of U.S. and European coal supplies, including
Polish coal exports to Western Europe. Although not a Marshall Plan
participant, Poland was a member of the ECE and its Coal Committee,
as were the members of the OEEC. Members of the ECE had established
a voluntary cooperative regime of agreement among them for the quar-

terly allocation of coal supplies, including Ruhr coal exports, which the Tri-Partite powers placed at the disposal of the allocation process.

The operations of the ECE Coal Committee were performed by a highly competent international secretariat that had the confidence of the members and assisted in the negotiation of the allocation agreements among the members. When voted on by the Coal Committee of the ECE, the agreements were adopted by the Coal Committee of the OEEC. Thus a rather meaningful but little known collaboration existed between the two international organizations and their members.

The benefits were mutual. Poland was a traditional exporter of coal to Western Europe and needed the foreign exchange earnings from continuing such exports, while the Western European countries needed Polish coal. When Yugoslavia broke with the Soviet Union in 1948, its supplies of Soviet coal were cut off and it requested an allocation of Ruhr coal from the ECE Coal Committee, which was approved by the members.

In 1950, I was transferred to the Economic Cooperation Administration from the Department of State and served as chief of the OSR Coal branch. The Coal branch was responsible for U. S. Representation on the OEEC Coal Committee and its subcommittees, including Coal Allocation, Production and so forth. It collaborated with and supported the country missions and ECA Washington on the administration of ECA coal related programs, including the supply of American coal to Marshall Plan countries.

I served briefly as Chairman of the OEEC Coal Committee until early in 1951 when I was detached from my duties with OSR, at the request of the Secretary General of the of the OEEC, who requested my service as a consultant to him on coal. Later that year, I was transferred to ECA Washington to serve as chief of the Central Europe branch (West Germany, Austria, and Yugoslavia). By then Marshall Plan programs were winding down, the Korean War had started, and the emphasis of U.S. foreign assistance programs was shifting to more direct support of American security interests. ECA became the Mutual Security Agency. President Truman's Point Four Program, with its focus on technical and economic aid to developing countries soon following, was administered by the Foreign Operations Administration. The MSA then became the International Cooperation Administration.

I continued to serve with the foreign assistance agencies until 1962, when I resigned from my position in the International Cooperation Administration, as Chief of the South Asia Division, after having served in India as Assistant Director of the U.S. Economic and Technical Assistance Mission. Thus I participated in and experienced first-hand the evolution of our foreign assistance policies and programs in the years from my departure from Europe in 1951 to my resignation in 1962. My observations pertaining to my experience with the Marshall Plan in Europe are written from that perspective, as well as the viewpoint of the unfortunate consequences of policies pursued after World War I. The Marshall Plan is generally regarded as having been remarkably successful in the achievement of its objectives of European economic recovery after World War II; the creation of institutions of economic cooperation, such as the Organization for European Economic Cooperation; and, the adoption of free trade policies by the participating countries. The Plan was completed ahead of schedule for less than its estimated cost. Its benefits in terms of improved relations among the participant countries, policy reforms that encouraged competition, and closer European unity will be felt indefinitely.

The success of the Marshall Plan may be attributed to several factors, of which perhaps the most important was the soundness of the principles stated by George Marshall himself in his founding speech at Harvard University. American aid was to be conditioned on actions and commitments by the recipient countries to share resources, cooperate with each other to jointly plan the use of their and U. S. resources made available under the Plan, and develop an overall plan on which Marshall Plan assistance would be based.

A selective bilateral approach to planning American aid to European countries would have been unrealistic, and would have encouraged the historic nationalistic tendencies of the individual countries. The emphasis on the Marshall Plan principles of joint planning of resources and policies would move the disparate countries into a European framework and away from policies and practices associated with almost continuous hostilities and warfare that had persisted for centuries. After the most destructive war in European and world history, European countries were probably ready for the changes embodied in the Marshall Plan. Fortunately, they had the leadership to put them into practice.

The Europeans themselves were largely responsible for the success of the Marshall Plan. They had well-developed political and economic institutions; a largely well-educated and well-trained people; and, a strong will to rebuild what had been destroyed in the War. A reverence for their own history also played an important part.

Unlike most successor foreign aid programs, the Marshall Plan had a definable, measurable, and achievable goal. The U.S. was the only realistic source of external resources required to accomplish this and give Europe the confidence it needed in its own future. The public interest of the U.S. in the economic recovery of Europe was identical to that of the European countries themselves. Anti-democratic forces were asserting themselves and threatening political instability. The U.S. motivation was seen as broadly based on the political and economic well-being of Europe itself, rather than narrower nationalistic interests and U.S. aid was offered and administered accordingly.

In my experience in Europe I saw and participated in the administration of the Marshall Plan, working closely with a number of European nations and their institutions, living with and observing the realization of George Marshall's ideals and principles. I never observed or experienced anything but genuine respect, trust, friendship and acceptance by our European colleagues.

Beyond its immediate program objectives of economic recovery, its major impact was the impetus it gave to European initiatives toward closer unity among themselves on economic and political affairs, including integration. The OEEC, now the OECD, was the forerunner, followed by the European Coal and Steel Community, the European Union with its parliament, and now the establishment of a common currency.

However, its implications for future foreign assistance policies and programs, however are problematic. The Marshall Plan occurred at a unique time in modern history, and under unusual circumstances. The Korean and Cold wars and their impact on foreign policy and assistance programs has already been mentioned. They continue to have an impact on foreign aid policies and priorities. In recent decades, more emphasis has been given to use of foreign aid to support the American economy, military assistance, and the financing of military equipment exports.

The U.S. is now confronted with a complex of foreign policy problems for which economic assistance may be an appropriate response, but for which the experience of the Marshall Plan is less appropriate than it was at the time. Conflicts between countries are an obstacle to regional cooperation, but they are less susceptible to modification within the framework of U.S. foreign aid programs.

For example, when I was serving as Chief of the South Asia Division in ICA in 1960-62, our fiscal year budget submission to the director of the Agency and the Budget Review Committee included a proposal for the initiation of modest use of our budget for South Asia to promote greater regional cooperation. It was presented to the director and the Committee and was dismissed without discussion.

Encouraging Democratic Labor Movements

JOHN D. WALKER

In July 1948, I joined the staff of Ambassador Harriman as Assistant Director of the European Labor Division under the brilliant direction of Boris Shishkin. The leaders of the various Divisions came from ranging backgrounds, but they were nearly all involved and motivated by a sense of purpose, easily approachable, and willing to exchange ideas and suggestions. At that time, the United States and Americans in Paris were well received by European countries participating in the program. Shishkin compensated for his lack of managerial abilities by giving his staff wide latitude in implementing their own agendas. One of the major activities that I carried out was to obtain Shishkin's blessing for projects I had in mind, or were already being carried out.

This was a time when the hold of communist organizations posed a serious threat to democracy. In a very interesting atmosphere, I met many leaders of these organizations, which proved to be of great interest and, sometimes, value. On one occasion, we sent two members of the communist dominated French Trade Union, the CGT, to the United States on a trade union exchange. We somehow sneaked them through the scrutiny which would have denied them visas. One came back, left the CGT, and became a leader in the "free trade union" movement. The other said he now realized how bad the U.S. was in comparison to the vaunted Soviet Union. (We cannot win them all.)

In addition to the regular staff, many recent graduates of outstanding universities had joined the Marshall Plan, beginning their careers as messengers for the OSR. As Harriman remarked, "We have the worst messenger service with the highest IQ of any messenger service in the world." Nearly without exception, they read most of the messages directed to a division, offered free advice, and quickly moved on to work for the division most appealing to them.

Another example, was that of a large steel mill which had requested a loan, not a grant. This company had one of the highest percentage of communist-dominated labor force in Europe, and coincidentally, one of the highest industrial accident rates. We stated that the loan would be granted only if conditions were improved. This condition was fulfilled. The loan was granted and the communist presence disappeared almost overnight. This led a small group of us to approach Harriman to start a technical assistance program. Continuing successes led to a wide expansion of the program.

In conclusion, I would like to mention a personal aspect of the Marshall Plan which aptly captures what was accomplished over time. I idolized Ambassador David Bruce and desperately wanted to meet him at an international trade union conference we were both attending. Bruce's secretary consented. When we arrived, the secretary remarked quite pointedly in front of the ambassador, "Don't forget, you only have five minutes." Bruce stared at her, and talked to me, an unimportant person, for nearly half an hour and then walked to the front door of the embassy with me. I departed, awe-struck, by his reception. I never forgot this encounter, nor the Marshall Plan which had indirectly made the meeting possible. Some years later, Amb. David Bruce became his country's Foreign Minister and proffered a secure and firm relationship with the United States.

Observations on Labor and the Marshall Plan

HERBERT E. WEINER[1]

A n assignment to London at the end of 1947 thrust me willy nilly into
the middle of the Marshall Plan and into an area of the Marshall
Plan, specifically the role of labor, which is little spoken about now but
which has been a very important part of American diplomacy since the
end of World War II. I find, however, that there are considerable
misconceptions about the Marshall Plan itself and about the role of labor
in the Marshall Plan.

Promoting Democracy as a Foreign Policy Goal

As I recall it, the two most important perceptions that existed right
after World War II were that people had a clear recollection of World
War I and its aftermath and nobody wanted to repeat the mistakes which
had been made. The term, "return to normalcy," which had been popular
after World War I, became a phrase of derision after World War II.

After World War I there was mass unemployment and poor currency
conversion arrangements. People thought of the period after World War
I as being a time of heavy unemployment and social pain. to my personal
knowledge, by the end of World War II, plans had already been drawn
up by the British government, for what you might call "a brave new
world."

It may be not be popular today in terms of current political
perspectives, but there was at that time tremendous support throughout
Britain for a break with the past in economic and social policy and therefore

for the Labour Party. In the United States two things were recognized: one, the United States was now an international power whether it wanted to be or not; isolationism was out. Two, the government had to play a larger role in the economy because the individual did not have very much influence or control over serious social and economic problems, but did have the pain.

A lot of that increased government involvement had started under Roosevelt with the Social Security System and so forth. There was a great deal of suspicion among working people about governments and doubts about the benefits of the free market system. Roosevelt recognized early on that he needed the support of working people in the United States for his domestic policies.

It was also recognized that if American foreign policy were going to be successful, it had to concentrate on several things. First, the guiding political principle in our foreign policy was that we did not want a resurgence of dictatorships. In those days, the issue was a resurgence of a Nazi Germany, a Fascist Italy or a militaristic Japan. These were the targets. The Soviet Union was considered to be our ally, not one with which we were particularly happy, but a convenient ally. I remember well the remark Churchill once made: "I would get in bed with the devil if he is on my side." The point was that politically there was to be no return to dictatorships of any sort, and the promotion of democracy became enshrined in American foreign policy as an objective. The feeling was that wars are bred in a crucible of dictatorship, and that democratic governments are unlikely to go to war.

Secondly, there had to be economic growth; and thirdly, the benefits of this economic growth should go to the whole population. We could not have extremes of rich and poor. If a country is going to be unified and economically vibrant, everybody has to feel that he or she is benefiting from economic growth; everybody had to feel that he or she could participate politically; and everybody has to feel that he or she is a free individual

Within that framework, there were subsets, for example, the feeling that you had to obviate war in Europe. And there was much also public discussion of an old issue, namely the unification of Europe. People saw the United States of America as prosperous, big, and vibrant. What if it had a counterpart in Europe, say a United States of Europe? Ours was not a new idea. It had been advocated at the end of World War I as well.

The argument ran that by integrating the economies in Europe, and more particularly weaving together the German and French economies, you would reduce a major cause of the wars in Europe that had taken place for a whole century before. Economic integration would eliminate a source of war in Europe and it would also promote economic growth through a more effective division of labor, the creation of large markets, and mass production. These would be good things.

There is a tendency today to say that promoting democracy is our newest foreign policy goal. Democracy has been an active, specific part of the foreign policy of the United States since the end of World War II. We have an interest in it. That doesn't mean that every democratic government is going to be friendly. Some will be friendlier than others at various times. But by democracy we are not just talking about a parliamentary process. We are talking about building institutions that have a stake in democracy for their existence, and would collectively constitute a sort of balance of power in society. Sometimes some groups would be more influential than others, but there would be others to offset them.

The labor aspect became very important right after World War II and everybody could see the need. I recall my arrival in London. I was amazed. We had not really suffered in the United States during the war. As a matter of fact, we had done very well. There had been a tremendous expansion of the economy. The standard of living in the United States was higher after the war than before the war. The gross national product, I think, was just about double what it had been. Unemployment had disappeared. Real wages were up. Whole new industries had developed.

In Britain, you could see there was destruction. London was in rubble. If you went to a restaurant to eat, you had the choice of having bread or a "sweet" (dessert) with your meal; and there was a five shilling limit on the charge for a meal. I remember one time soon after I arrived, one of the fellows said, "Let's go to lunch." I said, "Where?" "Oh, well, there's a bombed out movie theater, and the only thing left is the lobby. They have turned the lobby into a little restaurant." So despite all the rubble, there was a feeling of optimism. There was a feeling you had to do something. Not only want to do, but can do.

The Importance of Productivity

My real education in economics came in London on a very interesting day, February 12, 1948. The House of Commons had been destroyed during the blitz when the Germans were sending the VE rockets over London, so the House of Commons was meeting in the old House of

Lords and there were very few seats for outsiders. The House of Commons was having a great debate on economic policy, in particular, on incomes policy. I was the assistant to the Labor Attache and I was sent there to see whether the government would get the cooperation of the trade unions to restrain wage demands, to work longer hours, and to reduce or eliminate strikes. A big claim to power of the Labour government was that it had the confidence of working people, so that a Labor government could ask for restraint and sacrifices. A Tory government, on the other hand, would not have had that kind of confidence, and that confidence was essential. And so I went to the House of Commons. We had only one ticket in the embassy, and I was given that very treasured ticket.

The debate in the House began at 11 am and went on until 10 pm in the evening. I sat there afraid to give up my seat, crunched in the gallery of the House of Lords, leaning over the rail; and I saw an all-star show of some of the greatest economic and political minds of the day. I heard Sir Stafford Cripps, who was Chancellor of the Exchequer and then considered a brilliant political and economic mind, lay out what a British economic policy of restraint should be. The issue was restraints on wages, prices, and profits. The theory behind the policy was that everybody had to restrain themselves, and the buzz word was productivity. After Sir Stafford Cripps had spoken, Churchill spoke for the Conservatives, then Clement Davies, the leader of the Liberal Party, then Herbert Morrison, the powerful Home Secretary in the Labor Government and in the Labor Party.

Clement Attlee was Prime Minister and he spoke next. Then came the heart-searing left, Aneurin Bevan, who got up and spoke with his heart in the coal mines. He talked about the Welsh miners truggling in the pits, who are soaking in all that coal dust. Then his wife, Jennie Lee, who could bring you to tears, spoke. This was the greatest political theater I have ever seen in my life. I learned more about economics and its interrelationship with politics sitting there for 11 hours in my seat in the House of Lords than anywhere else in my life. And believe me, I had to go, but I wasn't going to give in, so I sat there. I think I had a piece of candy in my pocket, and that's all I had that day. I listened to the debate and I don't think that I have ever forgotten the lessons I learned about economic and political policy, and how you combine them to make people understand what they must do to save the country. Knowing about government policy by itself was not enough. Would the British Trade

Union Congress support the government? Did it, in turn, have the support of its members? You had a lot of union members, about 8,000,000 in the British Trade Union Congress, and possibly another 1,000,000 in independent unions, accounting for 40 percent of the labor force. Unions covered every major industry in the country.

Productivity was the big buzz word, and here's where the importance of organized labor came in. We knew, and governments throughout Western Europe knew, that productivity had to be increased if there was going to be more to eat and more to live on. It was simple. And it couldn't be achieved without investment and without the cooperation of working people. We kept driving home one lesson: increases in productivity come only a little bit from working harder. Big increases in productivity come from working smarter with more and more capital.

The big obstacle to increases in productivity was not a question of working harder. British workers were working harder than anybody I had ever seen in my life. They were working long hours, but the results were hardly enough. They were working with antiquated or broken down machinery. Assembly lines were short, where they should have been long. Moreover, there was great distrust left over from the Depression period, when increased productivity meant losing your job. You produced more; you lost your job. Why? Because there was a mentality, which, I believe, still exists to a large extent in many parts of Europe, that there is just so much "in the pie" or "it only grows a little," so that when you cut that pie, its at the expense of somebody else.

We have a normal subconscious concept of a growing pie in this country, and I believe it explains why we often run into problems in our dealings with Europeans. In the American view, each one gets more of a growing pie. Europeans think of a fixed pie, and a lot of that has to do with their suspicions and the way that their societies are constructed. The question was, how do you get British workers to understand the benefits to them of increased productivity. Governments cannot talk to them because they do not trust governments, which they believe have always sided against the working man. Even a Labour government have had this trouble. Certainly they are not going to believe the American government. America is the heart of capitalism. We hoped, however, that they would believe American workers.

Bureau of Labor Statistics Advisor
James Silberman and Labor Exchanges

And here is where what others called a silly, crack-pot idea began to bear fruit. In 1948, a man from the Bureau of Labor Statistics' new Productivity Office, Jim Silberman, came out to our Embassy. I think that was the only time in my life that I have ever seen him. He had came up with an idea and as the "kid" in the Embassy, it was my job to shepherd him around to meet various people.

He said, "It's no good to send an economic mission of experts from Britain to the U.S. or from the U.S. to Britain and so forth. What you have to do is send workers, not one or two, but hundreds of them, thousands of them. Let them get to know each other's cultures. Let them learn. Workers will listen to other workers where they won't listen to their employers or to governments." And that was the beginning of "people-to-people diplomacy." Nobody else in the Embassy would touch him because they said he was a "crack pot." "What does he mean we are going to send hundreds or thousands of workers? He's a nut case." I went around with him. They figured, "Well, Herb is okay. He's a youngster. No one will blame him for anything. He can get away with it."

So, the American Federation of Labor (AFL) and the Congress of Industrial Orgnaizations (CIO) began to send representatives to Europe under the aegis of the Marshall Plan. The labor attache in London at that time was Sam Berger. He had been hired initially by W. Averell Harriman as labor consultant for the Harriman Special Economic Mission to Britain during the war. Harriman recognized the importance of the idea of knowing what Labour people wanted. At the war's end, Sam Berger became the labor attache at the Embassy in London, where Ambassador Lewis Douglas recognized the importance of labor's role in the post-war reconstruction of Britain. As a matter of fact, Sam (who died on February 12, 1980) was becoming a legend by that time. He was the one in the Embassy who had predicted the Labour Party's victory in Britain's 1948 general election. He seemed to knew everybody in the Labour Party and he had links to the Cabinet. The other people in the Embassy were still dealing only with the old British establishment and the gentility of British society. But they didn't know what was going on in the guts of the country. I went to the coal mines, to the pubs; I lived with these guys. There was a tendency among the old line political officers in the embassy to ask, "Who are these socialist upstarts?" But these socialist upstarts had power in the factories, and that's where "the war" was going to be and where the economic war and the peace was going to be won. Workers had to see that they were going to get something for their efforts and that things were going to improve.

Ambassador Harriman had recognized that and had hired Sam Berger, who had been a captain in the U.S. Army but had earlier specialized in labor affairs while he was in the United States. Sam had studied labor relations at the University of Wisconsin with Selig Perlman, who was the dean of the labor economists in those days. Anyway, Jim Silberman was not getting any hearing until one day he seemed to hit pay dirt. He ran into a fellow who was the principal back room advisor to Herbert Morrison, who was a very powerful cabinet minister in the Labour government. In Labour Party ideological terms, he was about in the center. The advisor sold the idea to Morrison, who in turn sold it to Sir Stafford Cripps. And sometime afterwards, Sir Cripps went to Paris for a meeting with Harriman, who, I think, by this time had been appointed head of the Marshall Plan for all of Europe and was headquartered in Paris. Out of the blue, Cripps and Harriman announced the creation of the "Anglo-American Productivity Committee." Among other things, its projects involved having working people visit back and forth to try to get a transference of culture and attitudes towards production. I remember the announcement that the Anglo-American Productivity Committee had been set up, and I was just sitting there gloating, but dared not say anything because someone would have smacked down the saucy kid. I thought Jim Silberman's recommendations had come good, and that he had been vindicated.

Soviet Union's Opposition to the Marshall Plan

By now, however, the big complicating political factor was the rise of the Soviet Union. There we ran into a real problem. During the war, and this was true throughout Western Europe, the communists had gained an enormous amount of popular credibility for their role in partisan warfare, particularly among working people, and in the trade unions in France, Italy, and to a large extent in Britain. As a result they had considerable influence. Also, they had a "papacy," and the "papacy" was in Moscow. The Soviet Union, as a conscious political decision, decided to fight the Marshall Plan. The communists claimed it was a device for the United States to dominate Europe and to impose capitalism on it to isolate the Soviet Union.

And so the Soviet Union took "the war" to the factory floor. At the time popular speculation about possible Soviet ambitions focused on a possible military sweep through Western Europe since all the Western armies had virtually been dispersed. But we realized soon afterwards that what the Soviet Union couldn't take earlier by force, they thought they could win without military action by warring on the factory floor, by preventing increases in productivity, by strikes, and by industrial warfare. That was the key to their plan.

The Marshall Plan as the Arena for the Cold War

One of the things I have heard people say, which bothers me and may be a generational gap, is that the Marshall Plan was our answer to the Cold War. The Marshall Plan took root for different reasons, and the Cold War evolved after the Marshall Plan was underway, although there were already suspicions in the West about the post-war intentions of the U.S.S.R. mixed with the hope that somehow the wartime alliance would cooperate to rebuild Europe. The Soviet Union chose to make the Marshall Plan the arena for the Cold War.

The Marshall Plan was specifically aimed at the economic reconstruction of a physically devastated Europe. And as soon as it was announced, the leading statesmen of Western Europe began to organize a conference, which took place on July 12, 1947 in Paris, to coordinate their positions on the Marshall Plan.

The Marshall Plan was finally passed by Congress in March of 1948, and the conference became the organizational entity, the Organization for European Economic Cooperation (OEEC). The reaction was immediately positive. This was not a long considered reaction. Somewhere I have seen references that the Marshall Plan was a reaction to what was really only a monetary crisis. It was a lot more than that. Everybody could see the damage. You could walk around Europe and see it. There was no question.

The atmosphere at the time was that the Soviet Union had been an ally, and had suffered terribly during the war with heavy casualties, physical damage and so forth. There was no real love for the Soviets, but there was a tremendous amount of communist influence in Western Europe, particularly in the various ranks of organized labor. Not domination, but enough influence to affect policy. Each time the Soviet

Union took a step, people were rather puzzled. The Cold War was not something that was declared and nobody even used the term "Cold War." It sort of crept up on us incrementally. We took a "What are they up to?" kind of approach.

A defining moment was when the Soviet Union pressured Czechoslovakia, Poland, and Yugoslavia not to become members of the Marshall Plan. They were all at different stages in their deliberations on the Marshall Plan. I think that Poland had actually accepted an invitation to the July 1947 conference and was then told to pull back. Czechoslovakia had been about to accept, and then President Edvard Benes was called to Moscow and was told he would have to give up the idea. Tito in Yugoslavia was considering it and let out hints, but never went in. Then the Soviet Union itself, which had been offered an invitation, denounced the Marshall Plan as a plot for the capitalist Americans to establish hegemony over Western Europe.

Dock Strike Over Canadian Freighter

War broke out on the factory floor in Britain, France, Italy, and the Low Countries and the communist-dominated or influenced unions began to call strikes. This even took place in Australia, where I was transferred in late 1949. The same Cold War was being fought in Australia through strikes in the coal mines and steel mills, called on the flimsiest of excuses using industrial issues for in effect politically motivated strikes. It is interesting how skillful the communist union leaders were. For this reason, I have always argued that you don't need a majority, just a purposeful faction to do damage. At one time communist trade union leaders almost succeeded in tying up Marshall Plan shipments in the North Atlantic. I remember working feverishly over a weekend with my boss, Sam Berger, to prevent a general tie up of the North Atlantic sea routes.

A freighter arrived from Canada, which had been organized by a small communist-dominated seaman's union called the "Canadian Seaman's Union." The American seaman's union, the Seafarers International Union, also had a very powerful branch in Canada. When the ship docked in London, the seamen called a strike aboard ship, complaining about working conditions and so forth. And the parties could not settle the strike.

When you get into labor negotiations, you can never tell which are the real issues and which are the surface issues. Sometimes you spend most of your time trying to figure out what is really bothering the parties, "which tooth really hurts," so to speak, because you can't tell. The vessel itself was not of any great importance, but the communists were very skillful. They said, "Well, the men said they're not going to work." So the company flew a new crew over. This was not very common, but the company felt strongly enough that it actually flew in a crew from the United States. These crewmen were all members of the Seafarers International Union, the American union, which had a branch in Canada and was still the biggest of the seamen's unions then.

"Ah-hah," said the leaders of the local strike on the ship, "they are sending in strike breakers from the SIU. This ship is declared black, meaning boycotted. There was strong communist influence in those days on the British docks. You didn't have to explain the issue. They would simply say "If they're out, we're out." So, the London dockers initially struck in sympathy against American ships.

"Well," said the captain of the ship, "that's all right. We won't unload in London; we'll go to Liverpool." So they arrived in Liverpool, and the fellows on the docks in Liverpool said, "Well, how do you like that? That ship is black." So, the Liverpool dockers wouldn't work the ship either. So the ship went on to Bristol, and the Bristol dockworkers declared the ship black too. Before you knew it, starting from this one obscure incident, about 20,000 dockers were out on strike in sympathy and protest, tying up all the shipping.

The American dockers, the International Longshoreman's Association (ILA) at the time, said "if the British dockers are going to boycott our ships, we are going to boycott British ships." All the Marshall Plan shipments in the North Atlantic were thus threatened by a complete tie up. That's how skillful this operation was.

Sam Berger and I worked like dogs sending cables to the State Department. The man who was in charge of labor affairs in the State Department at that time was Daniel Horowitz. He had been the first American labor attache. Sam was sending cables saying, "Please get to the International Longshoremen's Association (ILA) and tell them not to strike British ships in retaliation." Meanwhile, we were contacting the General Secretary of the British Transport and General Workers Union, Arthur Deakin, an anti-communist although nominal President of the World Federation of Trade Unions, part of the communist-dominated International Labor Confederation.

The American labor leaders were informed, "Look, this dock strike is a political game. Don't fall for it. Get somebody here so you can talk it over with the head man," i.e. Arthur Deakin. (Mind you these strikes were called locally, and they would just catch fire.) And so the two top U.S. and U.K. dock union leaders somehow got in touch with each other. The American said, "Look, call your guys off. We won't do anything to your ships." Then Prime Minister Attlee got on the radio to ask people in the name of the Labour government go back to work. (The dockers would never have done that for a Tory government.) Troops were not the answer because that would have inflamed the situation in protest. If you had troops out there, you would have had every union in the country out on a general strike. So out of loyalty to the Labour government and with pleas from their own top labor union leadership, the dockers began to go back to work. There was also tremendous public pressure on the dockers not to jeopardize the interests of the country. The American longshoremen worked the British ships, and eventually the strike died. But this was an illustration of how the communists tried to disrupt the economy through labor unrest. Now, multiply that by what happened in the coal mines, in the steel industry, and just about anywhere you turned. This kind of warfare was carried on in Europe, at least all through Western Europe, especially in France, where the Central Labor Federation fell under communist control, and in Italy, where the central federation had also fallen under communist control.

Dispute With the World Federation of Trade Unions and Formation of the International Confederation of Free Trade Unions

During the days of the wartime grand alliance and early post-war period, the British Trade Union Congress and the Soviet All Union Central Council of Trade Unions laid the groundwork to form in 1945 what was called the World Federation of Trade Unions (WFTU). It was fed by a hope that the wartime alliance would carry into a common effort, on the labor level, to rebuild a world in which workers benefited from the prosperity of their countries. The post-World War II world was going to be "the brave new world."

However, once the Soviet Union denounced the Marshall Plan, the communists—and here the communists again were very clever, very skillful—demonstrated their control of the WFTU Secretariat by placing Louis Saillant, a French communist, as General Secretary. The top WFTU names were not communists. Arthur Deakin, the General Secretary of the Transport and the General Workers Union, the biggest union in Britain with about a million to 1.2 million members, was President of the WFTU and, if anything, an anti-communist. Jim Carey, who was the Vice President of the WFTU, had a reputation for defeating the communists in the Congress of Industrial Organizations (CIO) and was trying to get the WFTU to support the Marshall Plan. The WFTU, however, took the position, " We are a trade union organization. We are not political. We do not support it, because we are not political." Moreover, their affiliated organizations were looking for a lead. Some non-communist affiliates said, "The WFTU is neutral. Okay, we are neutral, too." That was not what the U.S. wanted. We needed support.

In essence, the WFTU did split over the Marshall Plan. There were other technical issues, but the basic issue was support for the reconstruction of Europe. And later on in November 1949, a new international federation, the International Confederation of Free Trade Unions (ICFTU) was formed. The big survivor, it is still in existence and very important. Both the AFL, which would never join the WFTU because of the democracy issue, and the CIO joined in the founding of the ICFTU.

The foreign policy differences between the CIO and the AFL were reflected in the tendency of the CIO and the Trade Union Congress of Britain (TUCB) to take the position that the communist-controlled unions could be brought around to reasonable positions if you kept talking and maintained contact. The AFL said, "No. It isn't only a matter of their support for the Soviet Union." The leadership in those organizations, they believed, saw labor unions as a political instrument to bring about the destruction of free society and did do not want a free society. Democratic unions have to have a stake in democracy, so that they can be independent. Free unionism means independent of government, independent of the employer, independence to organize, and independence to make their own decisions. The labor unions in the Soviet Union are tools of the government and tools of a political party. These were the principles at stake in the U.S. in the battles for control of the garment unions, the United Automobile Workers Union (UAW) and other U.S. unions when the communists at one time tried to capture the leadership of the unions. The AFL argued the communist unions were using associations with non-communist unions to gain acceptability for themselves.

I knew two of the men personally involved in the international trade union wars over the Marshall Plan, Jay Lovestone and Irving Brown.

Lovestone (December 15, 1897- March 7, 1990) had been a founding member of the U.S. Communist Party and at 29 became its General Secretary. Over the years after his expulsion from the Soviet Union by Stalin in 1927, Lovestone became an uncompromising anti-communist and eventually Director of the AFL/CIO International Department as well as a very close advisor on international affairs to George Meany.

Lovestone's emissary during the Cold War was Irving Brown, AFL Representative in Europe (Paris) for some 40 years before his death in 1989. In time, Brown became very close to Lane Kirkland, Meany's successor. In later years, Brown's relations with Lovestone became strained in a personality conflict, which both sought to hide from their common political enemies. Lovestone and Brown argued: "It's not just that a union is a collection of workers; it's a question of whether you believe in democracy. We're not saying what form of democracy, but democracy in a sense that they believe a union should be totally independent to act on behalf of its membership. That is, the union must be free to be independent of the government, political parties and employers. It must be free to bargain and free to act within the law. It must have a stake in democracy."

The ICFTU had taken that position. The British TUC, the CIO, and the Netherlands Confederation of Free Trade Unions (NVV) walked out of the WFTU in January 1949 and were central in forming the International Confederation of Free Trade Unions in November 1949. The AFL also joined as a founder and driving force in establishing the ICFTU. And from then on, it became a question, not only of contests in Western Europe, but subsequently throughout the world, to establish free trade unions in the newly independent areas in Africa, in Asia, and in Latin America.

Attitude of British Labor Towards the Marshall Plan, Class Struggle, and Socialism

The British miners union, the National Union of Mine Workers (NUM), has now just about disintegrated, together with the coal industry. When I was in Britain, there were 600,000 unionized miners. Now the NUM claims possibly 18,000 members. They were a big power in the Labour Party, and a big power in the TUCB. They were the "aristocrats" of the labor movement. In the public mind they personified organized labor, and there was great sympathy for miners because they had such dirty jobs.

I did not really appreciate this until my turn came to crawl on my belly through a hundred year old mine in Doncaster. The president of the mine workers union said, "Herb, if you really want to be a labor attache and want to understand us, you have to come with me and crawl through a mine." I did. Boy, I never forgot that experience! I suddenly began to realize that a hot shower was a hell of a lot more important than just any shower. It was not like bathing in the morning. It became an industrial necessity, because your ears, your nose, every pore of your body had coal dust in it. I had to stand under that hot shower for I don't know how long to wash out that dust, and even then it didn't wash it out completely.

And I began to understand why, for example, a miner would walk out if he had cold tea instead of hot tea, because that was the only thing he had to keep him going or give him a break. I began to understand that these are not just personal comforts. I began to understand why it was so important to dock workers that there be covering for them in the rain. You put on your rain coat and go for a walk in the rain, but to a dock worker, those are his working conditions. If he stands outside pulling boxes or managing loading something, he will be pretty well beat if he doesn't have any covering. People say, "Ah, what are they making such a fuss about? They walked out because it is raining." I began to understand the difference between personal comfort and what things are crucial to working people.

In terms of the attitude of working people towards the Marshall Plan, there always was a mixture of feelings. I wrote my doctorate on the attitude of British Labour towards public ownership, and it dealt a bit about where socialism fit into Labour thinking. This socialism colored the thinking and the views of people who were trade union members and/ or affiliated to the Labour Party. Their attitude towards the United States, towards productivity, and towards the reconstruction of Europe was that they wanted everybody to benefit and not just "the capitalists." It was the capitalists that sent them to war in World War I, but World War II was the "people's war." They fought it. And so their attitude was, if anybody's going to make money, they wanted to share it. Additionally, there was always a tendency, which still exists among the more doctrinaire elements in the Labour Party, of seeing the United States ideologically as the bastion of capitalism.

When the Soviet Union became an important power, it was seen, especially in the early days, as "the workers state." There was a tendency among British socialists to say, "Oh, but the dictatorship is temporary; it is a passing phase," and so forth. "The communists are socialists in a hurry." There was also a tendency to put a mild interpretation on the excesses of the Soviet Union, even Stalinism, and to see the United States as being the home of unbridled capitalism, trying to propagate capitalism to the disadvantage of the workers. But in the end, the relationship between the United States and Britain, whether with a Labour government or a Tory government, became "we are the two primary democracies. And so the relationship between the United States government, whether a Republican or a Democrat administration, and the British Government, whether Tory or Labour, was built on the feeling of mutual interest.

The feeling of suspicion towards American capitalism among British socialists was always there. The counterpart feeling among Conservatives was, "Who are these upstart Americans who want to take over our empire?" There was some of that attitude in Britain, and there still is, some of that around, but it is not a governing feature of Tory politics.

American policy toward Europe in the 1940s was forged as a pragmatic response to a mounting economic and political crisis. The vast destruction of European production capacity was threatening the collapse of social order in much of Europe. Shortages of food and fuel, particularly coal, Europe's overwhelming source of energy, were becoming severe, with adverse chain reactions in the work force and in the production of goods needed for reconstruction, for example, steel and machinery. Inflation was accelerating. Governments, having used much of their income producing foreign assets and reserves to pay for the war, were becoming desperately short of foreign exchange as U.S. loans and grants ran out. It is estimated that between 1938 and 1947, on the average, Europeans' standard of living, per capita gross national product in constant dollars, fell by more than eight per cent. In Italy, the decline was over twenty-five percent. In West Germany more than fifteen percent. In France, nearly ten percent. In the Low Countries, six to seven percent. In Austria and Greece, about forty percent. In contrast, per capita GNP in Britain had increased by about four percent, and in the United States almost fifty percent. That comes right out of official State Department publications.

Summary Statement on the Cold War and Its Significance

There's a tendency to say that the Cold War is over, and to ask what do we do now? Some have even said that the U.S. policy of furthering democracy is a current foreign policy gimmick. Looking at it as someone who saw the Cold War from its beginnings right through to its end, I want to emphasize that the furtherance of democracy has been an American foreign policy objective since before the Cold War. Looking at it in large historical terms, the Cold War was a test of our perseverance and an effort to subdue dictatorships without war and not on terms that were set by the "cold warriors." Now, the question for democracy is not whether or not there is a Soviet Union. The question is: Do we want to build institutions that perpetuate themselves in a democratic form?

In terms of labor, the question is not whether unions are organizations of working people. Communist-controlled unions do not have much in common with unions that are not communist controlled. I have talked with some of the leaders of the former official communist unions in Russia. A lot of their union behavior—and this can't be measured or determined in an objective way—has to do with outlook. People from the old official unions still see unions as a device for political power. They have no particular dedication to a democratic form of government. Many leaders of the old official unions, although they say they are independent of government, keep up their relationships with "their fellow apparatchiks" who manage the various formerly government-owned industrial enterprises, with the benefits going to the old communist party bureaucrats, and they see their function in terms of gaining power again. They are driven, in many cases, ideologically. There aren't communists anymore; but it doesn't really matter what the label is. They think in terms of political power and the use of industrial power to gain and perpetuate political power. They do not allow very much for the kinds of change that come with democratic forms and processes.

The issue of democracy thus remain the same. All through Eastern Europe and in what was the Soviet Union, democracy is not an automatic successor to absolutism. Democracy is rather the most difficult kind of government to make work, because it depends upon a delicate balance, and it depends upon a culture. It can work, but it's tough; it's not easy, and once you lose it, it's even tougher to get it back.

Notes

1. This is an excerpt from the text of a video interview with Herbert E. Weiner conducted by Linda and Eric Christianson. It was filmed on June 8, 1993 and recorded on February 17, 1994 for a proposed film documentary marking the 50th anniversary of the Marshall Plan.

   In World war II, Mr. Weiner served in the Japanese theater, in New Guinea and in two invasions of the Philippines (Leyte and Luzon). Mr. Weiner is a career Foreign Service Officer, and he is currently a consultant in the Office of the Special Assistant to the Secretary of State for International Labor Affairs.

Personal Retrospectives

V. The Legacy of the Marshall Plan

The Marshall Plan and the New Europe

RAGNAR ARNESEN

The staff recruited to implement the Marshall Plan was of very high caliber, beginning with Averill Harriman (known fondly to his staff as "Honest Ave the hairsplitter").

In 1947, I was only one of the young people who flocked to France after World War II to study. A number of us found work in the U.S. embassy as guards or messengers, or in the Office of the Special Representative (OSR) in Paris as junior staffers in order to continue our studies or simply to survive.

I started out in October 1949 in a temporary clerical job in Paris and, in January 1950, was given a position as clerk/typist in the Personnel Office of OSR. I sought an opportunity to participate in the substantive work of the Marshall Plan, and I was later transferred to The Hague as an Industrial Analyst. That assignment included analysis and presentation of the Netherlands' requests for priority raw materials, such as tin for tinplate and coal for the blast furnaces, etc. It also involved purchase of raw materials for U.S. stockpiles, such as industrial diamonds, quebracho bark, etc.

I remained in the Mission to the Netherlands until 1955, when I was assigned to Madrid and thereafter pursued a career in the U.S. foreign aid agencies.

Impact of the Marshall Plan

There is little point in my attempting to deal here with the history of European economic recovery, which has been adequately covered by professional journals and even the general press. However, a few anecdotal comments may be of interest.

One of the first slogans of the Marshall Plan—symbolizing a critical problem of the cooperating countries—was closing the "dollar gap." This was succeeded by the "productivity gap." As such, Productivity Centers were set up at U.S. suggestion in the various cooperating countries. I was involved in supporting the Dutch Productivity Center, arranging for technical assistance missions to observe American industrial and management methods, recruiting American consultants, and providing technical training films and other forms of assistance. The technical training films, covering all sorts of shop methods, were translated into Dutch and made widely available to industry and commercial firms. American industrial consultants visited Dutch factories to give advice on methods and manufacturing techniques, ranging from time and motion study to general management. Combined with the visits of Dutch industrialists to their counterpart industries in the U.S., the work of the productivity centers made the "practice of management" almost a shibboleth in industrial circles and the names of Peter Drucker, Taylor et al became bywords in those same circles.

This sort of technical assistance was a part of U.S. aid programs under the Marshall Plan in all the cooperating countries and continued long after. There is little doubt that modern American management and marketing methods left a permanent mark in the cooperating European countries.

Implications for the Future

As we look to the future, we can remember, the extremely important role of the Marshall Plan in setting the stage for the eventual integration of Europe, and recognize on the other hand the time and distance we are now from from that gloriously enthusiastic and optimistic aura which surrounded the efforts of far-seeing statesmen like Marshall, Truman, Monnet, Schumann and numerous others.The insistence of the United States on a cooperative effort among the European nations began what is now a tradition of working together, which bolstered visionaries of a greater Europe and resulted in the building of the institutions which led up to the Treaties of Rome in 1957 and Maastricht in 1992, confirming the reality of a new Europe.

Today's generation of leaders was born in the year the Marshall Plan was announced and were ten years old when the Treaty of Rome was signed. For the most part, they have known neither the trauma of such a war and its devastation, nor the hopes and confidence that were inspired by the Marshall Plan. Instead, their world is now observing the fragmentation of nations into separatist racial groups seeking independence in Yugoslavia, Chechnya, Zaire, Sri Lanka, Indonesia, and elsewhere. The fundamentalist wave, with which the separatist tendency is associated, is affecting developed societies alike, even the United States and Europe. This phenomenon is hardly conducive to an integrated Europe, but it can be diminished by nurturing the more moderate forces in the affected societies.

Currently, the economic recession in Europe is lessening support for the strict policy measures necessary to conform to the conditions set forth in the Treaty of Maastricht. The United States can again play an important role in facilitating the European leadership's attempts at reform by minimizing economic and market rivalries.

Reflecting on the plight of Europe at the war's end and her ability to emerge and create a new set of continental institutions and attitudes inspires hope that there will be progress toward the goal of true European integration—economically and, in one form or another, politically and socially. It is not out of the question—indeed, with time, it will become imperative—that Eastern Europe must gradually be included in this new Europe and thus realize the opportunity foreclosed by Stalin when he decided to exclude the Soviet bloc from participating in the Marshall Plan.

Rewards of the Marshall Plan

E. ERNEST GOLDSTEIN

In 1952, the Mutual Security Agency recruited me from my position as General Counsel of the House of Representatives Committee on the Judiciary, Subcommittee on the Study of Monopoly Power. I served as Restrictive Trade Practices Specialist in USRO Paris, and as a representative to the Productivity and Applied Research Committee of the Organization for European Economic Cooperation (OEEC).

My primary mission in Paris and in the OEEC Member States was to encourage and to assist in the development of legislation which would make the various economies more competitive. In short, to encourage the development of antitrust laws tailored to meet the special legal and economic needs of the Marshall Plan beneficiaries. Funds had been earmarked for this purpose, and they were generally referred to as "Moody money," because Senator Blair Moody of Michigan had fostered the antitrust program.

During my tenure at USRO, France, Ireland, Germany, the United Kingdom, Norway, Denmark, and the Netherlands took positive steps toward creating competitive economic climates. Italy expressed interest in encouraging competition, but the post-World War II government continued in force pre-Mussolini voluntary cartel control legislation. It was not until Italy joined the Common Market that positive changes began to take place. Greece was a total disappointment. Neither meetings at the Chateau de la Muette headquarters of the OEEC in Paris, nor meetings in Athens with other government officials produced positive results.

The Marshall Plan experience was most rewarding. It played a major role in my subsequent activities, produced long lasting friendships and eventually influenced my decision to spend twenty-eight years living in Europe.

In 1955, I joined the Faculty of the Law School of the University of Texas, Austin. Thereafter my teaching and writing directly benefited from the Marshall Plan experience. My book, *American Enterprise and Scandinavian Antitrust Law*, Austin, TX: University of Texas Press, 1963, is one example. Other examples include articles such as "France's First Discount House," *Harper's Magazine*, December 1956, pp. 53-56; "National and International Antitrust Policy in France: An Interview with M. Antoine Pinay, Minister of Economic Affairs and Finance," *Texas Law Review*, 1958, pp. 188-197; "Effects of Foreign Antitrust Laws on United States Business," a chapter in Matthew Bender ed., *Institute of the Antitrust Laws*, Albany: Southwestern Legal Foundation and Co., 1958, pp. 199-283; and "Administrative Shaping of French Refusal to Deal Legislation," *American Journal of Comparative Law*, Vol. 11, No. 4, 1962, pp. 515-538.

I returned to Europe many times during my teaching career, which ended in December 1965, when I returned to Paris to join the Coudert Freres international law firm. I left the firm in 1967 to serve as a Special Assistant to President Johnson, and rejoined it in 1970. During my Coudert career, I had the opportunity to meet and work with many of the European friends who dated back to the Marshall Plan days.

Looking at Europe today, it is obvious that the Marshall Plan worked. The legislation regarding competition in force in the European Union and its member states is evidence that the "Moody money" was well spent. The OEEC has been replaced by the OECD, thereby bringing the Marshall Plan antitrust philosophy to all the major, developed nations.

The aid programs, which many developed nations and international organizations extend to developing nations, demonstrate the validity of the concept of the Marshall Plan. The Marshall Plan would not have been a success without the great support received from officials, academics and journalists of the OEEC member states. In my field, I would mention: France: Monsieur Rene Jaume, Administrator of the Laniel Decree; Monsieur Claude Lasry, Conseiller d'Etat; Professors R. Plaisant and Y. Loussouarn; and Monsieur Jean-Claude Servan-Schreiber, journalist; Ireland: Hon. Padhraic O'Slatarra, the Fair Trade Commission; United Kingdom: Hon. R. L. Sich, Registrar of Restrictive Trading Agreements; Belgium: Professor Jean Limpens; Germany: Dr. Eberhard Gunther, Bundeskartellamt, and Dr. Arved Deringer; Denmark: Mr. Soren

Gamelgaard and Mr. W. Boserup of the Monopoly Control Authority and Mr. Ernst Klaebel, journalist; Norway: Hon. W. Thagaard and Mrs E. Boe of the Price Directorate; and the Netherlands: Hon. P. Verloren van Themaat, Director, Industrial Organization, Department of Economic Affairs; Count Dick de Milly and Professor I. Samkalden.

Each of those mentioned were among those who were most instrumental in shaping European competition policy during the post-World War II era, and for many years thereafter. I truly regret not being able to attend the George Washington University meeting. I would have liked to see some old and dear friends, notably Ev Bellows. Being part of the Marshall Plan was a great and wonderful adventure, I believe that what we did will have a lasting and positive legacy.

Successful Phase-outs

HERMAN KLEINE

I joined the Marshall Plan in October 1949 as an economist with the mission to the Netherlands on a one year's leave of absence from the faculty of the Worcester Polytechnic Institute in Worcester, Massachusetts. That led to a career in international economic development that continued for more than 35 years with all the successor agencies of the Economic Cooperation Agency (ECA), the MSA, FOA, ICA, and USAID and with a multilateral agency, International Development Bank (IDB), for eight years.

My work with the Marshall Plan began as assistant finance officer under Weir Brown on detail from the U.S. Treasury as Mission Finance Officer. When he departed I became Finance Officer and by the time I was transferred to Washington in March of 1953, I was the Mission Finance and Program Officer. I left because the Program was being phased-out. The Netherlands was the first of the Marshall Plan countries to renounce aid voluntarily because the Program objectives had been fulfilled.

In Washington, my initial assignment was as French Desk Officer (at the time France was termed "the sick man of Europe"). Not long after, I was named French and Yugoslav Area Officer. This was occasioned by the split that occurred between Tito's Yugoslavia and the Union of Soviet Socialist Republics. The U.S. joined France and the U.K. in providing assistance to support the breakaway. During this period, 1953-1957, when I served in Washington, the Marshall Plan throughout Europe was in a phase-out mode, which entailed the closing out of programs including counterpart funds, all of which called for extensive and intensive negotiations with host country governments. During the last year of that period, I served as Acting Deputy Director of the European Region under Stuart Van Dyke, the Regional Director. When I was appointed as Director of the U.S. Mission to Ethiopia in August, the Marshall Plan was pretty much a matter of history—a glorious chapter for the U.S. and its partners.

I am convinced that the overall interests of the U.S. require continuing involvement in foreign economic assistance through bilateral and multilateral programs. The questions that must be continuously asked are how much, what kind, and what combinations of bilateral and multilateral aid is needed. I am also convinced that more is not necessarily better. Indeed, in certain situations less or no assistance may be the best approach. Experience has convinced me that external aid can also not substitute for commitment to domestic measures and policies taken by developing countries. Where such efforts are not present to offer incentives to the local economy, external assistance serves only as an expensive, short-term palliative. The underlying problems will remain and dependence on aid will steadily increase.

I have always stressed efficiency, effectiveness, and accountability in the allocation and use of human and financial resources, giving close attention to the absorptive capacity of recipient governments and institutions. Ineffective aid is wasteful to both donors and recipients; it discredits and threatens the whole fabric of international economic cooperation.

My greatest satisfaction has come from phasing-out programs when their objectives have been achieved. Such phase-outs, when appropriately timed and staged, enhance the credibility of the role of foreign assistance. The history of the Marshall Plan bears witness to this view. Too often, short sighted decisions for phasing-out programs have been resisted for reasons not related to the basic purposes of economic assistance.

We Happy Few of the Marshall Plan

HENRY S. REUSS

Recently, I received a plain brown envelope out of which tumbled a document bearing the sinister label "Known Marshall Plan Participants." My name was included among some 200 other participants. Just as I was resolving never to name any of my co-participants to the inevitable Committee of Inquisition, I read on, to discover happily that nothing more was afoot than to celebrate the 50th anniversary of George Marshall's famous speech of June 5, 1947.

In this celebration of the Plan I gratefully join—for what it accomplished, for what its shining example may mean in the future, and for the great joy I got from being a part of it.

Paul Hoffman had just been appointed chief of the fledgling Economic Cooperation Administration when he came to my hometown of Milwaukee for a speech in the fall of 1948. We talked about my joining the legal staff of the Plan in Paris. By Thanksgiving Day, along with my wife Margaret and our two young sons, our plane was approaching Paris, where for the next 14 months I was to be Assistant, then Deputy, then Acting General Counsel, under Ambassador Milton Katz. It was a bumpy sky as we came in for a landing at Le Bourget, and our youngest son Mike, roaming the aisle, bloodied his nose when he hit the overhead rack. The welcoming Ambassador diplomatically declined to take note of the gore.

The legal office of Economic Cooperation Administration (ECA)/ Europe was a young lawyer's dream. There were four of us: Milt Katz, later for many years the head of Harvard Law School's international legal studies; Kingman Brewster, who later became President of Yale; Roger Fisher, still active at Harvard Law School and inventor of the negotiating process known as "getting to yes;" and me, Wisconsin congressman 1955-1983 and chair of the Banking and the Joint Economic committees. Our little law firm believed that we were engaged in a great enterprise. We believed that rather than live a life apart we should mix and mingle with the Marshall Plan's administrators and economists, and that our pronouncements should be written in a language that was easy to understand and a pleasure to read.

Above all, we believed with the Marshall Plan's leaders that our role was not to direct the Europeans but to help them to help themselves. We worked closely with the sixteen countries that made up the Marshall Plan's governing body, the Committee for European Economic Cooperation, out of which was to develop the present flourishing Organization for Economic Cooperation and Development. I can remember helping draft the European Payments Agreement, which opened up trade between what had been fiercely projectionist nations; consulting in Frankfurt with the drafters of the Basic Law for the new Federal Republic of Germany; going to Dublin to aid our Mission to Ireland re-open mines that had first been worked in the days of the Caesars; to accompanying Deputy Administrator Bill Foster back to Washington to construct a system for visits by European workers to study American productivity.

Our Paris office in the Hotel Talleyrand on the Place de la Concorde was a model of bureaucratic democracy. We of the lesser ranks were encouraged to speak our minds. In fact, some of us who were used to grabbing a croque monsieur for lunch at the snack bar formed our informal "Snack Bar Policy Board," economist Taylor Ostrander, labor specialist Sol Ozer, journalist Wally Nielson, and administrator Everett Bellows among them. Together, we pondered long over many a "great question"— how to get the Common Market and the European Community started; how to encourage labor unions that were neither communist nor limp; how to ensure that three Franco-Prussian wars in a century were enough.

One reason Marshall Planners were a happy breed was because we admired our bosses. They were supposed to be Democrats and Republicans in equal proportions, but it was hard to tell by their actions which was which. As in the brave days of old, "Then none was for the party, and all were for the state."

Getting on with the job was the leitmotif of our leaders, Republicans like Paul Hoffman who made good Studebakers and, later, a better world; Bill Foster, who looked as if he had been sent by Central Casting to play the clean cut American executive, and conducted himself accordingly; Democrats like the Bruces of the old Tidewater aristocracy with their sense of civic duty; and Averell Harriman, determined to excel at everything from international diplomacy to lawn croquet. What a delight and an inspiration they all were . . . and how we need them now.

What was the Marshall Plan's accomplishment, from the vantage point of fifty years? Rather than drown in statistics, let us look at the life of the people of the tiny village in southwest France where we have been spending our summers in recent years. Back in the Forties, the women did the family laundry by beating it against the rocks at the river's edge. Water had to be carried by hand up the steep bluff. Glad that the war was over, men worked long and hard for low wages. There were no telephones.

Today all is prosperity. World War II is almost forgotten, and a German family recently moved into the village without incident. Running water permits washing machines. All have telephones, often equipped with the cute little Minitel computers that make life easy. Some already have high-definition television. All enjoy health care, and other services from day care to elder care, as a matter of right.

The Marshall Plan was not carried out in order to wring gratitude from its recipients, but to a surprising extent it has done just that. The Germans have concocted the German Marshall Fund, which brings to America all sorts of examples of contemporary European culture, from city planning to early education. The British have founded the Marshall Scholarships, to give young Americans a touch of the British university. I was delighted to go to Vienna a few years ago as the guest of Chancellor Bruno Kreisky to dedicate a memorial to the Marshall Plan in front of the historic Stefansdom. Finally, could the Marshall Plan, designed to reconstruct a war-devastated Europe, be a model for other worthy activities? Hardly a month goes by without someone's suggesting a "Marshall Plan" for impoverished Appalachia, for our stricken cities, or for troubled Africa. Usually, this focuses on the $13 billion check the United States wrote as the material component of European recovery.

But the Marshall Plan was much more than about money. Its genius lay rather in its emphasis on cooperative planning and action by the Plan's beneficiaries, each of whom had to agree on how to divide the money, and how it was to be spent. This habit of working together engendered by the Plan was shortly put to even more important use in the building of the European Union. This liberating core of the Marshall Plan, the need for cooperation, deserves to be more frequently invoked.

For the future, I have some suggestions. At home, if our federal system is creaking, if the carrying out of most functions of government should be as close to the people as possible, if the federal government is best able to administer an equalizing revenue system of progressive income and estate taxes, if state and local governments are today failing to carry out their responsibilities, particularly in metropolitan areas because they have failed to modernize their relationships, then why not share federal revenues with states and localities provided the states, on a regional basis, work out for themselves a modern government plan worthy of federal support?

I introduced congressional legislation to this effect back in the seventies. It was favorably reported out of committee, but was sunk without trace on the House floor when the special interests combined against it. Abroad, recently Ambassador John W. Tuthill and I have proposed a "Concert of the Democracies" in which the world's industrialized democracies, old and new, would be given a representative organization (replacing some five present duplicating and ineffectual institutions) to find common strategies for solving common political and economic problems. Perhaps its day will come.

The Marshall Plan gave us not only a restored Europe, but a grand design for a cooperative approach to many other challenges facing humankind. Not bad for one short commencement address!

Implications for the Future

FRED SANDERSON*

I t is generally agreed that the Marshall Plan played a major role in the spectacular postwar recovery of Western Europe and the twenty-year economic boom that followed it. There is less consensus on the particular features of the program that proved to be most effective—initially and ultimately. The total transfer of resources from the U.S. to Western Europe was unprecedented—nearly \$13 billion in the years 1948-51. But as de Long and Eichengreen point out in their sober assessment, it still amounted to only about 2.5 percent of the aggregate GNP of the receiving countries.[1] They conclude that the conditions attached to this aid—the insistence on economic liberalization and financial discipline, the emphasis on economic cooperation and integration, the liberalization of trade and investments within Europe and globally, and the encouragement of competitive free enterprise—were the crucial elements in the program's success. At the same time, the Marshall Plan permitted, and indeed, facilitated, the development of strong social safety nets and the orderly resolution of social conflicts. These are the aspects of the Marshall Plan that are most helpful in serving as lessons for the present transition problems in central and eastern Europe and the countries of the former Soviet Union.

But we should not underestimate the important initial role of American aid in alleviating resource shortages. This assistance started immediately after the war and already ran at about \$4 billion a year before the Marshall

* Senior Fellow, National Center for Food and Agricultural Policy, Washington, D.C.

Plan was launched. A majority was spent on primary products and intermediate inputs. With Europe's agricultural production running at fifty percent of prewar figures, food and fertilizer supplies were critical. The coal shortage was a severe constraint on the recovery of industrial production—reaching a low of 60 percent of prewar performance. In its first year, food still accounted for half of all Marshall Plan aid; fuel comprised one-sixth. American assistance was the only way to meet these needs.

My participation in this effort, while modest, was a source of great personal satisfaction to me. Beginning in 1943, I was part of an inter-agency team responsible for projecting complete food balances for the countries to be liberated. My office, in the Research and Analysis branch of the Office of Strategic Services (OSS), went on to develop regional food balances, particularly important for Germany, which was to be divided into four occupation zones. In 1945, I spent six months in Germany for OSS to report on food conditions there. (Here again, we assembled an inter-agency committee of experts in Berlin to develop agreed estimates.) Upon my return to the U.S., we transferred our expertise and responsibility for food balance analysis to the newly established Food and Agriculture Organization of the United Nations (FAO), along with Henry Jacoby, one of our staff members, who later became FAO's representative at the European office of the UN in Geneva.

Following the transfer of OSS/R&A to the State Department, as chief of the Central European economic section I devoted much of my attention to coal supplies, which had become a major bottleneck in the industrial recovery of West Germany and of neighboring countries that had been traditionally depended on coal imports from Germany. Coal was still a major concern when I was detailed to Germany in 1948 to work with Don Humphrey, who was serving as deputy economic advisor to General Clay. There could have been no more exciting time to spend in Berlin than amidst two momentous events—the Soviet blockade of the city and the currency reform which opened the door to economic recovery in Germany. My principal contacts there included some of the American experts involved in the currency reform, Manny Gottlieb and Taylor Ostrander, who were concerned with the economic and social problems that might be expected from the reform. I also got marginally involved in issues of currency policy for Berlin. After a trip to the Ruhrgebiet, I proposed a reform of coal miners' incentive schemes to focus them more on increasing productivity per man rather than merely encouraging labor supply and attendance. I also covered equipment shortages in both coal and steel. I supported the British policy of offering Labour a role in the management of the coal and steel industries, an issue that was controversial on the American side of military government.

Later in 1948, I participated in a bizonal exercise in Frankfort, trying to project Germany's recovery potential in the European Recovery Program. As it turned out, the American projections fell far short of predicting the full extent of the German's "Wirtschaftswunder" that was about to unfold, although we were less pessimistic than our British counterparts (among them Schumacher, who later became chief economist of the British Coal Board, better known as the author of "Small is Beautiful").

Upon my return to the State Department, I was appointed chief of the Western European Economic Branch in the Division of Research for Western Europe. In that capacity, I worked on Marshall Plan issues with Harold van Buren ("Van") Cleveland, whom I remember as an official of broad vision and intellect. On coal, I worked with Louis Lister at the ALD Agency. It was the emerging European Economic Community that increasingly captured my attention. It became the main focus of some of my subsequent work: a year of study on the European Coal and Steel Community from 1956 to 1957, due to a Rockefeller Public Service Award; a year as chief of the Division of Research on Western Europe; a four-year assignment to the U.S. Mission to the OEEC in Paris; and 20 years (1973-1992) teaching a course at the Paul H. Nitze School for Advance International Studies, Johns Hopkins University, on the Economics of European Integration.

Note

1. de Long, Bradford, and Barry J. Eichengreen, "The Marshall Plan: History's Most Successful Structural Adjustment Program," National Bureau of Economic Research, Working Paper No. 3899, November 1991.

The Marshall Plan:
The Process As Prototype

DAVID J. STEINBERG

The Marshall Plan has long been a handy metaphor signifying large-scale U.S. government aid considered vital for solving critical regional problems in or outside the United States. The Marshall Plan's quantitative characteristics are undeniable. Seldom mentioned is the Marshall Plan as a process- a U.S. government initiative requiring aid recipients to craft a coordinated strategy to achieve agreed to objectives in accordance with basic standards set as a condition for that assistance. Inviting country candidates for economic assistance to craft and coordinate their own development or reconstruction programs has many advantages, none more important than diverting these countries from the narrowly (at times dangerously) nationalistic inclinations to the mutual cooperation essential to sound, durable solutions essential to world peace.

There has been a need to apply the Marshall Plan process to various regions of the world since the success of that strategy in Western Europe. Three such regions are Central America (a focus of U.S. concern during the Cold War), the remnants of the original Yugoslavia (scene of international aggression, including the abomination of "ethnic cleansing"), and the former republics of the Soviet Union. The opportunities for U.S. initiatives along the lines of the Marshall Plan (taking appropriate account of the huge differences between the needs of these areas today and those of Western Europe 50 years ago) have been missed. Such initiatives could have been undertaken even though the United States (unlike its capacity in the wake of World War II) can no longer be the sole source of economic assistance.

The following comments concern missed opportunities with respect to the former Soviet republics.

In the years since the dissolution of the Soviet Union, the United States has been urged in various quarters to mount a new strategy of aid to Russia and other former Soviet republics. For example, a *New York Times* editorial of March 18, 1992 advocated a U.S. initiative, together with Western Europe and Japan, to get Russia and Ukraine to subordinate nationalism to cooperation in the interest of economic progress and peaceful coexistence. In a letter to the *Times* (unpublished), I cited Secretary of State Marshall's historic speech of June 5, 1947 as a useful prototype, supplemented by appropriate economic and other standards as conditions for U.S. and other foreign assistance. "Besides providing a basis for the most productive use of external assistance," I explained, "the dynamics of inter-republic consultation and cooperation- through a coordinating council comparable with the Organization for European Economic Cooperation in Marshall Plan days- could be the catalyst for resolving a wide range of controversial issues."

Pressed to do more to help the former Soviet republics, President Bush had said he was handicapped by "constrained resources." My letter to the *Times* responded that "in concert with our allies, he could do much more with the modest amounts at hand. His real problem is less with the limitations of financial resources than with a shortage of policy resourcefulness."

Reacting to its understandable laments (March 23, 1992) on the adequacy of U.S. policy toward the former Soviet republics, I told *Business Week* magazine it had overlooked "a potential policy initiative for which an historic prototype awaits adaptation" (the Marshall Plan initiative). I noted that, in his lecture to President Bush (a lecture *Business Week* endorsed), former president Nixon's only object of nostalgia was President Truman's 1947 decision to help Greece and Turkey stave off communist incursion from abroad and insurrection at home. At least equally helpful, I said, would be the example set that same year by Truman's Secretary of State.

On February 16, 1993, I wrote Strobe Talbott (then Special Assistant to the Secretary of State regarding Russia and the other former Soviet territories):

From virtually the time of the disintegration of the Soviet Union, I have felt there has been something very important missing in the crafting of U.S. diplomacy toward these republics. I don't sense a coherent, readily identifiable U.S. initiative to catalyze greatly needed coordination of their economic, military, armaments disposal, human rights and other policies as the basis for- indeed an essential condition for- governmental assistance from the United States and allied countries (United Nations agencies as well). Inter-republic coordination need not mean and should not mean . . . tight control by a central authority (like Moscow in Soviet days). However, the Commonwealth of Independent States seems a far cry from the coordination I believe is necessary. What seems like (for the most part) a hodgepodge of bilateral arrangements with individual republics is itself a far cry from what needs developing. Encouraging the republics to be democratic and market oriented is commendable, as are the few agreements I think we have negotiated on nuclear and other matters, but much more is needed (in our interest and theirs). . . . One of many reasons for a well-coordinated regional strategy is the need to ensure that everything is done to make the most of the limited resources of these republics, and equally to ensure the most efficient use of the limited resources the United States and allied countries and international agencies are able to allocate to an aid program. . . . Something dramatic will be necessary to energize such coordination on the part of fiercely nationalistic republics, and a coherent, cohesive aid strategy in response. I have in mind something like what sparked the Marshall Plan.

On March 10, 1994, William Safire's column in the *New York Times* faulted President Clinton's "Russia policy troika" for sticking to "outdated partnership rhetoric rather than wrestle with grand theory." In a letter to Mr. Safire, I offered something that might fit what Zbigniew Brzezinski called "the consolidation of geopolitical pluralism within the space of the former Soviet Union." Objecting to the hodgepodge of U.S. bilateral (occasionally trilateral) agreements limited to too narrowly defined subjects, I proposed adaptation of the far-reaching, fully multilateral process of the Marshall Plan as the framework not only for the worthy objectives of economic development, privatization, and progress toward democracy, but as "the engine that drives enforceable progress on nuclear, security, human rights, and other tough issues beyond the scope of the IMF, World Bank and other forms of strictly economic aid."

In an op-ed appeal in the *New York Times* (October 9, 1994), urging a non-imperialist economic union of Russia and the other former Soviet republics, Grigory A. Yavlinsky (identified as leader of a democratic opposition party in Russia's legislature) advocated a regional economic bloc and other forms of policy coordination. I wrote the *Times* (unpublished) that this appeal should kindle memories of Marshall's historic message to postwar Europe and, in doing so, should spark a long overdue initiative in U.S. relations with these countries.

A *Wall Street Journal* article on May 28, 1996 concerning Russia's economic plight cited the view of experts in Rome that the West missed the chance to do much more for Russia by its unwillingness to "mount a Marshall Plan-style bailout in the days following the collapse of the Soviet Union." In a letter dated May 30 (unpublished), I responded:

> This reference to the Marshall Plan seems to project only a quantitative view of the aid the West might have provided, and to Russia alone. The most significant replication of the Marshall Plan would have been a strategy relating not bilaterally to Russia but multilaterally to all the republics of the former Soviet Union acting cooperatively, i.e., to as many as were willing to accept the standards on which the donor countries and international agencies would have insisted.

The kickoff for these and other efforts I have made urging adaptation of the Marshall Plan process for U.S. policy toward the former Soviet republics was a letter dated December 14, 1991 to Ambassador Robert S. Strauss in Moscow. (The letter was not acknowledged.) Emphasizing the need for compliance with standards concerning economic policy, human rights, labor rights, nuclear policy and other priority issues, I concluded:

> The coalescing of these republics into a regional economic cooperation entity, perhaps like the old Organization for European Economic Cooperation (OEEC) in Paris during the Marshall Plan days, may be likened to the forging of centripetal forces . . . in concert with the centrifugal forces [, the forces toward independence,] to energize a wheel of progress for the participating republics. . . . The dynamic of inter-republic cooperation for foreign-aid purposes would nurture inter-republic cooperation for other purposes as well.

We who are celebrating the Marshall Plan on the 50th anniversary of General Marshall's Harvard speech should be engaging in more than prideful recollection. We should be urging our government to apply lessons from that epic achievement in U.S. foreign policy to crises that keep erupting in other parts of the world. With extremely few exceptions, I don't sense such an effort.

Prelude to European Unity

LEONARD B. TENNYSON

It may be a singular distinction to have worked for the Marshall Plan in Europe (1949-53) and then as an American for the European Common Market in the United States (1954-1974). It happened more by chance than by forethought.

Like most men who'd gone off to war fresh out of college, I was eager in 1946 to put four years of war behind me and to get on with life. For me, it meant a news job in New York City, where as a rewrite man on the United Press Association's Foreign Desk I had an on-the-job crash course in international economics and European contemporary affairs.

Later, while a news correspondent in London, I went to Vienna in the fall of 1949 on assignment for the *London Observer*. While there, I learned the Vienna ECA Mission needed an information officer. I got the job. In the ensuing years beating the drum for the Marshall Plan in Europe, I gradually became a proponent of European integration, aware that a Western Europe of fragmented states could not survive, despite massive aid, without economic unity. How that would come about I could not then envision. The "plan" proposed by France's Foreign Minister Robert Schuman in May of 1950 did not, at the time, ring a bell with me. It should have done so.

In January 1952, I transferred to the mission in Rome. The next year, Eisenhower became president. His envoy to Rome was Claire Booth Luce, his European hit man in the ECA was Harold Stassen, and back home, Joe McCarthy was helping sanitize the government aided by the Cohen-and-shine road show boys. It was time to go home and I left that spring.

With wife and two children tucked away in suburban Connecticut (the kids were born in Vienna and Rome), I started commuting to a rewrite job at the *NY Daily News*. Earlier, the *News* had named W. Averell Harriman winner of a U.S. Presidency straw poll in the New York City area. One day, I encountered a former ECA Paris colleague and friend Waldemar Neilson. He remarked that Harriman was looking for a speech writer and general public affairs factotum. I went to see him at his East 82nd Street house. Taken by my *Daily News* connection and its perceptive poll, he hired me. Alas, I never asked him what he wanted me to write speeches about. He didn't tip his hand then about his state gubernatorial ambitions.

The chef of cabinet role for Harriman was not my bit. I also know nothing about New York state politics. Inside of six months another field beckoned. This time it was Washington. I'd met a lawyer from there by the name of George W. Ball. We'd hit it off well. He'd been Adlai Stevenson's campaign manager and a friend and advisor of Jean Monnet.

Ball invited me to come down to DC and help set up a U.S. office for the European Coal and Steel Community (ECSC), the progenitor of the European Union (EU). It was June 1954. Monnet, the architect of European unity and then president of the executive branch of the ECSC, saw that the apparent progress of European unification could be slowed by a setback vote in the French National Assembly. To him, it appeared certain that the proposed European Defense Community (EDC) treaty would be turned down. He was right; it was. He feared Americans would interpret this as a collapse of progress toward European economic integration, which was seen as the touchstone of U.S. European policy. Thus it was essential to inform and reassure the U.S. public that the process was still proceeding along economic lines by way of the ECSC.

A modest information office for the ECSC opened in June 1954. I became its director. It became the U.S. Headquarters for the Common Market from 1958 to 1973. After the 1973 enlargement of the Community from six to nine members, including Britain, it became the formal Diplomatic Delegation of the Nine. Being an American, I stepped down as head of the office and left at the end of 1974.

Notes on the Marshall Plan— A Connection to European Unity

Leaders of the Marshall Plan (Paul Hoffman, Paul Porter, W. Averell Harriman, Milton Katz, and many other Marshall Plan foot soldiers) recognized early on that the ultimate success of the Marshall Plan in rehabilitating Western Europe would be limited by the patchwork quilt of small nation-state economies each protected by national barriers, unless the Europeans pursued the goal of a United States of Europe. These nations were too small to vie individually with economies of continental scale such as those of the U.S. and the Soviet Union. Yet, to secure this goal was beyond the scope of the Marshall Plan.

The creation of the Organization for European Economic Cooperation (OEEC) did require Marshall Plan recipient nations to consult with each other within that framework on basic economic and monetary problems. The OEEC's European Payments Union for the settlement of accounts among members came closest to having an economic/political decision-making structure that bypassed the rule of unanimity, but there was no institutional framework in place to ensure this.

In its implicit proposition of a united Europe, the Marshall Plan did much to set the stage for real European integration. European leaders, such as Jean Monnet, Paul-Henri Spaak, Robert Marjolin, and Walter Hallstein acknowledged this. But, the organizations spawned by the Marshall Plan—the OEEC and its successor the organization for Economic Cooperation and Development (OECD)—did not contain the seeds of integration. They required decisions taken not by majority agreement, but by unanimity—effectively making decisions of real consequence impossible to reach.

The greatest and most enduring consequence of the Marshall Plan was the setting of the stage in May 1952 for the first step toward a "United States of Europe." Six Continental OEEC nations signed a treaty surrendering limited (but real) sovereignty over their coal and steel economies to federal-type bodies of the newly-created European Coal and Steel Community, the first "supranational" institution of Europe. By 1958, a generalized European Economic Community treaty came into force and the rest is history. The Community expanded from six to nine and then to fifteen members. Today its single market possesses a population of 371.5 million citizens and a gross domestic product totaling $8.586 trillion, making it number one in the world.

The European Union (EU) as it is called today is still in the process of formation. One clear political achievement is that its creation has made future wars between France and Germany, two great European nations which had been traditional foes for over 200 years, impossible.

Today, the two nations have compelling economic and political ties forged by mutual interests and the rule of law that are too vital to abrogate.

Two Marshall Plan Snapshots

The Doyenne: The guardian of State Department passports and diplomatic correctness, Mrs. Shipley, toured the nether reaches of her empire in 1950. She came to Vienna where the Mission Chief presented a luncheon in her honor. At the table, she eyed us coolly, waved her diplomatic passport, and, with a slight curl to her lip, said: "You don't deserve these. You are 'diplomatic gypsies.'"

The Adventurers: Mrs. Shipley was right. Adventure spurred most of the men and women who joined the Marshall Plan. It held out the challenge to get an interesting job done and get out. Job security was not included. There were a wide assortment of types who came along to help sell the Marshall Plan to recipient countries—just in case they hadn't received the message. Along with the essential bakers and candlestick makers of the administration came artists, filmmakers, designers, writers, and specialists of every ilk. The message was delivered.

The Continuing Impact
of the Marshall Plan

H. LAWRENCE WILSEY

The most concise possible summing up of the lessons of the Marshall Plan is that of Walt W. Rostow in *Foreign Affairs* (May/June 1997). The three dimensions of the Plan, which he cites as increasing in significance with the passage of time, are:

- ". . . the Plan's role in producing a postwar global economy that would avoid the problems that plagued the West between the two world wars including those that led to the Great Depression;"
- The help the Plan gave in shaping "The military and political events of the late 1940s and early 1950s and was in turn shaped by them;"
- ". . . the Marshall Plan's role in promoting the move toward European unity;"

As Rostow emphasizes, "Americans undertook the Marshall Plan as a national effort. It involved the Executive Branch and Congress, Democrats and Republicans, and private sector and trade unions, farmers, and a significant proportion of the electorate. Only the major war that had preceded it had more fully mobilized American society."[1]

The success of the Marshall Plan is all the more impressive considered in the light of America's retreat from Western European cooperation following the first world war and its even earlier traditions. Historically

American "culture has been intensively nationalistic and for the most part isolationist; it has been fiercely individualistic and capitalistic."[2]

In the late 1940's, as Marshall Plan concepts were being formulated, "America was facing an historic challenge: to assume, more or less suddenly and by default, world leadership while preserving and enlarging democratic practices at home. To reconcile global imperium and isolationist, technocratic tradition was a gargantuan task that could never be mastered, only fitfully attended to. . . . Under the threat of our own new and mortal rival, the U.S.S.R., . . . we quickly switched from a Morgenthau spirit of vengefulness to the generosity of the Marshall Plan, a splendid act of practical, self-serving idealism."[3]

In the perspective of the past half century, it is clearly fortunate that, "in the realm of economic policy, Western diplomacy—led by Secretary of State George C. Marshall, Under Secretary of State Dean Acheson, and Under Secretary of State for Economic Affairs William L. Clayton— was led by a desire to avoid the experience of the inter-war period, during which the United States had withdrawn behind a barrier of steadily rising protective tariffs and left Europe to its fate. In contrast, Washington now became the leading exponent of a cooperative economic order, which in turn encouraged a new generation of European leaders . . . to develop new economic structures that had often been talked about in the past but never attained."[4] Fortunately, the new generation of European leaders was well distributed among the nations which participated in the Marshall Plan. For those who had the privilege of serving in country missions and in the Marshall Plan's regional office in Paris, it was these leaders with whom we had the opportunity to work on a day-to-day basis and with whom we continue half-century friendships.

Those of us who were graduate students in economics in the mid-1940's did not have the opportunity to participate in conceptualizing and shaping the Marshall Plan. A few of us were, however, privileged to participate in implementing the plan. Some were to be given the opportunity to continue on after the termination of the plan in Europe as officers of the Mutual Security Agency, subsequently the Foreign Operations Administration and Agency for International Development. Some joined the professional staffs of NATO, ILO and other multi-national bodies. A few of us transferred to the Far East where what were originally technical assistance programs were increasingly becoming economic assistance and mutual security programs.

While I was a graduate student at Cornell University I followed the course of development of the Marshall Plan. The opportunity to join the Marshall Plan did not present itself until I returned to the University of Southern California to teach finance and to my responsibilities as Assistant Dean of the School of Business.

In February 1950 a cable, a word rarely encountered in the academic world of the 1950's, arrived from Paris addressed to me. My Cornell faculty advisor, Shaw Livermore, who had become Lincoln Gordon's deputy in ECA Paris, asked if I could obtain a leave of absence to join the Marshall Plan office in Oslo as International Finance and Trade Officer. The dean agreed to the leave (from which I have not yet returned). I drove home to consult with my wife, Luana, who was engaged in washing the floor of our just purchased house. I asked if she would be willing to go to Norway, taking our three-year-old daughter, Kathryn. She agreed, with the only proviso that she be allowed to finish cleaning the floor before packing, a reasonable request.

Thus began a journey and career which has never taken us back to live in southern California. But that journey, starting with the privilege of serving as one of the 630 or so Marshall Plan officers, has been long, diverse, service-oriented and, I believe, always in keeping with the highest standards of those who served as Marshall Plan officers.

I joined the ECA mission in Oslo in March 1950. John Gross, a Colorado labor leader, was Chief of Mission, relating well to leaders of Norway's Labor government. Alice Bourneuf was extremely effective as Program Officer, even often chided by ECA Paris colleagues as being "more Norwegian than the Norwegians." Warren Wiggins assisted Alice most ably. Emmett Wallace served as Industry Officer. Emerson Waldman was a very effective public information officer, and he later held a similar post in Bangkok. Mark Leiserson and Donor Lion joined the small staff later. Erik Brofoss, then the Minister of Commerce, and subsequently governor of Norges Bank, was the principal cabinet officer responsible for Marshall Plan relationships. He had assembled an outstanding professional staff, including a number of economists who had completed graduate work at Harvard University, the University of Chicago and other American universities. Key government officers included Johan Cappelen, who subsequently became Norwegian Ambassador to the United States and later to Brazil and other countries who is now retired and living in Oslo. Evind Erickson, who also retired to Oslo, served as senior economist in the Ministry of Commerce, ultimately holding highest responsibilities in the Ministry of Commerce and Ministry of Foreign Affairs. Dagfin Juel, assisted by a small staff of economists, headed the office in day-to-day liaison with the ECA Mission.

Controlling inflation and restoring the merchant fleet and industry, which had been destroyed during the war, were priorities pursued by the Norwegian government with assistance from the United States through the Marshall Plan. Norway focused on these priorities as it provided leadership among the smaller nations in the development of multinational Western European economic, political and ultimately mutual defense efforts.

Fortunately for those of us in the Oslo Mission, the Norwegian government, along with the British government, was a leader and far advanced in the development of national accounts statistics. The Central Statistical Bureau as well as the Ministry of Commerce provided the most detailed GNP, production, trade and balance of payments statistics. The Norwegian government and the Oslo Mission never had difficulty in providing data requested by ECA or by OECD, NATO and other agencies.

Today Norway continues to have a strong, stable economy characterized by high productivity and social responsibility. Still, too, Norway contributes to international cooperation and development measures beyond the size of the country's population. The Marshall Plan contributed at least in a small way to the Norwegian nation's and peoples' progress and well being.

In mid-1952 I transferred from the Oslo ECA/MSA Mission to the Republic of the Philippines. In Manila I was able to draw upon my Norwegian Marshall Plan experiences, since many of the post-war reconstruction problems of the two countries which had suffered severely under enemy occupation were similar. The program in the Philippines was, however, far more one of providing direct technical assistance in a variety of fields important to the people of this 7,083 island nation. The American economic assistance program did little to advance the development of the Philippines as an industrial nation. Program emphasis was never on industrial production as it was in Norway, Germany and the other states of Western Europe.

The Philippines, along with other Southeast Asian nations, was assisted through bi-lateral agreements with the United States. The interests and policies of America were different vis-a-vis each. And, most important, aid to Southeast Asia was never a "national effort" of America as was the post-war reconstruction of Western Europe. American assistance in

Southeast Asia and the Philippines, therefore, never achieved the three dimensions of success cited by Rostow.

The Manila mission was headed by Roland Renne, President of the University of Idaho, and overseen by Ambassador Raymond Spruance, an outstanding diplomat as well as a naval hero greatly admired in the recently liberated Philippines. Directly employed as well as contracted technical assistants included nationally recognized leaders of agriculture, Dean Leland Call of the University of Kansas; education, Professor Paul Hanna of Stanford University; public health, public administration and other fields. Two other former Marshall Plan officers, Ed Prentice and Warren Wiggins, transferred to the Philippines as Deputy Directors of the Mission. Our day-to-day focus was on "project" analysis rather than balance-of-payments and national accounts analysis, a contrast to our work in Western Europe.

The Philippine Council for USAID (PHILCUSA) was headed by Filemon C. Rodriguez, general manager of the National Power Corporation. An outstanding executive and professional, he served later as chairman of the National Economic Council under President Magsaysay and President Marcos and represented the Philippines in the 1966 Tokyo Ministerial Conference for the Development of Southeast Asia. He was a true parallel of those Western European leaders with whom we worked in the Marshall Plan and who achieved a degree of economic integration still far in the future for the Philippines and other Southeast Asian nations.

When I met with him last in March 1974, Filemon Rodriguez had fallen from grace with President Marcos for his actions, his opposition to the practices of those in positions of government and business leadership, and for two books strongly critical of political and economic conditions in the Philippines and proposing change.[5] He was truly a man who, given access to sufficient resources and a different political climate, could have led in the Philippines and Southeast Asia an economic recovery program parallel to that of the Marshall Plan in Western Europe.

At the end of 1954 I returned to Washington to head the China Division of USAID. The Quemoy-Matsu crisis was at hand, as was Secretary of State Dulles' application of the certainty/uncertainty principle.[6] Of course, "China" meant the Republic of China on Taiwan and the adjacent islands, not today's "China."

The China aid program was more like the later phases of the economic and military assistance programs in Western Europe than the aid programs in the Philippines, Indonesia and Thailand which emphasized technical assistance for public sector activity.

In mid-1955, I received and accepted an invitation to move from the public service to the management-consulting firm of Booz Allen and Hamilton, headquartered in Chicago. I accepted on the assurance that I would be working for public and international clients. (The financial inducement to change careers was a modest reduction in salary and elimination of the allowances we enjoyed while abroad.)

From 1955 through 1976 I served as a Consultant, Partner and Senior Vice President of Booz, Allen and Hamilton as well as a Director and President of BA&H of Japan. I served clients as I do today as an "independent" consultant, largely in the fields of development banking, public health, education, and government and occasionally in commercial banking and industry.

The experience and perspectives I gained as a Marshall Plan officer and in subsequent service in the Philippines and China have been beneficial to me and to the clients I serve. Certainly all that I did and learned in economic assistance programs in Europe and Asia was applied for the client's benefit in projects for the World Bank in Chile and Venezuela, for three major development banks in Brazil, for the Minister of Finance of the Kingdom of Saudi Arabia and its three development banks for industry, agriculture and housing.

During my consulting career I was joined by former ECA officers Maury Arth, Donor Lion and Ed Prentice, and former Manila Mission officers Carl Burness and Tom Haynes. Each contributed as a consultant and went on to careers as university executives, government officials or specialized consultants.

The Marshall Plan, therefore, continues to have a continuing impact on my life, the lives of my colleagues and, even today, on the development and effectiveness of my clients. All this in addition to the three-dimensional impact on Europe and the United States cited by Professor Rostow.

Notes

1. Walt W. Rostow, "Lessons of the Plan. Looking forward to the Next Century," *Foreign Affairs,* volume 76, no. 3 (May/June 1997), pp. 205-296.
2. Richard Hofstadter, *The American Political Tradition and the Men Who Made It.* (New York, 1948).
3. Fritz Stern, *Dreams and Delusions. The Drama of German History*, (New York, 1987), p. 222.
4. Gordon A. Craig and Francis L. Loewenheim, "Afterward" in *The Diplomats 1939-1979* (Princeton 1994). p. 703.
5. Filemon C.Rodriguez, *Our Struggle for Power* (Quezon City, 1967) and *Our Strategy for Survival* (Quezon City, 1971).
6. Richard D.Challener, "The Moralist as Pragmatist: John Foster Dulles as Cold War Strategist" *in The Diplomats 1939-1979,* edited by Gordon A. Craig and Francis L. Lowenheim (Princeton, 1994), pp 152-155.

Personal Retrospectives

VI. Illustrative Lives of Public Service

Paul H. Nitze
  At the Center of International Decisions 1941-1989
Theodore Tannenwald
  Remembering Averell Harriman
Morris Weisz
  Labor issues and the Marshal Plan
Maurice P. Arth (1921-1997)
  From Norway to Yugoslavia: Maurice P. Arth (1921-1997)
    by H. Lawrence Wilsey

At the Center of International Decisions, 1941-1989

PAUL HENRY NITZE

A mbassador Paul H. Nitze has been diplomat-in-residence at the Paul H. Nitze School of Advanced International Studies (SAIS), The Johns Hopkins University, in Washington DC, since his retirement from the State Department in April 1989. He is also a distinguished professor in strategic studies and American foreign policy.

From January 1985, Mr. Nitze served as Special Advisor to the President and the Secretary of State on arms control matters. In May 1986, President Reagan also appointed him Ambassador-at-Large, a position he held until his retirement. He was awarded the Presidential Medal of Freedom by President Reagan on November 7, 1985. Prior to this, from 1981-83, he was head of the United States Delegation to the Intermediate-Range Nuclear Forces negotiations with the Soviet Union.

During the Nixon Administration, Mr. Nitze was the representative of the Secretary of Defense to the United States delegation to the Strategic Arms Limitation Talks (SALT I) from 1969-74.

Under President Johnson, from 1967-69, Mr. Nitze served as Deputy Secretary of Defense to Robert McNamara and Clark Clifford. In 1963, President Kennedy nominated him to be Secretary of the Navy, a position which he held until 1967. As Secretary of the Navy, he served on the Executive Committee, advising Kennedy during the Cuban Missile Crisis. From 1961-63, Mr. Nitze was Assistant Secretary of Defense for international security affairs. In this role, he was closely involved in the Berlin Crisis of 1961.

From 1953-61, Mr. Nitze was President of the Foreign Service Educational Foundation, the fundraising vehicle for SAIS, the school he had co-founded with Christian Herter in 1944. Mr. Nitze also taught at the school and wrote widely.

In the Truman Administration, Mr. Nitze served in various positions in the State Department, first as Deputy Director of the Office of International Trade Policy. In 1948, Secretary of State George C. Marshall, named him deputy to the Assistant Secretary of State for Economic Affairs. In 1949, he became Deputy Director of the State Department's Policy Planning Staff. From 1949-53 he was Director of Policy Planning, under Secretary of State Dean Acheson, during which time he co-authored NSC-68, the cornerstone document of U.S. Cold War containment policy.

During the Roosevelt Administration, Mr. Nitze served in various positions. In 1940, he helped draft the Selective Service Act under General George C. Marshall. In 1941, he became Financial Director, Office of Inter-American Affairs, at the State Department, before leaving for the Board of Economic Warfare in 1942. From 1943-44 he was Director of Foreign Procurement and Development for the Foreign Economic Administration. In 1944, Mr. Nitze was appointed a director and then, in 1945, vice chairman of the United States Strategic Bombing Survey, which evaluated the effect of U.S. bombing upon German and Japanese industry, including the atomic bombs at Nagasaki and Hiroshima.

Mr. Nitze was graduated cum laude from Harvard University in 1928 (BA) and subsequently joined the New York investment banking firm of Dillon, Read and Company, which he left for Washington in 1941. He is the author of the books *From Hiroshima to Glasnost: At the Center of Decision. A Memoir*, (1989), and *Tension between Opposites: Reflections on the Practice and Theory of Politics*, (1993), and numerous articles.

Born in Amherst, Massachusetts on January 16,1907, Mr. Nitze was married to the late Phyllis Pratt. They had four children, Heidi, Peter, William, and Anina. In 1993, he married Elisabeth Scott Porter, who is President of Antique and Contemporary Leasing, Inc., and a political activist. They maintain their legal residence in Washington, DC, and also have a home in Bel Alton, Maryland.

I Remember Averell

THEODORE TANNENWALD

My initial association with Averell Harriman began in mid July 1950 when I joined him as his counsel and member of a five-man staff he recruited to help him carry out his new role as Special Assistant to the President for Foreign Affairs. The staff was very small, but it might well be considered to have been the embryonic staff of the National Security Council. The NSC had an Executive Secretary but little more than that at the time. We covered a variety of problems in the international field and, in particular, the relationship between the State and Defense Departments.

I had no direct contact with the operations of the Marshall Plan, which was ongoing at that time, but I did get involved in a variety of problems arising out of coordination of our military, economic, and technical assistance programs. At this point, I note that I did have an indirect contact with the Marshall Plan in early 1947. At that time, consideration was given to legislation authorizing military assistance. This was stimulated by President Truman's extending small arms and ammunition aid to France and Italy to help those governments deal with the internal threats of their communist parties. The only legal basis of Truman's actions at that time was his constitutional authority as Commander in Chief of the Armed Forces. In order to deal with the situation, Nate Goodrich of the General Counsel's Office at the Defense Department and I drafted the first military assistance act, which was to have been Title VI of the European Recovery Act. However, at the last minute, Senator Vandenberg on the Senate Foreign Relations Committee decided that the act was not an appropriate vehicle for military assistance, so the matter was dropped. Of course, military assistance came into being about one and one-half years later via the Military Assistance Act of 1949.

I continued in the role as Averell's counsel until October of 1951 when the Mutual Security Act of 1951 was passed. That Act created the office of Director for Mutual Security, and Averell was named to that job. I became Assistant Director for Mutual Security. Averell had two primary functions as Director for Mutual Security. The first was his role as technical head of the old ECA, which was then known as the Mutual Security Agency that handled all economic assistance. John Kenney, who also was an Assistant Director for Mutual Security and had previously been the head of ECA, became head of MSA and was given a free hand in carrying out the operations of the agency.

The second role Averell was given was responsibility for coordinating the military, economic, and technical assistance programs. It was in the implementation of this role that I became his Chief of Staff. Incidentally, this two-prong structure was created by the Conference Committee (without the benefit of Executive branch participation) as a compromise between the House and Senate versions, one of which made MSA part of the State Department and the other continuing the MSA as a totally independent agency, as the ECA had been. The relationship of the aid program to the State Department had been, and continues to be, a controversial issue. Witness the position of Senator Helms that USAID should be merged into the State Department.

The two and one-half years I spent with Averell in carrying out the above-described activities provided the foundation of a friendship which lasted the rest of his life, and included acting as an advisor to him when he was Governor of New York. In this connection, he had asked me to go to Albany as counsel to the Governor, but for personal reasons I declined. We remained close personal friends to the day he died. My wife and I frequently visited Middleburg in the last years of his life to keep him company and, during those sessions, we often talked about the experiences we had together.

About 12 years ago, I decided to record some of my memories of Averell. Given the long span of our personal and working relationship, my recollections obviously cover periods long after the end of the Marshall Plan. However, he was such a key figure in the Marshall Plan that I believe his personal characteristics over all the years I knew him were involved in the period preceding my association with him, a period which covered the creation and initial implementation of the Marshall Plan. It is in this context that I append my recollections under the rubric *I Remember Averell.*

Others have written and will continue to write about Averell Harriman, the world statesman and public servant, one of the giants of the history of the Twentieth Century. From my perspective, none will exaggerate the enormous contribution he made to the well-being of our nation. But there was another Averell Harriman—a human being with great personal qualities known only to a few who were close to him. I was one of those few, and I write to record some vignettes of his life which reflect those qualities. My friendship with Averell spanned more than three decades. It was a treasured personal relationship and evokes treasured memories which defy description.

It all began one warm Wednesday in July 1950. Averell, who had just returned to Washington to be President Truman's Special Assistant for Foreign Affairs, had seen Secretary of Defense Louis Johnson at a Cabinet meeting that morning and had asked him to recommend someone to serve as counsel on the five-man staff Averell wanted to recruit. My name had been suggested to the Secretary. The result was that I saw Averell at 6:30 that evening—having postponed my return to New York. He was running late and asked me to ride with him to the Chevy Chase Club, where he was to have dinner with the then Secretary of State, Dean Acheson. As we rode in his car, Averell described his job and what he wanted me to do. Then as we crossed the Taft Bridge on Connecticut Avenue, he turned to me and said, "There's one very important question that I have forgotten to ask you. I don't care whether you vote Republican or Democrat (I found out later that deep down he really did care), but I must know whether you believe in the principles FDR stood for, because, if you don't, I don't want you." The episode was revealing. It showed me very early in the game that Averell was more interested in substance than labels—a trait that showed up time and again in subsequent years.

One of the jobs Averell had was to try to bridge the gap in the relationship between the Secretaries of State and Defense. Averell sent me as an observer to an executive session of the Senate Foreign Relations Committee. Secretary of Defense Johnson was scheduled to testify on the subject of military aid to Spain and Spain's relationship to NATO. After the session, Johnson offered me a ride back to the Executive Office Building. On the way up Pennsylvania Avenue, he sounded off in the most vitriolic terms about how terrible a person Acheson was and how he hoped Averell would help him get the president to fire Acheson so that Harriman could take Acheson's-place. Averell was appalled at this outburst when I told him about it. He felt that Johnson had shown that he was unfit to hold this office and that he (Averell) owed it to the president to tell him what had happened. A month later, Johnson was fired. Averell's sense of loyalty not only reached upward to his superiors but also found full flower in his support for people who had worked for him. The years 1950 and 1951 were the heyday of the McCarthy witch hunt, and several of Averell's former colleagues in the Commerce Department came under attack. Averell never hesitated to testify or furnish affidavits to help their cases. His sense of loyalty was intense and, as far as I know, he never was concerned about the possible impact of his display of support on his own position. This lack of concern reflected itself on a broader scale when Averell was the only Cabinet officer to recommend that President Truman veto the McCarran-Walter Immigration Act in 1950.

One of the most popular subjects of comment about Averell Harriman is his penchant for telephoning his staff very early in the morning. I can't begin to count the number of times the phone bell jangled at 7:00 a.m. and a voice would say, "Ted, what did you think of Arthur Krock's column this morning?" Averell never understood why I didn't get the *New York Times* at home (the *Times* didn't offer home delivery in those days and Averell got his only because his butler went to the nearest drug store every morning). Eugene Bannigan, who was speaker of the state assembly when Averell was Governor of New York from 1954 through 1958, often told the story that one day shortly after Averell took office the telephone rang at 8:00 a.m. in his room at the Ten Eyck Hotel in Albany. Bannigan answered, and a voice said, "Gene, this is Averell; I hope I didn't wake you up." To this, Bannigan replied, "Not at all, Governor; I've been sitting up all night waiting for your call."

Another telephone call was the one that came from Hyannisport. Averell had gone there for the weekend to consult with Bobby Kennedy about whether Bobby should run for the Senate in New York in 1964. About 11:00 on Sunday morning, my telephone rang and the operator asked me whether I would accept a collect call from Governor Harriman. Averell came on the line and said, "Ted, I hope you don't mind my calling collect, but I didn't want to put this call on Bobby's bill."

This episode brings me to the subject of Averell and money. Obviously, he never suffered from any lack of that commodity. However, he rarely carried any cash on his person. He just assumed that one of his aides would pick up any tabs and get reimbursed (the fact is that most of the time reimbursement did occur, but that was not always feasible).

One Saturday in 1951, Averell had an appointment with the president (we had worked through the lunch hour and he asked me to walk across

West Executive Avenue with him to finish off the matter we were discussing). As I turned away at the door to the West Wing of the White House and started back to the Executive Office Building, I heard a voice calling. Averell was standing in the doorway and pointing to the vending machine just inside. He asked for a nickel and took it to buy a Hershey bar. Then he spotted a peanut machine. I pulled three pennies out of my pocket; which he took and promptly put into the machine. Then, with the Hershey bar in one hand and the peanuts in the other (bought with my eight cents), he went up the stairs to keep his date with the President.

In September 1954, the day after Averell was nominated for Governor of New York, I took up a variety of matters with him at campaign headquarters. As we were finishing up, I handed Averell $500 in $5 and $10 bills, explaining to him that now that he was a candidate he should be prepared to tip doormen, bellhops, etc., as he traveled around. He looked a little puzzled but he took the money—only after I assured him that it was his personal money. Seven weeks later, he gave me back $495!

Speaking of the gubernatorial campaign leads directly into the four occasions on which Averell sought to run for elective office—twice for president and twice for governor. The first occasion was 1952. Averell had come back from the session of the NATO Wise Men during the latter part of 1951. He decided to try for the presidency. People have often speculated as to why he did this, and again why he ran for Governor in 1954. I think there was a good reason- totally apart from the egoism which I believe motivates every candidate for elective office. I believe Averell was always troubled that his positions in the federal government had come his way, not because of his competence, but because of his money. He wanted to show people that, notwithstanding his background, he could make it on his own.

The 1952 quest for the presidency evokes a host of memories. There was the speech Averell gave in Constitution Hall on the occasion of the Third Anniversary of the North Atlantic Treaty in April. It is no secret that Averell's public speaking ability left much to be desired, but this speech was one of the best he ever gave- completely in keeping with the ultimate model of a great presidential decoration. It was a perfect example of how good a speaker Averell could be when he not only knew his subject matter but had a burning conviction of the correctness of what he was saying. He showed his mettle in this regard when he spoke at Roosevelt's grave at Hyde Park in May of the same year.

And then there was a Saturday afternoon in May 1952 when Averell returned to his office from a visit with President Truman. He was in no mood to talk about several important foreign aid matters which required his attention. He was on cloud nine: Truman, according to Averell, had promised to support Averell's candidacy. To this day, I am convinced that Averell heard what he wanted to hear, not what was actually said. I have no doubt that the president encouraged Averell to pursue his candidacy—after all, Adlai Stevenson was playing very hard to get. But I am convinced that the President did not promise to support Averell. It was too far ahead of the convention for him to do that- besides, Adlai might make up his mind to run, and Truman would not want to be inhibited by a prior commitment. Four years later, in 1956, Truman did support Averell at the Democratic Convention in Chicago, but to no avail. Adlai was renominated, only to lose to Ike again.

That Averell, if elected, would have made a good president is beyond question as far as I am concerned. That he would have been a winning candidate is extremely doubtful. I do not think he could have beaten Ike in either 1952 or 1956. Perhaps he could have beaten Nixon in 1960, but he was never in the running for the nomination. The American public was not yet prepared to accept a 68-year-old freshman president.

Averell was a hard taskmaster, but he was a human, kindly person. I remember the card that accompanied a huge bouquet of flowers which my wife received from him. Averell and I had a succession of days and nights of work, and one night I had warned him that the following night I had to be home for dinner because it was my wife's birthday. The card read, "Happy birthday. Hope you can keep Ted home tonight. Where has he been all week?"

Averell exuded the aura of the patrician that he was, but it was always tempered by an inner quality of humbleness. On my bookshelf is a copy of the *Forrestal Diaries* (Forrestal was the first Secretary of Defense and an old friend of Averell's.) It was a present from Averell. In the book, Forrestal is unstinting in his praise of Averell. On the flyleaf is the inscription, "To Ted Tannenwald. I hope you don't keep a diary. I'm afraid I wouldn't do so well."

Averell had a prodigious memory. Perhaps the best example involves his famous Yalta Statement, which he submitted to the Senate Foreign Relations Committee in June 1952 in lieu of testifying at the MacArthur hearings (as he had planned to do), because he had to go to Iran to negotiate with Mossadegh about the oil well seizures. The night before he was to leave, we had dinner together at his home on Foxhall Road and then spent most of the night going over the draft statement which I had prepared. After careful examination of the files containing cables, memoranda of conversations and so forth, I thought my draft was very complete and more than satisfactory, but Averell still worked many changes. He wanted to flesh-out the statement, as only he could do, with episodes and conversations which had not been recorded. His memory was phenomenal, and obviously the statement was vastly improved by the additions he made.

Averell's hearing had been a problem for a long time, and his difficulty hearing and his stubborn unwillingness to get a hearing aid almost cost him a place in the Kennedy Administration. One afternoon in December 1960, I received a telephone call from Mike Forrestal (the son of the first Secretary of Defense and an old friend and confidant of Averell's). It seems that Mike had been to a small luncheon Averell had given for Hugh Gaitskell at the house on East 81st Street. The newly elected President, John F. Kennedy, had been there. As the luncheon broke up, Kennedy got hold of Mike and asked if there was a place where the two of them could talk privately. Mike allowed that the only place at hand was the powder room off the foyer. And to the powder room they went. Kennedy told Mike that he wanted to appoint Averell Roving Ambassador but he hesitated to do so because of Averell's hearing difficulty; he was afraid Averell wouldn't hear the things he should hear at negotiations and other diplomatic gatherings. Kennedy asked Mike if there wasn't some way that Averell could be persuaded to get a hearing aid. It became Mike's and my task to persuade Averell to get a hearing aid. Happily, we succeeded, and Averell came back to public life (he had been pretty much out of it after his defeat for re-election as Governor of New York in 1958) and he gave distinguished service for almost 20 more years.

Speaking of the 1958 gubernatorial race, I have a very sad recollection of Buffalo in September, and New York City in November. At the convention, Averell had been nominated for Governor on Monday evening, although the issue of who was to be his running mate had not been settled. Some of us had urged Averell not to permit his name to be placed in nomination until the matter was settled, but our advice did not prevail. As a result, Averell was faced with the necessity of going to the convention the following evening (Tuesday) knowing that his candidate, Tom Finletter, would be rejected and Carmine De Sapio's candidate, Frank Hogan, nominated. Averell was so hurt and so angry that he did not want to go. But his wife Marie (supported by George Backer, Charles Van Devanter, and myself, who were the only ones with him in his hideaway above the convention floor in Buffalo) prevailed upon him to go. That night was the beginning of a disastrous campaign which culminated on a rainy night in November, when my wife and I were the only ones to say goodbye to him at his car before he and Marie left the Democratic headquarters at the Biltmore Hotel to go home and lick the wounds of defeat. "The King is dead, long live the King!"

There was another campaign incident which showed me how determined Averell could be. The day after the New York convention in 1954 when he was first nominated to run for Governor, he went to his doctor in New York City, presumably for a check-up. When Averell came back to campaign headquarters, he announced that he was giving up smoking on doctor's orders. And give it up he did (he had been smoking one to two packs a day), and, as far as I know, he never touched a cigarette again. Keep in mind that the next seven weeks were probably as hard and stressful a period as Averell had ever experienced.

There are many more stories and episodes involving Averell, but these are the ones I remember the best. No one can come close to him in terms of his long years of varied experience, and there is no doubt that, as the years went by, his experience was probably the most meaningful element in his ability to analyze and advise on important issues of foreign affairs. But beyond his experience and his other qualities, Averell had "intuition," a characteristic which I find difficult to describe. He had an uncanny ability to size up an important issue and know instinctively what needed to be done. On innumerable occasions, in top-level conferences which dealt with the great issues of the time, he would listen to others talk and then state his own views in a few words. Sometimes many of the details of why he felt the way he did were not articulated as clearly as one would want. But almost without exception his judgments were proved to be correct by subsequent events. It was this plus factor that made Averell's advice and counsel so invaluable to presidents over a span of almost 50 years.

But beyond everything else, Averell Harriman was a man of confidence, faith, and vision. He never wavered in his belief that world peace and a better life for mankind could be achieved. The only question was how this could be done. We would do well to remember this great man of history and to look to the future, as he always did: asking not whether, but how, we can achieve our ultimate goals.

Labor Issues and
the Marshall Plan

Morris Weisz

I am the only child in a family of seven to have been born in the United
States. Our parents were typical central European migrants to the
United States. Our father arrived first, together with my siblings who
were old enough to work. They all obtained whatever jobs were available
in order to earn enough to bring the younger children and our mother to
join them.

It was thus not some work ethic, but rather sheer need, which projected
my parents and elder siblings into the sweatshops. It was, however, my
father's socialist ideology and the international concerns he brought with
him from Europe, combined with the Jewish tradition of the importance
of education, which propelled us all into the excellent free school system
then available in New York City—a 1920's version of what later became
the GI Bill of Rights.

The sacrifices which my parents and siblings endured during my
youth permitted me to be the only member of our family to go to college
as a full-time student, working only during summers to earn the modest
funds needed for subway and street-car fares, lunches, engineering
equipment for my courses and other related fees, and for a very limited
amount of entertainment—mostly movies and only on very special
occasions to the live theater, of which I have been a devotee all my life.

The City College (CCNY) experience of campus politics, being a
member of the Student Council as a delegate from the conservative
Engineering School, provided the opportunity for gaining a very broad

education which was later to serve me well in my international work. I took courses in European history with Professor Henry David, who once graded one of my papers with the comment "What are you doing in the *Engineering* School?," and whom I was later able to appoint to a senior position in his field at the OEEC; logic, with professor Morris Raphael Cohen, whose experience as an immigrant from Czarist Russia was blended with his Yale University training, teaching us how to fight any type of authoritarian regime, with special reference to the threat of Stalinism, in both theory and practice, as we faced it daily from so many of our communist fellow-students; and public speaking, which I put to use in college debates and on street corners in the Bronx from the age of sixteen, and later in speaking tours to over 40 countries, while serving abroad in various US Foreign Service, OECD and academic posts.

My courses in French, unlike many of my my fellow Marshall Plan associates, enabled me to come to Paris with courses in Corneille, Racine and Moliere under my belt, helping me confront the French disdain of American cultural deficiencies and aided me in becoming adept at bargaining with the numerous Paris flea market merchants who normally used a Yiddish-ized version of French, understood only by customers having my unique cultural history. My English literature classes were with William Bradley Otis, whose classes were so crowded that we lined up outside his lecture hall as early as possible, just to hear him read plays, especially Shakespeare, or poetry in his imposing manner. This experience made me a life-time devotee of the theater. And it motivated me to engage in my hobby of collecting playbills as I traveled abroad.

During this period of my CCNY education, I also had the wondrous advantage of exposure to New York City politics in the age of Mayor Fiorello LaGuardia, who was famous for his ability to address many of his constituents in their own native languages and dialects, as later made famous in the Broadway musical "Fiorello." Through my socialist involvements, I came to know trade union and political leaders, including such nationally known personages as Norman Thomas, and many local figures, including August Claessens, the perennial Long Island Socialist candidate for any vacant office, and the Yiddish orator, B. Charney Vladeck, who led an entire generation of youth to understand the fundamental linkage between secular doctrine and communal obligation.

Employment

After graduation from CCNY in 1934, I made an easy transition to volunteering for a trade union, because it was virtually impossible for engineer to find paid employment during the Depression. My school and political activities made me a logical candidate to work as a non-paid organizer in a local union of the socialist-oriented International Ladies' Garment Workers' Union, (ILGWU) led by David Dubinsky.

By the next year, I was actually a *paid* employee of the union ($12 per week!), functioning variously as an organizer, assistant educational director and editor of the local's monthly news letter—also responsible for physically distributing it to the union members working in the garment area shops under our broad jurisdiction.

Soon the trade union movement had to give way to more personal interests the following year, when my future wife and I decided to plan for a more secure life, even if that meant leaving my trade union job, and my fiancee's tuition-free education at Hunter College, the women's CCNY branch in Manhattan, and all our families and friends in New York City.

Encouraged by Phil Travis, a former fellow socialist at CCNY who had become a messenger in the Federal Government, I took the Civil Service entrance examination. I was soon notified that I had passed and was offered a clerical position, at the Census Bureau, at a salary considerably greater than the ILGWU felt it could then match.

The head of our local union, who was also an ILGWU Vice President, approved my leaving so readily because he could not otherwise explain any additional effort to keep me, when my more senior colleagues in the local were earning much more modest salaries than that offered me by the U.S. government. This was part of the tradition that working for the ILGWU is a special privilege reserved for youth. Two decades later, however, when I introduced my old trade union chief to my new boss, Secretary of Labor Tobin, he proudly mentioned that I had been one of the "boys" he had trained, and whom he might one day even lure back from government to the ILGWU! With the blessing of my trade union colleagues then, I accepted the offer immediately and left New York within a week, arriving in Washington on May 19, 1935.

Upon arriving in Washington on an overnight excursion-rate train trip from New York, I was greeted warmly by Travis, who helped me find a rooming house where I could stay until I got married. I returned to New York on July 14, for a traditional synagogue wedding held in the

Bronx, near our childhood homes, close to James Monroe High School, from which we had both graduated. Though the date of our marriage fell on Bastille Day, we did not know at the time that we would later celebrate the holiday in Paris on many joyous occasions. Most recently, on our 50th wedding anniversary in 1985, we found ourselves attending the first concert performed at the new "People's Opera House" located in the working-class area of the city, on the actual site where the French Revolution had been proclaimed by hordes of all classes of citizens who tore down the detested prison where so many had suffered under the Bourbon regime.

Our marriage was followed immediately by a train trip to Washington. We were never again to be residents of New York, although we visited there frequently, either on official business, to see friends and family, or to attend one of the city's vibrant theater performances. We had a one-day honeymoon, during which I introduced my bride, Yetta, to many of the new friends I had made since my arrival in Washington—chiefly in the socialist group there. I then returned to my job and Yetta was left with a formidable task for a 19-year old who had never been away from home before: adjusting to the strange situation of rooming-house living, cooking in a minuscule kitchen, and searching for a free college in which to continue her education.

I remained at the Census Bureau for two years (1935-1937), learning some valuable lessons in statistical procedures while preparing a number of monthly industrial production reports which the Bureau compiled for the National Recovery Administration (NRA). The Bureau also offered us young "fast-track" employees, special courses in statistics, given by high officials of the Bureau.

In my spare time during the monthly cycle of preparing the NRA reports, I also became active in the Department of Commerce Lodge of the American Federation of Government Employees (AFGE). Then, much to the dismay of a few of the Bureau veterans, one of whom complained that she had entered the Bureau to work in the "aught" (1900) census and was still waiting for a promotion, I was promoted one grade within a year of my original appointment.

In April, 1937, through the efforts of two socialist friends, I was asked to apply for a clerical job at the National Labor Relations Board (NLRB), under the Board's Chief Economist, David J. Saposs. During the interview, Saposs told me that, since the Wagner Act had just been declared constitutional, the Board needed a statistical clerk to help prepare economics reports ensuring that respondents in Board proceedings were engaged in interstate commerce.

My Census Bureau experience had included NRA industry studies of the type which, Saposs told me, could be of value to the work of his staff and he offered to transfer me to a clerical position in his Division, at my present grade and salary. I accepted with glee, shifting from my permanent Census job to a 90-day temporary one on the Board's Division of Economic Research. I remained at the Board (except for my transfer from 1942-46 to the War Production Board) until entering the Department of Labor in 1948. I learned later that, typical of his personnel recruitment procedure, Dave Saposs had taken the precaution of questioning my friends who had recommended me regarding my trade union experience and political background. He had been impressed to learn that my sister, a Garment Workers' union activist, had been one of his students at the Brookwood Labor College, which he had directed just before he came to the NLRB.

At the NLRB, with the practical experience and training from the Division's senior staff members, and by enrolling at American University for graduate courses in trade unionism, labor law, and administrative and constitutional law, I was soon able to be promoted from clerical grades to professional positions (with commensurate pay) as an economist, even without having taken many of the formal economics courses required for graduate degrees.

Saposs became my friend and mentor, in both domestic and international assignments until his death in 1986. I am reasonably certain that Saposs consciously directed me to my own later practice of using a combination of specialized training, practical experience and teaching a variety of courses to serve as a substitute for earning formal graduate degrees for which I did not have the appropriate pre-requisite courses. I was not the only one of Saposs's friends, co-workers and professional colleagues who were assisted in this way. Nor did we ever learn the particular circumstances which lay behind his selection of those who came under his wing. Saposs motivated many other participants in The George Washington University 50th Anniversary Conference, including, notably, another of his proteges, Joseph Mintzes, who died recently. Mintzes was already known as an accomplished statistician when he first came to Dave's attention, having already earned an economics degree at Temple University in Philadelphia. We met first when he arrived in Washington as a very young bachelor, and he was offered the rare opportunity to be Saposs's tenant in the spare bedroom of their Belmont

Street home. It was there that Dave and his multi-talented wife, Bertha, hosted the many dinners where we young NLRB economists met the Saposses' circle of friends, many of whom were world-renowned experts in a variety of disciplines.

The method Saposs used to select members of his Division's staff was novel. Because of his experience in Wisconsin, he understood the need to train people in many aspects of formal economics, but he also instilled in us an appreciation of the need to engage in the practical work of actually administering public policy. This was the "Wisconsin idea" of Wisconsin's Progressive Party, led by Senator Robert M. La Follete Sr., who was famous for having rejected the Republican ticket to run on the Progressive Party ticket in 1924. The importance of teaching to those trained in the Wisconsin tradition was instilled in me by two close personal and political friends, George Brooks and Jack Barbash, also on the NLRB staff under Saposs.

Brooks, among my supervisors at the NLRB (and later at the War Product Board) left government service at the end of the war to become the director of education for an old AFL union, heading its newly-established Washington office. At the same time, he also gave an evening course in Labor History at American University. Since his work required considerable travel, he suggested that I replace him when he was absent on union business, using some of the notes from graduate courses I had been taking. After observing a few of his excellent lectures I did so and, beginning with the late forties, followed his excellent course outline when his union duties required him to leave Washington. I found this to be an enjoyable experience, and professionally rewarding since it soon led to my teaching other courses at the university. Brooks left full-time union work entirely a few years later, to become a distinguished Professor of Economics and Industrial Relations at Cornell University. He now conducts the university's Washington Semester Program, where I have lectured on occasion before my own retirement.

Jack Barbash and his wife Kitty became our closest family, political and personal friends from the day Jack reported to work at the NLRB in 1939. For the next few years we jointly rented three homes in Washington, and then actually bought a fourth home, in Bethesda, a nearby Maryland suburb. There we raised the first four children of our joint family. This rare arrangement amazed our friends, and caused considerable neighborhood gossip—all of which has been the subject of family lore for decades. Unfortunately, it also later became the basis for FBI investigations.

Beginning with the early forties, Barbash would spend many weeks each summer teaching at the famous Workers' School of the University of Wisconsin (UW) in Madison. By 1946 he arranged to have me invited to teach at the School whenever I could take annual leave from the NLRB. This was not only professionally rewarding, but had the further advantage of allowing our families to renew their ties. The faculty of the School itself included stimulating personalities from the regular UW faculty, but also from trade union, management, and academic circles from all over the world.

From then on, I would return to Madison from wherever I would be serving in the Washington area, or elsewhere in the Foreign Service, to lecture on different aspects of my work. By 1957, Barbash had left trade union and government service entirely, and in 1976 was appointed to the prestigious post of John P. Bascom Professor of Economics and Industrial Relations. And, in 1979, at his urging, I was appointed Visiting Professor of Economics and Industrial Relations, and spent two years there until I returned to Washington in 1979.

The teaching experience to which I was introduced by Brooks and Barbash was not only pivotal to my work career, but was also crucial to the perception of what I call the Legacy of the Marshall Plan. I have continued teaching and lecturing until now, and I am eternally grateful to Brooks and Barbash for initiating me into this secondary career.

As far as my employment is concerned, I remained at the NLRB during a period which exposed me to some events beyond labor law administration, and which were later quite relevant to issues raised in the Marshall Plan experience: the internal conflict between the pro-AFL and pro-CIO staff members, as well as the attempts of the small number of pro-communists on the staff to direct Board decisions in favor of communist unions.

Much has been written about the Labor Board during that period, and Saposs was engrossed in it as a strong critic of the pro-communists, based on his Wisconsin background and experiences there. The details of this internecine battle within the NLRB are beyond the scope of this paper, but they represent the precursors to many of the issues faced after World War II, even before the Marshall Plan was formally in place, and they continued in one form or another for many years thereafter.

Even at the NLRB during the late thirties, a number of issues arose which seemed strange to those of us who were politically active. Although none of the alleged pro-communist attorneys lost their jobs in this struggle, somehow a group of conservatives in the Congress were able to mount an attack on Saposs as an alleged pro-communist, based on a cruelly misinterpreted article he had written as a young, very *anti-communist*, researcher. As a result, the entire budget of our division was eliminated, and Saposs remained unemployed for some time, until "cleared" some years afterwards, due to the efforts of an exceptionally fair, conservative member of Congress.

Meanwhile, with Saposs dismissed from the NLRB, a few members of the decimated economics staff were retained, but were transferred to the legal staff, and, explicitly prohibited from doing any research, were restricted to computing back-pay under Board-ordered decisions-a virtually clerical, albeit complicated task, that had been part of my duties earlier.

As head of this small back-pay unit, I remained with the Board until I transferred to the War Production Board (WPB) in 1942. (This was the first time I was to replace Saposs—at his suggestion—in a career during which he was to recommend me to replace him at least four times. So much so, that when Saposs finally retired, a friend asked me how I would ever be able to find employment again!)

I left the Labor Board in 1942 for a job in the WPB's Labor Production Office, directed by a WPB Vice Chairman, Joseph Keenan, who had been a high official in the AFL's Chicago City Central body and head of the International Brotherhood of Electrical Workers. Another Board Vice Chairman, Clinton Golden, came from the CIO Steelworkers Union and headed what was called the Manpower Requirements Office. Both Keenan and Golden had small personal staffs from the trade union movement, but also received technical support from professional economists on the staffs of both Vice Chairmen. My own position was one of these and it fell under George Brooks, who had been a top assistant to Saposs before the Division of Economic Research had been abolished.

My duties at the War Production Board, from 1942-46, concerned recruiting workers in a variety of industries, ranging from printing and publishing, where my task was frequently to limit recruitment severely, since that industry was not deemed as important to the war effort as others, to the radio and radar industry, where I was also named labor advisor, and which had a priority for recruiting workers second only to that of the Hanford project which, we learned after the war, produced the atom bomb.

The administrative device for determining the relative priority for allocating scarce materials was the Controlled Materials Plan (CMP), under the authority of the brilliant economist (and later a top State Department official) Lincoln Gordon. It was at the frequent sessions of the CMP which Linc Gordon chaired that the various WPB operating Divisions would exercise their claims for steel, paper, or other critical materials in short supply.

As the labor and training advisor to the Radio and Radar Division, I was also able to use some of my engineering background, which was later to prove valuable since it gave me a top security clearance that turned out to be helpful during my Marshall Plan security problems discussed below.

I stayed on at the WPB for a few months after the end of the War to write a chapter of its history relating to the work of the Labor Production and Manpower Requirements staffs, and resigned in March, 1946. For personal family reasons, I decided to take advantage of my re-instatement rights at the NLRB, and to postpone my own international work for a few years. Meanwhile, however, the United Auto Workers (UAW)-CIO was in the midst of a strike against the General Motors Corporation, in 1946, and I volunteered to use some of my annual leave in order to help the union's Washington Office staff —and, incidentally, to delay taking the considerable cut in wages involved in going back to my NLRB pay-scale.

Since I had worked on a number of UAW cases at the Board and knew many of its leaders, including the Reuther brothers, I offered to prepare a memorandum on GE's strike-breaking history which had been exposed by Senator La Follette in hearings before his Senate Labor Committee. Some years ago, the Labor Board had assigned some members of its investigative staff to assist the Committee in its work, and I had collected its published hearings for labor courses I had taken at American University (AU). On the basis of this background, I was able to prepare the needed memorandum in a few weeks, for which I was thanked more profusely than this small task deserved.

My return to the Labor Board in March, 1946 was not a happy experience for a number of reasons, but chiefly because the work failed to challenge me as much as had my duties at the WPB. Additionally, the 80th Congress elected that year brought in a Republican legislature which quickly amended the Wagner Act of 1935 by adopting the Taft-Hartley Act, considered by many trade unions to be "slave labor" legislation.

I did not agree with this simplistic characterization of the new legislation, especially since the Board still retained powers which could be used effectively to advance labor's appropriate interests. After all, there still existed a backlog of court decisions enforcing earlier Board doctrines, and these could proceed through the courts, which were still led by Roosevelt appointees. Nevertheless, I had been so involved in preparing testimony opposing the new Act, that I began seeking a transfer to another government agency.

The opportunity for me to transfer to the Department of Labor came in late 1948, again with the help of Dave Saposs. In the Labor Department Bureau of Labor Statistics (BLS), the newly-appointed Commissioner was Ewan Clague, an old friend of Saposs's from the University of Wisconsin. Clague had just established labor and employer research advisory committees to help him deal with questions relating to the Consumer Price Index, now regularly being used to adjust wages under many joint labor-management collective bargaining contracts.

Clague asked Saposs to fill the labor research advisory post and also to serve as his staff assistant on a variety of other matters. Saposs accepted, and remained in the post for two years, until, in mid-1948, the head of the Labor Division in the Paris Headquarters of the U.S. Mission to the OEEC (and later to NATO) asked Saposs to return to Europe as the Division's trade union advisor. The problem of replacing Saposs at the BLS was solved by Dave's suggesting that I transfer to the BLS, since I had already expressed an interest in leaving the NLRB. I accepted his suggestion eagerly, and it was supported by Commissioner Clague. We all agreed that I would fill the BLS job for one year, subject to yearly renewals, depending on Saposs's personal situation. I then transferred to the BLS, arriving there a few days after President Truman's triumphant 1948 election. At the time, Saposs had suggested that I might prefer to take a specialist assignment on the OEEC staff rather than his BLS post, but Yetta and I felt our children were too young at the time for us to consider such a step. So, in spite of my interest in international labor affairs, we decided to postpone going abroad.

As it turned out, the BLS job was quite different from what it had been under Dave. The trade union advisory committee work continued to have first priority on my time; it was enjoyable and not at all difficult, since I had known most of the union researchers from my days in the union movement and at the Labor Board. The other part of the assignment, as a sort of senior labor advisor to Commissioner Clague, did not work out that well, mainly because I was not an old friend of his, as Dave had been. (Many years later, when we had gotten to be very good friends and the Commissioner was visiting us in our Paris home one evening, Clague confessed he had originally been a bit suspicious of me, although he had accepted Saposs' recommendation that I be appointed, but he was quite concerned about the campaign which my research friends seemed to have initiated on my behalf!) In the Labor Department, my services were found to be useful in ways different from Saposs's work. While Dave had spent more time handling Clague's relations with unions, I became more involved in the Department's legislative program because of my NLRB experience.

With the Truman victory in 1948, the President had embarked on a campaign to repeal the Taft-Hartley Law which the 80th Congress had passed over the President's veto. In this battle, I became a sort of adjunct to the office of the Department's Solicitor, where I worked most closely with the Associate Solicitor for Legislative Affairs, Kenneth Meiklejohn, a dear friend from my earliest days in Washington. Our first joint effort, at the specific request of the newly appointed Secretary of Labor, Maurice Tobin, was to write a long speech to be made two days later on the floor of the Senate by the newly elected Senator from Minnesota, Hubert Humphrey. He had been given the assignment on the theory that the intervening time could be used to convince a few Southern senators to change their votes. Ken covered the labor law aspects of the repeal effort while I condensed my lecture notes from the labor history course I was then giving at AU. Two days later we sat at the rear of the Senate floor and heard Humphrey speak for ten hours, brilliantly interpolating aspects of his own experience into what we had written.

Later the speech was entered into the Congressional Record. At the suggestion of Max Kampelman, Humphrey's chief of staff, it was published as a pamphlet and used by many trade unions in the campaign to repeal the Taft-Hartley Law. Hubert Humphrey became a good friend, and a great supporter in my foreign service career. (In New Delhi, Yetta was to chair the volunteer Committee to elect President Johnson and Senator Humphrey in the 1968 campaign.)

Secretary Tobin was quite impressed by our efforts for Humphrey, and asked Clague whether I could also prepare a few addresses for him to give on special occasions. Commissioner Clague approved the idea, but with the understanding that these chores had to fit into the time schedule of the labor research advisory meetings, and that I should limit the time spent on each speech to only two weeks. This became a new career for me, in terms of my relations with the Secretary, my work in the BLS, and the opportunity to expand the scope of my research, especially in the direction of my later international labor and Marshall Plan assignments.

With Tobin's approval, the speeches I prepared for him concentrated on three areas which I knew were close to Tobin's immediate political concerns, but also relevant to my own background and interests. These subjects were: (1) the labor relations aspects of a variety of current issues; (2) the social policies of the Catholic Church, in which I had become interested at CCNY, due to my friendship with a fellow Engineering School student with whom I was re-examining and comparing my faith; and (3) the Department of Labor's increasing responsibility for supporting Marshall Plan aid programs by assisting the productivity teams coming from abroad, with special emphasis on how our respective interests conformed with one another.

It was during this period that I first became involved in the domestic aspects of international labor issues. During the Korean War, Phil Kaiser, then Assistant Secretary of Labor for International Labor Affairs, was hosting the Joint Productivity Teams coming from countries receiving Marshall Plan funds. Kaiser's staff, together with representatives from other Department Bureaus, had to expose the teams to our methods of dealing with productivity issues, during the difficult domestic circumstances of the Korean emergency.

Here, the trade union and labor-management issues I had been working on in the domestic area were dominant and had to be understood by teams visiting the United States to study how their political and economic needs intertwined with our own problems. In fact, this was precisely the subject of the talks I gave to all incoming foreign service officers beginning with 1950, and to labor attache conferences in Cuba in 1950, and in Paris in 1951, during my first trip to Europe.

In fact, I adapted one of the talks I had prepared some months earlier for Secretary Tobin for Kaiser to use in an address he was to make before the American Club of Paris. This address also became the basis for part of Kaiser's formal presentation to the ILO Conference in Geneva that year, in his capacity as head of the U.S. Delegation; he also arranged for me to join the Delegation for a few days, to acquaint me with International Labor Organization (ILO) procedures as he expected me to work on ILO matters in the future.

The 1951 trip to Paris gave me the opportunity to speak to Dave Saposs about his own plans, and since I had been taking his place in the

BLS only on a year-to-year basis whether I should begin to explore job opportunities elsewhere. I told Dave that Tobin had offered me a political job on his staff, but that I would take it only on a temporary basis, and had already opened up negotiations with a few union research departments; what did he think? Dave replied that he was thinking of his own retirement in a few years, and would probably return to the BLS in 1952 for a while, and then seek an academic post where he could resume research and writing. I used some of my annual leave that week, spending as much time as possible before going on to Geneva walking around Paris, bewitched by a city I had always loved from afar. Upon returning home I told the family that I wanted to find any job in Paris as soon as possible, and was thinking of seeking a specialist's position at the OEEC, which Dave said could probably be arranged, if Yetta agreed to leave Washington.

Working in Europe

The following spring I received a letter from Saposs, announcing that both he and Mintzes, his economist, would be returning to Washington in the summer. Dave added that it was really time for me to take an international assignment and that, with this in mind, he had asked the head of the Labor Division to nominate me to become the trade union advisor in his place. Furthermore, he continued, Nelson Cruikshank, who then headed the Labor Division (an old AFL friend of mine and Dave's) had welcomed the idea, and could the family arrive in Paris as early as in August!

What followed was another indication of Dave's wisdom in using a particular form of training to prepare a staff member to take over an assignment: I was invited to come to Paris without the family, in July, so that I could accompany Dave on a one-month trip around Europe to help me become oriented to the content and scope of my future assignment.

Thus, we spent a month visiting major Marshall Plan missions, meeting the countless friends and contacts Dave had accumulated over the years in academic, trade union, political (including socialist and Catholic party) circles, as well as the U.S. labor attaches, United States Information Service (USIS) and Productivity staffs, and the labor officials of some other governments. In carrying out my OEEC duties for the next five years in the Labor Department, the OECD and foreign service activities as well as in all my academic work since then I continued to profit from Dave's thoughtfulness in this regard.

I flew back to Washington to pick up the family and we boarded a ship, a luxury then permitted foreign service families going to a new post, and arrived in Paris on August 11, 1952 (the second birthday of our youngest child), where Dave's secretary had arranged for a baby-sitter to stay at the hotel with the children so that we could change clothes and rush to the Cafe du Paris, where the staff had arranged a combined farewell reception for the Saposses and a welcome for us. The next day we joined many old and new friends at the Gare St. Lazare to say farewell to Dave and Bertha Saposs.

Early that spring, Saposs had already arranged for us to rent an old four-story "charming" wreck of a villa in Garches, a suburb of Versailles, which Fiora and John Houghteling, colleagues of ours at the WPB, were due to leave at about the time of our family's scheduled arrival. This again left the task of settling into a new home to Yetta, but now with even more problems than she had confronted when we first came to Washington as newlyweds. We can now recall our adventures in that home with laughter, but the daily problems there, combined with the children's challenges as they confronted language and food predicaments in their French schools, not to mention the French government bureaucracy, were hard to take for the next eighteen months.

In March 1954, however, we were fortunate to be able to move to Boulogne-sur-Seine, a contemporaneous, Corbusier-designed flat close to Paris, near the Longchamps race track in the Bois-de-Boulogne. We enrolled the children in an excellent bi-lingual school, and I joined a car pool commuting to my SRE office daily.

Upon being sworn in at our SRE Mission, I became a member of what was then known as the United States Delegation to the OEEC, NATO and other European Regional Organizations (USRO). My duties were broad in geographic range, all of Europe, including the USAID missions in each of the OEEC countries; but quite narrow in scope, comprising only the limited labor field, important as that was. I spent less than a year as the international trade union advisor to the Director of the Labor Division, as Cruikshank had already left Paris even before my arrival to return to a post at the AFL National Headquarters in Washington.

Cruikshank's successor was Joe Heath, a traditional AFL trade union organizer who was very different from his predecessor. I grew to admire Heath's basic good qualities and great sense of humor, but with the election of President Eisenhower that November, Heath was not able to remain very long. I was offered the Director post, but rejected it, insisting that it should be offered instead to a trade union political appointee. I did agree to serve in an acting capacity, however, until such a person could be found. This took more than two years to arrange. The ultimate replacement was a trade union friend of mine, with whom I was to share the Labor Division responsibilities in total satisfaction until we both left Paris in 1957.

At the time I was sworn in, the Labor Division reported to the USRO Ambassador for Economic Affairs, whom I had known for years as a leader in the Wisconsin socialist movement and as the Labor Secretary of the party until he resigned in 1940 in a disagreement with his old friend Norman Thomas, on the issue of aid to Great Britain before we entered the war.

The duties of my Paris assignment included direct supervision of the Mission's general labor policy and functional oversight of the important productivity and information activities, to determine their impact on overall labor policy. I was responsible for: supervising anti-communist research studies; reviewing operations of the AFL and CIO resident representatives in Europe, Irving Brown and Victor Reuther; maintaining membership on the OEEC and NATO Manpower Committees, alternating chairmanships with Cullingford; dealing with security problems such as the Mcleod and Norman Thomas issue, the burning of books in Germany by McCarthyites Cohn and Shein, and the political problems of defending our friends and thwarting communist attacks; the selection and assignment of OEEC staffers, American and European, from Missions, trade unions, etc; debriefing recipients of USAID support and reporting on their progress to Washington; representing the SRE at international trade union congresses and USG meetings where Marshall Plan issues are involved, usually with the U.S. Embassy Belgium labor attache; and, filing joint State/SRE reports to State Department and USAID headquarters.

A truly significant contribution to my career in the Marshall Plan period was Norman Thomas's insistence on appealing personally—and successfully—to President Eisenhower when Secretary of State Foster Dulles, a fellow active Princeton alumnus, had refused to over-rule the Assistant Secretary's public statement that no socialist should be permitted to remain in the Foreign Service. Thomas was then pleased to send me a copy of the *New York Times* article describing the President's reversal of Dulles's position which Eisenhower had permitted Thomas to give to the newspaper. A few years ago, I related this story in an article for the *Foreign Service Journal*, and it has since been used in labor attache training courses I and my successors have given. Thomas was also always happy to write letters of introduction to his friends in the democratic socialist movements in Italy, India, Germany, Scandinavia and Japan, where he felt it would help me establish valuable contacts.

Another example of welcome assistance from persons who knew of my political background was that offered by Vice-President Humphrey. On my departure for India in 1965, in recognition of my 1949 speech-writing chore for him and at the suggestion of my friend Hy Bookbinder, at that time the Vice-President's Poverty Program spokesman, Vice-President Humphrey sent me off with a picture of both of us on the steps of the Capitol. I therefore arrived in New Delhi with well-publicized connections which our USIS there used effectively, not only in its own publications in English and in a dozen Indian language editions, but also in its news releases to the Indian press.

The Legacy of the Marshall Plan

Two excellent biographies recount the details of the Marshall Plan's origin, both pointing to the decisive importance of the Truman Doctrine as its forerunner. David McCullough's 1992 scholarly masterpiece, *Truman*, as well as Robert Donovan's 1977 partial biography of Truman, *Conflict and Crisis 1945-1948*, both describe the efforts within the Department of State's Policy Planning Staff to pull together for the Secretary of State the policy alternatives for facing Western Europe's dreadful predicament of human hunger and indigence, and the need to confront simultaneously both its predicaments at home as well as the existing military hazards presented by the Soviet Union and its voluntary and unwilling allies.

Marshall's genius was firmly rooted in a number of concepts that had served him well as he advanced in both his military and then diplomatic career: first, to recruit an imaginative staff; second, to stimulate its members to generate a wide range of policy choices for him to explore; third, to test these alternatives thoroughly and promptly; and, fourth, to decide on a course of action and execute it promptly.

In 1947, with misery rampant in Europe, Secretary of State Marshall looked to George Kennan, the State Department Policy Planning Staff (PPS) Director—a long-time student of Soviet affairs who had been brought to Washington from his post in Moscow to prepare a series of policy papers on the situation in Europe, with special reference to the mounting threat of Soviet influence over its neighbors. The picture was grim and Kennan and his staff had made it clear that Western Europe's plight was not only a danger to its own people, but could also threaten our own country and its allies.

Marshall brought together a group of his "wise men" from within the State Department, including Under Secretary Dean Acheson, Assistant Secretary for Economic Affairs Clayton and the President's Special Advisor, Clark Clifford, to discuss the implications to be drawn from the PPS's research. Also involved was Charles Bohlen a fellow-expert on the Soviet Union who had been brought in from his post in Moscow, where he had once actually acted as the Russian language interpreter for President Truman during one of the President's visits to Moscow. And, as was customary from his experience in the military, he also brought into the discussions some of his brightest young colleagues, such as Paul Nitze, who was later to rise in the diplomatic policy world.

Marshall reviewed some of his tentative conclusions with the President, and was authorized to visit our major allies in Europe and then proceed to Moscow to attempt to enlist Stalin's help to adopt a common policy for all of the wartime allies to revive Europe's economy. Meanwhile, the President took upon himself the political task of building a bipartisan domestic consensus in Congress and the public for aiding Europe during a crisis that was as grave for the world as the one President Roosevelt had faced in 1940.

Accordingly, Marshall went on to Moscow, stopping en route in Berlin and Paris to brief General Clay at OMGUS and the supreme military headquarters staff on his mission to obtain Stalin's support for an economic assistance program to aid all of Europe. In a series of meetings with Stalin related to the signing of a peace treaty with Germany, it quickly became clear to Marshall that the Soviets had no desire for such a program. So, in his final session with Stalin on April 14, Marshall informed Stalin directly that this was his conclusion, adding that he would inform President Truman of this immediately upon his return to Washington. He left Moscow convinced that "Stalin viewed drift and crisis as auspicious for Soviet purposes" (Donovan, *Conflict and Crisis*, p.288).

Although the Secretary still felt that it had been wise to conduct his failed effort to enlist Stalin's endorsement for rebuilding Europe, he did not hesitate to reject Stalin's ploy that their conversation had only been an overture which would ultimately lead to some compromise on Germany.

Therefore, while stopping in Berlin on his way home, he asked General Clay to proceed vigorously with an economic development program in the three zones of Germany under the administration of our allies, leaving the Soviet Zone completely isolated from our economic assistance plan unless they reversed course and so advised us. Immediately upon his return to Washington, Secretary Marshall and his staff designed the details of what was to be the program for aid to Europe and conferred with the President on whether his ideas conformed with the results of the President's efforts to arrange for Congressional and public endorsement.

Thus was born what became known as the Marshall Plan. Marshall wanted it to be called the Truman Plan, as a logical sequel to the Truman Doctrine which had saved Greece and Turkey. However, the President insisted on naming it after Marshall, not only because he admired the Secretary, but also to emphasize that the program was bipartisan, and thus credit Republican Senators such as Arthur Vandenburg with a share of the acclaim for seeing it through Congress.

Ever since Marshall's return from his last talk with Stalin on April 15, Kennan and his staff had been preparing its report "Certain Aspects of the European Recovery Problem From the United States Standpoint," and it was delivered to Marshall on May 25. The American response to world problems must be more than simply a defensive reaction to communist pressure, it urged, but ". . . should be directed . . . to the restoration of the economic health and vigor of European society" (McCullough, *Truman*, p.562).

With President Truman's approval, Marshall took advantage of an earlier invitation from Harvard University to receive an honorary degree at its commencement exercises on June 5th. The speech, written by Bohlen in two days, was simple and direct, but with little specificity, since the details of the Plan were still to be determined. Large scale economic assistance was envisaged, but the participating countries would be expected to merge their requests for assistance and together apply as an entity for any funds to be made available from U.S. appropriations.

Within those general parameters, the presentation was explicit in a few important respects: first, the Plan was not directed at any country or ideology; second, the U.S. government would co-operate with any country willing to assist in the task objective of European recovery; and, third, on the other hand, any country which seeks to block the recovery of other countries must not expect any U.S. assistance.

The speech avoided any specific definition of Europe in the sense of identifying which countries were eligible to apply for aid, leaving open to any individual countries the opportunity to join with all others choosing to apply for assistance. With the U.S. assistance program announced, and in spite of Marshall's April 15th admonition to Stalin that President Truman would be informed of the Soviet leader's indifference to our plans to aid Europe, Stalin sent his Foreign Minister, Molotov, to lead a Soviet delegation to Paris at the end of June, for a three-power conference called by the British and French to take advantage of the Plan's offer of aid to all of Europe.

Using the justification that the Plan, with its proposal to integrate the economic plans for all of Europe, constituted an unreasonable interference in the Soviet economy, Molotov and his colleagues stated that they would walk out of the conference. Britain and France then countered by calling a conference of all European nations interested in joining the Marshal Plan. Molotov also rejected any participation in the Plan by Poland, Yugoslavia, and Rumania. And when the desperate Czechs asked Stalin about their participation, he replied "We look upon this matter as a question of principle, on which our friendship with Czechoslovakia depends. . . . All the Slavic states have refused. . . . That is why, in our opinion, you ought to reverse your decision. . . . If you take part in the conference, you will prove by that act that you allow yourselves to be used as a tool against the Soviet Union." (Donovan, p.290). Tito soon broke with Stalin and joined the OEEC, but the Czechs would have to wait four decades before they were free to join Europe.

Although my specific responsibilities lay within only labor aspects of USRO, they fitted into the overall pattern of what we called the three M's; that is, the ultimate goal for all of Europe to achieve: first, free trade (the free flow of materials); second, free flow of money, or financial transactions; and, third, free flow of manpower. While these were the long-term purposes of the original Marshall Plan, it is clear that they were never attained; but they were nevertheless approached to a remarkable degree. Upon my return to Paris in 1972, for the OECD assignment, it was clear that the original SRE membership was on its way to taking on the burden of extending to the developing world what had been done for Europe.

From Norway to Yugoslavia: Maurice P. Arth (1921-1997)

H. Lawrence Wilsey

Maurice Arth served as a Marshall Plan officer from mid-1949 until its end at the close of 1951. Thereafter, he continued with the Mutual Security Agency and Foreign Operations Administration until late 1958.

Shortly before his death in March 1997, Maury reminisced that his truly meaningful and gratifying years had been those in which he participated in the Marshall Plan. He appreciated the opportunity to contribute to history's most significant and successful multinational cooperative economic effort. He saw that the leadership and material contributions of the United States stimulated a cooperative effort among European nations, which not only continues but has become increasingly multi-dimensional. Finally, he treasured the associations he had with other Marshall Plan officers; many of whom he continued close friendships with throughout his life.

Maury would like to be remembered for his contribution to the Marshall Plan. He would most assuredly wish to be among those listed as endorsing the Marshal Plan Conference mission statement "The Marshall Plan and Its Consequences."

All of Maury's memories of the Marshall Plan were proud and favorable ones, with one possible exception. He enjoyed and thrived on the challenges of the work, even the eighteen-hour days. His one adverse, and still vivid, memory was of his first official visit to Norway. He, Eivind Erickson, senior representative of the Ministry of Finance, and a number of members of the Norwegian cabinet flew west in a small military aircraft for the purpose of inspecting industry reconstruction needs in the Bergen area. As they flew west and began to ascend to cross the high snow-covered Folgetonna mountains, it became increasingly apparent that the plane did not have enough power to carry such a heavy load across the mountains. They "scraped" the snow on the crest and began their descent only to land in the tidal waters of Hardangerfjorden. Both Maury and Eivind had attested that they will remember that moment forever.

With the Marshall Plan (ECA), MSA, and FOA, Maury served in Paris (1949-1950) as chief of the Scandinavian and Greek/Turkish branches; in Vienna (1950-1951) as program officer; in Washington (1951-1955) as division director in the Office of the Director of Mutual Security (with a one-year appointment to the National War College); in Belgrade (1955-1957) as deputy director of the USAID mission to Yugoslavia; and, in Teheran (1957-1958) as deputy director of the USAID mission to Iran. (In Teheran, Francie Arth contracted hepatitis and ultimately died of its effects in 1977).

Maury made effective use of his Marshall Plan and subsequent government service experience in the private sector as a consultant and executive. He served government and non-profit clients and became a senior officer of the international consulting firm of Booz, Allen & Hamilton (1958-1963 and 1967-1973). Additionally, he directed corporate planning for Exxon Corporation (1963-1967). He was Executive Vice-President of the University of Alaska (1976-1977) and then Vice-President of Cuyahoga College, Cleveland, Ohio (1977-1981). Finally, he served as Vice-President of Finance and Administration of Barnard College, Columbia University until his retirement. For the past ten years, he lived in his home state of California and served effectively as an arbitrator and mediator in securities disputes.

Maury is survived by six children, two sons and four daughters, numerous grandchildren, and a great grandchild. They, along with his many friends, will miss him.

Conference: The Marshall Plan, Perspectives of the Participants Fifty Years Later, June 2, 1997— Excerpts from the proceedings

The Administration of the Marshall Plan

HAROLD SEIDMAN

After fifty years we are still debating whether the foreign aid agency should be independent, under the policy direction of the Secretary of State, or integrated within State. In the 1990s, principal proponents of integration have been conservative Republicans such as Sen. Jesse Helms. This was not the case 50 years ago.

Republicans made their support of the Marshall Plan contingent on its administration by an agency independent of State. A group headed by Congressman Christian Herter insisted that the Economic Cooperation Administration (ECA) not only be independent, but organized as a government corporation, which, by definition, would be a business. The Herter Committee argued that those whom they caricatured as the elite—striped pants, cookie pushing, tea drinkers from State—were incapable of making tough economic decisions and could not be trusted with the expenditure of billions of dollars.

The Bureau of the Budget (BOB) was the principle advocate of integration. It accepted the orthodox doctrine that agencies should be organized according to their major purpose in a limited number of Executive departments. It stressed that the U.S. should speak with one voice abroad and cited the "Little King in Italy" incident in support of its position.

A working group of which I was a member prepared a comparative analysis of plans for the administration of foreign aid published by the House Select Committee on Foreign Aid. The ECA clearly did not meet the criteria for a corporation established by President Truman. Herter accepted a compromise authorizing the Administrator to create a corporation if needed.

President Truman opted for the independent agency and assured its support in Congress by announcing in advance that he would name Paul Hoffman as Administrator. Experience demonstrated that this was the right decision and that integration with State would have been disastrous.

The BOB, in preaching orthodoxy, ignored State's culture and the identification of its mission as representation, reporting and negotiation. Diplomats were not activists. The power centers were the geographic desks, not the functional bureaus. The foreign service system discouraged specialization in those skills most demanded by the Marshall Plan— economic analysis and management. The Treasury and Agricultural attaches were the best able to make the transition. State did not want to assume responsibility for a program which would fundamentally alter its mission.

The clash of culture and values soon surfaced in the operation of the country teams. The foreign service voiced its displeasure with the ECA's interfering in domestic affairs and conducting negotiations through ministries other than the foreign office.

The country teams was willing to acknowledge the authority of the Ambassador, but not if it was delegated to the Deputy Chief of Mission (DCM). The DCM, labeled a representative of State, was a co-equal, not a superior. Coordination of foreign aid also became a major problem as there were three ambassadors in Paris. This coordination was the task of the office headed by Averell Harriman.

The Innovations of the Marshall Plan

Theodore Geiger

T he main innovations of the Marshall Plan were of three types. The first were included or implicit in Secretary Marshall's Harvard speech and required actions by the Europeans:

1. the Europeans were to cooperate in preparing a single coordinated recovery program.
2. the Europeans were to establish an international organization which would be responsible for (a) collectively reviewing the recovery policies and programs of each participating country, (b) recommending to the United States the division of aid among them, and (c) preparing and implementing a regional program for trade liberalization and new monetary payments arrangements. The Organization for European Economic Cooperation (OEEC) was subsequently established for these purposes.

The second type of innovation was in the organization and operation of the Economic Cooperation Administration (ECA) established by the Congress to administer the European Recovery Program (ERP):

3. ECA was an independent agency reporting directly to the President.
4. ECA missions were stationed in each participating country.

5. the U.S. would participate (without voting) in the activities
   of the OEEC, and the Office of the Special Representative
   (OSR) of the ECA was established in Paris for this purpose.
6. 80% of the aid would be grants and the remainder loans.
7. the ECA would contain a labor policy division and a
   productivity program.
8. Allied-occupied Germany would participate in the ERP.

The third type of innovation were the procurement authorization
procedures and the counterpart funds:

9. procurement authorizations (PAs) were documents issued to
   recipient governments which they used to pay for specific
   goods and services purchased in the United States or other
   sources under their approved aid programs. PAs were
   deposited by the recipient governments in U.S. banks, which
   then paid the dollars directly to the suppliers and were
   reimbursed by the U.S. Treasury. Thus, no Marshall Plan
   dollars passed through the hands of foreign bureaucrats or
   politicians, thereby minimizing opportunities for corruption
   and pleasing the U.S. Congress.
10. counterpart funds were the local currency funds obtained by
    recipient governments when they sold ECA-financed imports
    to manufacturers, construction companies and consumers in
    their countries. Five percent of the counterpart funds were
    reserved for the expenses of the U.S. government in the
    country; 95 percent were the property of the recipient
    government but could only be used for specific purposes
    approved by the ECA, thereby also helping to inhibit waste
    and corruption, and ensuring that the use of counterpart would
    contribute directly or indirectly to recovery.

In the implementation of the ERP, there were five centers of decision
and action, with multiple interrelations among them, that had to be
coordinated: European governments and ECA country missions in the
national capitals; OEEC and OSR in Paris, and ECA headquarters in
Washington. Their operations were directed and coordinated largely by
two men: Robert Marjolin in Paris and Richard Bissell in Washington.
Robert Marjolin was Secretary General of the OEEC and had outstanding

intellectual and diplomatic capabilities, which enabled him to supervise OEEC activities and reconcile the differing interests of 16 governments—no small feat. Richard Bissell was the Assistant Administrator for Program of the ECA and was stationed at headquarters in Washington.

From the beginning, Paul Hoffman, the Administrator of the ECA, delegated to Dick Bissell authority for determining (a) how much aid each country would get and for what purposes, and (b) how much counterpart funds would be released to each government and for what purposes. Given this authority, Bissell in effect directed the substantive work of the ECA. Bissell, too, had outstanding intellectual and managerial capabilities. His analytical keenness was extraordinary and he had an uncany ability to identify the determinative elements of a problem and how they could be influenced. He was willing to delegate important responsibilities to people whose judgment he trusted. He encouraged new ideas and was willing to take risks and push his authority to the limits, if necessary. Withal, he was unassuming and he shunned self-promotion and avoided publicity. I have always been convinced that the capabilities of these two brilliant men were necessary conditions for the success of the Marshall Plan.

Finally, I want to comment briefly on two of the ways in which the lessons of the Marshall Plan have been misinterpreted or overlooked during the past 50 years. Unfortunately, I have time only for broad generalizations and not for the qualifications and exceptions that should accompany them.

First, there have been recurrent proposals for new "Marshall Plans" for other groups of countries but, in all cases, these proposals have misinterpreted the essential prerequisites for participating in such a program. Only the West European nations have possessed them. Western Europe already had fully developed market economies and governments capable of managing them—indeed, the modern market economy was its invention. European governments were willing and able to cooperate in reviewing and coordinating each others' recovery plans and in implementing regional integration. Moreover, in the early postwar years, the United States had unprecedented prestige and power to influence the behavior of European governments, which have never since been so dependent on U.S. support.

Second, in subsequent aid programs, the priorities and balanced nature of the ERP were often overlooked. In the first year of the ERP, the highest priority was on increasing production to relieve the severe shortages of producers' and consumers' goods; in the second and third years, attention gradually shifted to national macroeconomic policies and regional trade and payments integration. However, developing-country aid programs for decades overemphasized project aid and, until recently, underemphasized macroeconomic policies, thereby encouraging inflation and capital flight, as well as the self-defeating import-substitution strategy. In contrast, aid to Eastern Europe and the former Soviet countries initially gave a very low priority to increasing production, despite the drastic fall in output, and instead overemphasized fiscal and monetary policies, thereby helping to delay and distort the transition to a market economy and imposing unnecessary hardships on the people.

In conclusion, I would like to pay a tribute to all of the Marshall Planners. In 1940, Winston Churchill said of the Royal Air Force's victory in the Battle of Britain, "never have so many owed so much to so few." ECA qualifies for the "few" category—for most of its short life, it was a very small agency. So, my Churchillian tribute to us Marshall Planners is, *"Never in the history of the U.S. government—before or since—have so few civil servants—spent so much money—to such good effect—and with so little waste and corruption."*

Never Again
Another Such War

JACOB J. KAPLAN

My Role on the Team

My first experience with multilateral coordination of Europe's need for U.S. aid occurred in 1944. I was sent to London to participate, as a U.S. member, on the Combined Working Party on European Food Supplies. It sought to reach agreement on food needs as Allied forces liberated each of the occupied countries on the Continent.

Later that year, I went to Italy, where my duties required considerable travel around a large area south of Rome. I witnessed widespread poverty, which was incredibly disheartening, even to one whose adolescence coincided with the Great Depression.

In 1945, I went to Vienna with an advance party under General Mark Clark, who was charged with negotiating with the Soviets for the joint occupation of Austria. My assignment was to explore the food situation in Vienna and estimate how much imported food would be needed in the zones to be occupied by the Western Allies. There I encountered an entire population that was literally starving. Living off the land, the Soviet army had seized every stored supply of food.

Before returning to the U.S., I traveled all over occupied Germany, including Berlin. My photographs of the devastation and destruction soon became indistinguishable; every city looked like every other one.

I joined the State Department early in 1946, one among many whose primary motivation was "never again another such war." Providing Europe's people with reasonable expectation of a better future seemed to be the sine qua non. Reconstructing Europe's economy was the essential first step.

When the last UNRRA appropriation passed the Congress in 1946, I was told then-Undersecretary of State Acheson had announced sadly that he did not think the Congress would enact additional foreign aid. I therefore greeted Marshall's speech and the immediate European response with considerable enthusiasm. I eagerly agreed to Van Cleveland's request that I prepare the supporting material for an interim aid appropriation for Italy. At that time, the Marshall Plan was being negotiated and prepared. Several countries had needs that could not wait.

I then prepared the data for Italy included in the "brown books"—the State Department's supporting material for the first Marshall Plan appropriation, covering April 1948-June 1949, produced under the jurisdiction of Charles Kindleberger. They consisted of 389 pages of statistics, projecting needs for every commodity, the source of their supply, and the balance of payments of the participating countries. The Congress must have been overwhelmed by the enormity of the data, because the appropriation passed within weeks of their issuance.

Exhausted by the effort but gratified by the result, I took leave for the summer of 1948 and left government service in the fall to join the Institute for International Studies at Yale University. I returned to ECA two years later as Assistant Chief (and later, Chief) of its European Regional Staff. That staff was responsible for backstopping and providing policy guidance to the U.S. delegation to the OEEC and for ECA/MSA interests in NATO and other European regional organizations, such as the European Coal and Steel Community. At first, I was largely concerned with financing the proposed buildup of NATO forces. We worked with the Department of Defense's controllers, who provided cost estimates for the buildup. Collaborating with the U.S. delegation to the OEEC, we estimated the expenditures that Europeans could reasonably be expected to provide and sought to reconcile them with both the Defense Department's cost estimates and expected Congressional appropriations for defense support.

Early in 1953, I arranged for an OEEC delegation to come to Washington to meet the new Eisenhower Administration as incoming President Eisenhower was a strong supporter of European integration. Thereafter, I focused principally on British proposals for convertibility and the European Payments Union (EPU). I served as principal advisor on the U.S. delegation to the OEEC Ministerial Examination Group on

Convertibility. Early in 1955, I became the U.S. Representative to the Managing Board of the EPU and moved to Paris. I also served as Director of the Finance Division of the U.S. delegation to European Regional Organizations (NATO and the OEEC). I remained in that position until 1959, by which time the move to convertibility had taken place, and the EPU had been liquidated, having successfully completed its tasks.

The Crux of the Plan

In recent years, I have been impressed by how poorly the Marshall Plan is remembered and how much it is misunderstood. A decade ago, a younger European economist came excitedly into my office. He had just read Secretary Marshall's speech and was surprised that it contained no plan. Indeed, it would not be very fruitful to search for "a Marshall Plan." Neither the speech nor any of the reports and documents that followed took the form of the Monnet Plan for France or the Indian Five Year Plan, to say nothing of the versions conceived by the Comecon countries.

Marshall's speech contained nothing more than a powerful idea that energized the Europeans and the American public. It offered U.S. aid on only one condition: that European governments agree to cooperate and work together on behalf of European reconstruction. The materials subsequently prepared by the Europeans, the State Department, and ECA focused on the priorities of the European Recovery Program: achieving a high rate of production growth; satisfying needs for imported food, fuel, and raw materials from the dollar area to sustain such growth; and determining Europe's balance of payments prospects for financing its share of the cost of these essential imports.

Given the overriding priority of increasing production, each country proceeded with its own programs for increasing productive capacity with little regard for what others were doing. After a couple of years, the OEEC conducted a review of national investment programs, but it led to little more than an exchange of information. Collaborative planning of investments played no significant role in the operation of the ERP, yet production and European well-being improved far beyond the initial expectations.

A second misconception about the Marshall Plan concerns the importance of the amount of aid promised for a four-year period. Combining those sums of money with the experience and skills of European governments, businesses, farmers, and workers was indeed essential for the Plan's success. But, that combination alone was unlikely to suffice. In 1946 and 1947, Europe financed a larger dollar deficit than the aid it received in the subsequent years under the Marshall Plan, yet its economy was still shaky. The Golden Age of the 1950s and 1960s could hardly have shone so brightly if the ERP consisted solely of providing Europeans with $13.5 billion.

The crucial contribution of the Marshall Plan was institutional. First was the wholly unprecedented cooperation among European governments, under the auspices of the OEEC, in managing the recovery process. Responding to the only condition in Marshall's offer, they abandoned long cherished insistence on national sovereignty and non-interference in economic affairs. In the inter-war period, some governments, including France, had even regarded the League of Nation's requests for statistics as intrusions on national sovereignty. Now, however, they institutionalized their collaboration by forming and joining the OEEC. Between 1947 and 1949, they reviewed each other's production targets, need for dollar imports, and economic policies. They strove to reach agreement on how much aid each would need, and how U.S. aid would be divided among them. Thus, they came to accept each other's involvement in the management of their economies.

Moreover, they agreed to accept large, high-level U.S. aid missions in each of their capitals. These missions discussed at every level of government the country's economic programs, projects, and policies, as well as its needs for U.S. aid. The governments to which they were accredited thus accepted U.S. intervention into their economic sovereignty as well.

A third misconception is that the U.S. sought to impose an economic ideology on the Europeans in return for aid. In fact, the U.S. approach was completely pragmatic. To be sure, the U.S. wanted controls to be eased, budgets to be balanced, inflation to be controlled, and trade restrictions to be lifted. But, so did almost all European governments. The U.S. urged policies that it considered appropriate. However, it required no timetables, set no quantitative goals, laid down no economic conditions that had to be met before money would be provided. Individual countries reached for the ideal of a free market economy at their own pace, taking account of their individual capabilities and the inclinations and priorities of their electorates. For the most part, the pace at which restrictions and controls were removed resembled more the peeling of an onion layer by layer than a single bold stroke of a machete.

Modern commentators appear to understand least of all the significance that rebuilding intra-European trade bore to its economic reconstruction. Opening up their markets to competition with each other was critical for achieving competitive economies. The Europeans understood this; yet their confidence in the very possibility of competitiveness was weak. What loomed large to them was the possible loss of scarce dollars if trade barriers were lowered.

After two years of the ERP, intra-European trade had not reached prewar levels, though industrial production was 15% larger. The need for dollar imports was diminishing, but neither the U.S. nor the Europeans were confident about the future if U.S. aid were to come to a halt after two more years, as the ERP envisioned. A better intra-European trading system was needed both to reduce further reliance on U.S. aid and to lay the ground for competing in the dollar area. This led to the European Payments Union Agreement in mid-1950. It made all European currencies convertible into one another, suspended the bilateral trade agreements, and enabled countries to reduce or eliminate the quantitative restrictions that hobbled intra-European trade. More significantly, each signatory implicitly agreed to maintain a balance over time in their transactions with all others as a group and accepted the creation of an expert Managing Board to supervise the execution of the Agreement. The Board was able to make recommendations about economic policies needed to attain such balance to both creditor and debtor members. Moreover, it was successful in persuading governments to heed its counsel. Thus, under OEEC auspices, it created an operational system for managing European cooperation.

Through the EPU, the Europeans themselves became the first to introduce the idea of conditionality, as it has come to be used by international institutions that extend loans to governments. In dealing with its first crisis, Germany, during its early months the Managing Board conditioned a special EPU credit upon specific German commitments to budgetary discipline and credit restrictions. The results were impressive, and the crisis was overcome within a few months.

The intensity of economic cooperation under the EPU not only assured the success of the Marshall Plan, but also provided a firm basis for growing European prosperity and for full and free participation in the global economy after the move to convertibility at the end of the decade. It established a degree of European economic integration that has continued to intensify to the present day through the Common Market, the European Monetary System, the Single Market, and the European Monetary Union.

Success has many fathers, and even more would-be heirs. Who would not like to see the success of the Marshall Plan repeated as new problems emerge and seem intractable? But, those who blithely call for new Marshall Plans should carefully study and understand the precedent they invoke.

Making a Difference

Dr. Arthur Schlesinger

I had the great good fortune in the summer and early autumn of 1948 to be invited by Averell Harriman to work as one of his special assistants, in the period of setting up the Marshall Plan in various countries. And though my direct participation was only of short duration, as thereafter, when Averell Harriman came back to the United States, I was summoned to Washington to help prepare speeches and messages on mutual security and Marshall Plan issues.

I think we all felt that, as so much of life seems to consist of spinning wheels, one could look back on the Marshall Plan experience as an experience where we really made a difference. I think that is why we have all come here today.

Our first speaker, Amb. Lincoln Gordon, is someone who was involved in the Marshall Plan from the beginning. Soon after Secretary Marshall gave his famous speech at Harvard, Lincoln Gordon left Harvard to join the State Department, and work on the program. He was the original program director in Washington, and then for several years in Paris. There's no one who saw the Marshall Plan more from incubation to maturity.

The Three Major Accomplishments of the Marshall Plan

AMB. LINCOLN GORDON

I want to focus on three long-term institutional developments which could not have taken place at all without the Marshall Plan.

The first, was the reincorporation of West Germany, the Federal Republic of Germany, into full and responsible partnership in the community of civilized Western European nations. This important event was symbolized in October 1949 by the presence, for the first time, of a German cabinet minister at a meeting of top level OEEC ministers. He was a namesake of the famous Prussian marshal, who was Wellington's partner in the final defeat of Napoleon at Waterloo, so his was not necessarily a name particularly beloved by the French.

Although this minister spoke English better than he did French, he chose very diplomatically to speak in French, and he gave a beautifully tactful speech. I was sitting right behind Paul Hoffman, who was our ministerial representative, and Averell Harriman, who was the head of the Paris office. I must say the occasion was something that for me is unforgettable as I listened to this, the first speech of a German official in the first international organization after World War II to which the Federal Republic was admitted as a full and equal participating member. From then on West Germany played a very constructive part in working out the further implementation of Marshall Plan and its collaboration there.

Of course, the West German currency reform that was introduced in 1948, and Ludwig Erhart's policy, called a "social market economy," also helped launch West Germany on this famous economic miracle, which in a few years made it Europe's leading economy.

The second closely-related institutional development was the movement toward European political and economic integration, starting with French Foreign Minister Shuman's plan in 1950 for the European Coal and Steel Community (ECSC). This was followed by the abortive proposal for a European defense community in 1951, which was defeated by the French Chamber of Deputies in 1954, and therefore never came into being. The successful ECSC led to the Treaty of Rome in 1957, which created what has now become the European Union, which plans to have a common currency in circulation by 2001.

All of these institutional developments derived from the ideas of Jean Monnet, and his hope for the ultimate goal of European integration. I am not sure that it was his goal already in 1950, when the Shuman Plan was launched, but certainly by 1957 Monet's goal really was a United States of Europe-a genuine political federation in addition to economic integration.

There are some historians—most notably Michael Hogan, who has written the longest single book about the history of the Marshall Plan - who believe that this aim was not in Marshall's mind when he asked in his famous June 1947 Harvard address that there be "some agreement among the countries of Europe as to the requirements of the situation so that the program should be a joint one agreed to by a number, if not all European nations."

Looking back at the Administration's proposals to Congress in the Economic Recovery Act of 1948, which I was involved in drafting during the summer and autumn of 1947, there is no evidence of the purpose of a European political federation. There is reference to the dismantling of quantitative trade restrictions, reduction of tariffs interconvertibility of European currencies, all of which were successfully accomplished by 1951 through the OEEC, and the working of the Marshall Plan.

In 1949, when Paul Hoffman came to the October meeting in which West Germany participated for the first time, he was urging the economic integration of the participating countries. He clearly favored some kind of European economic federation. He saw the United States as a model to be copied if possible in Europe. However, U.S. Secretary of State Acheson vetoed Hoffman's proposed use of the word "economic unification."

Proposals such as the Shuman plan, first came as a surprise in Washington and it was enthusiastically received in the U.S., as was the proposal in 1951 for the European defense community.

One of Foreign Minister Schuman's initial purposes in 1950, was in my view, to avoid German dominance of steel production. France had hoped to accomplish this through a series of initiatives, such as effective international control of the Rhur Valley, the principal center of German iron and steel production and many coal mines, as well as by the actual transfer of the Saar Valley to France. As it turned out, by the late 1940's it was clear that both of those initiatives were not going to succeed.

In effect, to use an old American slang expression, Monnet said, "If you can't beat 'em, join 'em." And that I think was the basic origin of the Shuman Plan. By 1957, Monnet, with support from Adenauer, had set his sights much higher, and kept them higher.

While the Marshall Plan can not claim the direct ancestry of the European Union, it can claim that it created the economic conditions without which the European community could not have come into being. It also facilitated the necessary political conditions, by bringing the Federal Republic of Germany in as a full partner in late 1949.

The third long-term creation was the North Atlantic Treaty Organization (NATO). The Marshall Plan can not claim credit for the origin of the treaty, which was signed in 1949. But the North Atlantic treaty, which still exists, was merely an assurance of American non-neutrality in the event of another European War. It did not call for an organization; it did not call for a joint military force in Europe. It called for recognition that an armed attack on any member would be regarded as an attack on all, and each member would decide through its own constitutional processes how to respond.

But, in June 1950 after the outbreak of war in Korea, the North Atlantic Treaty became transformed into the North Atlantic Treaty Organization (NATO). This resulted in the creation of a supreme allied headquarters near Versailles, first commanded by General Eisenhower, which was later moved to Brussels, and an elaborate structure of subordinate military commands. Then after 1952 a political entity, the North Atlantic Council, was established, with a prominent European as Secretary General, a council of permanent representatives, periodic ministerial meetings, and summit meetings of chief executives at least once a year.

In 1951 I was Harriman's deputy to the Temporary NATO Council Committee, which made the recommendations for this political super structure, and the move of the headquarters from London to Paris "to reconcile requirements of collective security, with the political and economic capabilities of the member countries." And I can say with certainty that we could never have come even close to that goal, without the economic recovery and the political cohesion achieved by 1951, with the help of the Marshall Plan.

What is the relevance of the Marshall Plan experience to the issues of today? In 1991, Professor Grahm Allison of Harvard proposed a "grand bargain" of Western financial support to help Russia stabilize the ruble, using the analogy of the Marshall Plan. To disregard the absence in Russia of the institutional prerequisites for a successful market economy, prerequisites fully available in the Western Europe of 1947, seemed a good idea to me in 1991, and it still does.

Those prerequisites are gradually coming into being, but Russia has problems other than a dollar shortage. If Russia were to establish the proper kind of partnership with the international oil industry in the reconstruction of their oil and gas production and reserves for example, its foreign exchange problems could be solved. Other problems constitute obstacles to Russia's transition to a successful market-based economy.

In 1997 there was an effort by the Clinton Administration, to make an analogy between the Marshall Plan and the proposed enlargement of NATO. That has become a leading foreign policy initiative of the Administration which I believe is not persuasive and I agree with Jack Kemp's opposition to NATO enlargement.

This analogy with the Marshall Plan was analyzed well by the historian Ronald Steel recently in *The New York Times*. There is, in my view, a possible analogy between the treatment of defeated Germany in the late 1940s, and today's treatment of the succession states of the defeated Soviet Union, the most important of them of course being Russia. Unlike Germany however, the Soviet Union was not defeated militarily, and of course it was not occupied by foreign troops. It collapsed from within, and the parts of the former Soviet republics, with the notable exception of Belarus, one of the smaller republics, shook off their ideological blinders.

Russia still possesses an immense stock of intercontinental nuclear missiles, constituting a far greater potential security threat to North America than any visible sign of Russian military aggression in central

Europe. There are also Russian and Ukrainian scientific experts on other weapons of mass destruction, and on possible means of controlling them.

In my view, no effort should be spared to draw these former Soviet countries, particularly Russia, fully into the Euro-American community of democratic and peaceable nations, prepared to face collectively the challenges of internal and external security and economic cooperation. To abandon that objective would risk an outcome in Europe more similar to the failures of 1919 than the successes of 1947.

Finally, I thought perhaps that you might enjoy two very short anecdotes about working for Averell Harriman.

The first has to do with working with him in Washington in 1951 on the draft of some testimony to Congress. Harriman was meticulous with respect to the words that were put in that kind of testimony. It was very trying to his assistant, because he would sweat over a particular sentence for ages.

I had finished working with him at his house, now the site of the German Embassy residence on Reservoir Road, and arrived home at about 2:00 in the morning. I was awakened out of a sound sleep at 7:30 by this bright cheerful voice from Averell, saying, "Linc, what's new?" I said to him, "Averell, how in God's name do I know what's new? I last saw you at your house at 2:00 in the morning, and you just awakened me out of a sound sleep." He never did that again.

The other has to do with my youngest daughter, who now has two rapidly growing boys. At that time she was six years old and one day my wife called her for dinner and she put a little toy telephone to her ear and said, "Don't bother me, I'm talking with Averell."

Completing What the Marshall Plan Began

PAUL R. PORTER

We are so accustomed to friendly relations with our former enemies of the Second World War, that we fail to marvel at the huge American achievement of converting vanquished foes into friendly, prospering democracies.

For 50 years they have cooperated with us, and have been our allies in maintaining peace, and raising the standard of living of our respective peoples. I submit that in the history of nation states, there is nothing comparable to this triumph of good sense.

A fitting name for it would be the "community of prospering democracies." That community has been broadened beyond its North Atlantic base, to include prospering democracies in Asia and in Latin America.

Today I want to talk about the new situation that arises from the fact that we won the Cold War. Just as our enemies of the Second World War were transformed, it is in our national interest to help our former adversaries in the Cold War to become stable democracies with thriving market economies.

The failure of Russia to make such a transition could well result in an embittered and aggressive nationalist regime that in time could present a new threat to peace. Joining with Lincoln Gordon, let me say that we should never overlook the big stock of Russian missiles that must be kept from reckless hands.

This is not to suggest that the transition will be easy. Centuries of absolutist rule by Czars, and 70 years of communism have deprived the Russian people of democratic practice. The current decline in their living standards threatens their present venture in democracy. As among other states of the former Soviet bloc, democracy rests on a fragile foundation, and in some cases there is no democracy at all.

But, even though it will not be easy to make the transition, and though today we may also have advantages that we did not have then, we have the support and participation of the nations that were beneficiaries of the Marshall Plan. For them, helping the nations of the former Soviet bloc makes this a transition in their national interest just as much as it is in ours.

The Marshall Plan drew upon $13.3 billion in U.S. funding, about $90 billion today, and that was important. Our aid was only a part of Europe's remarkable recovery. At least as important was the effective contribution by European participants in the Plan. Without their efforts, our billions would have had little lasting effect.

The stimulus that brought this potential to life was the boldness of the American initiative as expressed in the Marshall Plan. The vision, the courage, and the spirit of mutual endeavor that were expressed in General Marshall's speech was transmitted to our European associates. Those of us who had the good fortune to serve in country missions could see a new vision, courage, and spirit of mutual endeavor take root and grow in the governments of the countries to which we were assigned as well as in many private bodies.

Today, there are many bilateral arrangements whereby Western governments and private agencies give aid to former Soviet countries. What is largely missing, however, is the quality and magnitude of the spirit of mutual assistance and domestic initiative that was central to the Marshall Plan. Thomas Schelling is the author of a phrase that I think cannot be improved upon, "reciprocal scrutiny." And it was reciprocal scrutiny that played a major part in converting France and Germany into allies. The Marshall Plan drew nations together in cooperative undertakings, but the former Soviet bloc nations are moving apart. This trend was beneficial to the break up of communism, but to the development of prospering democracies it is detrimental. We need thorough "mutual scrutiny" to bring the former Soviet bloc states together with the participation of the beneficiaries of the Marshall Plan, and our own nation. Just as France and Germany became allies after World War II, I suggest that the Czech Republic and Russia should become allies through "mutual scrutiny" in developing democracy in their respective countries.

Our Marshall Plan experience is relevant in another way, and that is the kind of aid that is appropriate today. I do not believe that Russia or any other member of the former Soviet republic needs aid as a gift in the way that the Marshall Plan countries did. The World Bank and the International Monetary Fund can meet their financial needs with loans. There is no need for any big ticket type of expenditure to help them to become prospering democracies. The help they need most is mainly of threefold.

One is help in devising and strengthening democratic institutions. The chairman of our conference, Dr. Constantine Menges, has written with perceptive insight on this subject. I commend his "strategy to encourage democracy in Russia" in a book which he edited, entitled, *Transitions from Communism in Russia and Eastern Europe* (1994). There are many private organizations today that can also be helpful in promoting a transition to democracy. I shall mention only one, because it has shown exceptional skill in transmitting stimulating ideas to democratic groups in other countries. That is the National Endowment for Democracy.

A second form of help is raising industrial and agricultural productivity. This is an area in particular, in which the Marshall Plan experience can be of great value.

A third lesson from the Marshall Plan is the importance of promoting easier trade between the countries of Eastern Europe and the Western democracies. On May 21, 1997, the House of Representatives approved a resolution reaffirming the U.S. commitment to European security and prosperity expressed in the Marshall Plan, and commending the countries that benefited from it for their efforts to assist the former Soviet bloc countries in developing market economies and democratic political systems. President Clinton, speaking in the Netherlands in May 1997, also correctly identified the need to support the democratic aspirations of Eastern Europe.

These statements hold the promise of a new initiative, but someone must lead. No power can do it more effectively than the United States. The time is ripe for our government to invite the Marshall Plan beneficiaries and the nations of the former Soviet bloc to join with us in examining what we and they can do cooperatively to enable all of them to be full members of the community of prospering democracies.

Every generation has the potential for vision, courage, and mutual endeavor. It is the responsibility of leadership, as exemplified by President Harry Truman and General George Marshall, to bring forth these qualities. A new generation of Americans has the enviable opportunity to complete what the Marshall Plan began.

Spreading the Word of the Marshall Plan

WALDEMAR A. NIELSON

First of all, this reunion is characterized by as much passion, warmth, and fraternity as any gathering of adults that I have ever been present at. Why is that? It is because all of us, in one way or another, have shared in a tremendously important historic and deeply satisfying experience in the Marshall Plan. That is why we are such dedicated alumni; that is why there is so much nurturing and respect in this room. That says something about the continuing strength of the American idea of public service and public participation. In human terms, we constitute a beautiful miniature sample of those qualities.

A second perspective that I want to share is how a public figure can be transformed by his involvement in an enterprise as timely, and as important as the Marshall Plan. I am speaking of Averell Harriman. I had the pleasure of being Averell's assistant and I knew him very well. He was a rather cold and dispassionate man and one of the worst public speakers that I ever heard. Yet this individual became one of the most effective primary advocates for the Marshall Plan throughout the United States.

As Averell Harriman began the effort to win public support for the Marshall Plan, many thought that it was a pointless and unproductive initiative. Yet as we took off to fly around America in the old wobbly Department of Commerce DC-3 aircraft, Averell-and I had not fully realized this at the time-had been seized with a passion about the importance of the idea of the Marshall Plan which simply consumed him, and ultimately transformed him. It never turned him into a great public speaker, but it turned him into an extremely active one.

We took off in that old plane on a three-week expedition. Everyday in differrent cities and towns Averell Harriman made no less than four or five, deeply felt, public statements about the absolutely essential importance of the Marshall Plan. We talked to chambers of commerce, women's clubs and every kind of civic organization from, Ottumwa, Iowa, to Los Angeles, California. Averell was absolutely indefatigable. This was his mission, perhaps the first deeply felt personal mission in his adult and political life. He believed, out of his experience as ambassador to the Soviet Union and during the Second World War, that the Marshall Plan was an absolutely crucial initiative for the American people to support, and he was going to do whatever he could to help get pubic support.

I'd like to share just one anecdote that remains in my mind from that period. I was frankly dead tired and exhausted by our journey, but Averell was not. We were flying in that decrepit old airplane over the Rockies. It was a stormy, terrible night. Lightening was running up and down the wings, and the plane was bucking like a bronco. Averell asked me to confirm the latest figures on British gold reserves, because he wanted to be sure that at the next talk for a breakfast in Boise, Idaho, that he had the most up to date figures.

I replied, "Averell, my God, I don't know where the numbers are." I could probably have found them since we had stacks of research in the airplane. But, I said, "It doesn't seem to me it's absolutely essential that those numbers be found; and besides, I'm dead tired." Averell looked rather surprised, and said, "Oh, are you tired?" And I said, "Averell, I'm going to drop dead if we don't stop." But, that was the man. That was his mission, and he went at it with fervor. I think it was probably the most passionate political cause in his life.

The legislation was passed. Then came the task of organizing a staff in Paris, and in Europe, and Averell was appointed to head the European aspect of the program. He asked me if I would work with Al Friendly, who at that time had been the editor of *The Washington Post*, in organizing a public information program.

I had been trained as an economist, and had been active in political and legislative matters, and I thought that getting into public information activity was frankly a little bit unimportant and out of my area of expertise. But, out of respect for Averell, and increasingly for Al, as I came to know him, I began both to understand and appreciate the significance of a vigorous effort to explain to the public in Europe what the Marshall Plan was intended to be and what their role and potential benefits might be. That led to a vigorous public information program which ultimately produced a flow of current information about the program that newspapers throughout the continent carried.

I shall make three other points very briefly, about the whole process of information dissemination. First of all, since we are a democratic society, a huge and costly enterprise like the Marshall Plan depends upon continuing voter understanding and support. Therefore it was an absolutely essential element of the Marshall Plan in Europe to see that an effective flow of information about the development effort and its positive results got back to critical audiences in the United States.

More than public relations or publicity, it was an essential and necessary function in sustaining the foreign policy initiative that the Marshall Plan represented. In that particular respect, I think the information program did a good job. American journalists of high standing generally called the press office in Paris the best U.S. Government press office that they had ever dealt with in terms of prompt, knowledgeable responses to their requests of and requirements for information.

A second very important element of Marshall Plan information activities in Europe was the political and psychological defense of the program. The Soviet Union, its various satellites, and its many instruments of propaganda had declared open war on the Marshall Plan. From the very beginning, and increasingly throughout the Plan, they saw this as an American initiative and a profound threat to their long-term strategic interest. Therefore, they activated every communist party throughout Western Europe and there were open propaganda and political warfare campaigns underway throughout Europe through most of the Marshall Plan era. A key task of the information program was to counter, and deal with that massive, aggressive information initiative against the Marshall Plan.

Third, there was the need to maintain the flow, not only of information back to the United States, but information that would help sustain public interest and public support for the program. There were critics, and in some cases severe and highly influential critics, of the Marshall Plan in the United States.

Another task that the information program had to undertake, was to maintain a flow back to the United States, not of general happy talk about the progress of European recovery, but of specific examples of the recovery progress. This would help sustain the support of the American people and their belief that although this costly and burdensome program was not universally popular, it was something, on balance, in the American interest.

To close, I remember in the midst of these complicated efforts of information warfare, Bill Foster took me aside about six months after the program began. He was a very successful industrialist in the United States, and then as the Undersecretary of Commerce and he had become in effect the chief administrative officer of the program in Europe. He took me to the window of his office, looking out on the Place de la Concorde, put his arm around me said, "Wally, if there's one thing I've learned on this job, it is that there's one hell of a lot more to economic recovery than economics."

The Legacy of the Marshall Plan: New Opportunities for Assistance

Hon. Peter McPherson

It is good to be here and to be able to personally thank and congratulate you for your work.

When I was administrator of the U.S. Agency for International Development (USAID) we were in the same offices in the State Department where Secretary Marshall had his office. My colleagues and I often thought about Secretary Marshall because the Marshall Plan represented one of the most successful foreign aid efforts ever.

It is interesting to hear the stories about Averell Harriman who was so important to the Marshall Plan. As an aside, I did not know Mr. Harriman until he was quite elderly, but, early on at my time at USAID, I invited all the living former administrators of foreign aid to a lunch to get some advice. The Reagan Administration had just come into office and I wanted to encourage bipartisan support for foreign assistance. Halfway through this lunch, Mr. Harriman said "Mr. McPherson, could I see you a moment?" I remember it as clearly as yesterday. He took me aside and said, "Now, Mr. McPherson, you won't see me again" and he went on to give me some advice on several matters. He very effective. I listened carefully to the grand old man whom I would not see again!

The Marshall Plan was a vision of practicality, idealism and boldness. American foreign policy is most successful when we combine these qualities. Clearly, the Marshall Plan was a major step toward an international role for the United States, in contrast to our isolationism after World War I.

We sometimes forget that the Marshall Plan also represented a major commitment to free trade. We encouraged the Europeans to open their markets and we openeded up our own. With some disputes, it is a policy which has served us well in the decades since Word War II.

In addition, the Marshall Plan implied a commitment to continue U.S. involvement in Europe and to focus that involvement on some issues about which Europeans were dubious, in particular, the rebuilding of Germany. France was not so sure that it wanted to help rebuild Germany, but the requirement of the nations of Europe to work together in the Marshall Plan forced the matter. Clearly, rebuilding Germany was very wise.

There is no question that the goods and services provided by the Marshall Plan were very important to the rebuilding, yet, the confidence in the future of Europe engendered by the Plan was in many ways just as critical. That confidence allowed governments to reach across borders, allowed entrepreneurs to take risks, allowed banks to extend credit, and in many cases, allowed workers to set aside immediate gains in favor of long term recovery.

In his memoirs, Charles Bohlen talks about Western Europe as having had the qualified people and the institutional framework. What was needed was "an injection of economic blood to a system that had stopped functioning." But, this statement does not capture the whole of the Marshall Plan as I know Mr. Bohlen understood. In addition, there was an infusion of confidence and many new ideas and some very important new technology that came from America. The Europeans also helped themselves.

Why did the Marshall Plan work? Resources, confidence, technology and self-help.

In the two generations since then, America has frequently turned toward the Marshall Plan as an inspiration. We often asked ourselves in the USAID offices, how could we do this again?

There have been some very important projects that combined the Marshall Plan's practicality, idealism and boldness.

Think, for example, of America's effort to eradicate small pox around the world.

There was also the Green Revolution—begun with support from the Ford and Rockefeller Foundations and extended with U.S. government leadership at the World Bank. We almost forget that because of the miracle grains of the Green Revolution, there has not been a major famine in India since the 1960's. In fact, in terms of human lives saved, the Green Revolution is one of the most significant developments in the 20th century.

We should also remember a 12-month period in the 1980s, when USAID delivered two million tons of food to Africa during a massive famine. This included food delivered to then communist Ethiopia and Mozambique. President Reagan insisted that "a hungry child knows no politics."

The actions of President Clinton and Secretary of the Treasury Rubin during the U.S. bailout of the Mexican currency in 1994 were also bold. We need to watch the finances of Mexico carefully, but if we had not taken that action, the costs would have been very great.

Americans can take pride in many other examples that reflect the bold spirit of the Marshall Plan. Look at Korea right after the Korean War. South Korea was as devastated as Europe had been after World War II, but South Korea did not have the human resource base or the institutional structure. As a result, in South Korea it took ten to fifteen years to see the results of our efforts, compared with four or five years in Europe. We helped provide confidence and a sense of economic stability, and we helped build a human resource base.

The same thing occurred in Taiwan. It was not impacted by a catastrophic war in the same way as Europe or Korea; however, special assistance was required to help cope with the influx of millions of refugees fleeing the communist mainland. The successes of the economic development program in Taiwan, were due, in part, to our helping the Taiwanese build a human resource base.

What does all this mean in terms of Russia, Eastern Europe, and the new post-Soviet republics? Many of those countries are rich in human resources; however, they lack a history of entrepreneurship and many critical institutional and legal structures. It is hard to do business, for instance, without being able to count on enforceable contracts. There is much to be done and I congratulate the United States for making efforts to help build the necessary institutions.

It is clear that the economic reforms need to continue in Russia. There will be setbacks, but major reforms are never done in a day. Unfortunately, all the current changes are not reforms. Corruption is also a matter of deep concern and an obstacle to effective change.

It is my belief that we need to make substantial efforts toward building sustainable institutions in Russia, the new post-Soviet republics and Eastern Europe, but we should not have a huge resource transfer program. Some resource transfers may be required for purposes of confidence building and developing political relationships, but it is not a tool we should overuse.

Today, there are also some major opportunities to bring about change that we did not have in 1981 when I became the Administrator of USAID.

First there are international capital markets. In the last ten years or so, one of the most important new factors has been the rapid availability of capital to countries that have stability and good economic policies.

Second, literacy is more wide-spread and more mass media exists to disseminate information. When I was a Peace Corps volunteer in Peru in the mid 1960s, literacy in the Andes was about 20 percent. Today it is probably 70 percent or more. It is much easier to distribute knowledge and effect real change when people can read. Today, we also have mass media almost everywhere. There are, for example, camel drivers with transistor radios and the availability of television in large parts of China and many parts of Latin America and Africa. Mass media is a highly effective educational tool.

Third, information technology will help drive change rapidly and effectively. At Michigan State (MSU), for example, we graduate many excellent students from developing countries. But we know that when they go back home, some of them will be out of date for lack of access to new information in just a few years.

Today through the World Wide Web and e-mail, we can help graduates and current students keep up with new advances in knowledge. Through a private donor, we at MSU are giving technology updates to professors in four African universities in agronomy and other areas of agriculture through the World Wide Web. That is just the beginning. The networks will grow exponentially and we are going to be able to connect people and knowledge around the world as we never have before.

Fourth, biotechnology will speed up the development of new varieties of crops and help us deal with some medical issues more quickly.

In short, as I look at the trends which are present at the end of the 20th century, it seems to me that there is an opportunity to do more faster in developing countries than we have ever done before. It will take money, but this money should be carefully focused rather than being spent broadly on traditional aid efforts.

It is a pleasure for me to be here. I have tried to learn from you who worked in the Marshall Plan by reading your history and thinking about the lessons you conveyed to the generations of foreign aid workers who followed you. The world will remember the Marshall Plan, and the practicality, idealism, and boldness of your vision.

Ireland

AMBASSADOR DERMOT GALLAGHER

I am pleased, in this the 50th Anniversary year of the Marshall Plan, to contribute the following remarks in tribute to the imagination and farsightedness of the United States and its then Secretary of State, George Marshall, and in gratitude to those who worked tirelessly to implement the European Recovery Programme (ERP), or the Marshall Plan, as it is more popularly and deservedly known.

By all accounts, the commencement address given by Secretary of State Marshall at Harvard University on June 5, 1997, went largely unnoticed when delivered. It was a short speech and was not perceived as being particularly significant. But within it lay the germ of an idea which would soon lead to the economic rebirth of Europe which laid the foundation for what was to become the European Economic Community and, subsequently, today's European Union. History is full of such ironies.

In 1947, the Irish economy was in an extremely weak position and shared with other European countries the common problems of continued rationing, rising inflation, falling living standards, labour unrest, and unemployment. There was, as a result, an increased reliance on the United States. Imports from the United States had risen from 10.9% in 1938 to 26.5% in 1947, while Irish exports in the opposite direction were small. Also, Irish dollar reserves had been reduced through increased consumer goods imports.

From a U.S. perspective, the inclusion of Ireland in the Marshall Plan also had a broader purpose. It was believed that Ireland, through support of agricultural production, could act as a food producer for the rest of Europe, including neighbouring Britain. However, as Ireland was at that time importing more food than it was exporting, there was a need for external assistance if it was to be able to provide for not just her own needs but also those of others.

There was a third consideration, linked to general anxiety at the time, to protect a weakened Europe against communist aggression. While Ireland's ideological credentials, so to speak, were never in doubt, there was a concern that the country's economic weakness could be exploited.

Ireland's share of Marshall aid, received in the period between 1948 and 1951, totaled $148 million, or some 40 million pounds. This was made up of a grant of $18 million, technical assistance of $1.25 million and loans totaling over $128 million.

The Irish economy derived considerable benefits from Marshall Plan funding, with aid going to finance capital and other services of the Government as well as a considerable number of projects in the agricultural sector and rural areas (land reclamation, drainage, forestation, livestock improvement, rural electrification and educational visits by Irish farmers to the U.S.). The value to rural communities was significant. For example, one million acres of farm land was reclaimed. Also, during the period 1949-52, cattle output grew, and agriculture became more mechanized. In urban areas, Marshall Plan funding was used to increase the Irish housing stock. Other projects, in such areas as public health, telecommunications, schools, state building programmes and transport and tourism development also benefited.

After the Marshall Plan had officially ended, funds were still being put to good use into the late 1950's. In 1957, for example, the Scholarship Exchange Act between Ireland and the United States established the Scholarship Exchange Board. The capital investment of 500,000 pounds made in 1957 to establish the Board was funded by Marshall Plan assistance. Much later, in the 1980's, the Board applied for funding under the Fulbright-Hayes legislation of the United State Congress, and consequently the Fulbright Association of Ireland, which deals with the majority of academic exchanges between Ireland and the U.S., was established. Another major achievement came in 1958 with the establishment of the Irish Agricultural Institute. A sum of 1.84 million pounds, drawn from Marshall Plan funds, was provided to the Institute, which enabled it to make an effective start in putting relevant research programmes in place to support the subsequent development of Irish agriculture.

The objective laid down by the United States in the context of the Marshall Plan was that European countries should achieve economic and social recovery and greater European integration. From Ireland's economic point of view, a greatly expanded capital works programme of enormous social and infrastructural value was instituted. Unemployment fell and the volume of industrial output rose. There was also a positive long-term effect: participation in the Marshall Plan contributed to laying the groundwork for the subsequent emergence of the modern Irish economy, Ireland's participation in European integration, starting with our membership in the European Community in 1973, and our involvement in the OECD and the GATT/WTO.

In 1947, then Irish Prime Minister Eamon De Valera, described the Marshall Plan as "an act of unparalleled generosity from one nation to other nations." For Ireland, the significance of the Marshall Plan was not only the economic generosity that it represented, but the influence it had on Irish economic development in the late 1950's and much later. It can safely be said that, to a significant degree, we are what we have become today because of the start made through our involvement in the Marshall Plan.

Turkey

Ambassador H.E. Nuzhet Kandemir

I am certainly delighted to have this opportunity to share my thoughts with you on the meaning of the Marshall Plan for Turkey and on the significance of its legacy for the future, in which we all have a stake.

The history of the Marshall Plan is well known. Turkey's place in that history, however, is unique, testifying to the amazing depth and breadth of the Marshall Plan's vision. Indeed, in his historic speech in 1947 at Harvard University, then Secretary of State George C. Marshall extended an invitation to Europe's war-torn countries to join together in the quest for economic recovery and reconstruction to overcome, in his words, "hunger, desperation, poverty, and chaos." He firmly believed that economic stability was an indispensable prerequisite for world peace and democracy and committed the U.S. to providing support and assistance for the realization of this important objective.

Even though Turkey, due to its neutral stand during most of the Second World War, escaped devastation, the US decided to include it in the Marshall Plan as a bulwark at Europe's southern flank to contain the growing threat of communist expansion. While Turkey certainly benefited from the nearly $352 million in economic and military assistance it received from the U.S. between 1948 and 1952, our inclusion in the Marshall Plan was far more meaningful. It was, in short, a historic moment for Turkey, for in that decision, Turkey's European vocation was irrevocably confirmed. Our place in Europe, our commitment to democracy, and our espousal of common ideals and values were forever validated. It was a triumphant moment of inclusion, cooperation and solidarity when collective interests and shared values prevailed over divisiveness and discrimination based on religious and cultural differences.

With our participation in the Marshall Plan at such a crucial moment in time, Turkey subsequently grew to become a dependable and indispensable ally of the West throughout the Cold War and after. From the Korean War to the Gulf crisis, Turkey stood shoulder to shoulder with its American counterparts in the defense of peace, liberty, freedom, and democracy. Just as the Marshall Plan planted the seeds for European integration, it sparked Turkey's own drive to become a full member of a unified Europe. Hence, we are a member of NATO, the OECD and the Council of Europe as well as an associate member of the Western European Union and the European Union through a customs union agreement, anticipating full membership in the very near future.

The importance of the Marshall Plan, even fifty years after Secretary Marshall's speech, lie in the lessons and legacy it continues to offer. We live in an amazing time of immense challenges and unprecedented opportunities. We have survived the Cold War, whose very end one might arguably attribute to the tenets of the Marshall Plan itself. Now, at the doorstep of the next century, we need a new blueprint and vision to guide international relations—to address the "hunger, desperation, poverty, and chaos" of a vast and strategic region of the world stretching from the Balkans to the Caucasus and from Central Asia to the Middle East and Africa. These areas, like Europe after the second World War, are now experiencing the difficulties of securing independence, nationhood, civil societies, and economic development. These regions crave peace and stability. Clearly, the parallels between 1947 after the Second World War and 1997 after the Cold War are striking. The spirit and wisdom of the Marshall Plan's vision must be reinvented and, just like it saved Europe, save these areas as well by guiding them towards peace and stability predicated on sound economic development and growth. I believe our greatest commemoration and salute to the Marshall Plan rests in how well we rise to meet this challenge. In the eyes of future generations, we will be defined by how we choose to act, or do not act, in this regard.

My friends, The Marshall Plan was an act of hope, rebirth and rejuvenation for Europe after the devastation of the Second World War. It was a doorway into democracy, economic development and peace. Turkey learned about the Marshall Plan firsthand because it had the privilege of being touched and transformed by it. Let us pay ultimate tribute to the Marshall Plan, and those visionaries who devised it, by infusing its vision and spirit into those nations, in the post-Cold War era, who also seek the hope and development it promises.

Germany

AMBASSADOR JURGEN CHROBOG

I am honored to convey my greetings to you on the occasion of this historic conference. Your gathering pays tribute to the generous spirit of George Marshall and his collaborators, some of whom are present at this event to share their unique experiences and insights into the history and accomplishments of the Marshall Plan.

The Marshall Plan enabled Europe to recover from the ravages of war. It also provided the stimulus needed for Europe's move toward closer integration and eventual political union. The German people owe George Marshall a special note of gratitude. In the years following 1945, Germany had a particularly complex situation. A strong sense of humanity and a noble historic vision were needed to help the former adversary get back on its feet. The Marshall Plan not only fought against hunger, poverty and chaos but also helped Germany find its way back into the community of nations. Thanks to the material and moral support which the Plan provided, democracy could take firm root in Germany.

The spirit of George Marshall still has relevance for us today. Europeans listened closely to President Clinton's great speech in Amsterdam a few days ago. This speech was an impressive testimony to America's willingness to keep George Marshall's heritage alive and to extend it to the whole of Europe. We welcome with gratitude the President's message—America is willing to contribute to Europe's political future as it did in the past. America joins Europe's endeavor to overcome the scars of the divisions of the Cold War and to build a Europe that is undivided and free. There is no better way to commemorate George Marshall's legacy.

The Netherlands

AMBASSADOR ADRIAAN JACOBOVITS DE SZEGED

Fifty years ago, the Netherland's economy lay in ruins, destroyed by the Second World War. Despair was rampant, hope was fleeting, and the challenge of rebuilding the Dutch economy was bewildering. Inspiration was found, however, in the words and vision of George Marshall, a vision which restored the economies of Europe and the confidence of its people, sowed the seeds of cooperation among nations, and sealed forever the friendship and ties between Europe and the United States. As the Netherlands Prime Minister Wim Kok remarked during the Marshall Plan commemoration in the Hague on May 28, 1997 "Americans are our relatives by history and our friends by choice."

Marshall Plan assistance was invested throughout the Netherlands. Bolstered by this aid, Dutch initiative and ingenuity coupled with American know-how was unleashed, transforming the Dutch economy and countryside. It is in the city and port of Rotterdam, perhaps, where one finds a most vigorous testament to Marshall's vision of a peaceful, democratic and prosperous Europe. Rotterdam, completely ravaged during the war, was rebuilt with Marshall Plan aid and has since become the world's largest and busiest port, the business gateway to a Europe united in its commitment to commerce and democracy, and a source of great prosperity for both the Dutch economy and, we like to think, a benefit to the rest of Europe.

In the 1990's, the Netherlands has enjoyed a vibrant economy and a socially stable but lively democracy. Our prosperity rests upon a foundation of free markets, international trade, cooperation and consensus, ideas which animated General Marshall 50 years ago and ideas found at the core of the European Union, which celebrates its 40th birthday this year.

Today, as we celebrate the 50th anniversary of the Marshall Plan, I am honored, on behalf of the people of the Netherlands, to join you in paying our deepest respect to George Marshall and his vision, and I thank all Americans for coming to our aid in our time of need. All of us must work to extend Marshall's vision over Eastern Europe also, as Marshall originally intended. This will lead to a stable, prosperous and undivided Europe in a close, energetic partnership with the United States.

Greece

AMBASSADOR LOUCAS TSILAS

On the fiftieth anniversary of the Marshall Plan, we celebrate an initiative which truly reflected the traditional links of close friendship and partnership between the United States and Europe. As the Ambassador of one of the countries that benefited from this historic project, I would like to express Greece's appreciation.

As so many European countries lay destroyed and ravaged by the catastrophe brought upon the people of Europe by the miseries of World War II, it was the Marshall Plan that boosted European reconstruction. And it was thanks to the vision of the statesman who conceived this idea that the bonds linking the two sides of the Atlantic were further enhanced and strengthened.

Today, proud of the achievements of the Transatlantic Cooperation in the promotion of peace, security and economic stability, we can acknowledge that George Marshall and the other worthy leaders of his era knew not only how to win a war but also how to consolidate the peace.

On behalf of Greece, I wish to reiterate my warmest expression of appreciation as well as our determination to continue on the same path of working together, so that the trans-Atlantic link remains strong for the years to come.

Sweden

Ambassador Henrik Liljegren

The Marshall Plan was a program unique in its breadth and depth, in its generosity and in the farsightedness of its approach. Even though Sweden was spared the ravages of war, our country received $120 million (nearly $700 million in today's terms) from the European Recovery Program. This made it possible for Sweden to buy raw materials and produce goods needed for war-torn countries, thereby helping them as well as ourselves. The basic idea behind the Marshall Plan was that the best foundation for lasting peace is to weave people and nations together for mutual benefit. The spirit of transatlantic solidarity in which the plan was offered embraced all of Europe. Today, the fundamental changes in the European security situation have, for the first time, created conditions conducive to fulfilling Marshall's vision.

In the spirit of that vision, Sweden, as a member of the European Union, as an active participant in Partnership for Peace program and as a major contributor to the Baltic Sea Cooperation, shall not fail to share in the building of a new pan-European security order resting on a strong trans-Atlantic link and on the inclusion of a democratic Russia.

I would like to pay tribute to all those who have contributed to organizing this conference at The George Washington University and to all participants who have given their perspectives on the Marshall Plan, one of the most important U.S. foreign policy endeavors ever.

Norway

Ambassador Tom Vraalsen

On 10 December 1953, George C. Marshall was given the Nobel Peace Prize in Oslo, Norway, for a most visionary achievement, namely his efforts to restore the war-shattered economies of Europe. More than six years earlier, George C. Marshall had proposed the launching of a European Recovery Program, later known as the Marshall Plan. The Secretary of State did not present a detailed program, but suggested rather that the United States would be willing to provide assistance to a Europe devastated by war. Marshall was convinced that economic recovery and stability were vital underpinnings to successfully rebuild a democratic Europe, and he believed that the security and the continued growth of the United States were closely linked to Europe's well-being.

The total amount expended under the European Recovery Program from 1948 to 1952 is estimated to be $13 billion. According to American figures, Norway received $256 million, which corresponds to nearly $1.7 billion 1997 dollars. A Norwegian study, however, concludes that the American contributions to Norway between 1948 and 1952 totaled $460 million. In fact, no European country received more aid through the European Recovery Program per capita than Norway.

For Norway, the Marshall Plan was indispensable in several ways. First, it was invaluable to the modernization of industrial Norway in the early fifties. Heavy investments were made in the aluminum industry, and several mines in war-devastated northern parts of Norway were modernized and reopened. Many small and medium-sized companies also benefited in that they were able to buy new machinery and production equipment with foreign currency.

Secondly, the Norwegian state invested in housing and infrastructure projects, and purchased consumer products like grain, flour, fat, oil and sugar. Undoubtedly, the support through the Marshall Plan was a necessary and vital boost to the Norwegian economy, and helped lay the foundation for modern Norway as we know it today.

Perhaps even more important, the Marshall Plan promoted peaceful economic cooperation throughout Europe. By encouraging economic growth, democratic development and peace in a region ravaged by war for centuries, the European Recovery Program contributed significantly to the peace and stability Western Europe has enjoyed for the past 50 years. In that sense, I presume that the Marshall Plan has been one of the most successful U.S. foreign policy initiatives ever.

Denmark

Ambassador K.E. Tygesen

The willingness of the United States of America to help in a situation of transition and difficult economic circumstances stands out as an example to be admired. It goes without saying that we are thankful that the United States of America decided to assist Europe in its efforts to recover following the Second World War.

Denmark did not suffer as much as other countries during World War II. Nevertheless, the $278 million that Denmark received in Marshall Plan financial aid were a much needed injection into the economy. Stocks were depleted and machinery had become obsolete. About half of Denmark's merchant vessels were lost during the war. And there was a pronounced lack of dollars needed for the purchase of raw materials and new machinery abroad. As a result of the economic assistance, industrial and agricultural production and exports soared during the Marshall years and in the years that followed. Consequently, on 10 June 1953, the Danish government announced that foreign economic assistance was no longer needed. Thereby, one of the main goals of the Marshall Plan was fulfilled in the case of Denmark, namely that the assistance should help recipient countries to helping themselves, so that eventually they could manage without outside help.

The experience gained from the Marshall Plan and through the process of cooperation that followed is highly relevant with regard to the problems of the present European political agenda. Fundamental elements such as help to "self-help," abolishment of trade restrictions and integration into formalized structures of cooperation are relevant also in the case of Central and Eastern European countries today.

In the days of the Marshall Plan, at the end of the Second World War, economic assistance was in high demand. The same is the case today.

After the end of the Cold War, we are faced with the task of helping the Central and Eastern European countries in sharing the stability and wealth from which we have benefited. The EU and its member states have provided and do provide considerable amounts of aid to Central and Eastern European countries and the New Independent States of the former Soviet Union in support of reforms. This can be seen as a modern equivalent of the Marshall Plan.

However, economic assistance was not and is not the only element of the process. The assistance rendered by the United States after the Second World War led to the establishing of a broad European cooperation, beginning with the OEEC. Today, we are faced with the task of integrating the Central and Eastern European countries into the European structures of cooperation. It is the most important task on the European agenda. In 1947, these countries declined the offer of Marshall Plan assistance as a result of Soviet pressure. Today, we who benefited from the Marshall Plan have a moral obligation to help them enjoy the same kind of benefits as we enjoyed fifty years ago. The experience drawn from the Marshall Plan makes it clear that this will not only be in their interest, but that it will also be in our interest—in the interest of a peaceful and prosperous united Europe.

Conference Agenda, June 2, 1997

I. Genesis and Debate within the Truman Administration Persuasion of Congress and the Public

Paul R. Porter, Panel Chairman	Chief, Marshall Plan Mission to Greece; Assistant Administrator, Economic Cooperation Administration; Acting United States Representative in Europe
Philip Kaiser	Assistant Secretary of Labor for International Affairs in the Truman Administration; DCM in the United Kingdom, Ambassador to Hungary and to Austria
George McGhee	Coordinator, Greek-Turkish Aid; Under-Secretary of State; Ambassador to Turkey and to the Federal Republic of Germany; author
Ben Moore	Senior official, Department of State; Economic Counselor, U.K.; Director, Office of European Affairs; educator
David Richardson	Citizens for the Marshall Plan, Special Assistant to the Assistant Administrator of the European Cooperation Administration (ECA, Richard M. Bissell), European Steel and Coal Community, World Bank
Harold Seidman	Senior Official, US Bureau of the Budget; author; educator

II. Innovation and Implementation

Theodore Tannenwald, Panel Chairman — Counsel to Averell Harriman; Judge, United States Tax Court

Theodore Geiger — Special Assistant to the Assistant Administrator (Richard M. Bissell), Economic Cooperation Administration, Washington, DC; Distinguished Professor Emeritus of Intersocietal Relations

Jacob Kaplan — U.S. Representative to Managing Board, European Payments Union; Chief, Regional Staff, ECA; Director, Financial Division, Delegation to USRO

Thomas Schelling — Economic Advisor to Special Representative Harriman, economist, educator and author

Morris Weisz — Chief Labor Advisor in the ECA, International Labor Affairs, Deputy Assistant Secretary of Labor, OECD

III. Political, Economic and Institutional Results

Arthur M. Schlesinger, Jr., Panel Chairman — Aide to Special Representative Harriman, historian and educator

Lincoln Gordon — Chief of Planning for Averell Harriman; Chief of the ECA mission in the UK, Ambassador to Brazil; President, Johns Hopkins University, The Brookings Institution

Paul R. Porter — as above

Waldemar Nielson — Special Assistant to Averell Harriman; Chief of the Labor; Education and Information divisions at Marshall Plan headquarters; Ford Foundation; independent consultant on corporate social policy and philanthropy; author

IV. The Legacy of the Marshall Plan

President Stephen Joel Trachtenberg, Panel Chairman	The George Washington University
Honorable Robert E. Rubin	Secretary of the Treasury
Honorable Benjamin Gilman	Chairman, International Relations Committee, U.S. House of Representatives
Honorable Peter McPherson	Former director of the United States Agency for International Development and president of Michigan State University

The Marshall Plan: Design, Accomplishments and Relevance to the Present

DR. CURT TARNOFF*

Summary

Periodically, Members of Congress and others have recommended establishment of a "Marshall Plan" for Central America, Eastern Europe, the former Soviet Union, and elsewhere. They do so largely because the original Marshall Plan, a program of U.S. assistance to Europe during the period 1948-1951, is considered by many to have been the most effective ever of U.S. foreign aid programs. An effort to prevent the economic deterioration of Europe, expansion of communism, and stagnation of world trade, the Plan sought to stimulate European production, promote adoption of policies leading to stable economies, and take measures to increase trade among European countries and between Europe and the rest of the world.

The Plan was a joint effort between the United States and Europe and among European nations working together. Prior to formulation of a program of assistance, the United States required that European nations agree on a financial proposal, including a plan of action committing

---

* This essay originally appeared as a January 6, 1997 report by Dr. Curt Tarnoff for the Congressional Research Service, The Library of Congress, Washington DC.

Europe to take steps toward solution of its economic problems. The Truman Administration and the Congress worked together to formulate the European Recovery Program, which eventually provided roughly $13.3 billion of assistance to 16 countries.

Two agencies implemented the program, the U.S. Economic Cooperation Administration (ECA) and the European-run Organization for European Economic Cooperation. The latter helped insure that participants fulfilled their joint obligations to adopt policies encouraging trade and increased production. The ECA provided dollar assistance to Europe to purchase commodities—food, fuel, and machinery—and leveraged funds for specific projects, especially those to develop and rehabilitate infrastructure. It also provided technical assistance to promote productivity, guaranties to encourage U.S. private investment, and approved the use of local currency matching funds.

At the completion of the Marshall Plan period, European agricultural and industrial production were markedly higher, the balance of trade and related "dollar gap" much improved, and significant steps had been taken toward trade liberalization and economic integration. The Plan had contributed to more positive morale in Europe and to political and economic stability which helped diminish the strength of domestic communist parties. The U.S. political and economic role in Europe was enhanced and U.S. trade with Europe boosted.

Although the Plan has its critics, many observers believe there are lessons to be learned from the effort that are applicable to present foreign aid programs. However, the extent of the Plan's replicability is subject to question. Central Europe and the former Soviet Union may most closely fit the mold of war devastated Western Europe, but the vast differences in economic systems and environmental burden left by communist regimes, among other factors, mark the distinctions between 1947 Europe and the present. Undertaking an effort equivalent to the original would be an enormous task costing $88 billion in current dollars.

The Marshall Plan and the Present

Between 1948 and 1951, the United States undertook what many consider to be one of its most successful foreign policy initiatives and most effective foreign aid programs. The Marshall Plan and the European Recovery Program (ERP) that it generated involved an ambitious effort to stimulate economic growth in a despondent and near-bankrupt post-World War II Europe, prevent the spread of communism beyond the "iron curtain," and encourage development of a healthy and stable world economy. It was designed to accomplish these goals through achievement of three objectives:

- the expansion of European agricultural and industrial production;
- the restoration of sound currencies, budgets, and finances in individual European countries; and
- the stimulation of international trade among European countries and between Europe and the rest of the world.

It is a measure of the positive impression enduring from the Economic Recovery Program that, in response to a critical situation faced by some regions of the world, there are periodic calls for a new Marshall Plan. This was the case in 1984 when the Kissinger Commission proposed an $8 billion infusion of funds to the Caribbean and Central America. In 1987, Senators and Representatives from both parties, proposed a mini-Marshall Plan for the Philippines. In the early 1990s, Members of Congress recommended "Marshall Plans" for Eastern Europe and the former Soviet Union. And, more recently, international statesmen have suggested Marshall Plans for the Middle East and South Africa.[1]

Generally, these references to the memory of the Marshall Plan are summons to replicate its success or its scale, rather than every detail of the original Plan. Sometimes parallels are drawn between the crisis to be resolved by such assistance and that faced by Europe in 1947, when the Plan was first proposed. The replicability of the Marshall Plan in these diverse situations or in the future is subject to question. To understand the potential relevance to the present of an event that took place fifty years ago it is necessary to understand what the Plan sought to achieve, how it was implemented, and its resulting success or failure. This report looks at each of these factors and then attempts to derive some lessons for the future.

Formulation of the Marshall Plan

The Marshall Plan was proposed in a speech by Secretary of State George Marshall at Harvard University in June 1947, in response to the critical political, social, and economic conditions in which Europe found itself at that time. Recognizing the necessity of Congressional participation in development of a significant assistance package, General Marshall's speech did not present a detailed and concrete program. He merely suggested that the United States would be willing to help draft a program and would provide assistance "so far as it may be practical for us to do so."[2] In addition, Marshall required that it be a joint effort, "initiated" and agreed to by European nations. The formulation of the Marshall Plan, therefore, was, from the beginning, a work of collaboration between the Administration and Congress, and between the U.S. government and European governments. The crisis that generated the Plan and the legislative and diplomatic outcome of Marshall's proposal are discussed below.

The Situation in Europe

European conditions in 1947, as described by Secretary of State Marshall and other U.S. officials at the time, were dire. Although industrial production had, in many cases, returned to pre-war levels (the exceptions were Belgium, France, West Germany, Italy and the Netherlands), the economic situation overall appeared to be deteriorating. The recovery to date had been financed by drawing upon domestic stocks and foreign assets. Capital was increasingly unavailable for investment. Agricultural supplies remained below 1938 levels and food imports were consuming a growing share of the limited foreign exchange. European nations were thus building up a growing dollar deficit. As a result, prospects for any future growth were low. Additionally, trade between European nations was stagnant.

Having already endured years of food shortages, unemployment, and other hardships associated with the war and recovery, the European public was now faced with further suffering. To many observers, the declining economic conditions were generating a pessimism regarding Europe's future that fed class divisions and political instability. Communist parties, already large in major countries such as Italy and France, threatened to come to power.

The potential impact on the United States was severalfold. For one, an end to European growth would block the prospect of any trade with the Continent. One of the symptoms of Europe's malaise, in fact, was the massive dollar deficit that signaled its inability to pay for its imports from the United States.[3] Perhaps the chief concern of the United States, however, was the growing threat of communism. Although the Cold

War was still in its infancy, Soviet entrenchment in Eastern Europe was well under way. Already, early in 1947, the economic strain on Britain had driven it to announce the withdrawal of its commitments in Greece and Turkey, forcing the United States to assume greater obligations to defend their security. The Truman Doctrine, enunciated in March 1947, stated that it was U.S. policy to provide support to nations threatened by communism. In brief, the specter of an economic collapse in Europe and a communist takeover of its political institutions threatened to uproot everything the United States claimed to strive for since its entry into World War II: a free Europe in an open world economic system. U.S. leaders felt compelled to respond.

How the Plan Was Formulated

Three main hurdles had to be overcome on the way to developing a useful response to Europe's problems. For one, as Secretary of State Marshall's invitation indicated, European nations, acting jointly, had to come to some agreement on a plan. Second, the Administration and Congress had to reach their own concordance on a legislative program. And, finally, the resulting plan had to be one that, in the words of the Secretary of State, would "provide a cure rather than a mere palliative."[4]

The Role of Europe

Most European nations responded favorably to the initial Marshall proposal. Insisting on a role in designing the program, 16 nations attended a conference in Paris (July 12, 1947) at which they established the Committee of European Economic Cooperation (CEEC). The Committee was directed to gather information on European requirements and existing resources to meet those needs. Its final report (September 1947) called for a four-year program to encourage production, create internal financial stability, develop economic cooperation among participating countries, and solve the deficit problem then existing with the American dollar zone. Although Europe's net balance of payments deficit with the dollar zone for the 1948-1951 period was originally estimated at roughly $29 billion, the report requested $19 billion in U.S. assistance (an additional $3 billion was expected to come from the World Bank and other sources).

Cautious not to appear to isolate the Soviet Union at this stage in the still-developing Cold War, Marshall's invitation did not specifically exclude any European nation. Britain and France made sure to include the

Soviets in an early three-power discussion of the proposal. Nevertheless, the Soviet Union and, under pressure, its satellites, refused to participate in a common recovery program on the grounds that the necessity to reveal national economic plans would infringe on national sovereignty and that the U.S. interest was only to increase its exports.

The formulation of a proposal by the CEEC was not without U.S. input. Its draft proposal reflected the wide differences existing between individual nations in their approach to trade liberalization, the role of Germany, and state controls over national economies. As a result of these differences, the United States was afraid that the CEEC proposal would be little more than a shopping list of needs without any coherent program to generate long-term growth. To avoid such a situation, the State Department conditioned its acceptance of the European program on six factors. The participants must: make specific commitments to fulfill production programs; take immediate steps to create internal monetary and financial stability; express greater determination to reduce trade barriers; consider alternative sources of dollar credits, such as the World Bank; give formal recognition to their common objectives and assume common responsibility for attaining them; and establish an international organization to act as coordinating agency to implement the program. The final report of the CEEC contained these obligations.

Executive and Congressional Roles

After the European countries had taken the required initiative and presented a formal plan, both the Administration and Congress responded. Formulation of a response had already begun soon after the Marshall speech. As a Democratic President facing a Republican Congress that was highly skeptical of the need for further foreign assistance, Truman took a two-pronged approach that greatly facilitated development of a program: he opened his foreign policy initiative to perhaps the most thorough examination prior to launching of any program and, secondly, provided a perhaps equally rare process of close consultation between the executive and Congress.[5]

From the first, the Truman Administration made Congress a player in the development of the new foreign aid program, consulting with it every step of the way. A meeting on June 22, 1947, between key Congressional leaders and the President led to creation of the Harriman, Krug, and Nourse Committees. Secretary of Commerce Averell Harriman's Committee, composed of consultants from private industry, labor, economists, etc., looked at Europe's needs. Secretary of Interior Julius A. Krug's Committee examined the U.S. physical resources available to support such a program. The group led by Chairman of the Council of Economic Advisers Edwin G. Nourse studied the effect of an enlarged export burden on U.S. domestic production and prices. The House of Representatives itself also formed the Select Committee on Foreign Aid, led by Representative Christian A. Herter, to take a broad look at these issues.[6]

Before the Administration's proposal could be submitted for consideration, the situation in some countries deteriorated so seriously that the President called for a special interim aid package to hold them over through the winter with food and fuel until the more elaborate system anticipated by the Marshall Plan could be authorized. Congress approved interim aid to France, Italy, and Austria amounting to $522 million in an authorization bill signed by the President on December 17, 1947. West Germany, also in need, was still being assisted through the Government and Relief in Occupied Areas (GARIOA) program.

State Department proposals for a European Recovery Program were formally presented by Truman in a message to Congress on December 19, 1947. He called for a 4 1/4-year program of aid to 16 West European countries in the form of both grants and loans. Although the program anticipated total aid amounting to about $17 billion, the Administration bill, as introduced in early 1948 (H.R. 4840), provided an authorization of $6.8 billion for the first 15 months. The House Foreign Affairs and Senate Foreign Relations Committees amended the bill extensively. As S. 2202, it passed the Senate by a 69-17 vote on March 13, 1948, and the House on March 31, 1948, by a vote of 329 to 74.[7] The bill authorized $5.3 billion over a one-year period. On April 3, 1948, the Economic Cooperation Act (title I of the Foreign Assistance Act of 1948, P.L. 80472) became law. The Appropriations Committee conference allocated $4 billion to the European Recovery Program in its first year.

By restricting the authorization to one year, Congress gave itself ample opportunity to oversee the Plan's implementation and consider additional funding. Three more times during the life of the Plan, Congress would be required to authorize and appropriate funds. In each year, Congress held hearings, debated, and further amended the legislation. As part of the first authorization bill, it created a joint Congressional "watchdog" committee to review the program and report to Congress.

Implementation of the Marshall Plan

Profile of the Marshall Plan

In its legislative form as the European Recovery Program (ERP), the Marshall Plan was originally expected to last four and one quarter years from April 1, 1948, until June 30, 1952. However, the duration of the "official" Marshall Plan as well as amounts expended under it are matters of some disagreement. In the view of some, the program ran until its projected end-date of June 30, 1952. Others date the termination of the Plan some six months earlier when the Plan's administrative agent, the Economic Cooperation Agency, was terminated and its recovery programs were meshed with those of the newly established Mutual Security Agency (a process that began during the second half of 1951).

Estimates of amounts expended under the Marshall Plan range from $10.3 billion to $13.6 billion.[8] Variations here can be explained by the different measures of program longevity and the inclusion of funding from related programs which occurred simultaneously with the ERP. Table I contains one estimate of funds made available for the ERP (to June 1951) and lists the sources of those funds.

Table II lists recipient nations and gives an estimate, based on Agency for International Development figures, of amounts received in both current and constant 1997 dollars. According to these estimates, the top recipients of Marshall Plan aid were the United Kingdom (roughly 25% of individual country totals), France (21%), West Germany (11%), Italy (12%), and the Netherlands (8%).

Administrative Agents

The European Recovery Program assumed the need for two implementing organizations, one American and one European. These were expected to continue the dialogue on European economic problems, coordinate aid allocations, insure that aid was appropriately directed, and negotiate adoption of effective policy reforms.

Economic Cooperation Administration

Due to the complex nature of the recovery program, the magnitude of the task, and the high degree of administrative flexibility desired with regard to matters concerning procurement and personnel, Congress established a new agency, the Economic Cooperation Administration

(ECA), to implement the ERP. As a separate agency, it could be exempted from many government regulations that would impede flexibility. Another reason for its separate institutional status was a strong distrust by the Republican Congress for a State Department headed by a Democratic Administration. However, because many in Congress were also concerned that the traditional foreign policy authority of the Secretary of State not be impinged, it required that full consultation and a close working relationship exist between the ECA Administrator and the Secretary of State. Paul G. Hoffman was appointed as Administrator by President Truman.[9] A Republican and a businessman (President of the Studebaker Corporation), both requirements posed by the Congressional leadership, Hoffman is considered by historians to have been a particularly talented administrator and promoter of the ERP.

A 600-man regional office located in Paris played a major role in coordinating the programs of individual countries and in obtaining European views on implementation. It was the most immediate liaison with the organization representing the participating countries. Averell Harriman headed the regional office as the U.S. Special Representative Abroad. Missions were also established in each country to keep close contact with local government officials and to observe the flow of funds. Both the regional office and country missions had to judge the effectiveness of the recovery effort without infringing on national sovereignty.

As required by the ERP legislation, the United States established bilateral agreements with each country. These were fairly uniform- they required certain commitments to meet objectives of the ERP such as steps to stabilize the currency and increase production as well as obligations to provide the economic information upon which to evaluate country needs and results of the program.

The Organization for European Economic Cooperation

A European body, the Organization for European Economic Cooperation (OEEC), was established by agreement of the participating countries in order to maintain the "joint" nature by which the program was founded and reinforce the sense of mutual responsibility for success of the program. Earlier, the participating countries had jointly pledged themselves to certain obligations (see above). The OEEC was to be the instrument which would guide members to fulfill their multilateral undertaking.

TABLE I
Funds Made Available to ECA for European Economic Recovery[a]
(millions of dollars)

Funds Available	April 3, 1948, to June 30, 1949	July 1, 1949, to June 30, 1950	July 1, 1950, to June 30, 1951	Total
Direct appropriations[b]	5,074.0	3,628.4	2,200.0	10,902.4
Borrowing authority (loans)[c]	972.3	150.0	62.5	1,184.8
Borrowing authority (investment guaranty program)[d]	150.0	50.0	—	200.0
Funds carried over from interim aid	14.5	6.7	—	21.2
Transfers from other agencies[e]	9.8	225.1	217.0	451.9
Funds made available (gross)	6,220.6	4,060.2	2,479.5	12,760.3
Less transfers to other agencies[f]	—	—	225.4	225.4
Funds made available (net)	6,220.6	4,060.2	2,254.1	12,534.9

a. **Source**: Compiled from figures made available by the budget division of ECA and from figures published in the Thirteenth Report of ECA, pp. 39 and 152; and Thirteenth Semiannual Report of the Export-Import Bank of Washington. For the Period July-December 1951. Appendix I, pp. 65-66.
b. The Foreign Aid Appropriation Act of 1949 appropriated $4 billion for 15 months but authorized expenditure within 12 months. The Foreign Aid Appropriation Act of 1960 contained a supplemental appropriation of $ 1,074 million for the quarter April

(continued)

TABLE I (continued)
Funds Made Available to ECA for European Economic Recovery[a]
(millions of dollars)

2 to June 30, 1949, and an appropriation of $3,628.4 million for fiscal 1950. The General Appropriation Act of 1951 appropriated $2,250 million for the European Recovery Program for the fiscal year 1951, but the General Appropriation Act of 1951, Sec. 1214, reduced the funds appropriated for the ECA by $50 million, making the appropriation for fiscal 1951 $2,200 million.

c. The Economic Cooperation Act of 1948 authorized the ECA to issue notes for purchase by the Secretary of the Treasury not exceeding $1 billion for the purpose of allocating funds to the Export-Import Bank for the extension of loans, but of this amount, $27.7 million was reserved for investment guaranties. The Foreign Aid Appropriation Act of 1950 increased the amount of notes authorized to be issued for this purpose by $150 million. The General Appropriation Act of 1951 authorized the Administrator to issue notes up to $62.5 million for loans to Spain, bringing the authorized borrowing power for loans to $1,184.8 million.

d. The Economic Cooperation Act of 1948 was amended in April 1949 to provide additional borrowing authority of $122.7 million for guaranties. The Economic Cooperation Act of 1950 increased this authority by $50 million, making the total $200 million for investment guaranties.

e. Transfers from other agencies included: from Greek-Turkish Aid funds, $9.8 million; from GARIOA funds (Germany), $187.2 million; from MDAP funds, $254.9 million. The Foreign Aid Appropriation Act of 1950 and the General Appropriation Act of 1951 authorized the President to transfer the functions and funds of GARIOA to other agencies and departments. Twelve million dollars was transferred to ECA from GARIOA under Section 5(a) of the Economic Cooperation Act of 1950 and the remainder under the President's authority. The Mutual Defense Assistance Act of 1949 appropriated funds to the President, who was authorized to exercise his powers through any agency or officer of the United States. Transfers to ECA were made by Executive Order.

f. Transfers to other agencies included: $50 million to the Yugoslav relief program, $75.4 million to the Far Eastern program, and $100 million to India. The transfer to Yugoslavia was directed by the Yugoslav Emergency Relief Assistance Act of December 29, 1950. The transfer to the Far Eastern program was made by presidential order (presidential letters of March 23, April 13, May 29, and June 14, 1951). The transfer to India was made by presidential order (presidential letter of June 15, 1951).

From William Adams Brown, Jr., and Redvers Opie, American Foreign Assistance, Washington, The Brookings Institution, 1953, p. 247.

**TABLE II. European Recovery Program Recipients
April 3, 1948, to June 30, 1952**
(millions of dollars)

	Current Dollars	Constant 1997 Dollars
Austria	677.8	4,486.9
Belgium/Luxembourg	559.3	3,702.5
Denmark	273.0	1,807.2
France	2,713.6	17,963.6
Greece	706.7	4,678.2
Iceland	29.3	194.0
Ireland	147.5	976.4
Italy	1,508.8	9,988.0
Netherlands	1,083.5	7,172.6
Norway	255.3	1,690.0
Portugal	51.2	338.9
Sweden	107.3	710.3
Turkey	225.1	1,490.1
United Kingdom	3,189.8	21,115.9
West Germany	1,390.6	9,205.5
Regional	407.0	2,694.3
TOTAL	$13,325.8	$88,214.5

Source: U.S. Agency for International Development, November 16, 1971.

Percentage of Country Allocations

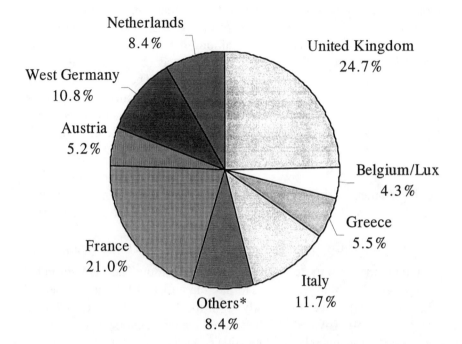

*Denmark, Iceland, Ireland, Norway, Portugal, Sweden, Turkey

To advance this purpose, the OEEC developed analyses of economic conditions and needs, and, through formulation of a Plan of Action, influenced the direction of investment projects and encouraged joint adoption of policy reforms such as those leading to elimination of intra-European trade barriers. At the ECA's request, it also recommended and coordinated the division of aid among the 16 countries. Each year the participating countries would submit a yearly program to the OEEC and then make recommendations to the ECA. The determination of assistance allocations was not an easy matter, especially since funding declined each year. As a result, there was much bickering among recipriant countries, but a formula was eventually reached to divide the aid.

Programs

The framers of the European Recovery Program envisioned a number of tools with which to accomplish its ends. These are discussed below.

Dollar Aid: Commodity Assistance and Project Financing

Grants made up more than 90% of the program. The ECA provided outright grants which were used to pay the cost and freight of essential commodities and services, mostly from the United States. Conditional grants were also provided which required the participating country to set aside currency so that other participating countries could buy their exported goods. This was done in order to stimulate intra-European trade.

The ECA also provided loans. ECA loans bore an interest rate of 2.5% starting in 1952, and matured up to 35 years from December 31, 1948, with principal repayments starting no later than 1956. Additionally, the ECA supervised the use of the dollar credits. European importers made purchases through normal channels and paid American sellers with checks drawn from American credit institutions.

The first yearly ERP bill provided $1 billion of the total authorized available only in the form of loans or guaranties. In 1949, Congress reduced the amount available only for loans to $150 million. The Administrator had decided that loans in excess of these amounts should not be made because of the inadvisability of participating countries assuming further dollar obligations which would only increase the dollar gap which the Plan was attempting to close. As of June 30, 1949, $972.3 million of U.S. aid had been in the form of loans, while $4.948 billion was in the form of grants. Estimates for July 1949–June 1950 were $150 million in loans and $3.594 billion for grants.

The content of the dollar aid purchases changed over time as European needs changed. The program began by supplying immediate need-related goods—food, feed, fertilizer and fuel—and it eventually provided mostly raw materials and production equipment. Between early 1948 and 1949, food-related assistance declined from roughly 50% of the total to only 27%. The proportion of raw material and machinery rose from 20% to roughly 50% in this same time period.

Project financing became important during the later stages of the ERP. ECA dollar assistance was used in combination with local capital in specific projects requiring importation of equipment from abroad. The advantage here was the leveraging of local funds. By June 30, 1951, the ECA had approved 139 projects financed by a combination of U.S. and domestic capital. Their aggregate cost was $2.25 billion, of which only $565 million was directly provided by Marshall Plan assistance funds.[10] Of these projects, at least 27 were in the area of power production and 32 were for the modernization and expansion of steel and iron production. Many others were devoted to rehabilitation of transport infrastructure.[11]

Counterpart Funds

Each country was required to match the U.S. grant contribution with a dollar's worth of its own currency for each dollar of grant aid given by the United States. The participating country's currency was placed in a counterpart fund that could be used for infrastructure projects (roads, power plants, housing projects, airports, etc.) to benefit that country. Each of these counterpart fund projects, however, had to be approved by the ECA Administrator. In the case of Great Britain, counterpart funds were deemed inflationary and simply returned to the national treasury to help balance the budget.

By the end of December 1951, roughly $8.6 billion in counterpart funds had been made available. Of the approximately $7.6 billion approved for use, $2 billion were used for debt reduction as in Great Britain; and roughly $4.8 billion were earmarked for investment, of which 39% was in utilities, transportation and communication facilities (electric power projects, railroads, etc.), 14% in agriculture, 16% in manufacturing, 10% in coal mining and other extractive industries, and 12% in low cost housing facilities. Three countries accounted for 80% of counterpart funds used for production purposes—France (half), West Germany, and Italy/Trieste.[12]

Five percent of the counterpart funds were used to pay the administrative expenses of the ECA in Europe as well as for the purchase of scarce raw materials needed by the United States or to develop domestic sources of such materials. By August 1951, more than $160 million was committed for these purposes, mostly in the dependent territories of Europe. For example, enterprises were set up for development of nickel in New Caledonia, chromite in Turkey, and bauxite in Jamaica.[13]

Technical Assistance

Technical assistance was also provided under the ERP. A special fund was created to finance expenses of U.S. experts in Europe and visits by European delegations to the United States. Funds could be used only on projects contributing directly to increased production and stability. The ECA targeted problems of industrial productivity, marketing, agricultural productivity, manpower utilization, public administration, tourism, transportation and communications. In most cases, countries receiving such aid had to deposit counterpart funds equivalent to the dollar expenses involved in each project. Through 1949, $5 million had been set aside for technical assistance under which 350 experts had been sent from the United States to provide services, and 481 persons from Europe had come to the United States for training. By the end of 1951, with more than $30 million expended, over 6,000 Europeans representing management, technicians and labor had come to the United States for periods of study of U.S. production methods.[14]

Although it is estimated that less than one-half of one percent of all Marshall Plan aid was spent on technical assistance, the effect of such assistance was significant. Technical assistance was a major component of the "productivity campaign" launched by the ECA. Production was not merely a function of possessing up-to-date machinery, but of management and styles of work. As one Senate Appropriations staffer noted, "Productivity in French industry is better than in several other Marshall-plan countries but it still requires four times as many man-hours to produce a Renault automobile as it does for a Chevrolet, and the products themselves are hardly comparable."[15] To attempt to bring European production up to par, the ECA funded studies of business styles, conducted management seminars, arranged visits of businessmen and labor representatives to the United States to explain American methods of production, and set up national productivity centers in almost every participating country.[16]

Guaranties

Guaranties were provided for convertibility into dollars of profits from American investments. The purpose of these guaranties was to encourage American businessmen to invest in the modernization and development of European industry by insuring that returns could be obtained in dollars. The original Act covered only the approved amount of dollars invested, but subsequent authorizations broadened the definition of investment and increased the amount of the potential guaranty by adding to actual investment earnings or profits up to 175% of dollar investment. The risk covered was extended to include compensation for loss of investment due to expropriation as well. Although $300 million was authorized by Congress (subsequently amended to $200 million), investment guaranties covering 38 industrial investments amounted to only $31.4 million by June 1952.[17]

Table III
Expenditures under the ERP by Type
(Approximate Figures in Billions of Dollars)

Grants	
General Procurement	$ 11.11
Project Financing	$ 0.56
Technical Assistance	$ 0.03
Total	$ 11.70
Loans	$ 1.14
Guaranties	$ 0.03
Counterpart Funds (equivalent in $ U.S.)	$ 8.60

How Programs Contributed to Aims

The individual components of the European Recovery Program contributed directly to some of the immediate aims of the Plan. Dollar assistance kept the dollar gap to a minimum. The ECA made sure that both dollar and counterpart assistance were funneled toward activities that would do the most to increase production and lead to general recovery.

The emphasis on financial and technical assistance and productivity helped to maximize the efficient use of dollar and counterpart funds to increase production and boost trade. The importance of this infusion of directed assistance to future economic growth in Europe should not be underestimated. During the recovery period, Europe maintained an investment level of 20% of GNP, one third higher than the pre-war rate. Since national savings were practically zero in 1948, this high rate of investment is largely attributable to U.S. assistance.

But the aims of the Marshall Plan were not achieved by financial and technical assistance programs alone. The importance of these American sponsored programs is that they helped to create the framework in which the overall OEEC European program of action functioned. American aid was leveraged to encourage Europeans to come together and act, individually and collectively, in a purposeful fashion on behalf of the three themes of increased production, expanded trade, and economic stability through policy reform.

The first requirement of the Plan was that European nations commit themselves to these objectives. On an individual basis, each nation then utilized its counterpart funds and American dollar assistance to fulfill these objectives. They also closely examined their economic systems with the analytical assistance of both fellow European nations under the OEEC and the American representatives of the ECA. Through this process, the ECA and OEEC sought to identify and remove obstacles to growth, avoid unsound national investment plans, and promote the adoption of appropriate currency levels. Thanks to American assistance, many note, European nations were able to undertake recommended and necessary reforms at lesser political cost in terms of imposing economic hardship on their publics than would have been the case without aid.

However, while contending with deeply felt sensitivities regarding European sovereignty, U.S. influence on European economic and social decision making as a direct result of Plan assistance was restricted. Where it controlled counterpart funds for use in capital projects, influence was considerable. Where counterpart funds were simply used to retire debt to assist financial stability, there was little such influence. Some analysts contend the United States had minimal control over European domestic policy since its assistance was small relative to the total resources of European countries. But while it could do little to get Europe to relinquish control over exchange rates, on less sensitive, smaller issues, the United States, many argue, was able to affect change.[18] On few occasions did the ECA threaten sanctions if participating countries did not comply with agreements. Italy was threatened with loss of aid for not acting to adopt recommended programs and, in April 1950, aid was actually withheld from Greece to force appropriate domestic action.

As a collective of European nations, the OEEC generated pressure that encouraged individual nations to fulfill their Plan obligations. The OEEC also provided a forum for discussion and eventual negotiation of agreements conducive to intra-European trade. For Europeans, its existence made the Plan seem less an American program. In line with the American desire to foster European integration, the OEEC helped to create the "European idea." As West German Vice-Chancellor Blucher noted, "The OEEC had at least one great element. European men came together, knew each other, and were ready for cooperation."[19] The ECA provided financial assistance to efforts to encourage European integration (see below), and, more importantly, it provided the OEEC with some financial leverage of its own. By asking the OEEC to take on a share of responsibility for allocating American aid among participating countries, the ECA elevated the organization to a higher status than might have been the case otherwise and thereby facilitated achievement of Plan aims.

The Sum of its Parts: Evaluating the Marshall Plan

How the Marshall Plan Was Different

Assistance to Europe was not new with the Marshall Plan. In fact, during the two and one half-year period from July 1945 to December 1947, roughly $11 billion had been provided to Europe, compared with the estimated $13 billion in three and one half years of the Marshall Plan. One of the factors that distinguishes the Marshall Plan from its predecessors is that the Marshall Plan was a PLAN. Because the earlier, more ad hoc and relief-oriented assistance had made little progress toward European recovery, a different, coherent approach was put forward. The new approach called for a concerted program with a definite purpose. The purpose was European recovery, defined as increased agricultural and industrial production; restoration of sound currencies, budgets, and finances; and, stimulation of international trade among participating countries and between them and the rest of the world. The Plan, as illustrated in the preceding section, insured that each technical and financial assistance component contributed as directly as possible to these long-range objectives.

Other aspects of its "plan-like" character were distinctive. It had definite time and monetary limits. It was made clear at the start that the U.S. contribution would diminish each year. In addition to broad objectives, it also supported, by reference to the CEEC program in the legislation and, more specifically, in Congressional report language, the ambitious quantitative targets assumed by the participating countries.[20]

The Marshall Plan was also a "joint" effort. By bringing in European nations as active participants in the program, the United States assured that their commitment to altering domestic economic policies, a necessity if growth was to be stimulated, would be translated into action and that the objective of integration would be further encouraged. The Marshall Plan promoted recognition of the economic interdependence of Europe. By making the Congress a firm partner in the formulation of the program, the Administration assured continued Congressional support for the commitment of large sums over a period of years.

Further, the Marshall Plan was a first recognition by U.S. leaders of the link between economic growth and political stability. Unlike previous post-war aid, which was two-thirds repayable loans and one-third relief supplies, Marshall Plan aid was almost entirely in the form of grants aimed at productive, developmental purposes. The reason for this large infusion of grants in peacetime was that U.S. national security had been redefined as the containment of communism. Governments whose citizens were unemployed and unfed were unstable and open to communist advancement. Only long-term economic growth could provide stability and, as an added benefit, save the United States from having to continue an endless process of stop-gap relief-based assistance.

The unique nature of the Plan is perhaps best emphasized by what replaced it. The Cold War, reinforced by the Korean War, signaled the end of the Marshall Plan by altering the priority of U.S. aid from that of economic stability to military security. In September 1950, the ECA informed the European participants that henceforth a growing proportion of aid would be allocated for European rearmament purposes. Although originally scheduled to end on June 30, 1952, the Plan began to come to a close in December 1950 when aid to Britain was suspended. In the following months, Ireland, Sweden, and Portugal graduated from the program. Further, the use of counterpart funds for production purposes was phased out. Additionally, to counter inflation, which resulted from the shortage of materials due to the Korean War, the ECA had begun to release counterpart funds. In the fourth quarter of 1950, $1.3 billion was released, two-thirds of which were used in retiring public debt.

Under the Mutual Security Act of 1951 and subsequent legislation, aid continued to be provided to many European countries, although in lesser quantities and in increasing proportion to defense. In the 1952-53 appropriations, for example, France received $525 million in grants, half of which was for defense support and the other as budget support. The joint nature of the Marshall Plan later disappeared as national sovereignty came to the fore again. Unlike during the Marshall Plan, France insisted on using its counterpart funds as it wished, commingling them with other funds and only later attributing appropriate amounts to certain projects to satisfy American concerns.

Accomplishments of the Marshall Plan

For many analysts and policymakers, the effect of the policies and programs of the Marshall Plan on the economic and political situation in Europe was broad and pervasive. While a direct connection can be drawn between American assistance and a positive outcome in some cases, for the most part, the Plan may be viewed best as a stimulus which set off a chain of events leading to the accomplishments noted below.

Did It Meet Its Objectives?

The Marshall Plan agencies, the ECA and OEEC, established a number of quantitative standards as their objectives, reflecting some of the broader purposes noted earlier.

Production

The overall production objective of the European Recovery Program was an increase in aggregate production above prewar (1938) levels of 30% in industry and 15% in agriculture. By the end of 1951, industrial production for all countries was 41% above the 1938 level, exceeding the goal of the program. However, aggregate agriculture production was only 9% above prewar levels and, given a 25 million rise in population during these years, Europe was not able to feed itself by 1951.

Viewed in terms of the increase from 1947, the achievement is more impressive. Industrial production by the end of 1951 was 64% higher than only four years earlier. Participating countries increased aggregate agricultural production by nearly 24% in the four crop-years between 1947-48. Total GNP rose by roughly 25% during the four years of the Plan.

The 1948 Senate report on the ERP authorization included a set of production goals that the Europeans had set for themselves, noting that they "seem optimistic to many American experts."[21] The participating countries, for example, wanted to increase steel production to 55 million tons yearly, 20% above pre-war production. By 1951, they had achieved 60 million. It was proposed that oil refining capacity be increased by 2 1/2 times that in 1938. By the end of the program, they managed a four-fold increase. The goal for coal production was 584 million tons, an increase of 30 million over pre-war production. By 1951, production was still slightly below that of 1938, but was 27% higher than in 1947.

Balance of Trade and the Dollar Gap

In 1948, participating countries could pay for only half of their imports by exporting. An objective of the ERP was to get European countries to the point where they could pay for 83% of their imports in this manner. Although they paid for 70% by exporting in 1938, the larger ratio was still sought under the ERP because earnings from overseas investment had declined.

Even though trade rose substantially, especially among the participants, the volume of imports from the rest of the world rose substantially as well, and prices for these imports rose faster than did prices of exports. As a result, Europe continued to be strained. One obstacle to expansion of exports was simply trying to enter the United States and South American markets where U.S. producers were entrenched. OEEC exports to North America rose from 14% of imports in 1947 to nearly 50% in 1952.[22]

Related to the overall balance of trade was the deficit vis a vis the dollar area, especially the United States. In 1947, the total gold and dollar deficit was over $8 billion. By 1949, it had dropped to $4.5 billion, by 1952 to half that figure, and by the first half of 1953 had reached an approximate current balance with the dollar area.[23]

Trade Liberalization

In 1949, the OEEC Council asked members to take steps to eliminate quantitative import restrictions. By the end of 1949, 50%, and by February 1951, 75% of quota restrictions on imports were eliminated. By 1955, 90% of restrictions were gone. In 1951, the OEEC set up rules of conduct in trade under the Code of Liberalization of Trade and Invisible Transactions. At the end of 1951, trade volume within Europe was almost double that of 1947.

Other Benefits

Some benefits of the Marshall Plan are not easily quantifiable, and some were not direct aims of the program.

Psychological Boost

Many believe that the role of the Plan in raising morale in Europe was as great a of contribution to the prevention of communism and stimulation of growth as any financial assistance. As George Kennan noted, "The psychological success at the outset was so amazing that we felt that the psychological effect was four-fifths accomplished before the first supplies arrived."[24]

Economic Integration

The United States viewed itself as a model for the development of Europe, equating individual countries with American states. As such, U.S. leaders saw a healthy Europe as one in which trade restraints and other barriers to interaction, such as the inconvertibility of currencies, would be eliminated. The ERP required coordinated planning for recovery and the OEEC was established for this purpose. In 1949, the ERP Authorization Act was amended to make it the explicit policy of the United States to encourage the unification of Europe.[25] Efforts in support of European integration, integral to the original Plan, were strengthened at this time.

To encourage intra-European trade, the ECA in its first year went so far as to provide dollars to participating countries to finance their purchase of vitally needed goods available in other participating countries (even if these were available in the United States). In a step toward encouraging European independence from the dollar standard, it also established an intra-European payments plan whereby dollar grants were made to countries which exported more to Europe as a group than they imported on condition that these creditor countries finance their export balance in their own currencies.

The European Payments Union (EPU), an outgrowth of the payments plan, was established in 1950 by member countries to act as a central clearance and credit system for settlement of all payments transactions among members and associated monetary areas (such as the sterling area). At the request of the ECA, the 1951 Congressional authorization bill withheld funds specifically to encourage the pursuit of this program since successful conclusion of the EPU depended on an American financial contribution. In the end, the United States provided $350 million to help set up the EPU and another $100 million to assist it through initial difficulties. Many believe that these and other steps initiated under the ERP led to the launching of the Coal and Steel Community in 1952 and eventually to the European Union of today.

Stability and Containment of Communism

Perhaps the greatest inducement to the United States in setting up the Marshall Plan had been the belief that economic hardship in Europe would lead to political instability and inevitably to communist governments throughout the continent. In essence, the ERP allowed economic growth and prosperity to occur in Europe with fewer political and social costs. Plan assistance allowed recipients to carry a larger import surplus with less strain on their balance of payments then would have otherwise been the case. It made larger investments possible without corresponding reductions in living standards, and could be used as a anti-inflationary device by decreasing purchasing power through the sale of imported assistance goods without increasing the supply of money. The production aspects of the Plan also helped relieve hunger among the general population. Human food consumption per capita reached the pre-war level by 1951. In West Germany, economically devastated and besieged by millions of refugees from the East, one house of every five built since 1948 had received Marshall Plan aid.[26]

Perhaps as a result of these benefits, communism in Europe was prevented from being elected into power. It is estimated that communist strength in Western Europe declined by almost one-third between 1946 and 1951. In the 1951 elections, the combined pro-Western vote was 84% of the electorate.[27]

U.S. Domestic Procurement

Champions of the Marshall Plan hold that its authorizing legislation was free of most of the potential restrictions sought by private interests of the sort to later appear in foreign aid programs. Nevertheless, restrictions were enacted which did benefit the United States and U.S. business in particular.

Procurement of surplus goods was encouraged under the Plan legislation, while procurement of goods in short supply in the United States was discouraged. It was required that surplus agriculture commodities be supplied by the United States and procurement of these was to be encouraged by the ECA Administrator. The ERP required that 25% of total wheat had to be in the form of flour, and half of all goods had to be carried on American ships.

By the end of the program, an estimated 83% of European purchases using ECA dollars were spent in the United States. Types of commodities purchased from the United States included foodstuffs (grain, dairy products), cotton, fuel, industrial and raw materials (iron and steel, aluminum, copper, lumber), and industrial and agricultural machinery. Sugar and non-ferrous metals made up the bulk of purchases from outside the United States.

Enhanced Role in Europe for the United States

U.S. prestige and political power in Europe were already strong following World War II. In several respects, however, the U.S. role in Europe was greatly enhanced by virtue of the Marshall Plan program. U.S. private sector economic relations with Europe grew substantially during this period as a consequence of the program's encouragement of increased exports from Europe and Plan grants and loans for the purchase of U.S. goods. The book value of U.S. investment in Europe also rose significantly. Furthermore, while the Plan grew out of a recognition of the economic interdependence of the two continents, its implementation greatly increased awareness of that fact. The OEEC, which eventually became the OECD (1961), with the United States as a full member, endured and provided a forum for discussion of economic problems of mutual concern. Finally, the act of U.S. support for Europe and the creation of a diplomatic relationship which centered on economic issues in the OEEC facilitated the evolution of a relationship centered on military and security issues. In the view of ECA Administrator Hoffman, the Marshall Plan made the Atlantic Pact [NATO] possible.[28]

Critiques of the Marshall Plan

Not everyone agrees that the Marshall Plan was a success. Many of the current criticisms of foreign aid- that it is a give-away program, that it is a waste of money—were heard then as well. One such appraisal was that Marshall Plan assistance had little effect. It is, for example, difficult to demonstrate that Plan aid was directly responsible for the increase in production and other quantitative achievements noted above. Critics have argued that Plan assistance was never more than 5% of the GNP of recipient nations and therefore could have little effect.[29] Some analysts, pointing out the experimental nature of the Plan, agree that the method of aid allocation and the program of economic reforms promoted under the Plan were not derived with scientific precision. Some claim that the dollar gap was not a problem and that the lack of economic growth was the result of bad economic policy on the part of Europeans, which could be resolved when economic controls established during the Nazi era were eventually lifted.[30]

Even at the time of the Marshall Plan, there were those who found the program lacking. If Marshall Plan aid was going to combat communism, they felt, it would have to provide benefits to the working class in Europe. Many believed that the increased production sought by the Plan would have little effect on those most inclined to support communism. In Congressional hearings, Congressmen repeatedly sought assurances that the aid was benefiting the working class. Would loans to French factory owners, they asked, lead to higher salaries for employees?[31] Journalist Theodore H. White was another who questioned this "trickle" [now called the "trickle down"] approach to recovery. "The trickle theory had, thus far," White wrote in 1953, "resulted in a brilliant recovery of European production. But it had yielded no love for America and little diminution of communist loyalty where it was entrenched in the misery of the Continental workers."[32]

In addition, many did not want the United States to appear to be assisting European colonial rule. Considerable concern was expressed that the aid provided to Europe would allow these countries to maintain their colonies in Africa and Asia. The switch in emphasis from economic development to military development which began in the third year of the Plan was also the subject of criticism, especially in view of the limited time frame originally allowed for the Plan. A staff member of the Senate Appropriations Committee's Special Subcommittee on Foreign Economic Cooperation believed that the original intent of the Plan could not be accomplished under these conditions.[33]

The tactics employed to achieve Plan objectives were often questioned as well. "Much of our effort in France has been contradictory," reported the Committee staffer. "On the one hand we have been working toward the abolition of trade barriers between European countries and on the other we have been fostering, or rebuilding, uneconomic industries which cannot survive unhampered international competition."[34] Another issue is the proportion of funding which went to the public rather than private sector. One contemporary writer noted that public sector investments from the Italian counterpart fund obtained twice the amount of assistance as did the private sector in that country. Another analyst has argued that the ECA promoted government intervention in the economy.[35] In the 1950 authorization hearings, U.S. businessmen urged that assistance be provided directly to foreign business rather than through European governments. Only in this way, they said, could free enterprise be promoted in Europe.[36]

From its inception, Members of Congress voiced fears that the ERP would have a negative effect on U.S. business. Some noted that the effort to close the trade gap by encouraging Europeans to export and limit their imports would diminish U.S. exports to the region. Amendments, most of which were defeated, were offered to ERP legislation to insure that certain segments of the private sector would benefit from Plan aid. That strengthening Europe economically meant increased competition for U.S. business was also not lost on legislators. The ECA, for example, helped Europeans rebuild their merchant marine fleets and, by the end of 1949, had authorized over $167 million in European steel mill projects, most using the more advanced continuous rolling mill process that had previously been little used in Europe. As the Congressional "watchdog" committee staff noted, "The ECA program involves economic sacrifice either in direct expenditure of Federal funds or in readjustments of agriculture and industry to allow for foreign competition."[37] In the end, the United States seemed to be willing to make both sacrifices.

Lessons of the Marshall Plan

The Marshall Plan was viewed by Congress, as well as others, as a "new and far-reaching experiment in foreign relations."[38] Although in many ways unique to the requirements of its time, analysts have attempted, over the years, to draw from it various lessons which might possibly be applied to present or future foreign aid initiatives. These lessons represent what observers believe were the primary strengths of the Plan.[39]

- Despite growing U.S. isolationism, polls showing little support for the Plan, a Congress dominated by budget cutters, and an election looming whose outlook was unfavorable to the President, the Administration decided it was the right thing to do and led a campaign- with national commissions set up and cabinet members travelling the country- to sell the Plan to the American people.
- Congress was included at the beginning to formulate the program. Because he faced a Congress controlled by the opposition party, Truman made the Plan a cooperative creation, which helped garner support and prevented it from becoming bogged down with private interest earmarks. Congress maintained its active role by conducting detailed hearings and studies on ERP implementation.
- The beneficiaries were required to put together the proposal. Because the Plan targeted changes in the nature of the European economic system, the United States was sensitive to European national sovereignty. European cooperation was critical to establishing an active commitment from participants on a wide range of delicate issues.
- The Plan had specific and limited goals—increased production, trade, and stability—and all resources were dedicated to meeting those goals. Furthermore, sufficient resources were provided for this purpose.
- In the main, the Plan was not a humanitarian relief program. It was designed specifically to bring about the absolute economic recovery of Europe and avoid the repeated need for relief programs that had characterized U.S. assistance to Europe since the war.
- The countries to be assisted, for the most part, had the capacity to recover; and they, in fact, were recovering, not developing for the first time.
- The human and natural resources necessary for economic growth were largely available; the chief scarce resource was capital.
- Aid alone was insufficient to assist Europe economically. A report in October 1949 by the ECA and Department of Commerce found that the United States should purchase as

much as $2 billion annually in additional goods if Europe was to balance its trade by the close of the recovery program.

- Parochial Congressional tendencies to put restrictions on the program on behalf of U.S. business were kept under control for the good of the program. American businessmen, for example, were not happy that the ECA insisted that the Europeans purchase what was available first in Europe using soft currency before turning to the United States.

- The Marshall Plan fully developed the use of counterpart funds that gave additional leverage to U.S. aid by requiring recipients to deposit local currency funds equal to the dollar amount of assistance in an account for use on projects agreed to by both U.S. and recipient country representatives. This method continues to be used in present day Agency for International Development programs.[40]

- Technical assistance, including exchanges, while inexpensive relative to capital block grants, may have had a significant impact on economic growth. Under the Marshall Plan, technical assistance helped draw attention to the management and labor factors hindering productivity. It demonstrated American know-how and helped develop in Europe a positive feeling regarding America. Both technical assistance and exchanges compose a large portion of today's foreign assistance programs.

- The foreign policy value of foreign assistance cannot be adequately measured in terms of short-term consequences. The Marshall Plan continues to have an impact in NATO, the OECD, the European Union, the German Marshall Fund, in European bilateral aid programs, and in the stability and prosperity of modern Europe, all America's chief allies.[41]

Is It Replicable?

Although many disparate elements of Marshall Plan assistance speak to the present, it is questionable whether the program in the main could be replicated in a meaningful way. The problems faced now by most other parts of the world are so vastly different and more complex than those encountered by Western Europe in the period 1948-1952 that the solution posed for one is not entirely applicable to the other.

Some aspects of the Marshall Plan are more replicable than others. The Plan was chiefly characterized by its offering of dollar assistance targeted at productivity, financial stability, and increased trade. This, however, is the aim today of only a portion of U.S. economic assistance to the developing countries, much of which goes for humanitarian relief or political security purposes. Surely developing and former communist countries would benefit by receiving large scale aid if it eliminated the necessity of going even deeper into debt to private or public sources. Such grant aid could also make radical policy reforms easier to adopt politically. However, many developing countries may not possess the human, industrial, or democratic base to make effective use of such aid and may need long term development-oriented aid, not a short term infusion of capital. Some suggest that, in many cases, a rapid infusion of large scale assistance would lead only to corruption and abuse of aid funds.

Another key feature of the Plan was its joint nature. Both individually and collectively, the European participants were collaborators with the United States in the Plan. It can be argued that the administrative systems of many developing countries remain inadequate for the formulation and implementation of such a significant program. Again long-term targeted interventions of technical assistance may be more appropriate at this stage.

There are, however, segments of the developing world that may be in a position to benefit from a Marshall Plan-type program. The advanced developing countries such as Thailand and Indonesia increasingly possess the appropriate industrial and human resources. In these cases, however, there is nothing in their current status to suggest they are at a crisis stage requiring extensive grant assistance rather than loans obtainable through the World Bank. In addition, for many such countries, private sector investment has supplanted the necessity for donor assistance.

More closely fitting the mold of an economically devastated post-war Western Europe are the nations of central Europe and the former Soviet Union. Although it could be argued that they were never very well developed to start with, these countries possess many human and natural resources, but are greatly lacking in investment capital and productive economic systems. To the extent that Marshall Plan grant aid was able to alleviate the political cost to European governments of difficult economic policy decisions, it is a useful model. But it should be remembered that an infusion of grant assistance was not the only thing that characterized the Marshall Plan. The environmental burden left by communist regimes, uncertain access to foreign markets, the strains of nationality questions, the unknown potential for regional development, and a host of other issues make clear how the situation in central Europe and the former Soviet Union is distinct from the post-war situation which provoked the Marshall Plan.

In the final analysis, however, even if there exist countries whose needs are similar in nature to what the Marshall Plan provided, the position of the United States has changed since the late 1940s. The roughly $13.3 billion dollars provided by the United States to the 16 nations over a period of less than four years equals an estimated $88 billion in today's currency. That sum surpasses the amount of economic, food, and military assistance the United States provided to over 146 countries and numerous international development organizations and banks in the four year period 1993-96 ($62 billion). In 1948, when the United States appropriated $4 billion for the first year of the Marshall Plan, outlays for the entire federal budget equaled slightly less than $30 billion. For the United States to be willing to expend 13% of its budget (that would be $203 billion in FY1996) on any one program, Congress and the President would have to agree that the activity was a major national priority.

Nevertheless, in pondering the difficulties of new Marshall Plans, it is perhaps worth considering the views of the ECA Administrator, Paul Hoffman, who noted twenty years after Secretary Marshall's historic speech, that even though the Plan was "one of the most truly generous impulses that has ever motivated any nation anywhere at any time," the United States "derived enormous benefits from the bread it figuratively cast upon the international waters." In Hoffman's view:

> Today, the United States, its former partners in the Marshall Plan and—in fact—all other advanced industrialized countries . . . are being offered an even bigger bargain: the chance to form an effective partnership for world-wide economic and social progress with the earth's hundred and more low-income nations. The potential profits in terms of expanded prosperity and a more secure peace could dwarf those won through the European Recovery Program. Yet the danger that this bargain will be rejected out of apathy, indifference, and discouragement over the relatively slow progress toward self-sufficiency made by the developing countries thus far is perhaps even greater than was the case with the Marshall Plan. For the whole broadscale effort of development assistance to the world's poorer nations—an

effort that is generally, but I think quite misleadingly, called "foreign aid"—has never received the full support it merits and is now showing signs of further slippage in both popular and governmental backing. Under these circumstances, the study of the Marshall Plan's brief but brilliantly successful history is much more than an academic exercise.[42]

References

Arkes, Hadley. *Bureaucracy, the Marshall Plan, and the National Interest*, Princeton, NJ: Princeton University Press, 1972.

Brookings Institution. *Current Issues in Foreign Economic Assistance*, Washington DC: Brookings Institution Press, 1951.

Brown, William Adams, Jr. and Redvers Opie. *American Foreign Assistance*, Washington DC: The Brookings Institution Press, 1953.

Cowen, Tyler. "The Marshall Plan: Myths and Realities," in Doug Bandow, ed. *U.S. Aid to the Developing World*, Washington DC: The Heritage Foundation, 1985, pp. 61-74.

Economic Cooperation Administration. *The Marshall Plan: a Handbook of the Economic Cooperation Administration*, Washington DC: Economic Cooperation Administration, 1950.

Economic Cooperation Administration. *The Marshall Plan: a Program of International Cooperation*, Washington DC: Economic Cooperation Administration, 1950.

Geiger, Theodore. "The Lessons of the Marshall Plan for Development Today," *Looking Ahead*, Washington DC: the National Planning Association, vol. 15, May 1967, pp. 1-4.

German Information Center. *The Marshall Plan and the Future of U.S.-European Relations*, New York: German Information Center, 1973.

Gimbel, John. *The Origins of the Marshall Plan*, Palo Alto, CA: Stanford University Press, 1976.

Gordon, Lincoln. "Recollections of a Marshall Planner," *Journal of International Affairs*, vol. 41, Summer 1988, pp. 233-245.

Hartmann, Susan. *The Marshall Plan*, Columbus, OH: Merrill Publishing Co., 1968.

Hoffmann, Stanley and Charles Maier, eds. *The Marshall Plan: a Retrospective*, Boulder, CO: Westview Press, 1984.

Hogan, Michael. *The Marshall Plan: America, Britain, and the Reconstruction of Western Europe, 1947-1952*. New York: Cambridge University Press, 1987.

Hogan, Michael. "American Marshall Planners and the Search for a European Neo-capitalism," *American Historical Review*, vol. 90, Feb. 1985, pp. 44-72.

Jones, Joseph. *The Fifteen Weeks (February 21-June 5, 1947)*, New York: Viking Press, 1955.

Kostrzewa, Wojciech, Peter Nunnenkamp and Holger Schmieding. *A Marshall Plan for Middle and Eastern Europe?*, Kiel, Germany: Kiel Institute of World Economics Working Paper No. 403, Dec. 1989.

Mee, Charles L. Jr.. *The Marshall Plan: The Launching of the Pax Americana*, New York: Simon and Schuster, 1984.

Milward, Alan. *The Reconstruction of Western Europe, 1945-51*, Berkeley, CA: University of California Press, 1984.

Organization for Economic Cooperation and Development. *From Marshall Plan to Global Interdependence*, Paris: OECD, 1978.

OECD. "Special Issue: Marshall Plan 20th Anniversary," *OECD Observer*, June 1967.

Pfaff, William. "Perils of policy," *Harper's Magazine*, vol. 274, May 1987, pp. 70-72.

Price, Harry Bayard. *The Marshall Plan and its Meaning*, Ithaca, NY: Cornell University Press, 1955.

Quade, Quentin. "The Truman Administration and the Separation of Powers: the Case of the Marshall Plan," *Review of Politics*, vol. 27, Jan. 1965, pp. 58-77.

Sanford, William F. Jr.. *The American Business Community and the European Recovery Program*, 1947-1952, New York: Garland Publishing, 1987.

Sanford, William F. Jr.. "The Marshall Plan: Origins and Implementation," *Department of State Bulletin*, vol. 82, June 1982, pp. 17-33.

Senator Tom Connally, U.S. Congress, Senate Committee on Foreign Relations. *Report on Western Europe*, 82nd Congress, 2nd session, Washington DC: U.S. Government Printing Office, 1952.

Smith, Kenneth. *The Marshall Plan Epoch in American Public Administration*, Fairfax, VA: Department of Public Affairs, George Mason University, May 1983.

Silberman, James M. and Charles Weiss, Jr.. *Restructuring For Productivity: the Technical Assistance Program of the Marshall Plan as a Precedent for the Former Soviet Union*, Bethesda, MD: Global Technology Management, Inc. for the World Bank, November 1992.

U.S. Congress Joint Committee on Foreign Economic Cooperation. *An Analysis of the ECA Program*, 81st Congress, 2nd session, Washington DC: U.S. Government Printing Office, 1950.

U.S. Congress Joint Committee on Foreign Economic Cooperation. *The ECA and Strategic Materials Report*, 81st Congress, 1st session, Washington DC: U.S. Government Printing Office, 1949.

U.S. Congress Joint Committee on Foreign Economic Cooperation. *Knowledge of the Marshall Plan in Europe: France*, 81st Congress, 1st session Washington DC: U.S. Government Printing Office, 1949.

U.S. Congress Joint Committee on Foreign Economic Cooperation. *The Proposed European Payments Union*, 81st Congress, 2nd session, Washington DC: U.S. Government Printing Office, 1950.

U.S. Congress Joint Committee on Foreign Economic Cooperation. *Report on Progress of the Economic Cooperation Administration*, 81st Congress, 1st session, Washington DC: U.S. Government Printing Office, 1949.

U.S. Congress Joint Committee on Foreign Economic Cooperation. *Shipping Problems in the ECA Program*, 81st Congress, 1st session, Washington DC: U.S. Government Printing Office, 1949.

U.S. Congress, House Committee on Appropriations. "Foreign Aid Appropriations for 1949," *Report on H.R. 6801*, 80th Congress, 2nd session, Washington DC: U.S. Government Printing Office, 1948.

U.S. Congress, House Committee on Appropriations, Special Subcommittee on Foreign Aid Appropriations. *Hearings on Foreign Aid Appropriations for 1950*, 81st Congress, 1st session, Washington DC: U.S. Government Printing Office, 1949.

U.S. Congress, House Committee on Appropriations, Special Subcommittee on Foreign Aid Appropriations. *Hearings on Foreign Aid Appropriations for 1951*, 81st Congress, 2nd session, Washington DC: U.S. Government Printing Office, 1950.

U.S. Congress, House Committee on Appropriations, Special Subcommittee on Economic Cooperation Administration. *Hearings on the Mutual Security Program Appropriations for 1952*, 82nd Congress, 1st session, Washington DC: U.S. Government Printing Office, 1951.

U.S. Congress, House Committee on Foreign Affairs. *Hearings on the Extension of the European Recovery Program*, 81st Congress, 1st session, Washington DC: U.S. Government Printing Office, 1949.

U.S. Congress, House Committee on Foreign Affairs. *Hearings on the Mutual Security Program*, 82nd Congress, 1st session, Washington DC: U.S. Government Printing Office, 1951.

U.S. Congress, House Committee on International Relations. *Foreign Economic Assistance Programs, Part I: Foreign Assistance Act of 1948*, Historical Series, Volume III, Washington DC: U.S. Government Printing Office, 1976.

U.S. Congress, House Committee on International Relations. *Foreign Economic Assistance Programs, Part II: Extension of the European Recovery Program*, Historical Series, Volume IV, Washington DC: U.S. Government Printing Office, 1976.

U.S. Congress, House Committee on International Relations, Subcommittee on International Operations. *Hearing and Markup on the Marshall Plan Resolution*, 95th Congress, 1st session, Washington DC: U.S. Government Printing Office, 1977.

U.S. Congress, House Select Committee on Foreign Aid. *Final Report on Foreign Aid*, 80th Congress, 2nd session, Washington DC: U.S. Government Printing Office, 1948.

U.S. Congress, Senate Committee on Appropriations. "Foreign Aid Appropriation Act for 1949," *Report on H.R. 6801*, Report no. 1626, 80th Congress, 2nd session, Washington DC: U.S. Government Printing Office, 1948.

U.S. Congress, Senate Committee on Appropriations. "Foreign Aid Appropriation Act for 1950," *Report on H.R. 4830*, Report no. 812, 81st Congress, 1st session, Washington DC: U.S. Government Printing Office, 1949.

U.S. Congress, Senate Committee on Appropriations, Special Subcommittee on Foreign Economic Cooperation. *Conditions in Europe in the Spring of 1951*, Staff Report, 82nd Congress, 1st session, Washington DC: U.S. Government Printing Office, 1951.

U.S. Congress, Senate Committee on Appropriations, Special Subcommittee on Foreign Economic Cooperation. *Report on the Strategic Materials Program of the Economic Cooperation Administration*, 82nd Congress, 2nd session, Washington DC: U.S. Government Printing Office, 1952.

U.S. Congress, Senate Committee on Appropriations, Investigations Division. *Report on the Foreign-Aid Program in Europe*, 83rd Congress, 1st session, Washington DC: U.S. Government Printing Office, 1953.

U.S. Congress, Senate Committee on Foreign Relations. *Hearings on the European Recovery Program*, 80th Congress, 2nd session, Washington DC: U.S. Government Printing Office, 1948.

U.S. Congress, Senate Committee on Foreign Relations. "European Recovery Program," *Report on S. 2202*, Report no. 935, 80th Congress, 2nd session, Washington DC: U.S. Government Printing Office, 1948.

U.S. Congress, Senate Committee on Foreign Relations. "Foreign Economic Assistance for 1950," *Report on S. 3304*, 81st Congress, 2nd session, Washington DC: U.S. Government Publishing Office, 1950.

U.S. Congress, Senate Committee on Foreign Relations, Subcommittee on United States Foreign Aid to Europe. *Hearings on United States Foreign Aid Programs in Europe*, 82nd Congress, 1st session, Washington DC: U.S. Government Printing Office, 1951.

U.S. Congress, Senate Committee on Foreign Relations and Committee on Armed Services. *Hearings on the Mutual Security Act of 1951*, 82nd Congress, 1st session, Washington DC: U.S. Government Printing Office, 1951.

United States Mutual Security Agency. *The Story of the American Marshall Plan in Greece*, Washington DC: Mutual Security Agency, 1950.

Weiss, Charles, Jr.. *The Marshall Plan: Lessons for U.S. Assistance to Central and Eastern Europe and the Former Soviet Union*, Washington DC: The Atlantic Council, December 1996.

Vandenberg, Arthur Jr., ed.. *The Private Papers of Senator Vandenberg*, Boston: Houghton Mifflin, 1952.

Wexler, Imanuel. *The Marshall Plan Revisited: the European Recovery Program in Economic Perspective*, Westport, CT: Greenwood Press, 1983.

Wilson, Theodore. *The Marshall Plan*, Headline Series 236, Washington DC: Foreign Policy Association, June 1977.

Notes

1. For example: Richard N. Gardner, "Time for a New Marshall Plan," *New York Times,* June 3, 1967. Robert A. Pastor and Richard Feinberg, "U.S. Latin American Policy: A Marshall Plan for the Caribbean?" *Vital Issues,* Vol. 33, No. 1, 1984. Alan Cranston, "Let's Have a Marshall Plan for Philippines," *Los Angeles Times,* September 13, 1987. Irwin M. Stelzer, "A Marshall Plan for Eastern Europe?" *Commentary*, January 1990. "'Global Marshall Plan' Urged for Environment," *Washington Post,* May 3, 1990. "Mandela Urges Marshall Plan for South Africa," *Reuters,* May 22, 1996. "Kohl Proposes a New Marshall Plan for the Middle East," *Deutsche Presse Agentur,* January 25, 1996.

2. Address at Harvard University, June 5, 1947, in Joseph M. Jones, *The Fifteen Weeks*, p. 284. The Jones book is an excellent description of events leading up to this speech.

3. The "dollar gap" was considered important because the United States was the dominant economy at this time, and it was assumed that U.S. goods would remain attractive enough to outcompete other nations' products for years to come. The dollar gap would be likely to grow. Until European countries were able to build up reserves, they would tend to divert their exports to and their imports away from the dollar area. This would force cuts in food imports and capital goods, further destabilizing Europe and slowing growth. The Marshall Plan sought to close the "dollar gap."

4. June 5, 1947 Address in Jones, p. 283.

5. The Chairman of the Senate Foreign Relations Committee called the version of the legislation which went to the floor of the Congress, "the final product of eight months of more intensive study by more devoted minds than I have ever known to concentrate upon any one objective in all my twenty years in Congress." Arthur H. Vandenberg, quoted in Harry Bayard Price, *The Marshall Plan and its Meaning*, p. 64. See also Quentin L. Quade, "The Truman Administration and the Separation of Powers: the Case of the Marshall Plan," *The Review of Politics,* January 1965, pp. 58-77.

6. See U.S. Congress, House Select Committee on Foreign Aid, *Final Report on Foreign Aid,* 80th Congress, 2nd session, 1948.

7. Many argue that the decisive support for the ERP came as a result of the Czechoslovak coup on February 25,1948, which brought the Communists to power there. This convinced many of those who saw the Plan as a "give-away" program that Soviet expansionism was a serious threat. Other major factors which swayed public and congressional opinion were the information dissemination activities of the "Public Citizens Committee" for the Marshall Plan, and support for the Plan from influential one-time "isolationist" Senator Vandenberg, Republican Chairman of the Senate Foreign Relations Committee.

8. Imanuel Wexler in *The Marshall Plan Revisited*, p. 249, offers a figure at the lower end. At the higher end is Susan Hartmann, *The Marshall Plan*, p. 58.

9. The original Administration proposal would have given State almost total control over the ECA. U.S. Congress, Senate Committee on Foreign Relations, "European Recovery Program," *Report on S. 2202*, Report no. 935, 80th Congress, 2nd session, 1948.

10. Brown and Opie, *American Foreign Assistance*, p. 237.

11. *Department of State Bulletin*, January 14, 1952.

12. As much as $1 billion in counterpart funds was never released by the ECA. Imanuel Wexler, *The Marshall Plan Revisited*, p. 87. U.S. Congress, Senate Committee on Foreign Relations, *United States Foreign Aid Programs in Europe,* 1951, p. 12 in Brown and Opie, p. 237.

13. About half of the funds were used for purchases and the other half for development projects. Another $25 million in U.S. dollars was provided by the ECA for development purposes. See U.S. Congress, Senate Committee on Appropriations, Special Subcommittee on Foreign Economic Cooperation, *Report on the Strategic Materials Program of the Economic Cooperation Association*, 82nd Congress, 2nd session, 1952, p.20.

14. *Department of State Bulletin*, January 14, 1952. p. 45.

15. U.S. Congress, Senate, Committee on Appropriations, Special Subcommittee on Foreign Economic Cooperation, *Conditions in Europe in the Spring of 1951*, Staff Report, 82nd Congress, 1st session, 1951, p.3.

16. U.S. Congress, House Committee on Appropriations, *Foreign Aid Appropriation Bill for 1960*, pp. 735-739. Brown and Opie, pp. 239-242.

17. Brown and Opie, p. 242. Wexler, p. 89.

18. Alan S. Milward, *The Reconstruction of Western Europe*, pp. 113-125.

19. Quoted in Harry Bayard Price, *The Marshall Plan and its Meaning*, p. 294.

20. U.S. Congress, *House Report 1585 on S. 2202* and *Senate Report 935 on S. 2202*, 1948.

21. U.S. Congress, Senate Committee on Foreign Relations, "Economic Recovery Program," *Report on S. 2202*, Report no. 935, 1948.

22. *OECD Observer*, June 1967, p.10.

23. *OECD Observer*, June 1967, pp. 10- 11.

24. In Charles Mee, Jr., *The Marshall Plan: The Launching of the Pax Americana*, p. 246.

25. This term was left undefined. An amendment calling for both political federation as well as economic unification was stricken in conference.

26. *State Department Bulletin*, January 14, 1952.

27. Changes in electoral laws also contributed to this outcome. U.S. Congress, Senate Committee on Foreign Relations, *United States Aid Programs in Europe 1951*, Washington DC: U.S. Government Printing Office, 1951, pp. 22-24.

28. U.S. Congress, House Committee on Appropriations, *Foreign Aid Appropriation Bill for 1950*, Washington DC: U.S. Government printing Office, 1949. p. 33.
29. For example, Kostrzewa, Nunnenkamp, and Schmieding, *A Marshall Plan for Middle and Eastern Europe?*, p. 7, a statistical analysis which shows only weak positive correlation between aid receipts in percent of GNP and the growth of exports and GNP during the ERP.
30. Tyler Cowan, *The Marshall Plan: Myths and Realities*, pp. 63-66.
31. U.S. Congress, Senate Committee on Foreign Relations, *U.S. Foreign Aid Programs in Europe 1951*, Washington DC: U.S. Government Printing Office, pp. 220-226.
32. Mee, Jr., pp. 258-59.
33. U.S. Congress, Senate Committee on Appropriations, *Conditions in Europe in the Spring of 1951*, Staff Report, 82nd Congress, 1st session, 1952, p. 2.
34. U.S. Congress, Senate Committee on Appropriations, *Conditions in Europe in the Spring of 1961*, Washington DC: U.S. Government Printing Office, 1962, p. 3.
35. U.S. Senate Committee on Appropriations, *Conditions in Europe in the Spring of 1951*, pp. 3-4. Cowan, pp. 66-68.
36. Brown and Opie, p. 172.
37. U.S. Congress, Joint Committee on Foreign Economic Cooperation, *Shipping Problems in the ECA Program*, 81st Congress, 1st session, 1949, p.12; and U.S. Congress, Joint Committee on Foreign Economic Cooperation, *An Analysis of the ECA Program*, 81st Congress, 2nd session, 1950, pp. 4-5,16-17.
38. U.S. Congress, House International Relations Committee, "House Report 1655 on S. 2202," *Conference Report on Foreign Assistance Act of 1948*, Discussion of section 124, April 1, 1948, Washington DC: U.S. Government Printing Office, 1948.
39. Some articles which discuss lessons and replicability are: Theodore Geiger, "The Lessons of the Marshall Plan for Development Aid Today," *European Community,* March 1967. William Pfaff, "Perils of Policy," *Harper's Magazine,* May 1987. Philip Gold, "The Marshall Plan 'Miracle' Looks Grand and Exceptional," *Insight,* June 8,1987. Lincoln Gordon, "Lessons from the Marshall Plan: Successes and Limits" in Stanley Hoffman and Charles Maier, *The Marshall Plan: A Retrospective*, 1984, pp. 53-58. Lord Franks, "Lessons of the Marshall Plan Experience," in OECD, *From Marshall Plan to Global Interdependence*, Paris: OECD, 1978, pp. 18-26. Wodciech Kostrzewa, Peter Nunnenkamp, and Holger Schmeiding, *A Marshall Plan for Middle and Eastern Europe?*, Working Paper No. 403, Kiel, Germany: Kiel Institute of World Economics, December 1989. James M. Silberman and Charles Weiss, Jr. *Restructuring for Productivity: The*

Technical Assistance Program of the Marshall Plan as a Precedent for the Former Soviet Union, Global Technology Management, Inc., November 1992. Charles Weiss, Jr., *The Marshall Plan: Lessons for U.S. Assistance to Central and Eastern Europe and the Former Soviet Union,* Atlantic Council, December 1995.

40. On a much smaller scale than the counterpart funds, the Plan leveraged private sector investment in recipient countries through the use of U.S. government guaranties. It also encouraged U.S. individual and charitable organization participation by continuing the earlier relief effort practice of subsidizing transport of private American donations.

41. One Plan activity actually remains in operation. Germany and Austria maintain revolving European Recovery Program Funds, originally repaid Plan money, which dispense loans to small business. "Germans in the East are still Getting Boost from Marshall Plan," *Wall Street Journal,* January 25, 1995.

42. Paul G. Hoffman, "Peace Building- Its Price and its Profits," *Foreign Service Journal,* June 1967, p. 19.

The
George
Washington
University
WASHINGTON DC

The George Washington University, founded in 1821, is a fully
accredited, private, nonsectarian, coeducational, institution; it is
classified as a 501 (c) (3) institution and contributions are tax deductible.
The University is dedicated to furthering human well-being and offers a
dynamic, student-focused community stimulated by cultural and
intellectual diversity built upon a foundation of integrity, creativity, and
openness to the exploration of new ideas. The George Washington
University, centered in the national and international crossroads of
Washington, D.C., commits itself to excellence in the creation,
dissemination, and application of knowledge.

The University provides a stimulating intellectual environment for
its students and faculty and fosters excellence in teaching. The University
offers outstanding learning experiences for full-time and part-time students
in undergraduate, graduate, and professional programs in Washington,
D.C., the nation, and abroad. As a center for intellectual inquiry and
research, the University emphasizes the linkage between basic and applied
scholarship, insisting that the practical be grounded in knowledge and
theory. The University acts as a catalyst for creativity in the arts, the
sciences, and the professions by encouraging interaction among its
students, faculty, staff, alumni, and the communities it serves.

The university enrolls 16,177 students, of whom 7,756 are graduate
and professional students. There are 1,420 full-time faculty members. It
offers 65 doctoral programs and 160 masters degrees in the entire range
of fields, including law, medicine, engineering, the sciences, humanities
and the social sciences. Faculty and students come from a variety of
ethnic groups and nationalities and 11% are from abroad.

The Elliott School of International Affairs, offers ten graduate and
four undergraduate programs to prepare future leaders for an
increasingly international and multinational environment. The Elliott
School enrolls approximately 1,000 undergraduate students and 500
graduate students from 31 countries. Integrated into a comprehensive

university, it offers an outstanding and informed faculty, an exceptionally able, diverse, and international student body, an urban campus and a tradition of late-afternoon and early evening classes for graduate students which permits employment while studying. With 104 full-time faculty members representing 15 disciplines, the Elliott School offers the opportunity to participate in the programs and research of the Institute for European, Russian and Eurasian Studies, the Sigur Center for Asian Studies, the Center for International Science and Technology Policy, and the Space Policy Institute.

The historical roots of the Elliott School can be traced back to 1898. In 1988, the School was renamed in honor of Evelyn and Lloyd H. Elliott, the President of The George Washington University from 1965 to 1988.

PROGRAM ON TRANSITIONS TO DEMOCRACY

Purpose

With a focus on Russia, other post-Soviet republics, China, and including other key countries, the ***Program on Transitions to Democracy*** combines education, research, publication, public forums and international cooperation. Established in 1990, the Program provides scholars, the public, the foreign policy leadership, and the media with objective information and analysis about the complex, often fragile—and sometimes reversible—process of movement from dictatorships toward political democracy and market oriented economies.

Activities

The Program has focused on the following activities:

- **Analytic reports**—each dealing with the dynamics of transitions in specific countries or with key conceptual or policy issues;
- **Perspectives of participants in the transitions**—these essays provide an opportunity for democratic leaders from countries in transition and those working to assist them to reflect on progress, problems and proposals for the future;
- **University forums on democratic and market transitions**— the Program convenes a series of public meetings at the university where democratic leaders from abroad as well as senior officials from the U.S. government and international organizations discuss the process of political and economic transition in specific countries and as a general field of public policy and intellectual inquiry;

- **Systematic collection, computerization and synthesis of data on transitions**—this provides an up to date information-base for analysis and is also available to other experts and scholars including from countries in transition;
- **Comprehensive reports and books on current political and economic trends;**
- **The US, Russia, China, Democracy and Security Project**—since 1998 has produced reports and published articles with a book in progress, *The United States, Russia and China—Geopolitics in the New Century.*

Organization, funding and leadership

The Director is Dr. Constantine C. Menges, Professor in the Practice of International Relations. Funding has been provided by private American foundations and doners. Dr. Menges has worked as a university professor, author, and senior federal executive for three U.S. presidents. His most recent public service included three years in the White House as Special Assistant to the President for National Security Affairs where his responsibilities included transitions to democracy. He has published a large number of articles and books: *Spain: The Struggle for Democracy* (1978); *Inside the National Security Council* (1988; paperback, 1989); *The Twilight Struggle: The Soviet Union and the United States Today* (1990); *The Future of Germany and the Atlantic Alliance* (1991); *Transitions from Communism in Russia and Eastern Europe* (1994, editor & contributor); *The Future of Russia* (monograph 1994), published in French as *Le Phenix Rouge* (1995); *Partnerships for Peace, Democracy and Prosperity* (1997, editor & contributor). He is the founding editor of the journal, *Problems of Post-Communism* and has appeared frequently on the national media to discuss international trends and issues. Dr. Menges speaks German, French, Spanish and Russian.

PROGRAM ON TRANSITIONS TO DEMOCRACY—
Selected Publications

Books

Partnerships for Peace, Democracy and Prosperity
editor and contributor, Dr. Constantine Menges, (Lanham, MD; New York; Oxford, UK: University Press of America), 1997
Le Phenix Rouge
by Dr. Constantine Menges, Brian Crozier, Hans Huyn, & Edouard Sablier, (Paris: Editions du Rocher), 1995
Transitions from Communism in Russia and Eastern Europe
editor and co-author, Dr. Constantine Menges, (Lanham, MD & London: University Press of America), 1994
The Future of Germany and the Atlantic Alliance
by Dr. Constantine Menges, (Washington, DC: AEI Press), 1991

Analytic Studies and Essays

Venezuela—Implications of the Emerging Radical Military Dictatorship
by Dr. Constantine C. Menges; September 1999
China: A Policy of Realistic Not Unconditional Engagement
by Dr. Constantine C. Menges; July 1999
Serbia After the Kosovo War—Prospects for the Democratic Political Parties
by Dr. Constantine C. Menges and Mihajlo Mihajlov; June 1999
Serbia, Kosovo, Iraq—International Assistance for Democratic Self-Liberation
by Dr. Constantine C. Menges; April 1999
Venezuela, Colombia, Panama, Mexico—New Challenges to Freedom
by Dr. Constantine C. Menges; January 1999
Russia—New Strategies for Assistance
by Dr. Ira Straus, January 1999
Russia Enlargement Proposals: Their Meaning for the Future
by Dr. Constantine C. Menges and Mihajlo Mihajlov; December 1998
Central America: A Marshall Plan to help our neighbors
by Dr. Constantine C. Menges; November 1998

Croatia, Democracy and Peace in the Balkans
    by Dr. Tereza Ganza-Aras; November 1998
Russia: The Political Roots of the Crisis
    by Dr. Constantine C. Menges; September 1998
The People's Republic of China: An Overview of Human Rights
    by Dr. Constantine C. Menges and Ms. Jill Schwartz; June 1998
China: More Than Trade in the Balance
    by Dr. Constantine C. Menges; May 1998
Kosovo: Déjà Vu
    by Mihajlo Mihajlov; May 1998
China-U.S. Relations—Two Futures
    by Dr. Constantine C. Menges; April 1998
US Relations With China—Lessons From the Cold War
    by Dr. Constantine C. Menges; January 1998
Russia and NATO
    by Ambassadors Vorontsov, Throbog, Banlacki, et. al.; February
    1997
Bosnia—Toward Peace or War?
    by Mihajlo Mihajlov; October 1996
Russian Organized Crime: Trends and Implications
    by Dr. Maryanne Ozernoy and Dr. Yuri Voronin; September 1996
Russia: Increasing the Prospects for Democracy
    by Dr. Constantine Menges; June 1996
Russian Election Update
    by Dr. Ira Straus; periodic updates May-July 1996
Russia: 1996 Presidential Election Results and US Policy Options
    by Mr. Ken Wollack, President, National Democratic Institute; Dr.
    John Sullivan, Executive Director, Center for International Private
    Enterprise; Dr. Constantine Menges; June 1996
Russia: Implications of a Communist Presidency
    by Amb. Jack Matlock, Dr. Constantine Menges and Mr. Mihajlo
    Mihajlov; June 1996
**Russia: the June 1996 Presidential Election and the US National
Interest**
    by Amb. Jeane Kirkpatrick, Mr. Lorne Craner, President, Inter-
    national Republican Institute, and Amb. Nelson Ledsky; May 1996
**Ukraine: Perspectives on the Development of Public Institutions and
Economic Reform**
    by Amb. Yuri Shcherbak; March 1996

US Aid to Russia, 1992-1996: a First Assessment of Results
by Dr. Constantine Menges; February 1996
On the Eve of the December 1995 Russian Elections
- **The Political Landscape**
  by Dmitri Glinski; December 1995
- **The Russian Military and the Parliamentary Elections**
  by Stanislav Lunev; December 1995

Preventing Communist Restoration—Implications for US Policy
by Dr. Constantine Menges; May 1995
Toward Peace and Freedom in the Balkans
by Joseph DioGuardi, President Albanian American Civic League; Shirley Cloyes, Publisher, Lawrence Hill Books; and, Iliaz Halimi, Member, Parliament of Macedonia; February 1995
The Future of Russia
by Dr. Constantine C. Menges; November 1994
The US, Russia and the Post-Soviet Republics
by William Perry, Secretary of Defense; March 1994
Russia: Profile of the Major Political Parties in 1994
by Dr. Andrei P. Tsygankov; February 1994
Russia: Perspectives on the Coming December 12, 1993 National Elections
by Constantine C. Menges; December 1993
Ukraine: Internal and International Trends
by Ambassador Oleh Bilorus, Ambassador of Ukraine to the United States; December 1993
Belarus: Assessing the Results of the Transition
by Ambassador Sergei Martynov, Ambassador of Belarus to the United States; December 1993
Kyrgyzstan: Current Political and Economic Reforms
by Ambassador Roza Otunbayeva, Ambassador of Kyrgyzstan to the United States; December 1993
The US and the Encouragement of Democracy—Experiences and Lessons
by Hon. Brian Atwood, Administrator, United States Agency for International Development; November 1993
The National Democratic Institute: its Purpose and Strategies
by Kenneth Wollack, President, National Democratic Institute; November 1993

Estonia: Progress and Prospects
by Ambassador Toomas Ilves, Ambassador of Estonia to the United States; November 1993

The Russian Crisis and the Clinton Administration
by Dr. Constantine C. Menges; October 1993

Problems of the Post-Communist Transitions
by Jiri Dienstbier, former Deputy Prime Minister and Foreign Minister of the Czechoslovak Federation; September 1993

Tajikistan: Tragedy and Prospects—Perspectives of a Democratic Leader
by Davlat Khudonazarov, pro-democratic opposition candidate in the 1991 Tajik Presidential elections; June 1993

The Political Crisis in Russia: Perspectives from Russian Democratic Leaders
by Sergei Sirotkin, Sergei Krasvchenko, Peter Filippov and Alexy Surkov, members of the Russian Parliament; May 1993

A Strategy to Encourage Democracy in Russia
by Dr. Constantine C. Menges; February 1993

US Assistance for Post-communist Democratic and Market Transitions—Approaches, Resources and Results
by Ambassador Robert Hutchings, Special Advisor to the Secretary of State for East European Assistance, Department of State; November 1992

The Former Soviet Union, the Economic Transitions and the World Bank
by Wilfried Thalwitz, Senior Vice President with responsibility for Eastern Europe and the post-Soviet republics, The World Bank; November 1992

The United States and the Post-Soviet Transitions
by Ambassador Thomas Niles, Assistant Secretary of State with responsibilities for Europe and the post-Soviet republics; October 1992

Russia: the Transitions and the Former KGB
by Vadim Bakatin, former Chairman of the KGB; General Oleg Kalugin, former Major General of the KGB; September 1992

Russia in 1992: the Institutionalization of Democratic Reforms—Progress and Resistance
by Thomas Baker and Dr. Constantine C. Menges; June 1992

The Economic Transitions in Post-communist Europe—the Role of the United States and the West
    by John Robson, Deputy Secretary of the Treasury; April 1992

The USSR, the Post-Soviet republics, Central and Eastern Europe: a Selected Bibliography on the Transitions
    by Alexander Henderson; April 1992

The New and the Old Parties of the Nineties in Romania
    by Dr. Petre Datculescu; April 1992

Romania: is there a Transition to Democracy?
    by Mr. Gyorgy Tokay, member of the Romanian Parliament and Mr. Dorin Tudoran, Publisher and Editor-in-Chief of the Romanian Newspaper, Meridian; April 1992

Hungary and its Role in the New Europe
    by Ambassador Pal Tar, Republic of Hungary; April 1992

Current Problems of Transition in Czechoslovakia
    by Ambassador Rita Klimova, Czech and Slovak Federal Republic; March 1992

Promoting Democratic Institutions Abroad—the Strategy and Experience of the US
    by Carl Gershman, President, National Endowment for Democracy; March 1992

The Future of Russia
    by Ambassador Andrei Kolosovskiey, deputy Ambassador of Russia; March 1992

Russia: Changes After the Coup and Problems of International Aid
    by Dr. Victor Sheinis, member of the Russian Parliament; February 1992

Romania: the Current Role and Development of Democratic Parties
    by Dr. Emil Constantinescu, President of the Romanian Civic Alliance; February 1992

Cuba: a Strategy for Peaceful Transition to Democracy
    by Dr. Constantine Menges; February 1992

Eastern Europe and the Post-Soviet republics—the Transition Strategy of the World Bank
    by Dr. Eugenio Lari, the World Bank; December 1991

Eastern Europe: the Role of Private Enterprise in the Transitions
    by Dr. John Sullivan, Executive Director, Center for International Private Enterprise; December 1991

Post-communist Europe: Impressions From Germany
   by Ambassador Vernon Walters; December 1991
Croatia's Struggle for Freedom and Democracy is Imperiled by Serbian Imperialism
   by Dr. Frone Golem; November 1991
The Danger of Continued Ethnic Violence in Yugoslavia
   by Mihajlo Mihajlov; November 1991
Slovenia Seeks International Support and Peaceful Resolutions to Serbian Aggression
   by Dr. Ernest Petric; November 1991
Peaceful and Lawful Mechanisms to Bring Peace to Yugoslavia
   by Dr. Miles Costick; November 1991
Serbian Aggression and US Policy
   by Phyllis Kaminsky; November 1991
Poland, Hungary, Czechoslovakia: Post-communist Trends
   by Professor Sharon Wolchik; November 1991
Hungary: Post-communist Trends and Prospects
   by Dr. Eniko Bollobas; November 1991
Czechoslovakia: Current Post-communist Trends
   by Dr. Irena Zikova; November 1991
Poland: Post-communist Trends and Prospects
   by Dr. Maciej Kozlowski; November 1991
The Present and Future of Hungary and a Europe in Transition
   by Dr. Jozsef Antall, Prime Minister of Hungary; October 1991
Assessing Soviet Political Changes During the Gorbachev years, 1985-1991
   by Thomas Baker and Dr. Constantine Menges; July 1991
Yugoslavia: Communism, Democracy, Fragmentation, or Civil War?
   by Dr. Constantine Menges; June 1991
Economic Transition in Eastern Europe: a First Assessment
   by Peter A. Clark and Dr. Constantine Menges; June 1991
Albania: Reform Communism or Transition to Democracy?
   by James M. Sheehan and Dr. Constantine Menges; April 1991
The East European and German Transformations—Conceptual Perspectives
   by Dr. Constantine Menges; March 1991
Bulgaria: a Second Opportunity for a Democratic Transition?
   by Dr. Constantine Menges; December 1990

Poland's Evolution, 1980-1990: Implications for Eastern Europe
by Dr. Constantine Menges; November 1990
Reunified Germany, the New Europe: Opportunities and Challenges
by Dr. Constantine Menges; November 1990
The Democratic Opening in Eastern Europe, 1989-1990
by Dr. Constantine Menges; August 1990
Bulgaria: Overview of 1990 Election Results, July 1990

Czechoslovakia: Overview of 1990 Election Results, July 1990

Romania: Overview of 1990 Election Results, July 1990

Hungary: Overview of 1990 Election Results, July 1990

East Germany: Overview of 1990 Election Results, July 1990

Eastern Europe: four national elections, 1990—Results and Implications
by Dr. Constantine Menges; July 1990

Comprehensive Reports

Russia: Contemporary Political and Economic Trends
by Dr. Constantine Menges and Mr. Thomas G. Baker; 1994
Uzbekistan: Contemporary Political and Economic Trends
by Dr. Constantine Menges and Mr. Thomas G. Baker; 1994
Ukraine: Contemporary Political and Economic Trends
by Dr. Constantine Menges and Mr. Kenneth Duckworth; 1994
Armenia: Contemporary Political and Economic Trends
by Dr. Constantine Menges and Mr. Robert Krikorian; 1994
Kazakhstan: Contemporary Political and Economic Trends
by Dr. Constantine Menges and Mr. Thomas G. Baker; 1994
Kyrgyzstan: Contemporary Political and Economic Trends
by Dr. Constantine Menges and Mr. Norman Offstein; 1994
Tajikistan: Independence and Communist Restoration
by Dr. Constantine Menges and Mr. Norman Offstein; 1994

Glossary of Frequently Used Abbreviations

CEEC—Committee for European Economic Cooperation

DCM—Deputy Chief of Mission

EDC—European Defense Community

ECA—Economic Cooperation Administration

ECE—Economic Commission for Europe

ECSC—European Coal and Steal Community

EECE—Emergency Economic Committee for Europe

EPU—European Payments Union

ERP—European Recovery Program

EU—European Union

FAO—Food and Agricultural Organization

GATT—General Agreement on Tariffs and Trade

ICA—International Cooperation Administration

IDB—International Development Bank

IMF—International Monetary Fund

ILO—International Labor Organization

MSA—Mutual Security Agency

NATO—North Atlantic Treaty Organization

OECD—Organization for Economic Cooperation and Development

OEEC—Organization for European Economic Cooperation

OSR—Office of the Special Representative

SRA—United States Special Representative Abroad

SRE—U.S. Special Representative for Europe

UNRRA—United Nations Relief and Rehabilitation Administration

USAID—United States Agency for International Development

USIA—United States Information Agency

USRO—U.S. Representative Office

WHO—World Health Organization

WTO—World Trade Organization